STUDIES ON MEDIEVAL AND EARLY MODERN WOMEN

In the same series

1 Christine Meek & Katharine Simms (eds), *'The fragility of her sex'? Medieval Irish women in their European context*
2 Christine Meek (ed.), *Women in Renaissance and early modern Europe*

Studies on medieval and early modern women

PAWNS OR PLAYERS?

Christine Meek &
Catherine Lawless

Editors

FOUR COURTS PRESS

Typeset in 10.5 pt on 12.5 pt Ehrhardt by
Carrigboy Typesetting Services, County Cork for
FOUR COURTS PRESS LTD
7 Malpas Street, Dublin 8, Ireland
e-mail: info@four-courts-press.ie
and in North America for
FOUR COURTS PRESS
c/o ISBS, 920 N.E. 58th Avenue, Suite 300, Portland, OR 97213.

© the various authors and Four Courts Press 2003

A catalogue record for this title is available
from the British Library.

ISBN 1–85182–774–9 hbk
1–85182–775–7 pbk

All rights reserved.
Without limiting the rights under copyright
reserved alone, no part of this publication may be
reproduced, stored in or introduced into a retrieval system,
or transmitted, in any form or by any means (electronic, mechanical,
photocopying, recording or otherwise), without the prior
written permission of both the copyright owner and
publisher of this book.

Printed in Great Britain by
MPG Books, Bodmin, Cornwall

Contents

LIST OF ILLUSTRATIONS	6
INTRODUCTION	7
A source for the depiction of Eve in the early-modern period: biblical Latin epic of the fifth and sixth centuries *John Flood*	18
Share and share alike? The marriage portion, inheritance and family politics *Claire de Trafford*	36
'I have nothing but through her': women and the conquest of Ireland, 1170–1240 *Brendan Smith*	49
The power of dower: the importance of dower in the lives of medieval women in Ireland *Gillian Kenny*	59
Freedom of movement? Women travellers in the Middle Ages *Diana Webb*	75
The gender of lordly women: the case of Adela of Blois *Kimberly A. LoPrete*	90
Women on the margins: the 'beloved' and the 'mistress' in Renaissance Florence *Catherine Lawless*	111
Women and violence in late medieval Ireland *Dianne Hall*	131
Theory in the absence of fact: Irish women and the Catholic Reformation *Tadhg Ó hAnnracháin*	141
'What will my sister think of me now': the role of sisterhood in sustaining resistance by the Port-Royal community *Carol Baxter*	155
'Hyr wombe insaciate': the iconography of the feminised monster *Samantha J.E. Riches*	177
BIBLIOGRAPHY	197
LIST OF CONTRIBUTORS	215
INDEX	217

Illustrations

1 Peter Gottland, St George and the Dragon – *Allegory of the Triumph of the New Faith over the Old* (1552) — 178
2 Lucas Cranach, *The Fall of Man* (late fifteenth century) — 182
3 Wenzel of Olmutz, *The Papal Ass* (*c.*1500) — 183
4 *Hercules at the Crossroads*, from Sebastian Brant's *Narrenschiff* (1498) — 186
5 *Luther's Game of Heresy* (1535) — 187
6 Albrecht Altdorfer, *St George and the Dragon* (1511) — 188
7 Leonard Beck, *St George Fighting with the Dragon* (*c.*1515) reproduced by kind permission of Kunsthistorisches Museum, Vienna — 194

Introduction

This book comprises some of the papers read at two conferences in Trinity College, 'Pawns and Players' on 4 December 1999 and 'Women at Home, Women Abroad' on 23 February 2001. The conferences and the book represent a continuation of a series, by now almost a tradition, begun in 1993 with the conference that resulted in the volume '*The fragility of her sex*'? *Medieval Irish women in their European context*[1] and continued with the conference on 22 November 1998 whose papers were published as *Women in Renaissance and early modern Europe*.[2] The sub-title of the present volume reflects this continuity, since it is borrowed from a phrase in Cormac Ó Cléirigh's article in the first volume.[3] At the same time it represents one of the main current preoccupations of women's history, that of agency. No longer content simply to find information about women, which was previously overlooked, or to present women as the victims of a patriarchal system that took little account of their interests, women's history, in Ireland as elsewhere, attempts to present a more nuanced picture. Women are seen in the context of the various societies that governed and shaped their lives, at times limited by their circumstances but at times empowered by the laws and institutions within which they lived, so that they were able to make decisions and exploit resources that not only affected their own lives, but also the lives of those with whom they came into contact. Linked to this, and a natural consequence of it, is an increased concern with gender, a concern for men as well as women, exploring their respective roles and societal expectations. Neither women nor men were wholly free agents, of course, since legal systems regulated vital questions of marriage and inheritance rights, while ecclesiastical law and social conventions dictated many aspects of religious life and moral conduct. The way in which women accepted or resisted or defied these rules and conventions, or exploited the space and opportunities that were afforded to them is explored in the papers presented in this volume.

In the first essay John Flood tackles the question of the figure of Eve, a matter of vital importance for the way in which women in general were regarded, since Eve was interpreted as representing womankind and anything said about Eve was applied by extension to all women. Feminist scholars have

---

1 Ed. C.E. Meek and M.K. Simms (Dublin, 1996). 2 Ed. Christine Meek (Dublin, 2000). 3 'The absentee landlady and the sturdy robbers: Agnes de Valence' in Meek and Simms (eds.), '*The fragility of her sex*', p. 117.

devoted considerable attention to Eve, represented by early Christian and medieval theological tradition as a secondary creation yet the first to fall into sin, thus necessitating the incarnation and redemption of man through another woman, Mary. John Flood concentrates, however, not on the theological tradition, but on early Christian epic poetry, which was also of significance for early modern literature and thought, since, as he demonstrates, it underwent a revival in the sixteenth century when a series of epics dealing with the Fall appeared in Latin and in a number of European vernaculars. Although the outlines of the Genesis story were fixed and the need to maintain the essentials of the divine message acted as a constraint of poetic creativity to some extent, certain embellishments and differences of emphasis were permissible, such as Cyprian's stress on the personal concern of God for his creation or Victorius' anxiety to underline the justice of God's sentence or Dracontius' focus on divine mercy. While these Genesis-based interpretations of Eve are all necessarily somewhat negative, they are also quite varied and none of them is vituperative. It is worth noting that Proba, the one woman among these early Christian poets, is hardly more generous to Eve than the male writers, applying to her terms that Virgil had used of Scylla, even while praising Eve's beauty. Cyprian was perhaps the most sympathetic towards Eve, graphically describing her fear the first time the darkness of night falls and attributing her disobedience to the serpent's promise that the light will return if she eats of the forbidden fruit, and her persuasion of Adam to her desire to share this gift with him, though Dracontius too stresses Eve's physical beauty and the sexual innocence of both Adam and Eve, soon to be brought to an end by the Fall, although the companionship they had enjoyed continued afterwards. Victorius is perhaps the most hostile, striking a sensual note in his emphasis on the love and desire Adam felt for the newly created Eve, while stressing Eve's unwisdom and credulity in yielding to the serpent's blandishments and then dragging her husband into temptation. Avitus, too, who depicts the psychology of his characters more fully than any of the other writers discussed, stressed Eve's beauty, but also her weakness and perversity, so that knowing it was wrong, she nevertheless dared to eat the forbidden fruit. These differences of emphasis, as John Flood points out, provided a precedent for a more nuanced treatment of Eve in the early-modern writers who are likely to have had access to these works.

In the first of a group of essays dealing with women and property in the social and political history of England and Ireland, Claire de Trafford discusses the role of the *maritagium* in England, that is the marriage portion or dowry given to a bride by her own family, as opposed to the better known dower, the life interest enjoyed by a widow on her late husband's property. Until the Statute of Westminster in the late thirteenth century the *maritagium* was an outright grant to a woman; she had a vital say in its disposition during her marriage and was restored to full possession of it in her widowhood. By a close study of the documents preserved in cartularies, Claire de Trafford is able to show that women themselves using their *maritagia* to make grants to younger sons or to daughters, who might in turn receive a *maritagium* from that of their mother. Men, too, might use the marriage portion, as land that had been acquired rather than inherited and was perhaps not central to the main family holding, to make provision for younger sons and daughters. There are interesting indications of 'women's land', land that might have been originally received as *maritagium* or alternatively land that had been used as a widow's dower, being used again in subsequent generations to provide for women members of the family. But the legal position was often complicated; the heirs might challenge the non-inheriting child's title to land from the mother's *maritagium*, the woman herself might have allowed a son to share it with her during her lifetime without actually giving him title to it or have favoured just one child at the expense of others. There are indications that while the *maritagium* might be used as more freely disposable land to mitigate the effects of an increasingly rigid primogeniture, it might also be a cause of family tensions. Much of the evidence comes in fact from the records of disputes, though some of these may have been fictitious lawsuits designed to give one party a better title to property. But until the Statute of Westminster any woman who had brought a marriage portion with her had to be considered when any disposal of it was proposed. As a widow she could alienate her marriage portion lands permanently away from the main heir to younger sons and daughters, or indeed to religious foundations, and could revoke any grants that her husband might have made from it during his lifetime. Claire de Trafford argues that this must have increased the status and power of the mother within the family. But a progressively less generous attitude towards provision for non-inheriting children, that may have lain behind the enactment of the Statute of Westminster, and the provisions of the statute itself, diminished women's freedom of action and consequently their position within the family.

The establishment of Anglo-Norman lords in Ireland brought the system of land tenure, primogeniture, *maritagium* and dower in force in England to Ireland too. Brendan Smith in his essay discusses, however, the period of the initial conquest of Ireland and the role of women in it, demonstrating that they were far more than simply conduits for the transfer of property or passive victims of acts of violence. Female victims there certainly were, but there were also women who played a far from passive role and might inflict violence on their own account, from the lower-class Alice of Abervenny, who beheaded some seventy Irish captives after the battle of Baginbun in revenge for the death of her lover, who had fallen in combat, to Isobel, daughter of Strongbow and wife of William Marshal, left in Ireland to uphold her husband's interest during his absence. Brendan Smith is able to point to a number of parallels, where women can be shown to be actively involved in warfare in England, on the

Continent or during the crusades. While active involvement in fighting was unusual for women in Ireland, many of the early conquerors of Ireland were accompanied by female relatives, who were thus put at risk should the fighting take an unexpected turn during the earliest and most dangerous stage of the conquest. Smith offers two explanations for this, firstly a desire to ensure that female relatives were not seized as hostages by the king during the absence of their men in Ireland and secondly the desirability of having unmarried women relatives to hand, since the arrangement of marriage alliances played a major role in the establishment and consolidation of English rule in Ireland. These were marriages among the Anglo-Norman families rather than between the invaders and the families of Irish lords, and since such marriages were an important means of forging alliances, achieving ambitions or consolidating a newcomer's position, they might seem to reduce the women involved to mere transmitters of land and status. While there is some truth in this, the poor rate of survival of the early conquerors militated against the establishment of a self-contained colonial baronage and opened up new possibilities for their women-folk, ranging from Basilia, sister of Strongbow, who after two marriages in Ireland ended her days in the convent of St Thomas the Martyr in Dublin, to widows and heiresses who might have Irish interests but spent much of their time out of the country. As Brendan Smith demonstrates the role of women in the conquests of Ireland was more significant and more varied than simply acting as channels for the transfer of property.

Gillian Kenny discusses women's property rights in Anglo-Norman Ireland once the colony was established, concentrating on the question of dower. Women were normally entitled to a life interest in a third of their husband's property as widows, and this could either be specific lands the husband had allotted to be his wife's dower or, where he had not designated specific property, an allocation judged to amount to a third. Since the widow held this property for life, her rights unaffected by any subsequent remarriage, and these rights gradually became extended from the property the husband had had at the time of the marriage to the frequently more extensive property he held at the time of his death, this could be a serious disadvantage to the heir. Gillian Kenny illustrates from the case of the inheritance of William Marshal the way in which an estate might have to support as many as four widows, where a series of brothers all died young and childless, with the heirs finding themselves dealing with powerful women and their relatives and second husbands. As it was common for women to marry extremely young, the heirs might have a long wait for the reversion of a widow's dower. Widows might on occasions have a struggle to establish their claim to dower and to obtain actual payment of agreed revenues from the heir, but there were writs to facilitate their claims and only in fairly rare circumstances, the proved invalidity or termination of the marriage, their own adultery, their husband's forfeiture for felony, would dower be denied.

If a widow remarried, as many did, her dower came under the control of her new husband along with any other property she might possess, and at the highest social level this rendered her liable to prohibitions on marrying without royal consent, or pressure to marry a particular man. Women could, however, purchase the right to remain unmarried, or even to have their own choice of second husband. One of the fears of the heirs was that the widow's dower lands might suffer 'waste', deterioration due either to administrative incompetence or even to deliberate profiteering, especially by a second husband, to the detriment of the long-term value of the estate. While this may sometimes have happened, Gillian Kenny is also able to quote examples of widows such as Roesia de Verdun, whose holdings as heiress of Nicholas de Verdun and widow of Theobald Walter made her a powerful figure in Louth in the first half of the thirteenth century. Roesia was an independent woman and a capable administrator, who built castles and defended her lands against raiders, as well as simply engaging in estate administration. There are other examples, too, of women, including some from more modest levels of society, engaging in litigation and vigorously pursuing their claims, but Gillian Kenny postulates that the twelfth and particularly the thirteenth century was the golden age for widows in Anglo-Norman Ireland. Even though a widow's legal position if anything improved subsequently with the extension to Ireland of the more favourable jointure system developed in England, the relatively peaceful and settled conditions in thirteenth-century Ireland gave way to a situation of endemic warfare in the fourteenth and fifteenth centuries, which among other effects made it very much more difficult, and sometimes impossible, for women to enforce their rights and actually enjoy the benefits to which the dower and jointure systems entitled them.

Diana Webb considers the potentialities and limitations of women's activity from a different point of view, and paints a nuanced picture. Women had far fewer occasions to leave home on business or on ecclesiastical, secular, legal or military affairs and undoubtedly travelled far less than men did. There were, however, occasions when women travelled impressive distances in sometimes hazardous circumstances from the Norwegian women of the Viking period, who might travel between Norway, Scotland, Iceland, Greenland and even Vinland in the company of or to join husbands or sons to royal and noble ladies who travelled hundreds of miles to marry foreign kings and lords. Women of more modest social level too might make one-way journeys to live and probably die abroad. What these journeys had in common was that the women travelled at the behest of their kin to further the interests of the group to which they belonged and not of their own volition or without good cause. The main category of journey which was not strictly necessary and which women might themselves choose to make was pilgrimage and a disproportionate amount of the information about women travellers in fact relates to pilgrimages. There were anxieties about women travelling even on pilgrimage and attempts to discourage both secular women and nuns from undertaking such journeys. Nuns in particular should remain enclosed and not be exposed to the dangers and temptations of life outside the convent walls, though some nuns were called upon to take part in the Anglo-Saxon missionary effort in Germany in the eighth century and might travel about there supervising convents. While women probably formed only a small percentage of the total number of pilgrims, women certainly did go on pilgrimage in some numbers and might be commissioned do so on behalf of deceased relatives. Nor were these pilgrimages necessarily confined to modest local shrines. Women might travel to distant sites, such as Santiago, Rome or Jerusalem, as in the well-known case of Margery Kempe. Women were conventionally, and probably correctly, regarded as especially vulnerable on such journeys and needed to be suitably escorted, something that was easier for ladies of status and resources, or to join a sufficiently large party for their own safety, in the case of humbler women. A woman alone or escorted by just one man might be an object of suspicion, and for a married woman the consent and if possible the company of her husband might be required. While pilgrimage did offer women some opportunity for mobility and adventure they might not otherwise have had, quite apart from its pious purposes, it still remained the case that women tended to operate in the private sphere close to home, while men were more likely to experience the stimulus of travel with its attendant excitements and dangers.

Against a rich conceptual background of both modern gender theory and medieval understandings of male and female roles Kim LoPrete discusses the activity of just one politically prominent woman, Adela of Blois, demonstrating the anachronism involved in categorising her either as a rare exception to general female powerlessness or as an honorary man. As the daughter of William the Conqueror, the wife of Stephen-Henry, count of Blois, Chartres and Meaux, and the mother of Thibaud 'the Great' of Blois-Champagne, Stephen, king of England and Henry, bishop of Winchester, her status and dynastic connections assured her of a role in European power politics. She had participated alongside her husband in all except military aspects of his rule as count and her early widowhood, after his years away on crusade, saw her well equipped and well able to exercise comital rule, at first on behalf of and later in association with her sons. She was able to intervene as a power in the land in negotiations with the kings of France and England, the emperor or the pope, to assist her brother Henry I of England and to consolidate and strengthen the territorial and dynastic position of her sons. Even after her retirement to a convent at the age of about fifty, she continued her intervention in political matters from time to time. She was also herself well educated and literate in Latin, and was an important and generous patron of ecclesiastics and monastic houses. The large quantity of legal documents, letters and poems, hagiographical and historical narratives concerning Adela depict her as a woman who was also a lord, neither categorisation detracting from the other. Kim LoPrete analsyses this material in detail, showing that Adela was depicted as a woman, physically attractive and sexually active within the bonds of marriage and motherhood, yet modest and chaste, and at the same time able to play a public role as lord and patron, while also mindful of religious obligations. While ecclesiastical writers might have their own agenda and occasionally condemn some of her actions, it is a tribute to her political skills that she met with no gender-based criticism. Using Adela of Blois as an example, Kim LoPrete is able to demonstrate that women not infrequently exercised lordly powers while playing out their gendered social roles in an aristocratic society, where since power was based in the family and household, the 'public' and 'private' spheres distinguished by modern theorists are hardly applicable and politically-active women generated little anxiety in men because they exercised lordly powers from within the household.

Catherine Lawless explores the position of a particular category of women who did not fit at all easily into either religious or social stereotypes, women who were the objects of amorous devotion on the part of prominent and influential citizens and on a more earthy level women who were mistresses, concubines and mothers of illegitimate children in Renaissance Florence. The women idealised as love objects were usually high-born ladies, who were celebrated in poetry or in art for their beauty, elegant manners and chastity, and since this was to a large degree a courtly game, it was possible for a prominent citizen to express his amorous devotion to a married lady very publicly without scandal. Nevertheless there was a certain tension in such relationships and the ladies risked criticism for extravagance and flightiness, if nothing worse, and for an unmarried girl like Marietta Strozzi, the combination of beauty and amorous attentions might give rise to gossip that seriously blighted her prospects of making a good marriage. Most of the women Catherine Lawless discusses did not have to worry about such tensions, however, because, with a few exceptions, concubines and mistresses were drawn from the lower classes, though some of them were married to someone else. Irregular relationships were common, ranging from men who had taken a mistress while living abroad as merchants, to nuns who caused scandal by becoming involved with men within their convent or who fled from it with a lover, to priests and friars who had mistresses and illegitimate children, to relationships between Florentine men, married or single, and women who might be from tradesmen's families, peasants, servants or slaves. While occasionally there is evidence of a long-term relationship, even of couples living together as man and wife, and occasionally the couple might belatedly marry, particularly in an effort to legitimise their children, usually the association was more temporary, casual or uneven. In many cases there is little information about the woman herself and the relationship was only referred to because it had resulted in illegitimate children, who might be cared for by their father at one extreme or deposited in the foundling hospital at the other. As Catherine Lawless points out the women involved in such relationships were marginal both in comparison with the upper-class women who were courtly love objects and with the virtuous women who lived as wives and mothers within the structure of a family, which formed the foundation of the Florentine state, but they are not negligible and should not be neglected.

Three essays deal with women and religion and the church, in somewhat different contexts and aspects, yet not without links and connections between them – indeed the first essay, that of Dianne Hall, provides another perspective on the activities of women in aristocratic society, since the protagonist, Elicia Butler, was almost certainly the sister of Piers Butler, recognised in 1537 as earl of Ormond. The trial and deposition of Elicia Butler from her position as abbess of the convent of Kilculliheen in 1531, the only known case of a religious woman being deposed by a bishop in Ireland, also provides an insight into religious life in Ireland in the last decades before the Reformation brought the dissolution of monasteries and convents. Dianne Hall sets the accusations against Elicia Butler, of mismanaging and dilapidating the goods of her house and of using excessive and unjustified violence against her nuns and against John McOdo, a neighbour's servant, in the context of religious and secular life of the period and of the proper role for women. The use of force and violence by an abbess against her nuns was not necessarily condemned, providing the motivation was to maintain discipline and correct faults. The monastic rule required that nuns should live harmoniously together, and this might require the use of force by the abbess against malcontents and transgressors. It would be wrong if, as alleged in Elicia's case, it arose, not from a desire to maintain proper standards of religious discipline, but from quarrelsomeness and bad temper on the part of the abbess. This particular example of the use of excessive and unjustified violence by a woman in the context of a religious house inspires reflections on the use of violence by women in secular life. Dianne Hall is able to quote a number of examples, some of them from Elicia Butler's own family, of women who engaged in warfare and violence or were thought to be the driving force behind vigorous action by their menfolk. Again the main criterion for the acceptability or otherwise of recourse to force by women was its motivation. In the context of parental discipline, or indeed warfare, recourse to force might be acceptable, but women who engaged in indirect acts of violence might be accused of treachery or deceit and also of 'unwomanly' conduct, though conversely they were likely to be punished less severely than men guilty of similar acts. The case of Elicia Butler, however, shows that there were limits to what was acceptable, even for a woman in her exalted social and ecclesiastical position.

Tadhg Ó hAnnracháin deals with the role of women in a very different religious context in Ireland, though interestingly the women he studies might also engage in acts of violence and count on being less severely punished than if the same actions were done by men. He discusses the role of women, and possible explanations for their special role, in the extension of the Catholic Reformation to Ireland and the consolidation of a Catholic identity throughout the island in the last decades of the sixteenth century and first half of the seventeenth. Contemporary Protestant observers were very conscious of the strong adherence of women to the Church of Rome and the influence they could exert in dissuading their husbands from the conformity to the Protestant Church required of them, and their transmision of their faith to their children, so that it was quickly diffused to other households through the marriage of their like-minded daughters. Though Protestant critics might regard the fact that the Catholicism was particularly supported by women as no recommendation for it and make accusations of impropriety in the relations of women and their Catholic priests, they were also conscious of these women as a force against evangelisation by the Protestant clergy, even able to prevent their menfolk gaining access to the ministrations of such clergy in case of sickness.

But the activity of women in support of the Catholic church was by no means confined to the domestic sphere. Women apparently took the intiative in riots aimed at rescuing Catholic priests from the authorities or disrupting attempts to conduct funeral services in a Protestant form. Although the women's prominence may be due in part to a belief that they were less likely to be prosecuted, it may also be an indication of a particularly strong bond with the local clergy and a sense of obligation to them. This seems to be paralleled in Gaelic Ireland, where the arrival unannounced of Catholic dignitaries, such as the papal nuncio GianBattista Rinuccini, quickly attracted a highly organised party of local ladies to greet them, somewhat to their consternation and inconvenience. Rinuccini also twice found his house surrounded by mobs of women complaining of their treatment at the hands of mutinous soldiers fighting for the papal cause, though there was also a political dimension to these demonstrations. These senior foreign clerics were impressed by the religious zeal and innocence of the Irish women with whom they came into contact, but on occasions found them over assertive and lacking in deference. The establishment in Ireland of a resident Catholic hierarchy by 1630 may have had provided some protection for women as well as establishing a stricter social control, and Tadgh Ó hAnnracháin ends his essay with a discussion of the limited evidence available for the differing reactions of men and women in Ireland to this new situation.

Carol Baxter deals with a convent very different from that of Elicia Butler and a religious situation very different from that of the adherents to Catholicism in Ireland, but her essay too is concerned with the relationships of women with each other and to the ecclesiastical authorities. Her essay centres on the nuns of the convent of Port-Royal, which became one of the centres of resistance to the condemnation of Cornelius Jansen's *Augustinus*, a synthesis of Augustinianism which the French Catholic Church regarded as heretical. The refusal of many of the nuns to sign the Formulary condemning this work resulted in increasingly severe measures against them by both ecclesiastical and secular authorities, culminating in their dispersal, the withholding of the sacraments and the destruction of their convent. Carol Baxter examines the reasons behind their remarkable resistance in the face of such pressure to conform. While the nuns were convinced that it was their religious duty to uphold what they saw as God's truth against the temptations to laxity and compromise and put a positive interpretation on persecution as a sign that they had been singled out for martyrdom, the circumstances of the history of their convent gave them a strong sense of solidarity, which stiffened their resistance. The reform of Port-Royal in 1609 had established strict cloistering and community of property, with entry to the convent determined by strength of commitment to the religious life rather than the availability of a dowry, and involved the replacement of family ties by the sisterhood of the convent. The strength of this sisterhood was revealed when the convent came under pressure, since very few of the nuns were willing to sign the Formulary, even when the leading members of the convent had been removed and imprisoned, revealing that resistance did not depend on the leadership of a few but was collective. Documents setting out their cause were produced after consultation of the nuns in general and agreed by all, although this did not preclude the existence of strong emotional bonds between individual resisters and among the community more generally. Resistance was seen as much as a sign of loyalty as a matter of personal choice, which meant that those who did sign the Formulary were seen as traitors, especially if they gained personal advantage from their submission. Waverers, including one sister who signed and retracted her signature more than once, were influenced by their affection for their fellow sisters and considerations of their reactions, and the authorities recognised that the nuns were more likely to submit if separated from the rest of the community. Those who were tempted by the fact that submission meant the restoration of the sacraments might then be racked by guilt that they were enjoying a privilege denied to their fellow sisters. While there were other factors, the resistance of the nuns of Port-Royal stands out as a remarkable example of a group of women united in a common purpose against all the pressure that the ecclesiastical and civil authorities could bring to bear upon them.

Samanatha Riches also deals with the period of the Reformation, but from a particular point of view, the use in both Catholic and Protestant visual propaganda of monstrous figures and more specifically of monsters who are visibly female. While only a small proportion of representations depict monsters as female, since most are not shown as belonging specifically to either sex, the feminised monster which appears in illustrations and descriptions in many European countries, gives rise to some interesting reflections. The serpent of the Garden of Eden was often depicted as female, with a serpent's body and a woman's head, her feminine and sexual character sometimes emphasised by conspicuous breasts, long hair and even a feminine headdress. She may be linked with Lilith, who is also presented in this form, and intended as a reference to the dangerous and untrustworthy character of the sexually-experienced female. When the composite figure of the Papal Ass was shown as female, it linked everything the Reformers saw as being wrong with the Church with female sexual depravity, and similar feminised, sexualised figures were used in anti-Reformation polemics. A particular case is illustrations of St George and the dragon, where the dragon is shown either with apparent female pudenda or with one or more little dragons. While the dragon's maternity and the presence of baby dragons risked making her a more sympathetic figure, the intention was probably to intimate that she was made yet more terrible by her ability spawn new evils. Samantha Riches interprets these representations in terms of a contrast between the dragon as female, sexual, evil and bestial and St George as male, chaste, good and human. The dragon and the virgin princess, depicted as female, chaste, good and human, would represent the polar opposites inherent in late medieval attitudes to women, the dragon an evil, sexual, bestial creature and the virgin princess, good, virginal and saintly, the worst and the best in female nature.

Many people have been involved in these conferences and the resulting publications, not just the editors and the authors of the papers given and the articles published, but also those who have assisted in making the conferences a success and given advice and assistance with the work of editing the papers for publication, Dr Ciaran Brady, Dr Edward Coleman, Dr Seán Duffy, Professor Corinna Salvadori Lonergan, Dr Mary O'Dowd and Professor John Scattergood who have chaired sessions and others who have encouraged us to continue with the enterprise. It has been a source of particular satisfaction that we have been able to extend the range of people involved to comprehend the universities of the whole of Ireland and also increasingly speakers from outside. We are reluctant to give hostages to fortune by giving this volume a number or undertaking to organise a conference each year, but we hope that there are many more of both yet to come.

A source for the depiction of Eve in the early-modern period: biblical Latin epic of the fifth and sixth centuries

John Flood

In 1560 Guillaume Morelle edited a one-volume octavo collection of the Latin verse of Pseudo-Hilary of Arles, Blossius Aemelius Dracontius, Claudius Marius Victorius, Alcimus Avitus of Vienne and Cyprian of Gaul (Cyprianus 'Gallus'), Christian poets of the fourth to sixth centuries, who had reformulated the story of creation within the conventions of the epic genre.[1] Morelle was no doubt trying to profit from the renewed interest in hexameral literature which had emerged due to the publication of editions of the Fathers (notably Basil the Great and Ambrose of Milan) earlier in the century.[2] The number of editions of the poets of Christian Latin epic testify to the popularity of the genre in the 1500s and 1600s. Dracontius' poem, for example, appeared in five editions between 1564 and 1651, while Avitus' work was published in thirteen editions between 1507 and 1654.[3]

Inspired by this body of work there emerged a series of Genesis-based biblical epics written in the vernacular. In European terms the most famous and

---

[1] Watson Kirkconnell in *The celestial cycle: the theme of Paradise Lost in world literature with translations of the major analogues* (New York, 1967), xix, mistakenly attributes this edition to Frédéric Morel (1552–1630), an understandable confusion considering the latter's output which included an edition of Basil's *Sermo de Paradiso*, a translation of the works of Philo Judaeus and Gregory of Nyssa, as well as Chrysostom's *In Genesin sermones*, and his *Discours sur la création des animaux et de la dignité de l'homme* (see Stanislas Gamber, *Le livre de la 'Génese' dans la poésie latine au Ve siècle* (Paris, 1899), p. 1). Before the age of the printing press, biblical Latin epics had been gathered together in groups of manuscripts, for example, Abbey of St Victor B.N. 14758 which Guillaume Morelle used for his text (Paris, 1560) and the ninth-century Laon Bibliothèque municipale MS. 273 which contains the work of Proba, Cyprian of Gaul, Hilary of Arles, Dracontius and Avitus (Daniel J. Nodes, 'Introduction' in Alcimus Avitus, *Avitus: The Fall of Man – De spiritalis historiae gestis Libri I–III*, ed. Daniel J. Nodes (Toronto, 1985), p. 10). [2] Erasmus had edited the works of Basil (1532) and Ambrose (1555). An edition of Ambrose's work had appeared earlier (1492) under the editorship of John d'Amerbach. [3] Claude Moussy, 'Introduction' in Blossius Aemilius Dracontius, *Œuvres*, vol. 1., ed. Claude Moussy and Colette Camus (Paris, 1985), 132;

influential of these was written by Guillaume du Bartas (1544–90) whose *La semaine* (1578) and *La seconde semaine* (1584) appeared in fifteen Latin, ten Dutch, seven German, six Italian and two Spanish editions.[4] In England du Bartas enjoyed a reputation second only to that of Erasmus[5] and parts of his poetry were translated by Sir Philip Sidney, James VI, Thomas Lodge and Joshua Sylvester.[6] Similar works were produced by poets of notable standing in other languages; Torquato Tasso composed *Le sette giornate del mundo creato* (1607), while in Portugal Luiz de Camões wrote *Da creacao e composicao do homem* (*c*.1580), and the Spanish Alonso de Acevedo's completed his *Creación del mundo* in 1615.[7]

This essay focuses on the manner in which Eve is represented in early-modern Europe. Part of this process involves examining her portrayal in the biblical Latin poetry which was popular at the time. As retellings of the beginning of all things, these poems are particularly relevant to examinations of attitudes to womankind in general, as their narratives deal with what was believed to be the foundational moment of human history by means of a story which depicts a woman at the centre of its action. This prominence places Eve in a position under scrutiny. Her chronological pre-eminence makes her not only the 'mother of all the living' (Genesis 3:20), but more specifically the prototype of all womankind, so that any judgement passed on Eve is by extension passed on her daughters.

The popularity of biblical Latin epic in sixteenth- and seventeenth-century Europe may have been a result of similarities which existed between the mindsets of the educated writers of late antiquity and the humanists of the early-modern era. Both sets of Christian writers faced the problem of reconciling the substance of revealed belief with the elegance of expression of classical literature. Both were committed simultaneously to the message of Christianity and to the stylistic richness to be found in pagan authors, who were the basis of their rhetorical education.[8] This reverence for two traditions – which were on

Nodes, op. cit., p. 5. **4** Maury Thibaut de Maisières, *Les poèmes inspirés du début de la Genèse à l'époque de la Renaissance* (Louvain, 1931), p. 57. **5** Anne Lake Prescott, *French poets and the English Renaissance: studies in fame and transformation* (New Haven and London, 1968), p. 144. **6** Sidney's work in this respect is now lost (See Katherine Duncan-Jones, *Sir Philip Sidney: courtier poet* (New Haven and London, 1991), p. 252). King James was a particularly ardent admirer of du Bartas' poetry: he rewarded du Bartas with a knighthood, an expensive golden chain and two thousand crowns in gold (Urban T. Holmes Jr and others (eds.), 'Introduction' in *The works of Guillaume De Salluste Sieur Du Bartas*, 3 vols. (Chapel Hill, 1935), i, pp. 20–1). A florid letter from the King to du Bartas extolling his poetic excellence has recently come to light (James Dauphiné, 'Le "Chevallier" Du Bartas: lettre inédite de Jacques VI d'Écosse', *Bibliothèque d'Humanisme et Renaissance* 59 (1997), 63–6). **7** Further vernacular treatments of the early chapters of Genesis are to be found in Watson Kirkconnell, op. cit. **8** Something like this is suggested by J.W. Binns, 'Biblical Latin poetry in

one level dichotomous – revived the practice of biblical Latin epic in the early modern period after it had been largely neglected during the later middle ages.

Biblical Latin epic had emerged in late antiquity as the recasting of the material of revelation in the language and style of Virgil. Educated early Christians saw that the more 'refined' Latin accounts of creation and paradise to be found in Virgil's fourth *Eclogue*, Ovid's *Metamorphoses* and Lucretius' *De rerum natura* were potential threats to the attractiveness of the cruder Hebrew narrative to be found in the Old Latin version of the Bible. This can be seen, for example, in the *Confessions* of St Augustine where he admits, 'when I studied the Bible and compared it with Cicero's dignified prose, it seemed to me unworthy'.[9]

Early Christian poetry is clearly an outgrowth of prose dogmatic apologetics, part of 'a syncretistic movement which parallels the articulation, begun earlier, of the Christian faith in the language and framework of Classical philosophy'.[10] Like dogmatic apologetics it evidently had a didactic purpose, but a didactic purpose whose focus was slightly different, as it engaged with faculties other than the purely cognitive:[11]

> The appeal of this poetry was directed to men of some culture and leisure, who, like the poets themselves, owed the whole atmosphere of their education to the public schools, and whose lukewarm Christianity might be transformed into something more serious and genuine by a method of instruction which would appeal to their aesthetic sense.[12]

Defences of the practice of writing Christian poetry were written by Lactantius, Hilary of Poitiers and Paulinus of Nola, amongst others. Lactantius expressed their arguments succinctly in his *Divinae institutiones* (*c*.305–11):

Renaissance England' in Francis Cairns (ed.), *Papers of the Liverpool Latin Seminar*, vol. 3 (Liverpool, 1981), p. 388.   9 St Augustine, *Confessions*, tr. Maria Boulding (London, 1997), p. 80 (*Confessions* 3:5:9). An outline of the sometimes uneasy relationship between early Christianity and classical poetry can be found in W. Evenepoel, 'The place of poetry in Latin Christianity' in J. Den Boeft and A. Hilhorst (eds.), *Early Christian poetry: a collection of essays* (Leiden, 1993).   10 Daniel J. Nodes, *Doctrine and exegesis in Biblical Latin poetry*, ARCA vol. 31 (Leeds, 1993), p. 1.   11 Christian Latin poetry could teach both dogma and rhetoric. Victorius and Avitus wrote that their work could profitably be used for the education of the young (Gamber, op. cit., p. 33). In addition to these, other works considered here such as the *Dittachaeon* of Prudentius and the *Cento* of Proba were used as pedagogical tools in antiquity, throughout the middle ages and into the early-modern period. See Nodes, op. cit., 1985, pp. 10–11; Ian Thomson and Louis Perraud (eds. and trs.), *Ten Latin schooltexts of the later Middle Ages: translated selections* (Lewiston, 1990), p. 89; Elizabeth A. Clark and Diane F. Hatch (eds. and trs.), *The golden bough, the oaken cross: the Virgilian Cento of Faltonia Betitia Proba* (Chico, California, 1981), p. 10; Evans, op. cit., p. 142, notes that Proba was on the syllabus of St Paul's while Milton was a student there.   12 F.J.E. Raby, *A history of Christian Latin*

... although the truth may be defended without eloquence, as it has often been defended by many, it ought to be illustrated and in a certain way asserted by a clarity and splendor of speech so that, equipped with its own force as well as adorned by the light of oratory, it may more potently seep into minds.[13]

The similarities between the intellectual milieus of early Christianity and early-modern Europe are emphasised in the continued necessity to account for the writing of Christian poetry. Boccaccio, both in his *Genealogiae deorum gentilium* (1360) and in his life of Dante, saw an obligation to harmonise the ostensibly immoral tales of pagan antiquity with divine revelation. Boccaccio's ideas in this regard were elaborated by his successors throughout the 1500s and 1600s.[14] One of these, Sir Philip Sidney (1554–86), pointed to the poetry to be found in the Bible and, claiming Jesus as his licence to write verse, echoed Lactantius in asserting that truth may be well served by rhetoric:

Certainly, even our Saviour Christ could as well have given the moral commonplaces of uncharitableness and humbleness as the divine narration of Dives and Lazarus; or of the disobedience and mercy, as that heavenly discourse of the lost child and the gracious father; but that His through-searching wisdom knew the estate of Dives burning in hell, and of Lazarus in Abraham's bosom, would more constantly (as it were) inhabit both the memory and judgement.[15]

The Latin tradition of the metrical treatment of biblical material appears to have been inaugurated by *Evangeliorum libri IV*, the hexameter paraphrase of the Gospels written by the Spanish priest Caius Vettius Aquilinus Juvencus (fl. c.330). The Old Testament, with its variety of heroic stories, more easily lent itself to epic treatment and it is in a late fourth-century work, the *Cento* of Faltonia Betitia Proba (fl. c.350–70) that one has the first extended poetic treatment of Genesis 2–3 in a poem which ingeniously combines Virgilian lines with the text of the Bible.[16]

---

poetry from the beginnings to the close of the Middle Ages, 2nd ed. (Oxford, 1953), p. 76. 13 *Institutiones* 1.1.10, quoted in Evenpoel, op. cit. p. 41. 14 Vernon Hall Jr and others, 'Renaissance poetics' in Alex Preminger and T.V.F. Brogan (eds.), *The Princeton encyclopedia of poetry and poetics*, 3rd ed. (Princeton, 1993), pp. 1024–5. 15 From *The defence of poesy* (Katherine Duncan-Jones (ed.), *Sir Philip Sidney, the Oxford authors* (Oxford, 1989), p. 223). 16 A cento 'is a poem or poetic sequence made up of recognizable shorter sequences from one or more existing poems', Stephen J. Harrison, 'cento' in Simon Hornblower and Anthony Spawforth (eds.), *The Oxford classical dictionary*, 3rd ed. (Oxford, 1996), p. 309. Proba's poem inspired three other Christian centos between the fourth and the sixth century.

Later poetry dealing with Genesis was less artistically constrained in its approach to Holy Scripture. Despite this there were obvious issues of authority involved in recasting the word of God. Stylistic concerns would not be sufficient to give warrant to an alteration of the divine message. Thus Paulinus of Nola (d. 431) promised:

> Though I use the poet's art, the song I will sing will not be invented. I shall tell it with an historian's truthfulness and without the poet's deceit, because a servant of Christ should not utter lies.[17]

In the same tone, the sixth-century bishop of Vienne (in Gaul), St Avitus (whose poetry will be examined at the end of this paper) wrote that for the Christian the licence to lie granted to secular poets and painters is not given to those dealing with revealed truth. If, in consequence, his work appears to lack skill, Avitus is undeterred, as he submits his case to the judgement of God and not to that of humanity.[18]

Consequently, the division between 'paraphrase' and interpretation of Scripture was a vital one. An appreciation of this is today hindered somewhat by the employment on the part of the Christian poets of methods of 'paraphrase' drawn from classical precedents based on the writings of Cicero, Pliny the Younger and Quintilian.[19] The application of ancient practices meant that 'paraphrase', as it was then understood, encompassed treatments exploiting regulations governing abbreviation, omission, conflation, *interpretatio* and certain forms of amplification.[20] Extensive developments of narrative threads present in the biblical original *might* then 'be thought of as stylistic embellishments, matters of *elocutio* not *inventio*'.[21]

It is worth approaching the treatment of Eve in the Latin biblical epics individually – even at the cost of spending some more time on them – as in doing so one gets a better idea of the differing approaches to the representation of Eve found in a series of works which are similar in outline. In examining these texts, the focus is on the effect they may have had on the manner in which Eve was regarded in early-modern Europe and, therefore, questions of the works' original theological context will be eschewed while their narratives, particularly as they deal with the Fall, will be closely scrutinised.[22]

---

[17] Carm. 20:28–30, quoted in Evenepoel, op. cit., p. 45. [18] Michel Roberts, 'The prologue to Avitus' *De spiritalis historiae gestis*: Christian poetry and poetic licence', *Traditio* 36 (1980), pp. 399–407 q.v. [19] Michael Roberts, *Biblical epic and rhetorical paraphrase in Late Antiquity*, ARCA vol. 16 (Liverpool, 1985), pp. 6–20 q.v. [20] Ibid., pp. 107–60 q.v. [21] Ibid., 162. [22] Because the *Metrum in Genesin (c.*430) of Ps. Hilary of Arles omits an account of the Fall, it will be passed over here (Hilary of Arles, *Metrum in Genesin ad Leonem Papam*, ed. Rudolph Peiper, *Corpus scriptorum ecclesiasticorum latinorum* vol. 23 (Vienna, 1891), pp. 231–9. Note that in the early-modern period the work was sometimes attributed to Hilary of Poitiers). Similarly, there

Before looking at some of the epics dealing with the Fall it is worthwhile mentioning the *Tituli historiarum* (often known as the *Dittochaeon*) of Aurelius Clemens Prudentius (348–post-405), a series of four-line stanzas which provide snapshots of the main action of key incidents from biblical history.[23] Due to their brevity the stanzas are of necessity condensations, focusing attention on what the author considers significant. Prudentius' summary of the action of Genesis 2–3 is as follows:

> In the beginning Eve was as white as a dove, but was after
> Stained by the serpent's dark venom when he enticed her to evil,
> And in turn she infected with foul taint the innocent Adam;
> Then the victorious snake gave them leaves to cover their nudeness.[24]

The action of this stanza turns on the contrast between innocence and pollution, light and darkness. *Both* Eve and Adam are white/innocent before the serpent corrupts them. However, the impression created on the reader by attributing action to the infected Eve while Adam remains passive (described only by the adjective 'innocent') clearly places the woman, rather than the man, on a step nearer evil.

At the head of the epic treatment of Genesis is the *Cento* of Faltonia Betitia Proba, the wife of Clodius Celsinus Adelphius, prefect of Rome in 351.[25] Proba's

---

will be no detailed examination of Ps. Prosper of Aquitaine's *Carmen de providentia Dei* (*c*.416) as, although it deals briefly with the Fall, it does so in a manner which focuses solely on Adam. Although this might be seen as excluding Eve from the culpability of the original sin, it is more likely that she was passed over as being incidental to the history of salvation, since as Romans 5:12 informs us, death came through one man, i.e. Adam. The relevant section of the text can be found in Michael P. McHugh (ed.), *The carmen de providentia Dei attributed to Prosper of Aquitaine: a revised text with an introduction, translation, and notes*. The Catholic University of America Patristic Studies, vol. 98 (Washington D.C., 1964), 273–5. **23** It has been theorised that it was written to inspire/accompany a series of pictures (Angelo DiBernardino and Nello Cipriani, 'Christian poetry' in Angelo DiBernardino (ed.), *Patrology*, vol. 4, trans. Placid Solari (Westminster, Maryland, 1986), p. 296; Ian Thomson and Louis Perraud, op. cit., p. 87. This chapter does not consider Prudentius's 'Hymnus ante cibum' in the *Cathemerinon* as it is mainly a paraphrase (in the modern sense) of the Genesis text (Prudentius, *The poems of Prudentius*, vol. 1, trans. Mary Clement Eagan, *Fathers of the Church* vol. 43 (Washington D.C., 1962), pp. 19–21 q.v.) I note that according to a reference in Gennadius of Marseille's *De viris illustribus* (*c*.480) Prudentius wrote a work on creation and the original condition of humanity which is now lost. Though Gennadius did not specify whether this work was written in prose or verse, given the nature of Prudentius's work, it is likely to have been the latter (Jacques Fontaine, *Naissance de la poésie dans l'occident chrétien: esquisse d'une historie de la poésie latine chrétienne du IIIe au VIe siecle* (Paris, 1981), p. 153, n. 259.) **24** Stanza 1 in Prudentius, *The poems of Prudentius*, vol. 2, trans. Mary Clement Eagan, *Fathers of the Church* vol. 52 (Washington D.C., 1965), p. 179. **25** Quotations are

retelling of the Creation and Fall occupy the first 277 lines of her 694-line survey of the Old and New Testaments. Interpreting her work is complicated by its form, as it operates on two levels, that of a straightforward narrative and that of a poem which is elaborated and constrained by its quotation of Virgil. An illustration of how these two levels may come into conflict can be found in the account of the formation of Eve:

> And suddenly arose a wondrous gift –
> Imposing proof – and shone in brilliant light:
> Woman, a virgin she, unparalleled
> In figure and in comely breasts, now ready
> for a husband ... (29)

On the face of it, this passage is one of praise of Eve, a *mirabile donum* created in beauty and light. However, as the description of her breasts as *pulchro pectore virgo* comes from *Aeneid* 3: 426, Virgil's description of Scylla, the passage can be interpreted in a more ominous fashion as both Scylla and Eve lure men to their deaths.[26]

At the level of the narrative Proba's Eve is sometimes treated in a positive light. Before her creation no other being was worthy enough to dare to approach the man, let alone be his helpmeet (29). In addition, Eve is not subjected to the gender specific punishment of childbirth to be found in Genesis 3:16. However, even without a knowledge of the Virgilian parallels, the text's descriptions of Eve as an 'impious wife' (33, from the description of Clytemnestra who murdered her husband Agamemnon), who was filled with 'madness' (37, like Dido before her suicide), 'Of all these ills the origin and cause' (43, Dido again), is enough to confirm that 'Proba's views on women were not more charitable than those of her male counterparts'.[27]

The Virgilian parallels would not have been lost on the scholars of the early-modern period and it cannot be objected that the negative descriptions of Eve are principally a consequence of the profusion of troublesome or malign women, harpies and furies of the *Aeneid*, as the references to the Virgin Mary clearly demonstrate the care with which Proba matched Virgil and the Bible.[28]

The *Heptateuch* (so called as it is composed of a series of paraphrases of the first seven books of the Old Testament) of Cyprian of Gaul (fl. *c*.397–425) may

---

taken from Clark and Hatch, op. cit., and are referred to by page numbers in parentheses in the body of the text. The Latin text is to be found in Carolus Schenkl (ed.), *Poetae Christiani minores*, Corpus scriptorum ecclesiasticorum latinorum, 16 (Vienna, 1888).
26 An observation made in Clark and Hatch, op. cit. p. 157.   27 Ibid., p. 159.   28 For example, Mary is introduced as 'Wearing a virgin's countenance and clothes' (53), a phrase from the description of Venus, the mother of Aeneas. This emphasises the parallel between the pagan hero (Aeneas) and the divine one (Christ). The later

have been an attempt to provide an Old Testament counterpart to Juvencus' Gospel-based poem.[29] As such, it sought 'to present a hexameter version of the biblical text which would be as close as possible to its original, shunning for the most part the addition of interpretative expansions'.[30] This description, combined with the relative brevity of the section of the poem which deals with Genesis 1–3 (one hundred and thirty-six lines), might give rise to the expectation that it does not contain much innovative material.

On the other hand, others have not been slow to recognise the specific exegetical interests and consequent elaborations of Cyprian.[31] Turning to the text, it can be seen that it not only provides an interpretation of the events of Genesis 2–3 which emphasises the merciful dealing of God with humanity despite the disobedience and sin of the Fall, but it does so by introducing novel elements into the narrative.[32]

The exceptional dignity of Adam is based on his privileged origin. Whereas light had been produced by the grand and impersonal *Fiat lux*, man's creation depicts God as having been more directly drawn into his work:

> 'Let us make man exactly similar to us in appearance
> And then he can have dominion over the whole world.'
> And although he could create man by his Word alone,
> Yet he was kind enough to lead him with his holy hand
> And breathed from his divine lungs into the insensible creature's Chest.
>   (ll. 27–31)

God's special involvement is also shown in the creation of Eve, although in keeping with the biblical text (Genesis 2:18, 20–22), she is intended as a helper for Adam:

---

references to Mary also avoid quotations associated with any of the female figures associated with Eve.   29 For the most part, quotations are taken from the translation of the section of the poem dealing with Genesis 2–3 to be found in Carolinne White (ed. and tr.), *Early Christian Latin poets* (London and New York, 2000), pp. 100–4. References to line numbers in this translation are given in parentheses in the body of the text. An English translation is also to be found in Alexander Roberts and James Donaldson (eds.), *The writings of Tertullian, Vol. III*, Ante-Nicene Christian library, vol. 18 (Edinburgh, 1870), pp. 293–300. The Latin text, edited by Rudolph Peiper, is to be found in *Cypriani Galli poetae heptateuchos accedunt incertorum de Sodoma et Iona et ad senatorem carmina et Hilarii quae feruntur in Genesin, de Maccabaeis atque de Euangelio*, Corpus scriptorum ecclesiasticorum latinorum, vol. 23 (Vienna, 1891). The first early-modern edition was that of Guillaume Morelle (1560). He later included it in his works of St Cyprian of Carthage (Paris, 1564). J.A. Fabricius produced an edition that same year (Basle, 1564). 30 Judith McClure, 'The biblical epic and its audience in Late Antiquity' in Francis Cairns (ed.), *Papers of the Liverpool Latin Seminar*, vol. 3 (Liverpool, 1981), p. 307. See also Raby, op. cit. p. 76.   31 Nodes, op. cit., 1993, p. 26.   32 J.M. Evans, op. cit.,

> When he [God] saw that man was formed in his own image,
> He judged that he should not remain alone to worry over nagging cares.
> And so he at once poured sleep over the creature's eyes
> So that he could gently remove a rib out of which to form woman,
> So the combined substance might strengthen the double limbs.
> She was given the name of Eve, signifying 'life'. (ll. 33–7)

In the biblical text Eve is named by Adam (Genesis 3:20) so Cyprian is treating the order of the original narrative freely. What is the effect of this reordering? It might be argued that the association between Eve and 'life' is strengthened by the fact that it is God who names her; however, it is more likely that he is combining Genesis 2:24 and 3:20, both passages which are concerned with children. On the other hand, if Cyprian's reordering of the story is a considered one, then the fact that the man names all living beings after Eve's creation (rather than before it as in Genesis 2:19–20) emphasises that it is 'Adam who has been granted practical understanding and ingenuity' (l. 43).

Eve is a 'loyal wife' (l. 64) and together with Adam she is told of the harmful apple. In this way Cyprian avoids a potential problem which St Ambrose had noted, namely, that in Genesis the divine prohibition is delivered before Eve was created and, in consequence, some might doubt that she had clearly been informed of God's command.[33]

Though Cyprian deals summarily with the Fall, his treatment of it is unusual in that he presents the serpent appearing to Eve during her first experience of 'the deep darkness of night'. The reader cannot but feel sympathy for her 'soft heart under her breast'[34] as she is interrogated by a serpent capable of 'outdoing all the other animals in cunning' (l. 73). Furthermore, his blandishments do not appeal to the woman's pride with promises of the divine exaltation mentioned in Genesis 3:5, rather, he merely assures her that if she eats of the forbidden fruit the light will return. Though Eve is reluctant, 'her weakness of mind overcame her resolve' (l. 82) and having eaten, true to the serpent's word, 'The clear sky, unblemished by a single cloud, shone bright' (l. 84). Eve is driven to pass on the gift (*munus*) to her husband and for him too the night is lighted up before the couple realise their crime in the revelation of the shame associated with their genitals.

Cyprian's style is sparse and he makes almost no attempt to explore the psychology of his characters. For the reader who has to reconstruct their motivations from external actions, the narrative cannot be seen as particularly

---

pp. 140–1. Evans' treatment of the poets in what was then thought to be their chronological order involves him dealing with Cyprianus Gallus after Dracontius, Victorinus and Avitus (thus invalidating some of his theories about their respective influences on one another).   33 *Patrologia Latina* 14, col. 302 (*De Paradiso* 1.12.54).   34 'sub pectore

condemnatory. Neither Adam nor Eve is motivated by pride or greed; they are innocents who long for the return of the brightness they are used to. Eve does not knowingly pass on an accursed fruit to her husband; rather she shares with him a 'gift'. Indeed, Cyprian's approach to the fruit of the forbidden tree is strangely ambiguous. As has been seen, eating of it does in fact produce some sort of illumination. Is this the double-edged sword of knowledge which deprives them of innocence (by revealing their nakedness) while lighting up their minds?[35]

Inevitably, however, God's punishment is meted out. The narrator describes the woman as 'pitiably tricked by ... treacherous persuasion' (l. 114), and while God gives her the struggles of childbirth before punishing Adam and turning them out of the garden, he is soon personally at work again, sewing the flayed hides of cattle together lest the couple feel cold (ll. 131–3).

If the abiding care of God is to be found in the *Heptateuch*, Claudius Marius Victorius (d. *c.*425–50) – who appears to have known Cyprian's work – is even more explicit on this point.[36] He opens his *Alethia* (*Truth*) with a prayer forbidding anyone to blame Adam for his sin, since by disobeying God he ultimately brought about the conquering of death.[37] Jacques Fontaine has suggested that each of the three books of *Alethia* ends with a typological reference to humanity's final salvation, and it is clear that, although the poet describes the horror of humanity's fallen condition at some length, he emphasises the fact that God's mercy exceeds his justice (Bk. 1, ll. 463–5 q.v.).[38]

The length of Victorius' treatment of Genesis (547 lines) allows him to interpolate more material than Cyprian. Despite this, he is less inventive than

mollia cordia', Peiper, op. cit., p. 176.   **35** Is it possible that Cyprian was influenced by Gnostic teaching? Though the rest of his poem is without any of the obviously heterodox interpretation of Genesis to be found in Gnostic commentaries, Cyprian's account of the Fall is closer to Gnostic ideas about the light of knowledge and understanding than to mainstream Christian thought. For a summary of Gnostic treatments of Genesis 2–3 see Giovanni Filoramo, *A history of gnosticism*, tr. Anthony Alcock (Oxford, 1990), pp. 93–8 and Kurt Rudolph, *Gnosis: the nature and history of gnosticism*, tr. Robert McLachlan Wilson (Edinburgh, 1983), p. 99.   **36** Victorius is not to be confused with Victorinus, bishop of Pettau (d. *c.*304), a martyr who wrote a (now lost) commentary on Genesis in addition to a treatise *De fabricia mundi*.   **37** The edition of *Alethia* used here is that of P.F. Hovingh in Joseph Martin (ed.), *Commodianus, Claudius Marius Victorius*, Corpus Christianorum series latina, vol. 128 (Turnhout, 1960) and is referred to by line number in the body of the text. For the English translation of this work I am grateful to Revd Prof. Thomas Finan (St Patrick's College, Maynooth). The text can also be found in Schenkl, op. cit. and *Patrologia Latina* vol. 61 (the latter should be used with some caution as it is ultimately based on Jean de Gagny's edition (Lyons, 1536), part of which was composed by de Gagny himself (Gamber, op. cit., p.16)). An English translation of the serpent's address to Eve appears in White, op. cit., pp. 119–25.   **38** Jacques Fontaine, op. cit. p. 242. Book I ends with the suggestion that just as life was lost through the wood of the forbidden tree, so might it be restored

his predecessor, insofar as his story proceeds along fairly conventional lines. Typical of such elaboration (and of his somewhat convoluted hexameters) is his description of Adam's feelings on the creation of a wife whom, as she was made from him, he finds deserving of care:

> a new grace touched Adam's soul, and desire (*affectus*), received through his eyes, entered into his viscera and penetrated into his bones with such heat that it already gave him to know, that the name of the woman was wife that children are dear and parents to be given second place to spouses. (Bk. 1, ll. 382–7)[39]

Here, Eve's creation is described in terms of the change she brings about in Adam. At this stage in the poem Eve's being is mediated through her effect on her husband, a particularly acute form of narrative subordination. Furthermore, the man's visceral reaction to the woman is erotically charged; the word *affectus* will later be used to describe the longing that one sex feels for the other (Bk. 2, l. 61), a longing which Adam uses to excuse his complicity in Eve's sin.[40]

While the poet is comparatively generous to Adam, the adjectives which Victorius attaches to Eve are unsympathetic. She is *incautam ... Evam* and *credula ... Eva*, easily open to the temptation of evil (Bk. 1, ll. 397; 411–2). Having broken the divine 'prescription with sacrilegious bites', she is become 'learned in evil' and seeking relief for her sin she 'easily drags her husband into the crime' (Bk. 1, ll. 412–14).[41] By contrast Adam is *miserabilis,* and even though he cedes to temptation, he has been overcome by a 'double enemy', namely, Eve and the serpent.

Evans notes that Victorius 'takes great pains to demonstrate the justice of His [God's] sentence'. One of the results of this is that 'Eve, who multiplied sin by corrupting her husband, is condemned to the pain of natural multiplication' while Adam 'who rebelled against God, is condemned to suffer the rebellion of the earth'.[42] What Evans does not note is that although the emphasis of the poem at this stage is placed on the fallen condition of humanity (*quam sit triste mori*, Bk. 2, l. 99), the poet introduces his own additions to God's judgement on Eve as found in Genesis 3:16 (the Vulgate version of which reads, 'multiplicabo aerumnas tuas et conceptus tuos in dolore paries filios et sub viri potestate eris

---

by wood (i.e. the cross); Book 2 ends with Moses and the Flood, a type of baptism, while Book 3 also refers to baptism at its end.   **39** 'tetigit noua gratia mentem/ affectusque oculis in uiscera nota receptus/irruit et tanto penetrauit in ossa calore,/ut iam scire daret, quod nomen coniugis uxor,/quod dulces nati postponendique parentes/ coniugibus'. Cf. Genesis 2:23–4.   **40** There is a contradiction here in that in Book 1, l. 430ff. Victorius notes that any bodily cares the couple have are due to the Fall. **41** 'rupit sacrilegis praescriptum morsibus Eua ... iam docta mali ... et in crimem facilem tractura maritum'.   **42** J.M. Evans, op. cit., p. 125. Cf. Bk. 1, ll. 486–522.

et ipse dominabitur tui').⁴³ In *Alethia* woman is to become 'a subject destined to feel the will of a *hard* husband' (emphasis mine) whose 'children will sometimes be a cause of death to their mangled mother' (Bk. 1, ll. 501–2; 507).⁴⁴

When the couple have realised their error and have been expelled from Paradise it is Adam who is the first to raise his head from the earth to address God in prayer and it is Adam who is the first to speak, suggesting to Eve that their initial action be the stoning of the serpent, thereby 'giving death to the death giver' (Bk. 2, l. 97).⁴⁵ In his speaking, he not only demonstrates his superior initiative (the natural state which was reversed to humanity's ruin in Book 1), but he also ties the travail of Eve to the heavy punishment of subsequent generations. It is a chilling vision:

> Then it will come to pass that Eve, having acquired wisdom and certain of salvation, will serve me and having experienced the hard sufferings of giving birth she will bring forth peoples, who will be struck by our crime, and a succession will expiate the sins of the fathers by the deaths of the descendants, making [for] eternal punishment. (Bk. 2, ll. 85–9)⁴⁶

The three books of *De laudibus Dei* (*The praise of God*) by Blossius Aemelius Dracontius (fl. *c*.494) are focused artistically and doctrinally on God's mercy.⁴⁷ The poet enjoyed no shortage of time to compose his work as he was supplied with a personal perspective which was likely to stimulate his fellow feeling for the grief of Eve and Adam, writing it as he did, *circa* 494 while incarcerated by the Vandal King Gunthamund.⁴⁸

Dracontius has a creative empathy for the human condition before the Fall. Adam is born into a naive questioning of life, a life which is lonesome while he is without a partner:

> But seeing from afar the beasts of burden in the green fields
> and silently asking of himself what these were all together
> and he considered why he had no companion with him. (ll. 356–8)⁴⁹

---

43 *Biblia Sacra: iuxta latinam vulgatam versionem* (1926). Ed. Henry Quentin. Rome, Typis Polyglottis Vaticanus. **44** 'praebebis famulare iugum subiectaque duri/arbitrum sensura uiri'; 'mortis nonnumquam lacerae sint causa parenti'. **45** 'auctorem leti leto dare'. **46** 'tunc erit, ut rerum compos et certa salutis/seruiat Eua mihi saeuumque experta creandi/supplicium pariat populos, qui crimine nostro/plecantur, purgetque patrum peccata nepotum/mortibus aeternam faciens successio poenam'. **47** Only the first book, 818 lines long, is written in the form of a biblical epic. It is of note that this book became separated from the other two and was circulated independently in the Middle Ages under the title *De opere sex dierum*. The best edition of *De laudibus Dei* is: Blossius Aemelius Dracontius, *Œuvres*, ed. Claude Moussy & Colette Camus (Paris, 1985). All quotation will be taken from this edition which will be referred to by line number in the body of the text. **48** Claude Moussy, op. cit., pp. 18–26 q.v. **49** 'at procul exspectat uirides iumenta per

It is in this context that the Almighty takes pity on him and creates woman, so that the couple will love one another and be of the same will (ll. 364–7). Dracontius' emphasis is on the mutuality of the married life, and it is to reinforce this that God forms Eve from the man's side, when he could instead have made her – like Adam – from the dust of the earth (ll. 377–80). God's new creation deserves a powerful description in her own right, even if – as in Victorius' *Alethia* – it is mediated through Adam's gaze:

> She stood before his eyes covered by no veil
> Her body snow white and naked, like a nymph of the deeps.
> The hair of her head was uncut, her cheeks blushing beautiful,
> Everything about her was lovely; eyes, mouth, neck and hands,
> As well as the Thunderer's fingers could form her. (ll. 393–7)[50]

This remarkably sensual description reminds us that most of Dracontius' work was secular in nature and that elsewhere he tackled conventional epic subjects such as Achilles, Hercules, Helen and Medea.[51] Despite the beauty of Eve's physical appearance, the pair are as sexually innocent together as Adam was naive when he was alone: 'They had their fingers and eyes and considered their genitals in the same light' (l. 443).[52] It is into this idyll that the 'venomous serpent, concealing gnawing envy under a front of modesty' is introduced to attack the 'soft heart of the girl' (ll. 463–7; 471).[53] The deadly fruit works its evil so that Eve believes that the time of Paradise which had gone before was wasted and, in a repetition of a familiar theme, 'the tempted woman seduces her husband' (l. 477).[54]

The sinners' story ends with their punishment. Unusually, the reader is told that Adam's blaming of the woman when confronted by God (Genesis 3:12) was not aimed at exculpating himself; rather its purpose was that he would have a companion to share in his misfortune. It is likely that in Carthage Dracontius would have had ample opportunity to encounter the writings of Augustine. The mention of companionship here may then be an adaptation of Augustine's

---

agros/et de se tacitus quae sint haec cuncta requirit/vel quare secum non sint haec cuncta uolutat'. **50** 'Constitit ante oculos nullo uelamine tecta,/ corpore nuda simul niueo quasi nympha profundi:/ caesaries intonsa comis, gena pulcra rubore,/omnia pulcra gerens, oculos os colla manusque,/ vel qualem possent digiti formare Tonantis'. **51** See David F. Bright, *The miniature epic in Vandal Africa* (Norman, Oklahoma and London, 1987). **52** 'Quod digitos oculosque, putant hoc quoque pudenda'. Is there a hint here of Augustine's belief that before the Fall Adam and Eve could voluntarily control their genitals just like their fingers. See *Patrologia Latina* 41, col. 431 (*De civitate Dei* 14.23.2) and Peter Brown, *The body and society: men, women, and sexual renunciation in early Christianity* (New York, 1988), pp. 417–9. **53** '... serpente uenenum/inuidiae mordacis habens sub fronte modesta'; 'mollia corda puellae'. **54** 'tempta seducta

assertion that Adam took the fruit from Eve, knowing it to be wrong, as he could not bear to be separated from her.⁵⁵ The difference between these two authors is that whereas in Augustine Adam's desire not to be separated from his wife leads to his being dragged down by Eve's transgression, in Dracontius it is the man who attempts to bring down the woman. The importance of the bond between the couple is, therefore, a theme to which the poet returns (ll. 536–43). When it comes to their punishment, the judgement of God is delivered as one sentence; death is ordained for man and woman and no mention is made of gender-specific chastisement (ll. 544–9). They are treated together, united as a married couple.

It has been suggested that as he was in Vandal Africa, Dracontius could show more freedom in his dealing with the text of Genesis.⁵⁶ However, this is to forget that in Carthage the Vandals had their own orthodoxy, Arianism, in defence of which they had persecuted both the Catholics and the Donatists.⁵⁷ This did not prevent Dracontius from describing Arius as *insipiens* (l. 738). Indeed, what one critic has said of his secular work might well be applied to his Christian poetry:

> Dracontius is not afraid to create new directions for his stories and to draw new lessons from them ... In pursuit of this goal Dracontius draws from whatever source or form will serve his purposes.⁵⁸

St Alcimus Avitus (c.450–518), bishop of Vienne, the last of the epic poets I will look at, represents not only the chronological culmination of the series I have been following (there is evidence that he knows the work of Cyprian, Victorius and Dracontius),⁵⁹ but he is sometimes seen as marking the high point of the practice of biblical Latin epic in Late Antiquity.⁶⁰ In part this is due to his innovative characterisation and his attempts to explore the psychology of the

---

maritum'.   55 *Patrologia Latina* 41, col. 419 (*De civitate Dei* 14:11); *Patrologia Latina* 34, cols. 209–10 (*De Genesi contra Manichaeos libri II* 2.17.26 to 2.18.28); *Patrologia Latina* 34, cols. 453–4 (*De Genesi ad litteram* 11.42, 59). Augustine needs to reconcile his account of the fall with 1 Tim. 2:14 which asserts that, unlike Eve, Adam 'non est seductus'.   56 Charles Wittke, *Numen litterarum: the old and the new in Latin poetry from Constantine to Gregory the Great*, Mittellateinische Studien und Texte V (Leiden, 1971), p. 178.   57 Bright, op. cit., p. 11.   58 Ibid., 248. An example of Dracontius's reworking a Fall-related topos is his account of the winds which appear in Hilary of Arles' *Metrum in Genesin* and in Victorius as agents barring Adam and Eve from Eden but which are manifestations of God's care in *De laudibus Dei* (see Daniel J. Nodes, 'Benevolent winds and the spirit of God in *De laudibus Dei* of Dracontius', *Vigiliae Christianae* 43 (1989), pp. 282–92).   59 Nicole Hecquet-Noti, 'Introduction' in Avit de Vienne, *Histoire Spirituelle, Tome I (Chants I–III)*, ed. and tr. Nicole Hecquet-Noti, Sources Chrétiennes, 444 (Paris, 1999), p. 59. See also the index of proper names in this edition. 60 Gamber, op. cit., p. 24; Nodes, op. cit., 1993, p. 55.

crucial moments surrounding the Fall. Avitus seeks to flesh out the story, not only with physical descriptions of the beauties of Eden, but also with attempts to explain the interior movements of the tale's protagonists.

Following the psychological action of Avitus' *De spiritalis historiae gestis* (*The deeds of spiritual history*)[61] is not always easy. The account of Adam's deep sleep as God forms Eve from his rib is 'interrupted' by a theological exposition of the Eve/Church typology which is in turn followed by a sustained comment on the nature of marriage (which, incidentally, stresses the necessity of the *woman's* remaining faithful to the bond). This tendency, combined with long Virgilian descriptions of Paradise, sometimes shifts the focus from the drama of the Fall, so that the modern reader may be less apt to appreciate Avitus' innovation in his approach to Eve and Adam.

Avitus' independence from his immediate predecessors in his treatment of Eve is evident from the moment of her creation. She is 'a form delightful in its grace and beauty ... that new apparition' (76), and as such she is created without being immediately subject to the approving eyes of Adam. The good bishop is not, however, one to let an occasion for didacticism pass, and readers are subsequently warned that the Devil often takes the form of 'a girl with a beautiful body' so that he may draw 'men's passionate gazes towards obscene joys' (81).

Despite initial appearances then, Avitus will prove to be lacking in deliberate pro-feminist credentials. The serpent (whose elaborate physical description has something of the erotic about it) is afraid that he will not succeed in tempting the man, so he 'began to pester the weaker ear' (83), an idea which Avitus may have found in Augustine.[62] The scenes which follow display the poet's rhetorical training in persuasion and controversy.[63] The serpent knows his mark, and aims at Eve's vanity with a touch or two of dramatic irony:

> O happy creature and glory of the earth, maiden most beautiful, you whom radiant grace decks with the blush of modesty, you who will become the parent of the race, whom the vast world looks to as mother, you, the first and faithful delight, the solace of your husband ... rightly

---

[61] All quotations from *De spiritalis* are from Avitus of Vienne, *The poems of Alcimus Ecdicius Avitus: translation and introduction*, ed. and tr. George W. Shea, Medieval and Renaissance Texts and Studies, vol. 172 (New York, 1997). Page numbers are given in parentheses in the main text. The preferred Latin texts of books 1 to 3 of *De spiritalis* are: Avitus of Vienne, *Avitus: The Fall of Man: De spiritalis historiae gestis libri I–III*, ed. Daniel J. Nodes (Toronto, 1985) and Avit de Vienne, *Histoire spirituelle, Tome I (Chants I–III)*, ed. and tr. Nicole Hecquet-Noti, Sources Chrétiennes, 444 (Paris, 1999). The poem is also to be found in *Patrologia Latina* vol. 59 and R. Peiper ed., *Alcimi Aviti opera*, Monumenta Germaniae Historica, AA 6,2 (Berlin, 1883). [62] *Patrologia Latina* 41, col. 386 (*De civitate Dei* 13.14). Augustine and Avitus could point to 1 Peter 3:7 (where woman is described as the *infirmiori vasculo*) for support of their views on the relative moral strengths of man and woman. [63] Fontaine, op. cit., p. 258.

your sweet spouse is subject to your love ... To you a worthy dwelling place has been granted on this summit of Paradise. (83)

Eve, on that summit in Eden, is ignorant of the wisdom of the Old Testament prophets with their warnings against female pride and their admonitions about the delusory nature of high places (see *inter alia* Isaiah 3:16–24 and Jeremiah 3:23 respectively). Like the Eve of Victorius she is 'open to seduction' and she greets the snake's 'shallow words' with a remark on their delightful potency. Avitus, in a moment which recalls a rhetorical explosion in one of John Chrysostom's *Homilies on Genesis*, is aghast at this inconceivable example of female idiocy: 'What stupidity, woman, clouded your mind? Did you feel no shame in speaking with the serpent ... ?'(83).[64] The understanding of the masculine mind fails to comprehend woman and the mysterious given of her openness to flattery and careless talk.

Regardless of this momentary hindrance Avitus is able to give Eve a long speech in reply to the serpent. Is there some hint of her being innocent, as she ends with the request: 'What He [God] calls death, do you now, *wise* serpent, graciously explain, since it is a thing unknown to us in our simplicity?' Avitus is adamant that this is not the case. The perceptive reader has seen that the serpent's putative wisdom consists in his recognition of Eve's excellence and that Eve's request is to be taken as *faux naïf*. The less perceptive reader has the narrator's word that the woman is 'too ready to believe', indeed, she is 'perversely gullible' (84).

Avitus then employs deft characterisation to explore the psychomachia experienced by the guilty Eve. In full knowledge of her sin – despite her earlier protestations of innocence – she breaks the divine proscription. The lamenting tones of Avitus, the tension of that decisive moment, and the palpable strain of the division in the mind of a free human agent do not blur the guilty knowledge of the woman:

> how often, stung by conscience, did she withdraw it from her lips and how often did her right hand, faltering beneath the weight of her own daring wickedness, yield and, trembling, flee from committing the crime! And yet she wanted to be like the gods, and that ambition's noxious poison stole through her. Opposites took hold of her mind. On one side tugged her longing, on the other her fear. Her pride dashed itself against the law and yet, even as it did the law came to her aid. The alternating surges of her divided heart seethed, as this harsh battle with self took place ... (84–5)

[64] Chrysostom asks: 'What kind of excuse could anyone find appropriate to the woman?' and 'O woman, what have you done'. John Chrysostom, *Saint John Chrysostom: homilies on Genesis 1–17*, trans. Robert C. Hill, The Fathers of the Church, vol. 74 (Washington D.C., 1986), pp. 212, 214.

Ironically, though he is not sympathetic to her, Avitus paints Eve in the fullest light in which she had thus far been depicted in literature. It is Avitus' malign characters who have the most developed psychology. The reader is given a glimpse of the thoughts of the snake too, as he is seen shrewdly holding back his joy in victory, in anticipation of further triumph. It can be suggested of Avitus, just as well as *Paradise Lost*, that the Devil has the best lines.

The ignorant Adam is truly one of life's innocents. Happily making his way through the pastoral landscape of Eden he meets his wife. '[D]aring then stirred the female madness in her spirited breast for the first time' and she demands of her spouse that he 'Give me your trust ungrudgingly, for it is wrong for a man's mind to hesitate over what I, a woman, could do'. The 'unlucky man listened to her words ... nor did he hesitate, as the woman had, over the first bite' (85). The moment is brief: it can hardly be denied that Avitus has drawn Eve more vitally than Adam.

The human drama of the story is somewhat deflated by an *exemplum* with the cue: 'Eve was not, of course, the only searcher after evil' (87). This is the signal for an idea which was to be found in Prudentius' *Hamartigenia*, namely the exploration of the similarities between Eve and the wife of Lot, both of whom sought after forbidden knowledge (88).[65] Sexual or at least sensual imagery is present here too; Satan, 'accustomed since his destruction of Eve to *touching* a woman's mind, *stirred* with his *coaxing* a *desire* in Lot's wife' (87).

Back in Eden, sexuality is still to the fore. The virtuous Adam is the first to sew leaves together to hide his shame and, the example given, Eve duly follows (90). God (and, the reader suspects, Avitus) has no equivocations about the situation. Having commented on nudity by noting an 'urge' which is 'disgusting' and 'foul', he is clear about the guilt of Eve, the 'treacherous woman' who dragged the 'masculine good sense' of Adam down from its virtuous height (92). While the punishment of Adam (despite the brambles and thorns) is focused on the now stained earth with its newly barren soil and grudging acres, the punishment of 'this fickle woman' is firmly related to the feminine body. Not only will she 'endure the domination of your husband in bed', obeying his commands and learning to 'accustom yourself to his male pleasures' (93), but there are the additional exquisite punishments of childbearing. Mother earth is not the only one who will bear fruit with difficulty from now on:

> Soon, when your womb conceives and feels the growing of life within it, you will testify to its burden with groans, and your uneasy belly will carry closed within you its growing load until, when the allocated time has passed, and your weariness is complete, an offspring, producing life, makes good nature's curse with the vengeance birth takes. This will be a

---

65 Prudentius, 1965, op. cit., p. 681. 741–2.

parent's punishment. And why should I speak now of the many different perils of motherhood in years to come? [Why indeed?] For when, woman, wearied with hard work, you have brought forth the child you longed for, giving birth in the manner I have described, it will sometimes happen that a child will be taken from you and you will weep for your meaningless suffering. (93)[66]

A negative note sounds the end of this excursus into the representation of Eve in early biblical latin epics. This is a fitting conclusion as it is representative of the general tenor of the way in which she is portrayed. However, the comparatively sympathetic approach of Cyprian of Gaul, the beauty of Eve in Dracontius and the strength of her psychological depiction by Avitus remind one that the literary treatment of the Fall contains a more diverse representation of Eve than that to be found in the parallel theological tradition upon which it sometimes drew (the latter reached back at least to the second century and Tertullian's condemnation of Eve in *On the apparel of women*).[67] The popularity of these Latin epics, outlined in the introduction, provided a venerable precedent which prepared the way for more nuanced treatments of the role of Eve (and consequently the nature of woman) which sometimes emerged in early-modern Europe.[68]

---

[66] This vision is in keeping with Avitus' views of the lot of married women which he expressed in a work he sent to his sister Fuscina celebrating virginity. Here he speaks of the hardship – consequent on the sin of Eve – of being oppressed by husbands who use their wives as sex slaves before they are forced to give birth in pain while running the risk of bearing a dead child or, indeed, dying themselves 'providing a double tomb'. (A translation of the passage on motherhood and marriage is to be found in White op. cit., pp. 157–8.)   [67] See Tertullian, *La toilette des femmes*, tr. Marie Turcan, Sources Chrétiennes, 173 (Paris, 1971), pp. 42–4.   [68] For a clear and readily available example of the more positive description of Eve and her actions see Aemilia Lanyer's poem *Salve Deus rex Judæorum* of 1611: Aemilia Lanyer, *Salve Deus rex Judæorum*, ed. Suzanne Woods (Oxford, 1993).

Share and share alike? The marriage portion, inheritance and family politics

Claire de Trafford

In the early Middle Ages, English custom, in common with continental practice, saw two gifts exchanged between bride and groom upon marriage at the church door, although it is unclear whether the gifts were exchanged prior to or after the ceremony. Dower was assigned by the groom's family to provide for the new bride in the event that she was left widowed. The other grant was known as the marriage portion or dowry, and is called *maritagium* in the sources – the same word, incidentally, as that used for marriage itself. Commonly a grant of land, rents or a combination of the two, and only rarely a straightforward sum of money, the *maritagium* was passed from the bride's family to the bride who, now under the *potestas* of her husband, immediately conferred legal rights in the gift to her spouse. Although, unlike dower, there was no formal legal obligation for a *maritagium* to have been granted, certainly in the eleventh, twelfth and thirteenth centuries it appears that there was a strong customary pressure on families to give a marriage portion with their daughters.[1]

Women in this period, particularly aristocratic women for whom records survive in the greatest numbers and detail, derived their power in society through the family. Their identity was closely bound up with first their birth family and then their marital family: a woman was generally known as the daughter of one family, or the wife of another, rarely as an individual in her own right. Hence status in society and particularly wealth generally devolved from within these families. In turn, however, a woman with land of her own could become a power within her family, for grants had to be made with her consent. Although the *maritagium* was not necessarily a large grant of land, in no way comparable to the lands even a minor heiress would bring with her, it nevertheless formed a valuable contribution to the estate of her husband. As we shall see, it could be, and was, used by many women to balance out the uneven distribution of land created by the system of primogeniture by providing for both sons and daughters. The possession of this land, and the ability to dispose

---

1 See C. de Trafford, 'The contract of marriage: the *maritagium* from the eleventh to the thirteenth century'. Unpublished Ph.D. thesis, University of Leeds, 1999.

of it where she would, must surely have given a woman, particularly in her widowhood, a measure of power over her family, status and respect. Originally this *maritagium* may have been intended to pass to the couple's heir, and indeed by the end of the thirteenth century restrictions to this effect had been placed on the gift in the Statute of Westminster known as *De donis*, ensuring that the couple did not alienate the gift to the heir's disinheritance. Prior to the enactment of *De donis*, however, the *maritagium* could be sold, or given outright to a monastery for spiritual gains. Further more, unlike dower, this land had no strings attached: it came from the widow's family and was an outright grant to her; in her widowhood the woman was restored to full possession of her *maritagium* and outright seisin. As we shall see, one of the common uses of the *maritagium* prior to *De donis*, by both widows and married couples, was to help provide for differing family members.

At the end of the twelfth century Matilda of Rimington granted land from her *maritagium* to both a daughter and a son. In one charter Matilda granted William of Whitewell six acres, a messuage and other land in Rimington (West Riding of Yorkshire), along with Alice her daughter, from her free marriage portion.[2] In another charter she also granted her son Warin, with the consent of Elias her son and heir, the remaining bulk of her marriage portion in Rimington.[3] It is not possible to contrast the two gifts but a crude guide to the comparative value of the two is perhaps provided by the terms on which each gift was held; William and Alice were to pay one pound of pepper in rent yearly, whereas Warin was to do service for approximately four carucates of land when called to do so ('doing the foreign service for a third part of the fee of one knight, where twelve carucates of land makes a knight's fee'). This example shows that a woman did not have to choose one child to grant her *maritagium* to wholesale; she could divide her land and share it. If she wanted, she could also retain some land for herself and grant away other portions. Two mid-twelfth-century charters survive which refer to the *maritagium* of Emma de Gant. One was a grant made by her son, Walter de Percy, of two carucates in Wold Newton, which had come to him from his mother's marriage portion: when he subsequently regranted them to one Erneis son of Besing, he stated that the lands were those 'which my mother gave me in Newton from her marriage portion'.[4] In fact we know from other charters that the Percy family held twelve carucates in Wold Newton from the Gant fee, three carucates in Ganton and six carucates in Saxton, all of which must have come to them with Emma in marriage and Emma herself donated one carucate of land in Wold Newton to the canons of Bridlington Priory.

2 *The Pudsay deeds*, ed. Col. R. Pudsay Littlejohn, Yorkshire Archaeological Society Records 56 (1916) no. 10 (temp. Richard I).   3 *Pudsay deeds* no. 9 (temp. Richard I).
4 'quas mater mea michi dedit in Neutona de matrimonio suo', *Early Yorkshire charters*, ed. W. Farrer (3 vols., Edinburgh, 1914–16) and C.T. Clay (vols. 4–12, Yorkshire

In many of the charters where a son has been granted the *maritagium* by his mother he is specifically noted as being a younger son. In the late-twelfth century Basilia de Dai gave Ralph, 'my younger son', half a carucate in Kirkby Wharfe (North Riding of Yorkshire), 'which Ascelinus de Day my late father gave me in free marriage', and this was to be held from William de Grimston her heir, who would have inherited the land along with his patrimony had she not made the grant.[5] Also referring back to the twelfth century a note found in the cartulary of Darley Abbey, concerning the mill of Copecastle in Derby, recorded that one Peter de Sandiacre had given the mill to William de Ruston in marriage with his daughter Albreda and that, after William's death, 'the said Albreda in her free widowhood gave the same mills to Richard de Ruston her younger son'.[6] In other cases we know from the pedigree of a family that the son was not the heir: in the example quoted above, for instance, Walter de Percy was a younger son. One school of historical thought has argued that the eleventh century saw a shift from inheritance customs involving the division of land between children to the narrower system of primogeniture or *parage*, and the granting of *maritagia* by widows to their sons may have arisen from this change.[7] The grant of the *maritagium* to sons may therefore have been a form of compensation in some cases.

Alternatively a widow could let her son live on the land whilst she herself kept seisin in her own hands, rather than granting it to him outright. This, of course, would increase the dependence of that child on his mother. In 1218–19, for instance, Philip Butler claimed land from his uncle Alan, which he said his father Adam had held; Alan denied this on the grounds that Adam had never been seized in demesne but 'the truth was that that land was the marriage portion of Adam's mother and Adam was in the land together with his mother'.[8] Furthermore Alan stated that Adam had died many years before their mother so that their mother had always been seized of that land as her *maritagium*. The jurors agreed with Alan and Philip was put in mercy; the actions of that widow had led to her grandson losing land.

It must have been fairly commonplace for a widow to release land to her younger sons, because we can find frequent disputes on the rolls where one

---

Archaeological Society extra series, 1935–65), vol. 2, no. 1202 (1142x54). (Hereafter cited as *E.Y.C.*) **5** 'juniori filio meo', 'quam Ascelinus de Day quondam pater meus mihi dedit in liberum maritagium', *E.Y.C.* vol. 3, no. 1613 (1180x1200). **6** 'predicta Albreda in libera viduitate sua dedit eadem molendina Ricardo de Ruston filio suo iuniori', *The cartulary of Darley abbey*, ed. R.R. Darlington (2 vols. , Kendal, 1945) vol. 1, p. 45. Hereafter cited as *Cart Darley*. **7** J.C. Holt, 'Feudal society and the family: II. Notions of patrimony in early medieval England', *Transactions of the Royal Historical Society* 5th Series 33 (1983), pp. 193–220, esp. p. 211. This belief can be traced back to French authors such as Duby and Schmid but ultimately to Frédéric le Play in the late-nineteenth century. **8** 're vera terra illa fuit maritagium matris ipsius Ade et Adam fuit in terra simul cum matre sua', *Rolls of the justices in eyre, being the pleas and assizes for*

brother claimed that *maritagium* land had been given to him, and his brother or family denied the claim. Philip of Stiffkey, for example, claimed in 1220 that his brother, Bartholomew, should warrant him for fifteen librates of land in three Norfolk villages, including Stiffkey itself, which their brother Peter had given him.[9] Bartholomew countered that Philip did not hold the lands claimed, for a number of reasons including the fact that one part of the stated land was the *maritagium* of their mother, which Philip had only held in co-seisin with her in order to provide for her needs ('que ei invenit necessaria'). Philip retorted that she had demised that land to Peter and that Peter had given it to him in turn. Bartholomew again denied this and they eventually purchased a licence in order to make a concord.[10]

Where the younger son could produce a charter to prove that his mother did indeed give him the land in her widowhood (rather than sharing or leasing it to him), as Everwin of Tintagel could in 1225, when his nephew Gervaise claimed a carucate in 'Hornacott' from him as the heir of the elder brother, that charter could only be countered with two claims: that the land was not held as *maritagium* but as dower, as Gervaise in fact claimed in this case, or that the mother was not legally empowered to grant the land, having remarried before the time of the grant.[11] No defence was ever made on the grounds that a woman could not grant away her *maritagium* land. In this case the jurors found that Matilda had indeed held the land as her marriage portion, but that she had died in possession of the land, regardless of her charter, and hence the land was Gervaise's by right of descent and not Everwin's by right of grant.

As land which was acquired rather than inherited, or perhaps as land which was not central to the main bulk of the family holdings, the marriage portion was also used at times by the men of the family, or in conjunction with the woman, rather than the widow alone, to make provision for sons or daughters. In the early-thirteenth century Mauger le Vavasour, for example, granted his son, Robert, land which he had purchased ('de perquisito meo') and land which he had in Elslack (North Riding of Yorkshire) of Robert's mother's *maritagium*.[12] At the opposite end of the thirteenth century Walter Collier of Througham and Alice his wife granted Alice's marriage portion to their son John and Agnes his wife in return for eight shillings.[13]

It was also not unheard-of for the heir himself to assign the marriage portion of their mother to a younger brother, or at least for the younger brother to claim

Yorkshire in 3 Henry III (1218–19), ed. D.M. Stenton, Selden Society 56 (1937), no. 218. 9 *Curia regis rolls* (hereafter cited as *C.R.R.*), (London, 1922–) vol. 9, pp. 67–8. 10 *C.R.R.* vol. 9, p. 221. 11 *C.R.R.* vol. 12, no. 348. 12 *E.Y.C.* vol. 7, no. 144 (before Michaelmas 1219). 13 *The cartulary of Cirencester abbey, Gloucestershire* vol. 3, ed. M. Devine (Oxford, 1977), no. 588 (late-thirteenth century). (Hereafter cited as *Cart Cirencester.*) This is the actual grant, which does not note that the land is *maritagium*. Registered in the same cartulary, however, is the charter of William de Pagenhull

that this had been the case. In 1239 Robert son of Henry quitclaimed his younger brother William of those lands which William already held 'of the inheritance of Henry son of Wulfric our father and of the marriage portion of Agnes of Througham our mother' in the manors of Upton in Blewbury (Berks.) and Cliveshale in Bisley (Glos.), in return for twenty marks and a horse (a 'rouncy') worth forty shillings.[14] This suggests that provision had already been made for William by his parents and that they were ensuring that their heir did not dispute the grant at a later date. It is evident from other legal cases that similar grants were common throughout this period. In 1202 William son of Osbert claimed two bovates of land in Hardwick in Nettleton (Lincs.), and one bovate in Hackthorne in the same county from his brother Thomas as land which was their mother's *maritagium*.[15] He also claimed six bovates at West Rasen (Lincs.), which was their father's inheritance. Thomas countered that whilst they were in the hands of the lord of the fee William had quitclaimed those lands for twenty shillings and twenty sheep, which William then denied. No conclusion survives. In 1220 Elias de Beauchamp produced a similar claim in defence of his seisin of one and a half carucates of land in Worle (Somerset), stating that 'since the same Elias was a young man without land, the said William, John and Andrew [his older brothers] granted him the whole right and claim'.[16] Elias lost his case but this was evidently a plausible reason for his seisin. In 1226 William, the son of Ennisan le Bret, claimed one hide in Berley (Wilts.) from his cousin Agnes and her husband for the same reason: that Ennisan had held the land on his death by the gift of his brother. Agnes stated that the land had been her grandmother's marriage portion which Ennisan had only held as a tenant and which ought now to descend to her as the heir. The jurors said that, although the land was *maritagium*, during his mother's lifetime Ennisan had received the land from his brother William and died seised, and hence Ennisan's heir regained the land. The defendants were given permission, however, to bring another writ because the jurors also stated that 'concerning William's entry ... they know nothing concerning that entry nor whether Agnes his mother devised it or not, since she was not seen in that county'.[17] This is almost certainly an example of a son appropriating rights over his mother's marriage portion during her lifetime.

---

granting this land to Walter with Alice his daughter in *liberum maritagium*, no. 585 (probably before 1290). **14** 'de hereditate Henrici filii Wulfrici patris nostri et de maritagio Agnetis de Thruham matris nostre', *Cart Cirencester*, vol. 2, ed. C.D. Ross (Oxford, 1964) no. 402 (28 July 1239). **15** *The earliest Lincoln assize rolls A.D. 1202–1209*, ed. D.M. Stenton, Lincolnshire Record Society 22 (1926) no. 260. (Hereafter cited as *Earliest Lincoln assize*.) **16** 'quia idem Elias fuit iuvenis sine terra, ipsi Willemus, Johannes et Andreas concesserunt ei totum jus et clamium', *C.R.R.* vol. 8, pp. 213–15. **17** *C.C.R.* vol. 12, no. 2522., 'de ingressu Willelmi ... nichil sciunt de ingressu illo nec si Agnes mater sua se dimisit vel non, quia ipsa non fuit visa in comitatu

A widow could, of course, grant any land which she held to her sons and it is, on occasion, difficult to perceive precisely how that land was held. In the earlier-thirteenth century Matilda, daughter of Michael de Velescines, burgess of London, and the widow of Arnold Brun, granted her eldest son and heir, John, all the land which Robert Brun 'father of the said Arnold ... conferred on the said Arnold when he married me', although Matilda was to have residence and free board in the house for the remainder of her life.[18] These lands may have been dower or marriage portion. Emma, widow of Wakelin of Wickenham, was noted on the roll for the 1248 Essex eyre as having given her son Ralph de Gosefeud, for his homage and service and, more importantly, ten marks, forty acres of land which she herself had recovered by plea of Henry of Bath's eyre at Chelmsford; she did not state what claim she had to these lands.[19] Margaret, countess of Warwick, used what appears to have been her dower to provide for a younger son in the early-twelfth century.[20] The lordship of Gower passed from Margaret's husband, Earl Henry who died in 1119, to her eldest son Roger and then to a Henry of Warwick who reclaimed the land from the Welsh. This Henry can be identified with Henry of Neubourg, youngest son of Earl Henry and Margaret, and his claim to rule the land seems to have been based both on his reconquest of the lordship and a claim through Margaret. Using the evidence of two of Margaret's surviving charters, and the fact that Henry's sons did not follow their father in possession of Gower, it is probable that Henry had been seised of Gower by right of Margaret and that Gower constituted part of Margaret's dower lands. Both dower and *maritagium* could thus be utilised by a widow to provide lands for a younger son but the Gower evidence shows the advantage of the marriage portion over dower (at least in the eyes of the son so provided for): Henry's sons, of which he had at least one, did not follow their father into seisin of Gower, which reverted to William of Warwick, as Margaret could not permanently alienate her dower lands despite her control over them in her lifetime. Had the lands been her *maritagium*, however, Henry's ability to pass the land to his children in turn would have been assured by his grant.

Other widows similarly acted to provide land for their daughters from their *maritagia*. The charter of Emma daughter of William Aluet, for example, granted her daughter Agnes her own *maritagium* land, one fore-earth and one acre at Haytesbury, seemingly as a free grant of land to Agnes.[21] Such grants, however, often took the form of *maritagia* grants themselves and this links in with a tendency within families to designate land as 'women's land'. This was

illo'.   **18** 'pater dicti Arnaldi ... ipsi Arnaldo contulit quando me desponsavit', P.R.O. E40/2241 (prior to 1231).   **19** P.R.O. JUST 1/231 m 17d.   **20** D. Crouch, 'Oddities in the early history of the marcher lordship of Gower', *Bulletin of the Board of Celtic Studies* 31 (1984), pp. 133–41.   **21** *The Hungerford cartulary. A calendar of the earl of Radnor's cartulary of the Hungerford family*, ed. J.L. Kirby, Wiltshire Record Society 49 (1994), no. 526 (probably late-thirteenth century). (Hereafter cited as *Hungerford cart.*)

land which had been obtained in *maritagium* and then immediately granted out again to a daughter or other relative as *maritagium*. Emma the widow of Walter Breton of Stedhowe, for example, gave Cecilia her daughter two bovates along with a toft and croft in Hutton, which Luciana her mother had given to her in *liberum maritagium*.

Both widows with and, apparently without, sons granted lands from their *maritagia* to their daughters. At the start of the thirteenth century, for example, Aveline, widow of Adam de Dodington, granted twelve pence rent per annum and half of her land in the field of monk's foregate at Shrewsbury from her *maritagium* to Adam son of Adam de Chetwynd with her daughter Hawise.[22] At the opposite end of the century Christina de la March granted half a tenement in Southampton to Michael Balaam with her daughter Alice in *maritagium*.[23] In contrast a charter of Agnes, widow of William de Blanchevil, made with the consent of her son Adam, noted that Agnes granted John Trite all the land, 'which William de Pesenhall my brother gave me in free *maritagium*' with the exception of the acre which she had given in *maritagium* to Juliana her daughter.[24] Similarly when Agnes de Percy granted land to her son Richard at the end of the twelfth century she excepted the land 'which I gave to John de Daiuill with my daughter in marriage'.[25] Isolde, daughter of Elias of Hutton granted her *maritagium* land in Hutton (Cumb.) to John Haydock with her daughter, Agnes, in the early-thirteenth century, and when they in turn granted the land to Cockersand abbey John and Agnes noted that this was 'known as Isolde's land'.[26] John and Agnes also stated that they had the charter of Elias granting the land in free marriage, that of Isolde granting the land in free marriage, the charter of Richard de Culchet, Isolde's second husband, granting the land in free marriage, and the charter of Isolde's brother Reginald confirming the grant. As the *maritagium* had originally been granted to one Henry son of Gilbert with Isolde, it seems that we have here the *maritagium* passing to the daughter of a second marriage. It is not entirely clear why widows with heirs should have granted land to their daughters for their marriage portion: this may have been due to an expectation that the marriage portion should be used as women's land, or, more probably, the daughter had not been endowed by her father before his death and the heir was unwilling or unable, perhaps due to his age, to do so. Alternatively these charters could be confirmations of grants made

---

22 *The cartulary of Shrewsbury abbey*, ed. U. Rees (2 vols., Aberystwyth, 1975) vol. 1 no. 177B (early-thirteenth century)   23 *The cartulary of the priory of St Denys*, ed. E.O. Blake, 2 vols., Southampton Record Series 24–5 no. 69 (c.1290–1330)   24 'quam Willelmus de Pesenhall frater meus dedit mihi in liberum maritagium', P.R.O. E40/3379 (undated)   25 'quas dedi Johanni de Daiuill cum filia mea in matrimonio', *E. Y.C.* vol. 2 no. 84 (1180x1204)   26 *The chartulary of Cockersand abbey*, ed. W. Farrer, 7 vols., Chetham Society, new series, 38–40, 43, 56–7, 64 (1897–1909), part 2, vol. 1, p. 417. This records a grant made by John of Haydock and Agnes to Cockersand (c.1240x56)

by the husband to which the widow needed to restate her consent, in identical granting language, in her widowhood; in the case of Isolde daughter of Elias, noted above, the fact that her second husband had given the land to John of Haydock with Agnes suggests that this was the case.

As acquired land the marriage portion was ideal for alienations to other families and to monasteries, and particularly suitable for alienations when the *maritagium* land was isolated from a family's main holdings; such lands may have been continually regranted until finally finding a family to whom they were more central and then been absorbed into the patrimony. Evidence for such chains of grants is, unfortunately, hard to locate over more than two consecutive generations but it seems probable that the practice would have often continued beyond this. The Wakebridge chartulary records the longest such chain of 'women's land' found: here land passed through three generations of women as a marriage portion. Peter of Wakebridge gave four shillings rent and twenty-two acres of land to Pagan de Ryley with Edelina his daughter; after the death of Pagan Edelina gave this land to Roger son of William the Clerk with Eva her daughter; Eva in turn granted the land to John of Cheshire and Amicia his wife, who was presumably Eva's daughter.[27] Amicia and John's son inherited the land and one of his descendants later granted the land to Wakebridge. Such practice was evidently not confined to England; in her article on the shift from brideprice to the marriage portion in medieval Europe, Diane Owen Hughes concluded that, where the *maritagium* consisted of land rather than being a cash settlement, such land came from a 'maternal estate and perhaps constituted a separate class of female, dotal property'.[28]

The practice of utilising land as 'women's land' seems to have been common in both the twelfth and thirteenth centuries, and hence probably in the eleventh century also, and evidence for it can be found in many cartularies or other sources. In one of the earliest charters referring to the marriage portion, dated 1127, Richard fitz Pons noted that he had given his wife an exchange of land in return for her original marriage portion, which he had given to Elias Giffard when he married their daughter Bertha.[29] Another charter which, although dating to 1268, refers back to events in the reign of Henry II, noted that John le Gros, parson of Grittleton (Wilts.), gave ten virgates there to William de

---

[27] *The chartulary of the Wakebridge chantries at Crich*, ed. A. Saltman, Derbyshire Archaeological Record Series 6 (1976) no. 99 (undated).   [28] Diane Owen Hughes, 'From brideprice to dowry in medieval Europe', *Women and History* 10 (1985), pp. 13–58 at pp. 34–5. Professor Hughes suggested that in Europe the preference seems to have been for cash dowries, but this does not seem to have been the case for England. This theme was further developed by K.H. Thompson in her article 'Dowry and inheritance patterns: some examples from the descendants of Henry I', *Medieval Prosopography* 17 (1996), pp. 45–61.   [29] *Ancient charters, royal and private, prior to A.D. 1200*, ed. J.H. Round, Pipe Roll Society 10 (1888) no. 12.

Ludyngton with his daughter, and William in turn gave the land to Richard de Dol with their daughter.[30] Also in the mid-twelfth century a grant was made by Elias son of Ralph to Simon de Borehard as a marriage portion when he married his daughter, of that land of Rushall (Wilts.), which he and his wife held as their marriage portion.[31] In 1222 Helen, daughter of Llywelyn and Joanna illegitimate daughter of King John, was married to John the Scot, heir to the earldom, and her marriage portion included two manors which John had granted to his daughter in *maritagium*.[32]

Most of the evidence for grants made in *maritagia* from the *maritagium* of the mother dates from the thirteenth century, but we have seen that, towards the end of the twelfth century, Matilda of Rimington granted William of Whitewell six acres, a messuage and other land in Rimington in *maritagium* with Alice her daughter from her own free marriage portion.[33] In addition we know that at least one charter of a widow granting land from her inheritance, as opposed to land from her marriage portion, does survive from the twelfth century.[34] This suggests that the lack of twelfth-century evidence for women passing *maritagia* on to daughters may be the result of poor survival rates rather than any other factor.

Land which had been used as dower could similarly be reused in the next generation as *maritagium*. In 1235–6 John le Pecher divided four houses in Oxford between his four daughters, Christina, Emma, Margaret and Galliana, which were the houses with which he had dowered his late wife; the charter stated that 'should it happen that any of my said daughters should die without children, the said four houses will remain to my three surviving daughters, so that they shall be divided among them in equal shares'.[35] The girls do not appear to have been John's heirs, however, as two later charters record John's son Gilbert giving Emma and Margery [Margaret in the previous charter] two messuages each, probably as the surviving sisters.[36] This suggests that the sisters were assigned the houses as their *maritagia*. Incidentally here the land was divided equally between the sisters. Similarly at the end of the thirteenth century, Walter Walsh gave Gilbert de Chalcore land in Goring (Oxon.), in

---

30 *The great chartulary of Glastonbury*, ed. A. Watkin, 3 vols., Somerset Record Society 59 and 63–4 (1947–56) vol. 3 no. 1202 (1268).   31 *Hungerford cart*. no. 189 (1151x74).   32 *Charters of the Anglo-Norman earls of Chester c.1071–1327*, ed. G. Barraclough, Lancashire and Cheshire Record Society 126 (1988) no. 411 (1222). See above also.   33 *Pudsay deeds* no. 10 (temp. Richard I). We have seen that Matilda also granted land to her son from her marriage portion, p. 217.   34 *The cartulary of Haughmond Abbey*, ed. U. Rees (Cardiff, 1985), no. 507 (1182x1201).   35 'si contingat quod aliqua dictarum filiarum mearum decedat sine liberis, tres filias meas antedictas supersitites dicte domus quatuor remanebunt, ut equis porcionibus inter dividant', *The cartulary of Oseney abbey*, ed. H.E. Salter, 6 vols., Oxford Historical Society 89–91, 97–8, 101 (1929–36), vol. 2 no. 935 (1235–6). (Hereafter cited as *Oseney cart*.)   36 Ibid. nos. 936 (2 messuages were given to Emma, probably summer 1245) and 937 (2 messuages are to go to Margery,

maritagium with his sister, 'which Isabella le Waleys my mother held as dower in the manor of Goring'.[37]

Maritagia were thus reused on occasion to form *maritagia* in the next generation and it is possible that an expectation that daughters had a special claim to the *maritagia* of their mothers arose as a result of such practices. When John son of Henry, for example, granted his mother's marriage portion to Oseney abbey around 1230 he received five marks but his three sisters also received two shillings each.[38] Such an explanation might also be construed from evidence contained in Bracton in which the question is posed, during a discussion of inheritance and *maritagium*, 'what if a mother in her liege widowhood gives one of her several daughters her whole *maritagium*?' We might perhaps take this to mean that a widow was generally expected to share her *maritagium* between all her daughters, rather than reserving the whole to one. In other cases we have seen that the marriage portion was granted to a younger son, a similar principle of providing for non-inheriting children, and it should therefore come as little surprise that the *maritagium* was often reused in order to provide for a daughter.

*Maritagi*a could also be used on occasion to provide for members of the woman's birth family. These cases are rare, probably reflecting the priority given to a woman's own children when making grants from her land, but they did take place. In the early-thirteenth century we can see that Margery de Rya, for instance, granted her brother, William son of William, in her widowhood a mill and five shillings rent which their father granted her in *maritagium*, 'I made this donation and quitclaim to William for the great damage and great destruction which king John did to him when Roger de Cressy married Isabella my daughter'.[39] The widow of John Pupplynton similarly granted her *maritagium* of property in Worcester to her brother John de Felp, perhaps also in his time of need.[40]

If we can see some families sharing out their lands, and women using their marital lands to provide for their children and in particular their non-inheriting children, we can also see, however, that the gift of the *maritagium* could create tension within the family unit. This is hardly surprising as both the initial grant of a *maritagium* to a woman, and her subsequent grant or sale of that land, reduced the patrimony of the heir. In a *cui in vita* plea by Richard le Scryneyn

---

probably summer 1245). **37** 'quam Isabella le Waleys mater mea habuit in dotem in villa de Garinges', *The Goring charters*, ed. T.R. Gambier-Perry, Oxfordshire Record Society 13 (1931) no. 60 (1295). **38** *Oseney cart.* vol. 6 no. 1063A (*c*.1230) **39** 'hanc donationem et quietam clamantiam feci Willelmo pro magnis dampnis et magnis destructionibus quas rex Johannes fecit ei quando Rogerus de Cressi desponsavit Ysabellam filiam meam', *Sibton abbey cartularies and charters*, ed. P. Brown, 4 vols., Suffolk Record Society, Suffolk Charters 7–10 (1985–8) vol. 2 no. 159 (after 1207). **40** *Original charters relating to the city of Worcester*, ed. J.H. Bloom, Worcester Historical Society 27 (1909) no. 1391 (no date). The name of the widow has been lost.

and Ermelina his wife, for example, over four acres at Pontefract (West Riding of Yorkshire), Robert son of Simon le Polet, the son of Ermelina's late husband, was called to warrant. When asked if Robert had any land with which to warrant, it was claimed that he had a messuage in Pontefract but Richard and Ermelina claimed that she was in seisin of that land by feoffment and that he had no other land.[41]

We have already seen evidence that the granting of the marriage portion to a younger son, or to a daughter, could occasion legal action (although significantly often only after the death of the woman). Where we can see women in court in disputes over their *maritagia*, rather than their descendants, it is clear that the same tensions arose. Roughly half of the pleas concerning women and their *maritagia* are disputes over the initial grant of the marriage portion. In many of these cases the other party to the suit was a close relative, often the heir of the grantor, and thus often the brother of the donee.

The most obvious explanation for this is that many heirs resented land being granted away from their inheritance, and attempted to reclaim it at all costs, as they similarly tried to evade doing service for *maritagium* land where they had accepted that the *maritagium* was valid. One of the earliest cases in the rolls, from Leicestershire in 1198, illustrates this point: John and Rohese de Sancto Laudo brought a plea of intrusion against Rohese's brother, Miles de Sancto Mauro, who had allowed Walter de Foleville to enter Rohese's *maritagium* of one carucate in Saxby. Miles was forced to concede that the land had indeed been granted as her *maritagium* after their father's charter was produced in court along with the concession charter of their elder brother.[42] This reluctance to accept the grant is hardly surprising as the *maritagium*, if the gift was proven, passed from the main line and into a cadet branch. Although legally speaking, the *maritagium* should be returned to the main branch in default of heirs before the birth of a third generation subsequent to the grant, and the consequent performance of homage by that heir, it was by no means a certainty that the land would in fact revert. Such reversion required families to keep in contact with distant kin, and maintain an encyclopaedic knowledge of family alienations. In addition, once homage was made, of course, the main branch lost all claim to the reversion of the land.

It is possible that some legal cases even reflect favouritism within the family being played out via the grant of the *maritagium*! At the start of the thirteenth century William de Rocheford, Beatrice his wife, and Herbert II de St Quentin, all tenants of the count of Aumale in Holderness, resolved their differences in court.[43] William and Beatrice gave up their rights to Brandesburton and in return Herbert gave them eighteen bovates in Thirkleby (East Riding of Yorkshire), instead.[44] The fact that the main manor of the St Quentin family in

41 P.R.O. JUST 1/1046 m.42.   42 *C.R.R.* vol.1, p. 41.   43 *Pedes finium eboracensis regnante Johanne*, ed. W. Brown, Surtees Society 94 (1897) no. 1199 (1202).   44 This

Holderness was at Brandesburton suggests that Beatrice was the daughter of Herbert I de St Quentin and sister of the Herbert involved in the suit. It is quite possible that Herbert I had assigned the core demesne to his favourite daughter and that it was left to the next generation to work out the problems which this grant had caused.

Other more generous explanations for these cases, however, include a means of registering title through the courts, perhaps in the event of a second marriage, or an entry fee paid to the heir by means of a court case. In 1198, for example, Walter de Burhont acknowledged that his father had given land to Emma, his sister, as a marriage portion; in return for this concession Emma and her husband Ralph gave Walter five marks.[45] In another case, from 1239, an element of blackmail may have been involved in the Yorkshire baron William de Percy's confirmation of his sister, Joanna's, *maritagium*.[46] William concede that the five bovates which their father had held in 'Friton' and the homage and service of Hugh of Howthorp was Joanna's *maritagium*, and in return for this William de Furneys, the husband of Joanna, released seventy marks due to William from the will of his father. In other cases it was the actual donor of the land who was forced to admit his grant in court: in a York case from 1208 Stephen of Upton acknowledged that one carucate of land in Upton was the marriage portion of Agnes daughter of Gamel, which he had given her. In return for this she gave him twenty marks.[47] Again there are a number of reasons why a donor should seek to deny his grant such as the need to reclaim the land.

It is evident, therefore, the *maritagium* could be used in a number of different ways within the family unit. The use of the *maritagium* within the family, however, has two main ramifications. The first reflects on the status of women within the family. Prior to the enactment of *De donis* any woman who brought a marriage portion with her (and I believe that the majority of women would have contributed something) had to be considered when disposal of that property was considered. Although a husband was free to make grants from her *maritagium*, he always had to be aware that his wife could negate his gift if she chose during her widowhood. Heirs must have similarly been aware that their mother could alienate her lands permanently in her widowhood and diminish the patrimony. Younger sons and daughters must have hoped that they would

---

was probably more a dispute over the location of the marriage portion than the initial gift; the main manor of the Quentin family in Holderness was at Brandesburton and they had other lands in Thirkleby. This suggests that Beatrice was the daughter of Herbert I de St Quentin and sister of the Herbert involved in the suit; B. English, *The lords of Holderness, 1086–1260* (Oxford, 1979), pp. 149–50.   **45** *Feet of fines of the tenth year of Richard I, A.D. 1198 to A.D. 1199*, Pipe Roll Society 24 (1900) no. 169.   **46** *Feet of fines for the county of York 16–30 Henry III*, ed. Col. J. Parker, Yorkshire Archaeological Society Record Series 67 (1925) no. 811 (13 October 1239)   **47** Brown, *Pedes finium ebor.* no. 337.

be given this land as their share. The net effect must surely have been to increase the status of the mother and her power within the family; to speak colloquially it was important to stay on mum's good side or risk losing out. After *De donis*, however, this influence must have been severely diminished and as a consequence the majority of women's position within the family may have become more precarious.

The second ramification is on the nature of inheritance in the early Middle Ages. Many families in the twelfth and thirteenth centuries seem to have been comparatively generous towards their daughters (even illegitimate ones), providing those who wed with *maritagia* of either lands, rents or goods and those who entered convents with a similar form of endowment. How widespread this practice was is impossible to state for certain but the evidence suggests that those families who could afford to cater for more than one daughter did so. Given that many women in turn passed their *maritagia* on to their sons and daughters, it is probable that the family in this period was more inclusive in terms of how it shared its land than in the later Middle Ages. It would appear from these charters that, although there was no doubt that one son would inherit the bulk of the family lands in the twelfth and thirteenth centuries, there was a moral obligation to provide for all members of the family no matter how small the amount of land given may have been. Over time, however, this generosity seems to have eroded, resulting in the legislation enacted in *De donis*. Prior to this period though, rather than rigorously enforcing primogeniture, it would appear that families used various strategies, including the use of the *maritagium*, to continue to provide for as many offspring as possible.

'I have nothing but through her': women and the conquest of Ireland, 1170–1240

Brendan Smith

> Of the Irish there were taken
> Quite as many as seventy.
> But the noble knights
> Had them beheaded.
> To a wench they gave
> An axe of tempered steel,
> And she beheaded them all
> And then threw their bodies over the cliff,
> Because she had that day
> Lost her lover in the combat.
> Alice of Abervenny was her name
> Who served the Irish thus.
> In order to disgrace the Irish
> The knights did this.
> And the Irish of the district
> Were discomfited in this way.[1]

The revulsion inspired by this description of the aftermath of the battle at Baginbun in May 1170 serves to draw attention away from one of its most interesting aspects. Alice of Abervenny, or Abergavenny, may impress first by her stamina and blood-thirstiness, but she has a more noteworthy claim to fame, being one of the very few non-noble secular women to be mentioned by name in the literary sources of Ireland and Britain in the twelfth and thirteenth centuries. The alliterative quality of her name perhaps owes something to the imagination of the author of the *Song*, but there is nothing improbable about the presence at Baginbun in 1170 of a woman of humble origin from the Welsh Marches.[2] Women

---

1 *The song of Dermot and the earl*, ed. G.H. Orpen (Oxford, 1892), p. 111, lines 1474–93. *The deeds of the Normans in Ireland. La geste des Engleis en Yrlande*, ed. E. Mullally (Dublin, 2002) unfortunately appeared too late for proper consideration in the essay. 2 For recent comment on the *Song* see P. Damian-Grint, *The new historians of the twelfth-*

usually accompanied men to war in the medieval West, and were even to be found in the ranks of that phantom force which Walter Map tells us was seen on the borders of Wales and Hereford in 1155.[3] Contemporary accounts usually portray such women as traders or prostitutes. Jean de Joinville, in his *Life of St Louis*, tells how during the Crusade of 1249 the Christian army was saved from a surprise Turkish attack at night by 'the butchers and other camp followers, including the women who sold provisions' who raised the alarm. At another point the happily-married Joinville tells us that 'my bed was placed in my pavilion in such a position that no one could enter without seeing me as I lay there. I did this to prevent anyone harbouring evil suspicions of me with regard to women.'[4] There is no suggestion that Alice was a prostitute – her violent actions were motivated by grief at the death of her lover – but whether she was engaged in any trade is unknown. Clearly she was a woman of considerable physical strength, if the account of her exertions on that dreadful day in May 1170 are to be believed.

The killing of men by women was sufficiently unusual to merit special mention by contemporaries, and the cold-blooded slaughter of prisoners at Baginbun carried with it a symbolism which was clear to all concerned.[5] Not only were enemy captives considered unworthy of being ransomed, they were so low that the knights added an extra element of humiliation to their deaths by allowing a woman to kill them. 'In order to disgrace the Irish, the knights did this.' To find a comparable contemporary example of male deployment of female violence we can turn to the account of the Crusade of 1189–91 contained in the *Itinerarium peregrinorum et gesta regis Ricardi*, which relates how

> The victors dragged the enemy galley back with them up on to dry land and left it on the shore to be plundered by our people of both sexes who came running to meet them. Our women dragged the Turks along by the hair, treated them dishonourably, humiliatingly cutting their throats; and finally beheaded them. The women's physical weakness prolonged the pain of death, because they cut their heads off with knives instead of swords.[6]

Alice of Abervenny deserved mention in the eyes of the author of the *Song* because her behaviour, if not her presence, during the military campaign in

---

century Renaissance: inventing vernacular authority (Woodbridge, 1999), pp. 79–81. See also *A new history of Ireland II. Medieval Ireland, 1169–1534*, ed. A. Cosgrove (Oxford, 1989), pp. 717–18; I. Short, 'Patrons and polyglots: French literature in twelfth-century England', *Anglo-Norman Studies* 14 (1991), pp. 229–49, esp. pp. 239–40.   3 *De nugis curialium*, ed. M.R. James, C.N.L. Brooke and R.A.B. Mynors (Oxford, 1983), p. 371.   4 Joinville and Villehardouin, *Chronicles of the Crusades*, ed. M.R.B. Shaw (London, 1963), quotes at pp. 233, 291.   5 J. Gillingham, 'Conquering the barbarians: war and chivalry in twelfth-century Britain', *Haskins Society Journal* 4 (1993), pp. 67–84.   6 *Chronicle of the Third*

Ireland was exceptional. Women usually featured in contemporary accounts of the conquest of Ireland as the helpless victims of violence. In his *History and topography of Ireland* Gerald relates how when Hugh de Lacy was going through Fore in Meath one of his archers 'dragged a woman into the mill and lustfully violated her there'. The purpose of Gerald's tale was not to criticise the act of rape *per se*, but rather to show the power of the local saint, St Fechin. Women were forbidden to enter either Fechin's church or the mill which he had constructed with his own hands, and the saint took appropriate revenge on the man who caused this prohibition to be violated. The archer, Gerald tells us, 'was stricken in his member with hell-fire in sudden vengeance and immediately began to burn throughout his whole body. He died the same night.' Elsewhere in the *History and topography* Gerald describes the fire at St Brigid's, Kildare, which only women were allowed to tend. The area around the fire served as a sort of sanctuary for women. When an archer in Strongbow's retinue crossed the hedge, Gerald tells us, he went mad.[7] Such places of safety for women in late-twelfth-century Ireland were few and far between; if they were not deliberately targeted during the conquest, they were certainly not exempt from its violent consequences. The Annals of Connacht give a disturbing account of the suffering of women and children during the English campaigns in Connacht in the 1220s and 1230s. 'A pitiful thing', says the annalist, describing the aftermath of an attack on a group of refugees in the Ox mountains of Sligo by a mixed English-Irish force led by Áed Ó Conchobair in 1225, 'the weirs were found to have their wattles full of drowned children'. In 1230 the activities of an English force near Loch Key meant that 'a multitude was there reduced to cold and hunger; women and children were killed, and those who escaped death were stripped bare'. At a higher social level Irish princesses enjoyed some protection from violence on account of their value as hostages. In 1227 when the wife of Áed Ó Conchobair was captured by the sons of his rival Toirdelbach Ó Conchobair she 'was afterwards delivered up to the English'.[8] The fact that in 1165 Henry II took out his frustration for a failed campaign in Powys by mutilating and beheading his Welsh hostages, including the noble women among them, serves as a reminder of the perils faced by such female captives.[9]

This 'shameful beheading of hostages' was condemned by Gerald of Wales in his *Expugnatio hibernica*, and his attitude towards women in his account of

---

Crusade: a translation of the 'Itinerarium peregrinorum et gesta regis Ricardi', ed. H.J. Nicholson (Aldershot, 1997), p. 89.   7 Gerald of Wales, *The history and topography of Ireland*, ed. J.J. O'Meara (Mountrath and London, 1982), pp. 88, 90–1.   8 *Annála Connacht, The Annals of Connacht (A.D. 1224–1544)*, ed. A. Martin Freeman (Dublin, 1944), s.a. 1225, 1227, 1230.   9 Roger of Howden, *Chronica*, ed. W. Stubbs, 4 vols., Rolls Series (London, 1868–71), i, p. 240. Lest it be thought that such ferocity was shown only to women from non-chivalric, Celtic, cultures, the fate of Matilda de Braose, starved to death in Windsor Castle by King John in 1210, should be borne in mind. R.V.

the conquest of Ireland was in general sympathetic.[10] It is true that early in the *Expugnatio* Gerald stated that 'almost all the world's most notable catastrophes have been caused by women', but when he moved from the general to the specific his approach was less judgmental.[11] He came from the same background as many of the noble women from Britain he mentioned in his Irish writings, and possibly knew some of them.[12] He avoided any criticism of them as individuals, in contrast to the vitriol he poured out steadily against so many of the men who accompanied them. While his account of the massacre of the Irish hostages at Baginbun does not mention Alice of Abervenny, it is also the case that the *Song* fails to include the descriptions of female suffering to be found in Gerald's writings on Ireland.[13] What both sources make abundantly clear, however, is the central role played by women in the enterprise as a whole.

That this role did not involve noble women in significant amounts of fighting may at first appear strange, given the numerical inferiority of the earliest invasion forces. Irish princesses had never been expected to engage in warfare, and this did not change after 1169.[14] Aife, daughter of Diarmait Mac Murchada, played no part in the military campaigns of her father in Ireland, but on the death of her husband, Strongbow, she came into possession of the de Clare estates in Wales, England, and Normandy and in 1183–4 led the defence of Chepstow castle during an invasion by the Welsh.[15] It was only when she moved from the Irish to the Anglo-French sphere that military action became a possibility for her. While many examples of aristocratic female warriors can be cited from contemporary France and England, the type of fighting in which such women engaged was very different from that which obtained in Ireland.[16] Chivalric warfare, which revolved for the most part around the taking and keeping of castles, involved less danger for women generals than the vicious

---

Turner, *King John* (London, 1994), pp. 13–14.   10 Giraldus Cambrensis, *Expugnatio hibernica. The conquest of Ireland*, ed. A.B. Scott and F.X. Martin (Dublin, 1978), p. 221.   11 Giraldus, *Expugnatio*, p. 25; T. O'Loughlin, 'Giraldus Cambrensis and the sexual agenda of the twelfth-century reformers', *Journal of Welsh Religious History* 8 (2000), pp. 1–16.   12 Karen Nicholas' assertion that 'Gislebert of Mons like other secular clerics who worked closely with aristocratic women thought of them in less misogynistic terms than monastic authors' might also be applied to his contemporary, Gerald. K. Nicholas, 'Countesses as rulers of Flanders', in *Aristocratic women in medieval France*, ed. T. Evergates (Philadelphia, 1999), pp. 111–37, quote at p. 113.   13 The author of the *Song*, which was first composed in the 1190s, does not seem to have known Gerald's work. It is noteworthy that both sources give seventy as the number of hostages killed at Baginbun. E. Mullally, 'Hiberno-Norman literature and its public', in *Settlement and society in medieval Ireland: studies presented to Francis Xavier Martin O.S.A.*, ed. J. Bradley (Kilkenny, 1988), pp. 327–44.   14 For a twelfth-century account of an eleventh-century Irish princess engaged in warfare see M.T. Flanagan, *Irish society, Anglo-Norman settlers, Angevin kingship: interactions in Ireland in the late twelfth century* (Oxford, 1989), pp. 92–5.   15 Flanagan, *Irish society*, pp. 124–30.

series of harrying and burning raids which characterised the conquest of Ireland.[17] The exception to the rule that women did not lead armed forces in arenas of frontier conflict in the British Isles in the twelfth century is found in the career of the Welsh princess, Gwenllian, whose last campaign in 1136 was described by Gerald of Wales in his *Journey through Wales*:

> It was in this region [around Kidwelly Castle, near Carmarthen], after the death of Henry I, king of the English, and at a moment when her husband, Gruffydd ap Rhys, prince of South Wales had gone to North Wales for reinforcements, that the Princess Gwenllian rode forward at the head of an army, like some second Penthesilea, queen of the Amazons. She was beaten in battle by Maurice of London, who ruled over the district at that time, and by Geoffrey, the bishop's constable. She was so sure of victory that she had brought her two sons with her. One of them, called Morgan, was killed, and the other, called Maelgwn, was captured. Gwenllian herself had her head cut off, and so did many of her followers.[18]

As Gwenllian's actions are ignored in the Welsh chronicles we are again indebted to Gerald for his habit of including the activities of women in his narrative. His neutral tone concerning her behaviour is also worthy of note, as it contrasts with the more dismissive approach of other contemporary writers in Britain towards female involvement in warfare.[19] Jordan Fantosme ridiculed the earl of Leicester for arming his wife in the rebellion against Henry II in 1173 and describes her subsequent discomfiture in gloating terms, saying

> My lady, the countess, has taken to flight,
> And found a ditch, in which she nearly drowns.
> Her rings disappear in the slough;
> They will not reappear in her lifetime.[20]

---

16 For France see the essays in *Aristocratic women in medieval France*, ed. T. Evergates (Philadelphia, 1999). Recent discussions of the situation in England include M. Chibnall, 'Women in Orderic Vitalis', *Haskins Society Journal* 2, (1990), pp. 105–22; M. Chibnall, *Empress Matilda: queen consort, queen mother, and lady of the English* (Oxford, 1991). **17** M. Strickland, *War and chivalry: the conduct and perception of war in England and Normandy, 1066–1217* (Cambridge, 1996), pp. 204–29; R. Kaeuper, *Chivalry and violence in medieval England* (Oxford, 1999), pp. 161–88; M.T. Flanagan, 'Irish and Anglo-Norman warfare in twelfth-century Ireland' in *A military history of Ireland*, ed. T. Bartlett and K. Jeffery (Cambridge, 1996), pp. 52–75. **18** Gerald of Wales, *The journey through Wales and the description of Wales*, ed. L. Thorpe (London, 1978), pp. 136–7. **19** William of Newburgh came close to blaming Eleanor of Aquitaine for the failure of the Second Crusade on account of the fact that 'she refused to be left at home and insisted on going with [her husband, King Louis] to battle.' N. Partner, *Serious entertainments: the writing of history in twelfth-century England* (Chicago, 1977), pp. 71–3, 104–5. **20** *Jordan*

While aristocratic women such as Peronelle de Grandmesnil, countess of Leicester, were willing to take up arms in support of their male relatives when necessary, the expectation was that warfare would normally be conducted and led by men. When such warfare occurred far from home the issue arose as to whether women should accompany their men on campaign. Orderic Vitalis' account of the Norman conquest of England suggests that in 1066 few women had initially crossed the Channel from France, since soon afterwards

> certain Norman women, consumed by fierce lust, sent message after message to their husbands urging them to return at once, and adding that unless they did so with all speed they would take other husbands for themselves. For they dared not join their men themselves, being unaccustomed to the sea-crossing and afraid of seeking them out in England, where they were engaging in armed forays every day and blood flowed freely on both sides.[21]

This absence of women at the earliest, most dangerous, stages of this venture stands in marked contrast to the situation in Ireland one hundred years later. Both Gerald of Wales and the *Song* emphasise the physical proximity of female relatives to the men at the eye of the storm which engulfed Ireland in the late twelfth century. When Diarmait Mac Murchada left Ireland in search of foreign support in 1166 he took with him 'his wife and beautiful daughter', Aífe, while the earliest of the conquistadores recruited by Mac Murchada, Robert Fitz Stephen, had his wife with him in Ireland by 1171 at the latest.[22] Gerald tells how Robert's half-brother, Maurice Fitz Gerald, who was besieged in Dublin in 1171, worried less about his own plight than that of Fitz Stephen 'and of his wife and children. They were in the midst of their enemies, trapped in a most ill-fortified castle' in Wexford.[23] It is heartening to imagine that Fitz Stephen, who had spent years in Rhys ap Gruffydd's prison, put his wife in such danger because he could no longer suffer separation from her, but Gerald's remark that Robert was 'excessively addicted to wine and women', suggests that other considerations may also have been at play.[24] Robert was not unique in having his female relatives close by him in the early days of conquest; Strongbow's sister, Basilia, was probably in Dublin during the siege of 1171

Fantosme's chronicle, ed. R.C. Johnson (Oxford, 1981), pp. 75, 79. Fantosme's negative attitude towards women was not representative of contemporary writing in French verse in the British Isles. The *Song* has no criticism of women, and the same is true of the *Histoire de Guillaume le Maréchal*. E. Mullally, 'The portrayal of women in the *Histoire de Guillaume le Maréchal*', *Peritia* 10 (1996), pp. 351–62.   **21** *The ecclesiastical history of Orderic Vitalis*, ed. M. Chibnall, 6 vols. (Oxford, 1969–80), ii, Book iv, pp. 218–21. **22** *The register of the abbey of St Thomas the Martyr, Dublin*, ed. J.T. Gilbert (London, 1889), p. 102.   **23** Giraldus, *Expugnatio*, p. 81.   **24** Ibid., p. 87.

with Maurice Fitz Gerald and her future husband, Raymond le Gros, and was certainly there by 1173. She was also in Dublin with her brother when he died in the town in 1176.[25]

Why did these men put their female relatives at such risk? Two reasons suggest themselves. Perhaps with Henry II's actions in Wales a few years before in mind, Robert and Strongbow brought these women to Ireland in order to ensure that they were not seized as hostages by the king. More positively, it could prove advantageous even in the most dangerous of circumstances to have in attendance unmarried daughters, sisters, nieces and cousins. Reading Gerald, or the *Song*, makes it obvious that the earliest conquerors of Ireland devoted almost as much energy to marrying off their female relatives as they did to beating the Irish. Strongbow, of course, was promised the hand of Aífe, and succession to Leinster, before he ever set foot in Ireland, and he wasted little time in claiming his prize after landing in the country. Immediately after the capture of Waterford in August 1170, which Gerald tells us was accomplished with 'large numbers of the citizens being slaughtered in the streets', Diarmait brought his daughter to the town and the marriage took place.[26]

The marriage of Strongbow and Aífe was but the first in a series of important marital alliances to be forged within a few years of the arrival of the conquerors. Strongbow wished to exploit both his new Irish base and his impressive collection of unmarried female relatives in order to improve his status in the wider Angevin world. He had at least one daughter from a previous marriage with him in Ireland as early as 1172, and in that year she married Robert de Quency at Ferns in Wexford.[27] The de Quencys, a Northamptonshire family with Scottish royal connections, in the next generation produced in Roger de Quincy an earl of Winchester and constable of Scotland.[28] This was the level of society with which Strongbow wished to tie himself by marriage, but unfortunately Robert de Quency died at the hands of Ó Díomusaigh soon after his marriage. The brief union did produce a daughter, Maud, who subsequently married Philip son of Maurice de Prendergast, scion of a rather obscure Pembrokeshire family of Flemish origin which was deeply involved in the conquest of Ireland.[29]

It was not the Irish who thwarted Strongbow's lofty marital ambitions, however, but rather the Geraldines, whom he seems initially to have tried to keep at arms length in Ireland. In 1173 Strongbow refused to grant the hand of his sister Basilia, to Raymond le Gros, with the result that Raymond returned to Wales, thereby seriously weakening the military position of the invaders in

---

25 Ibid., pp. 139, 165.   26 Ibid., p. 67.   27 *Song of Dermot and the earl*, p. 201, lines 2741–2750.   28 G.G. Simpson, 'The *familia* of Roger de Quincy, earl of Winchester and Constable of Scotland', in *Essays on the nobility of medieval Scotland*, ed. K.J. Stringer (Edinburgh, 1985), pp. 102–29; Flanagan, *Irish society*, pp. 158–9.   29 *Song of Dermot and the earl*, pp. 205, 207, lines 2801–26.

Ireland. Strongbow soon found himself besieged in Waterford and sent a message to Raymond agreeing to the marriage in return for his help.[30] Gerald tells us that 'Raymond was fired with a passionate desire to enjoy the embrace of a woman so noble and so desired by him' and so responded to Strongbow's plea, relieving Waterford and taking the earl to Wexford. Basilia was then summoned from Dublin and the marriage was concluded, and indeed consummated if we trust Gerald of Wales' comment that the next day Raymond set off against Ó Conchobair 'not in the least slowed down by the effects of either wine or love'.[31] The extent to which Strongbow's marital plans were now in the hands of the Geraldines quickly became apparent. 'In order that relations between the families should be cemented with more durable links,' Gerald tells us, 'on Raymond's urging the earl gave his daughter Aline in marriage to Maurice [Fitz Gerald]'s oldest son, William [baron of Naas].'[32] This was the same Raymond whom Strongbow had not wanted as his brother-in-law only a short time before.[33]

Gerald of Wales preferred to dwell on the ancient lineage of his family rather than on its more recent rise to prominence through these advantageous marriages, but he was well aware of how ambitious men might use the marriage market to scale the social ladder. While he declined to mention Strongbow's reluctance to allow his sister to marry beneath her by becoming Raymond's wife, he waxed indignant at the impudence of Hervey de Montmorency in attempting to improve his standing by marrying into his own family. Hoping 'under the cover of a marriage alliance' to crush Raymond le Gros 'because he would be off his guard', Gerald tells us, Hervey 'asked for and obtained as his lawful wife Raymond's cousin, Nest, the daughter of Maurice Fitz Gerald'.[34] Gerald accused Montmorency of many things, but never of stupidity, and this marriage was a clear sign that the Geraldine star was on the rise. Confirmation of this can also be found in the decision of Hugh de Lacy in 1183 not only to build the castle of Timahoe for Meiler Fitz Henry but also gave him his niece in marriage.[35]

---

30 Ibid., pp. 207, 209, 219, lines 2827–63, 2994–3039.   31 Giraldus, *Expugnatio*, pp. 139, 141.   32 Ibid., p. 143. It is not clear if Aline was the widow of Robert de Quency, or another daughter of Strongbow by his first marriage. J. Cottrell, 'Leinster, South Wales, Bristol and Angevin politics, 1135–1172. Some influences on the earliest English in Ireland' (unpublished Ph.D. thesis, University of Bristol, 2000), pp. 60–1.   33 After his death the Geraldines also made marriage alliances with some of Strongbow's most important supporters. Around 1193 Gerald son of Maurice Fitz Gerald married Eva, daughter of Robert de Bermingham, to whom Strongbow had granted Offaly. G.H. Orpen, 'The Fitz Geralds, barons of Offaly', *Journal of the Royal Society of Antiquaries of Ireland* 44 (1914), pp. 99–113, at pp. 102–3. A few years later Amabilis, sister of Meiler Fitz Henry, married Walter de Ridelsford. *Song of Dermot and the earl*, p. 285; E. St John Brooks, 'The de Riddelsfords', *Journal of the Royal Society of Antiquaries of Ireland* 81 (1951), pp. 115–38; 82 (1952), pp. 45–51.   34 Giraldus, *Expugnatio*, p. 143.   35 *Song of Dermot and the earl*, pp. 304–5; Giraldus, *Expugnatio*, p. 195.

These and other marriages made in Ireland in the first decade or so of English intervention, such as that between Mabel, sister of Raymond le Gros and Nicholas de Kantitun, Ralph, son of Robert FitzStephen and Margaret, daughter of Miles de Cogan, and Gilbert de Nugent, first baron of Delvin and his cousin, Roesia, sister of Hugh de Lacy, were only possible because of the physical presence in Ireland of marriageable women.[36] It is tempting to imagine that such marriages presaged the rapid emergence of a self-contained colonial baronage in Ireland with intimate familial and tenurial ties, but biological chance, the rules of inheritance, and the political realities of the Angevin world combined to work against such a scenario from the outset. Basilia, sister of Strongbow, made another marriage in Ireland on the death of Raymond in about 1189, and ended her life in the convent of St Thomas the Martyr in Dublin, but her exclusively Irish career was unusual.[37] Gerald noted the 'inscrutable but just judgement of God' which meant that few of the most important early conquerors had legitimate children to succeed them, and even those marriages which did prove fruitful did not necessarily dictate an Irish future for the offspring concerned.[38] Strongbow and Aífe's two children, Gilbert and Isobel, went with their mother to live on their late father's English and Welsh estates following his death in 1176. Gilbert died in 1185 before attaining his majority, and in 1189 Isobel married William Marshal.[39] While Isobel did spend some time in Ireland, many heiresses with Irish interests did not. This absence did not in itself imply neglect of Irish concerns, as Roesia de Verdun proved in the 1230s by overseeing the construction of Castleroche, 'which none of her predecessors was able to do', without it seems ever visiting the country, but it did remove an important point of contact between *domina* and tenant in a situation which demanded strong lordship.[40]

Both Gerald of Wales and the author of the *Song* traced the origins of the conquest of Ireland to the abduction by Mac Murchada, king of Leinster, of Derbforgaill, daughter of the king of Meath and wife of Tigernán Ó Ruairc, king of Breifne, in 1152. In 1186 Derbforgaill entered the Cistercian house at Mellifont in Louth, to which she had made a generous donation at its consecration in 1157, and died there at the age of eighty-five in 1193.[41] By then large parts of the kingdoms of Meath and Breifne had been subsumed into the de Lacy lordship of Meath, while Leinster had passed through the marriage of the grand-daughter of the man who had kidnapped her, Isobel, into the hands

---

36 E. St John Brooks, *Knights fees in counties Wexford, Carlow and Kilkenny (13th-15th Century)* (Dublin, 1950), p. 27; Giraldus, *Expugnatio*, p. 187; *Song of Dermot and the earl*, p. 314.   37 *Song of Dermot and the earl*, p. 302.   38 Giraldus, *Expugnatio*, p. 181. 39 Flanagan, *Irish society*, pp. 123–5.   40 For Roesia's career see M.S. Hagger, *The fortunes of a Norman family: the de Verduns in England, Ireland and Wales, 1066–1316*, pp. 72–83.   41 *Annála Uladh, Annals of Ulster*, ed. W.M. Hennessy and B. MacCarthy, 4

of William Marshal.[42] Marshal's biography, written in the 1220s, shows Isobel to have been an important source of personal support for her husband, particularly in his dealings with Irish affairs. In 1208 Marshal was required to return to England from Ireland by royal command, and rightly feared that at the instigation of King John his Leinster tenants would rebel in his absence. Before departing he told the assembled barons

> Lords! See the countess, whom I here present to you; your lady by birth, the daughter of the earl who freely enfeoffed you all when he had conquered this land. She remains amongst you, pregnant. Until God permits me to return, I pray you to keep her well and faithfully, for she is your lady, and I have nothing but through her.[43]

The Leinster rebels, led by the Geraldine Meiler Fitz Henry, were quickly subdued by Marshal on his return to Ireland, but his decision to treat them with leniency was taken against the advice of his wife, who urged stronger measures against them.[44] As Strongbow's daughter, Isobel perhaps knew of the frustrations experienced by her father at the hands of the Geraldines, though she was not to know that in 1234 they would be deeply involved in the death of her son, Richard, on the Curragh of Kildare.[45] Isobel's incitement to 'gran[t] cruelté' was ignored, but the incident reminds us that the role of women in the conquest of Ireland concerned much more than simply the transfer of property, and that the bloody actions of Alice of Abervenny were less extraordinary than might be imagined.

vols. (Dublin, 1887–1901), s.a. 1157, 1186, 1193. **42** G.H. Orpen, *Ireland under the Normans, 1169–1333*, 4 vols. (Oxford, 1911–20), vols. i–ii. **43** *L'histoire de Guillaume le Maréchal*, ed. P. Meyer, 3 vols. (Paris, 1891–1901), ii, p. 123, lines 13532–44. The translation is from D. Crouch, *William Marshal: court, career and chivalry in the Angevin Empire* (London, 1990), p. 100. For comment on the date and content of the *Histoire*, D. Crouch, 'The hidden history of the twelfth century', *Haskins Society Journal* 5, (1993), pp. 111–30. **44** *L'histoire de Guillaume le Maréchal*, lines 14021–100; Mullally, 'Portrayal of women', p. 353. **45** B. Smith, 'Irish politics, 1220–1245' in *Thirteenth Century England VIII*, ed. M. Prestwich, R. Britnell, and R. Frame (Woodbridge, 2001), pp. 13–22.

The power of dower: the importance of dower in the lives of medieval women in Ireland

Gillian Kenny

THE IMPORTATION OF THE DOWER LAW

The Anglo-Norman invasion of Ireland in the later twelfth century witnessed the importation of English laws and customs regarding the legal rights of widows into the new colony of Ireland. From the precarious beginnings of the colonisation through to the relatively settled conditions of the thirteenth and early fourteenth centuries, widows were backed by the law in claims to their dowers. Towards the end of this period, however, it appears that the use of jointures was becoming more common and the old legal insistence on the dower consisting (in most cases) of one third of the husband's lands or chattels was increasingly bypassed by the use of gifts and other devices to ensure a comfortable widowhood for many women. In this essay the concentration is on those initial hundred or so years after the invasion, when the dower was the primary source of income in widowhood for many women. Although it was recognised as a right and as a necessity, and was welcomed by women, the dower was not always of beneficial import in the lives of many women. While it could make them economically and socially freer and in freedom of action, more powerful, the repercussions could include familial strife and intense pressure to remarry.

THE DOWER

From the late twelfth century on, it was the prevailing practice in England for the bridegroom to name certain lands, a 'dos nominata' as his new wife's dower, to be enjoyed by her if he predeceased her.[1] Occasionally it consisted of chattels or money but nearly always it was land of which the bridegroom was seised,

---

1 *Glanvill, Tractatus de legibus et consuetudinibus regni Anglie qui Glanvilla vocatur* ed. & trans. G.D.G. Hall (London, 1965), vi, 1–2.

which was a far more secure option for the woman. Glanvill wrote, however, that there were two exceptions to this rule. First was the dower, which consisted of lands which the father or other ancestor of the groom was seised of but which the ancestor agreed should be named by the heir as dower. This was the dower 'ex assensu patris'. The second exception alluded to by Glanvill was where the dower was specifically named as being part of lands that the husband would acquire during the marriage. It seems that a public marriage with a pledge in the form of the wedding ring took the place of the delivery of seisin in this instance.

The dower was restricted to one-third of the lands of the husband if they were by military tenure; this was to be adopted by the common law courts in the thirteenth century but it did not apply, during the twelfth and thirteenth centuries, to lands he may have held in socage. If a husband did not name a dower, he was taken to have endowed his wife automatically of her share of the lands which he had held at the time of marriage, a so-called 'reasonable' dower. At the end of the thirteenth century when William de Vescy, a tenant in chief of the king in Ireland, died, the king ordered that a reasonable dower, 'according to the law and custom of those parts', be assigned by the justiciar to his widow, Isabella. The dower was to be taken from William's lands in Kildare but, as Isabella was to complain shortly after, the justiciar had not given her any of the monies due to her.[2] Dependence on the calculations of outside parties to ascertain their dowers was a common complaint for widows. In 1180 John de Courcy took steps to prevent the future naming of a reasonable dower by issuing a dower charter for his wife, Affreca, daughter of the king of Man. Her dower lands lay almost exclusively in Ulster with the exception of a virgate of land in Northamptonshire.[3]

Widows were essentially temporary custodians of the dower lands for the heirs and could not permanently dispose of any part of them without the heir's permission. They could and did utilise the profits of the dower lands, however, and in this way increase their personal wealth. When a widow came to make a will, there were no restraints on how she distributed her chattels and lands, at least part of which may have come from dower land profits, even though the heir had first choice of all chattels for himself. These might include jewellery, plate, weapons and books. According to the common law, widows and unmarried adults could dispose of their property as they liked. This contrasts with the position of wives who needed the consent of their husbands.[4]

Apart from dower grants, the parties involved often made other agreements among themselves, including gifts in frank-marriage and gifts of conditional

---

2 *Calendar of the Justiciary Rolls, Ireland*, i, 1295–1303, ed. J. Mills (Dublin, 1905) pp. 357, 401 (cited as *Just. rolls*). 3 A.J. Otway-Ruthven, 'The dower charter of John de Courcy's wife', *Ulster Journal of Archaeology* 3rd ser. 12 (1949) pp. 77–81. 4 Hall, *Glanvill*, p. 80.

fees to bolster the marital agreement. Grants between partners often had to be routed through a third party, because the law did not accept that a person could grant something to himself or herself. So if a woman wanted to be enfeoffed jointly with her husband, the land first had to go through a third party who would then give it to them jointly.[5] The law was hostile towards grants purporting to be in fee simple whilst also being conditional, that is on the eventual marriage and so couples planning a marriage and making grants had to conceal their reasons for making them. A third party made the grant less worthy of suspicion and made these transactions of land more difficult. Certain conditional fees such as the fee tail of *De donis* emerged, whereby an estate granted to a couple for the rest of their lives would automatically become alienable and inheritable upon the birth of an heir. These advances in law were often adopted officially in Ireland some time after they had come into force in England.

The dower was treated differently from a man's other lands in that it was not liable for the payments of his debts. The widow's rights were thus protected against her husband's actions. During his lifetime her husband could grant away most of his land or leave a substantial amount of it in his will. The dower lands were not included in these, however, unless it was with her express consent, given in the form of a fine before the king's justices.[6] In the community the fact of a woman holding land, even if only for her lifetime, conferred a social standing on her. The bigger the dower she received, the more influence she could wield in her locality. Also the provision of a separate house for her, a dower house, meant that she could retain an independent lifestyle and not have to live in her children's households, when they were grown up. This, of course depended on the wealth of the family involved. Only the richer families could afford a dower house. A widow had the right to stay in the marital home for forty days after the death of her husband until the heir assigned her a place to live.[7] In 1227, David, baron of Naas, assigned a dower and home to his mother. He granted to her,

> Lady castle with all its appurtenances and Tolachtyper with all its appurtenances for a third part of all the lordships which his father, William, baron of Naas, held on the day when he died.[8]

Less-well-off women may certainly have continued to live with their offspring and their family.

---

5 Robert C. Palmer, 'Contexts of marriage in medieval England from the king's court circa 1300', *Speculum* 59 (1984) pp. 42–67.   6 F. Pollock and F.W. Maitland, *The history of English law before the time of Edward I*, ii (Cambridge, 1911), p. 408.   7 D.C. Douglas and G.W. Greenaway (eds.), *English historical documents, 1189–1327* (London, 1953) 'Magna Carta' (1215), *c*.4 (cited as *E.H.D.*).   8 *Calendar of the Gormanston register, 1175–1397*, ed. J. Mills and M.J. McEnery (RSAI, Dublin, 1916) p. 146 (cited as *Gorm. reg.*).

DIFFICULTIES IN OBTAINING DOWER

By the thirteenth century the widow's dower rights were crystallising (Magna Carta included a clause expressly protecting the right of dower), but there were some limitations on what could be claimed as dower. One item, which a widow could not take as dower, was an advowson, as incorporeal rights could not be incorporated in a dower agreement. However, this was not always adhered to. In a case concerning the church of St Patrick in Kellystown in the early thirteenth century, Agnes the widow of Matthew Fitz Griffin attempted to claim the advowson of the church as part of her dower. She was awarded rights over it in the liberty court of Carlow but this was later overturned by the intercession of the king.[9]

In certain cases a widow was not entitled to receive a dower at all. She lost her dower if the couple divorced due to her misconduct or by a judgement, if her husband committed a felony or if she had consented to the alienation of it by fine. An interesting case of a thirteenth-century widow of a felon who did receive her dower is revealed in the justiciary rolls of 1295–1303. In a case before the justices at Limerick, Isabella, widow of the murderer, John Goes, claimed and received her dower, because her husband had died just before he had been convicted. Thus Isabella was able to exploit a loophole in this area of dower law.[10] In addition a wife lost her dower if she had committed adultery, but if the couple were reconciled then it was restored to her.[11]

If difficulties in obtaining an award of dower arose from a doubt over the validity of the marriage, then the ecclesiastical authorities were called in to determine that question. On some occasions, a widow's use of the processes of law could backfire to her loss. Margery, the widow of Emery de Derneford, sued Robert Bagod and John Daundon over her dower through her attorneys in Bunratty. She had been assigned a dower by the justices in early 1294 but they had deferred handing it over to her. Margery had sued Robert for a vill in Bunratty. However, when the time came to reassess her case, the escheator, Walter de la Haye, argued that Margery was never the wife of Emery and so had no right to dower. After an inquisition was made on the matter, this claim was upheld. The king, however, wrote to the bishop of Killaloe who certified that she had been married. The outcome was that she did not recover the lands she had demanded as 'the record sent did not find plainly for or against Margery, therefore execution could not issue thereupon'.[12] The fact that Margery lived

---

9 *Calendar of Ormond Deeds*, ed. E. Curtis, i (Dublin, 1932) no. 71, pp. 31–2 (cited as *Ormond deeds*). 10 *Just. Rolls*, 1295–1303, p. 340. 11 *Statutes and ordinances and acts of Parliament of Ireland, King John to Henry V*, ed. H.F. Berry (Dublin 1907), p. 155 (cited as *Statutes*). 12 *Calendar of documents relating to Ireland*, ed. H.S. Sweetman, iv, 1293–1301 (London, 1875–6), no. 161 (cited as *C.D.I.*).

in an age when marriages were more often than not clandestine proved to be disastrous for her, as the marriage needed to be proven for her to obtain her dower.

Despite the fact that a widow's right to her dower was enshrined in the Anglo-Norman law codes, there are numerous examples through the centuries of women who had enormous difficulties in obtaining their dowers, even those who were validly married. One example of a tenacious woman's appeals for her dower can be found in the case of Affreca Cordwainer, who fought for her dower rights in the 1230s. In May 1230, Affreca brought an assize of novel disseisin against Ralph de Trubleville. Ralph, she alleged, had entered on her dower lands in Ballimadun. What the court had to decide was whether or not he had entered, with his bailiffs, on the king's order. If so, he was without blame and would be acquitted of the twenty marks which he had already been fined for disseisin.[13] By July, the jurors had still not heard the case. Again, the issue rested on who had been in actual seisin of the disputed lands. The king's commands to the justiciar were clear and addressed the question of the actions not only of Ralph but also his relative (son?), Henry.

Affreca's accusation of disseisin extended to Henry and the important question to be decided by the jury was whether or not Henry's alleged disseisin had taken place while the land was in the king's hand after the first seisin of Ralph, or not. The king had, it seems, granted the land for life to Ralph in January 1230.[14] If it happened whilst in the king's hand, and as they were acting in good faith regarding their own rights of seisin, then there was no disseisin of Affreca. Therefore, she could not recover seisin against them and Ralph did not have to pay damages. The judgement went in Ralph's favour. He was to recover his seisin; Affreca, by then remarried to Roger Audoein, was to have the profits of the corn sown on the land. This judgement was delivered in July 1231. If one looks ahead thirty-two years into the future, there is a sequel to these events. In the inquisition on the death of Affreca in 1263, one finds that she had recovered her dower lands; it is not clear when but it is stated by the inquisitors that she held,

> 140 acres of arable land, 20 acres of meadow and 42 acres of pasture and moor, belonging to said land, every acre of which they extend at 13d. yearly; and also 5 marks and 7 pence rent of assise there yearly; and she rendered for royal service a third of the service of half a knight's fee, and to the chief lord of the fee a third part of a pair of leather gloves yearly, she held these in the name of dower in the free tenement of John le Cordwaner, her first husband, in Ballymacdon and not of the king's grace, because she recovered the premises as her dower by judgement of the court of the lord the king.[15]

13 *C.D.I.*, i, 1171–1251, no. 1828.   14 Ibid., no. 1865.   15 *Gorm. reg.*, p. 131.

Many widows of Anglo-Norman magnates possessed dower lands in Ireland, which they had never even seen. Other widows, attending to lands in other parts of the Angevin dominions, were too busy too attend personally to problems in Ireland. These women had to appoint lawyers in Ireland to oversee their rights and sue on their behalf if needs be. Avice, widow of William de Apeldrefeld, while staying in England, nominated two attorneys to deal with her affairs in Ireland in 1284.[16] In 1287, Lucia, widow of Guy de Sancto Amando, appointed two men to sue and take seisin of her dower in Ireland.[17] In a case which came before the justices in Dublin in May 1285 Emmeline, widow of Hugh de Aston, sued William le Deveneys and Ralph of Norwich for one carucate of land and nine marcates of rent in Balimony and Baliboth. Even the poorest of such widows brought pleas. In 1297, for example, there is the case of the widow Alice who reported her cow, worth half a mark, stolen. The culprit, David Ker, fled and was outlawed.[18]

GIFTS AND GRANTS

After the death of their husbands and once their dower was secure, widows often made grants and gifts especially to members of their families. They had gained a new-found freedom of action and perhaps wished to exert it. As widows, they no longer had a legal capacity akin to that of children. They were in control of lands, most for the first time, independently of their husbands, and these lands included the dowries, which they had brought with them into the marriage.[19] The Statute of Merton made it legal for them to bequeath the corn from all their lands including dower lands, for instance.[20] As widows they had to learn to manage their lands both for their own benefit and that of their heirs. Should they fail to do so, there were provisions to deal with widows who were careless and negligent of lands which were to be the heir's after their death. The rights of the heir were paramount and were always to be considered in all dower transactions. For example, the Statute of Westminster held that waste of lands held in dower was to be prohibited.

In many cases, grants from widows were to the heir and their families, as in 1270, when Joan, the widow of Hugh le Bigod, quit-claimed to her daughter and heir, Elizabeth, all the lands which she held in dower

> in the half cantred of Offinneglas at Moycreddin and elsewhere, namely what she has of the tenement of Sir Theobald or any other whether of the Cross or lay fee.[21]

16 *Calendar of the patent rolls*, 1281–92, 12 Ed. I, m. 7 (cited as *C.P.R.*). 17 *C.P.R.*, 15 Ed. I., m. 2. 18 *Just. rolls*, 1295–1303, 25–26 Ed. I, m. 8. 19 *E.H.D.*, 1189–1327 pp. 18, 19, 311. 20 Ibid., p. 352. 21 *Ormond deeds*, no. 165.

This was a straightforward enough transaction; perhaps Joan was unable to attend to her lands any more and so gave them up in favour of her daughter and her family. Often a widow did not have the time or inclination to attend to all her dispersed lands and so exchanges were made. In 1275 John de Brundeye and his wife, Marsilia, agreed with Thomas de Welend that they would exchange all of Marsilia's dower lands in England and Ireland from her previous marriage to William de Welend, for the manor of Middleton in England.[22] Possibly Marsilia and her new husband found it difficult to attend to her lands in Ireland. This arrangement must also have suited the heir, Thomas, as well, for him to enter into such an agreement.

By the mid-thirteenth century larger gifts on the part of the widow were becoming more and more common as her independence increased and as long as the heir consented to it. Her lord also needed to give his consent.[23] According to the Statutes of Gloucester, extended to Ireland in 1285, if a widow demised her dower to the detriment of the heir, then he should recover it when he came of age by a writ of entry.[24] An heir could encounter difficulties when trying to retrieve dower land which had been demised by the widow before the Statute of Westminster II. An example of this is the case of Henry de Audley, who was the heir of Adam de Audley, his uncle. Adam died seised of the manor of Renlys and after his death his wife Leyra, was endowed of it. She, in turn, demised the manor to John le Chen for a term, which had by then (April 1252) expired. Upon the death of Leyra, John continued to hold the manor, as no heirs of de Audley had come forward. After John le Chen died the king seized all his lands despite the fact that John was not a tenant in chief, but the king claimed the right by virtue of the lease. The king instructed that seisin be given, not to Adam de Audley, but to the heir of John le Chen, who was a minor and in the king's custody.[25] So Henry de Audley, the heir of the lands in question, was not allowed any title to them after all.

Dower and dower rights were constantly changing and being refined in the period in question. The rights and status of widows were assuming an increasingly concrete form. This era, which saw the establishment of a standard dower under the common law in cases of unnamed dower, correspondingly witnessed the gradual expansion of the rights of widows and increased protection of them and their dowers under the law. Also by the end of the thirteenth century the use of jointures by husbands and wives was rising in popularity, a move which was very beneficial for the women involved, as under a jointure agreement they were not restricted to one-third but could enjoy the whole property of certain lands after the death of the husband.

The only widows who appear to have been left out of these advances were the Gaelic widows of Anglo-Irish men. By taking an Irish wife many of the

22 *C.D.I.*, ii, 1252–84, no. 1165.   23 Bracton, *De legibus Anglie* ed. Sir T. Twiss, 6 vols. (London, 1878–83), 92b.   24 *Statutes*, 13 Ed. I., p. 95.   25 *C.D.I.*, ii, no. 21.

early settlers were pursuing an important political ambition in the colony, the legitimisation of the succession to their conquered lands by any heirs they might have and the sanction of the pre-existing families to their intrusion. Marriage was no more than a political tool by which to gain alliances, thus making the colonisation more acceptable and strengthening, not only their own claims on the land, but also those of their descendants. However, the two sides rapidly became more and more isolated from one another and a habit of intermarriage did not develop. Intermarriage appears to have been used more as a short-term tool than as part of the general marriage strategies of the invading nobility.[26]

Irish widows of settlers appear to have had no legal right to a dower unless they were first admitted to English law.[27] For example, in 1289, the king granted English law to an Irishwoman named Ismaya who was married to an Englishman, Bertram de Rapenteyn, 'because it is the custom in Ireland that Irishwomen may not take dower after the death of their husbands'.[28] In 1285, licence was given to Mariota, married to Ralph Burges, and to their children to use English law.[29] As an Irishwoman not admitted to the law, she was not allowed to bring an action of dower in the king's court. The Remonstrance of 1317 complained of this practice, which completely deprived the native Irish widow of the type of independence or wealth she might expect as an Anglo-Irishwoman. The failure of the invaders to bring the entire colony under one cohesive system of law and their insistence on alienating the native Irish through severe discrimination ensured the non-consolidation of the colony during this period, despite the gains made by Edward I in the thirteenth century. By 1331 it was provided that 'one and the same law be made as well for the Irish as the English ...'[30] By then, however, the fate of the two different female 'nations' were sealed.

YOUNG WIDOWS AND FEUDS

By the later twelfth century, the women of the aristocracy were generally some years younger than their husbands in a first marriage. This development of a late first marriage for men with an early age for women led to important social consequences for women. In spite of the dangers of childbirth, noble women especially had a good chance of outliving their husbands and reaping the rewards of the dower system and perhaps contracting subsequent marriages. One widow, who married several times, outliving each husband in succession,

---

26 Parallels between the Norman-English and Norman-Irish situations in this regard are drawn by Eleanor Searle, 'Women and the legitimisation of succession at the Norman Conquest', in R. Allen Brown (ed.), *Proceedings of the Battle conference on Anglo-Norman Studies* 3 (1980), pp. 159–161.   27 *Just. rolls*, 1295–1303, pp. 121–3; *C.D.I.*, iii, 1285–92, no. 558.   28 *C.D.I.*, iii, 1285–92 p. 252.   29 Ibid., no. 94.   30 *Statutes*, p. 325.

was Alice Bela Jambe, daughter of Walter Bela Jambe and self-styled 'lady of Colp'. Hers are the earliest of the series of charters from the owners of the manor of Colp in County Meath. Alice married three times and issued charters and donations to St Mary's abbey with and without her three spouses. Women like Alice could amass large amounts of dower land, increasing their economic power in their local community and outside it and keep those dowers for decades to the detriment of the eventual heirs. Still young, as widows, many of these noble women could block the transmission of the patrimony in its entirety to the younger generation for decades. This often generated odium towards the widow, as the heir could view her as an obstacle to inheritance. This was one of the less beneficial aspects of a dower for many women. Resentment by the heirs who had essentially to defer ownership of one-third of their lands for an unknown amount of time could lead to unpleasant and exhaustive family in-fighting.

Fighting over dower land is a familiar sight in the Irish records. Although it is unclear from the records whether or not the feuding was mainly between blood or step relations, the impact on familial relations and affections was often serious. In one instance of family conflict plucked from the records, the widow is, very unusually at that stage, suing for a dower made up of her husband's chattels. It was in 1299 in the liberty court of Trim and the accuser was Ismannia, widow of Nicholas Dyloun. Her suit was against a Thomas Dyloun, the heir of her late husband. He, together with his co-executor, Stephen Wolbot, had failed to assign certain items to her as dower. He did not come to the hearing and essentially after that nothing seems to have been done, with the seneschal of Trim repeatedly being given orders to detain him and, apparently, failing to do so.

In an age when, despite the opposition of the Church, marriages were still being contracted by very young children (or rather by their parents on their behalf), a widow who was underage at the time of death of the husband could run into serious difficulties with her in-laws when it came to retrieving her dower. When the sisters and heirs of Roger le Blound sued Theobald de Verdun in 1300 in a case of disseisin in the liberty court of Trim, Roger's widow, Joan, and her second husband Andrew de Buckingham joined them.[31] Theobald's defence rested on the fact that as Roger held of him by knight service, he had only entered on the lands because the heiresses were underage and held them until the sisters could prove their age, which the sisters claimed to have done on many occasions.[32] Andrew and Joan claimed to have held by reason of her dower and claimed it was assigned to them by Theobald, the chief lord. However, her step-children, the heiresses, and their husbands objected to this claim. They claimed that Joan ought not to receive a dower as when her husband died she was not of an age to 'deserve dower', as she had only been

---

31 *Just. rolls.* 28 Ed.I., m. 30 p. 365.   32 The problems inherent with underage heirs are recounted by S.S. Walker, 'Proof of age of feudal heirs in medieval England', *Medieval Studies* 35 (1973) pp. 306–23.

eleven years old at the time of his death. However, the court disagreed and in the final judgement, Theobald was ordered to restore seisin to all parties and pay a fine of 20 marks.

Sometimes the behaviour of the widow and her actions after the death of her husband could not fail to lead to quarrels within the family. It is not always clear from the records whether or not a widow was the mother of the dissatisfied heir in question. There is a lack of clarity in the family descriptions in the records which means that we cannot know for certain what level of kindred was involved and hence the amount of damage this caused to familial relationships. In the case of Joan de Kaerdif and Matilda de Kaerdif, it is not possible to determine whether or not they were related by blood. Matilda was the widow and Joan was the daughter (or step-daughter). Joan alleged that Matilda had kept chattels of her father's, which belonged to her (Joan) by right. Matilda denied this. However, the report of the jury found that Matilda had reserved certain chattels to herself to the value of 37s. 4d. The judgement was that Joan was to recover the chattels, although she did remit the damages due.

WIDOWS AND THE LAW

When blocked from entering their dower lands widows had immediate recourse to the law. A huge advantage of widowhood over the pre-marriage and married state and an indicator of an increase in power was that a widow could bring a suit of law to court independently. She needed no one else's permission. As a result, the records are littered with widows suing and counter-suing over their dower lands. Usually, the problem seems to have been a denial of entry to them, in which case they could derive no profits from the lands in question. In a case from Waterford in 1300 it was a prior who refused the woman in question entry onto her dower lands. The prior had demised to this woman's husband, John de la Bataille, twenty acres of land near Waterford to farm for seven years for 8d. per acre. John had died within this term of time and had died seised of the land, so the executor of the will had granted it to the widow. When she wished to enter the land the prior had her plough removed and generally impeded her.[33] So she immediately went to law to try and retrieve her lands.

Retrieving their dower lands from their lords, guardians or their king was a perennial problem for widows, especially those who belonged to the upper levels of society. On the death of Walter de Lacy in 1241, Meath had to be partitioned between the two heiresses of Gilbert, granddaughters of Margery de Lacy. As they were the heirs of a tenant in chief and important heiresses, the king ordered that they be sent over to him, commanding their grandmother, Margery, to hand them over to the justiciar.[34] They were deemed too valuable

33 *Just. rolls*, 28 Ed.I., m. 8. p. 300.   34 *C.P.R.*, 1232–47, 25 Hen. III, m. 4.

to be left in her care. Margery then began to sue for her dower, as her husband Walter's lands had been taken into the king's hand and then granted to Walter de Godarville.[35] Whilst awaiting the outcome of the inevitable inquisition and dower arrangements, Margery was assigned £100 out of Walter's lands and tenements in June 1241. The king then authorised Maurice FitzGerald, the justiciar, to assign her dower to her according to the custom of Ireland. She was also granted all the 'fruits and rents accruing from Walter's lands in Ireland from the time of his death'.[36]

These grants were made in October 1241, yet by the following September, Margery had still not received all her dues in Ireland. She requested that she have a third of the goods and chattels, to which the king assented. Margery's dower was ordered to be assigned to her in 1242.[37] As was common with women in control of lands, Margery had to be watchful lest advantage was taken of her. In 1244, for example, she can be found bringing a plaint against several people in the king's court in Dublin.[38] Later, in 1245, an agreement was made between her and the justiciar that her dower ought to consist of lands valued at £131 15s. 2½d. in England and £26 4s. 9½d. in Ireland, in Newcastle and Ardnurcher, which consisted of forty librates in all with liberties. In return for this she agreed to renounce all further claims to de Lacy lands.[39]

However, the wrangles did not end there. Six years after Walter's death, Margery's dower arrangements had still not been completely sorted out. Finally, on 30 July 1247, the king mandated the justiciar to arrange that, as part of her dower, she was to have, out of the value of the castle of Blathac and her portion of the vill of Drogheda on the Meath side, the third part of fifty marks which her late husband used to receive each year at the exchequer. The other two thirds were given to the two heiresses.[40] It appears that her dower arrangements were by then complete, and she could settle down to be the dowager of Meath.[41]

As part of their increased legal freedoms widows could make wills. In the will of Moldina Whitechurch (28 April 1456), a widow living in the Armagh diocese, she left a number of chattels to be disposed of.[42] This testament is dated later than the narrow span of time covered in this paper, but it serves to illustrate the type of chattels medieval widows might own and their concerns as evidenced in their wills. The majority of Moldina's worldly goods were to be left to her nephew, a Dominican friar, living in Drogheda, Co. Louth. The inventory of her goods included several valuable items such as,

---

35 *C.D.I.*, i, 1171–1251, nos. 2507, 2508.   36 Ibid., nos. 2542, 2547.   37 *C.P.R.*, 1232–47, 26 Hen. III, m. 3.   38 *Calendar of close rolls* (London, 1892–1963) 28 Hen. III., m.9 (cited as *C.C.R.*).   39 *C.D.I.*, i, 1171–1251, no. 2519.   40 *C.P.R.*, 1232–47, 30 Hen. III., m. 4; *Liberate Rolls*, 34 Hen. III, m.6.   41 *C.C.R.*, 1254–56, 38 Hen. III., m. 12.   42 *The register of John Swayne, archbishop of Armagh and primate of Ireland 1418–1439*, ed. D.A. Chart (Belfast, 1935), pp. 200–2.

a potte bound with silver with its covering – 10s.
a cup bound with silver – 12s.
5 silver spoons – 5s.
a girdle bound with silver – 6s. 8d.

Other bequests were money to the various religious orders resident in Drogheda.

Widows not only attended to their own wills, but they were often assiduous in attending to the wills of their dead husbands also. They were often appointed by executrices by their husbands. Some were kept very busy in recovering what was due to them. Isabella, widow of Gilbert Shank, was such a woman. In Cork in 1303 she pursued three different men for debts due to her dead husband. Along with the executors of her husband's will, who prosecuted with her, she sued, first of all, Richard Cod, for the sum of 6s. which she recovered. Next to be dealt with was John de la Pulle, who owed one crannoc of wheat, worth half a mark. Again, he was forced to hand it over. Finally, there was Nicholas de Montaigne who owed her one mark of silver and Thomas, son of Philip who owed her the sum total of 2s. 6d. The judgement here was also in her favour.

Isabella's actions reflect the determination of many widows, anxious to have debts to their husband's estate settled as well as their own. Isabella's seeking of restitution did not end there. She, along with the executors, also demanded of Eustace de Cogan, 15s. 9d. which he owed. Again here the judgement was that she recover the debts. There are three other instances, all in that same year, of Isabella, aided by the executors, recovering debts due to her husband. Sometimes damages were also awarded to Isabella, as when Richard Cod was again ordered to repay his debt and another 2s. was added onto it.[43]

WIDOWS AND THE CHURCH

With the addition of a dower to their resources, women's gifts to favoured religious institutions, sometimes perhaps censored by husbands, rose after their deaths. Widows utilised and enjoyed this new power of independent bequest. In the charters themselves, however, they often used a husband or father as identifier. More commonly, they name their dead husbands in their donations and gifts. In an entry from 1309 Elena Bretonn identified herself clearly as both a widow and as the daughter of Nicholas Page. There could be no doubt in the mind of her contemporaries as to who she was.[44] There are numerous examples of this in the Irish records. For example, in the chartularies of St Mary's abbey there is the charter of a Cecilia de Vernun, 'relict' of Galfrid des Auters.[45] 'De

---

43 Ibid., pp. 58–60.   44 Revd J.L. Robinson (ed.), 'Of the ancient deeds of the parish of St John (Dublin) preserved in the library of Trinity College Dublin', *Proceedings of the Royal Irish Academy* 33 (1916–7) C, no. 18, p. 183.   45 *Chartularies of St Mary's*

Vernun' was her maiden name, which she once again assumed after the death of her husband; she referred to herself in a charter of St Mary's abbey as the daughter of Rodulf de Vernun.

Evidence of widows' concern with supporting the church in Ireland can be found from the earliest days of the conquest. One prominent woman of that era was Basilia de Clare, sister of Earl Richard FitzGilbert de Clare, otherwise known as Strongbow. She married Raymond de Carew. Of Basilia, very little is known. Her dower agreement does not survive on paper, but some of it must have come from Raymond's new Irish lands, for she maintained an interest in Ireland after his death. His lands were in Leinster, the baronies of Forth and Idrone in Carlow and Glenscarraig in Wexford. Basilia can be found, as Raymond's widow, in the register of St Thomas' abbey, donating land around 1199–1200.[46] St Thomas' received a considerable number of grants from all of Strongbow's followers. Raymond, as one of his followers, was also a patron of Christ Church cathedral, along with Strongbow and Robert Fitz Stephen.[47] Basilia was eventually to be buried in St Thomas'.

Apart from aiding the church and easing their passage into the next life, a dower also furnished a means for many widows to provide some form of relief to the most needy in society, perhaps by diverting some of the profits from their dower lands, often accommodated through practical gifts to the church. These efforts provided an invaluable form of medieval welfare on a local level. The government did not have the resources or the desire to give attention to the area of relief of the sufferings of the poor and so it was up to private benefactors to do something. For example, in a document issued in 1235 by the 'prior and brethren of the Hospital of St John of Newtown by Trim', the prior granted to 'Nicola de Tuyt her heirs and successors, two beds in said hospital always ready with proper apparel for the use of sick persons whom she may choose, and this at the expense of the hospital for ever. For this Nicola gave to the prior and brethren forty marks.'[48] A common form of medieval philanthropy was also to provide dowries for poor girls.

THE NEED FOR REMARRIAGE?

Despite the obvious piety of many widows, and the desire of many to utilise their new importance in their locality for charitable or religious purposes, as a woman alone with an independent source of income and as a non-virgin the widow was often subject to whispers and insinuations concerning her supposed or actual sexual habits. Lascivious traits were assigned to widows; those who had known the

Abbey, Dublin, ed. J.T. Gilbert (2 vols., Rolls Series, London, 1884, 1886), no. 5. **46** *St Thomas the martyr, Dublin: register of the abbey* ed. J.T. Gilbert (Rolls Series, London, 1889), p. 111. **47** Edwin C. Rae, 'Architecture and sculpture, 1169–1603', in A. Cosgrove (ed.), *A new history of Ireland,* ii (Oxford, 1985), p. 744. **48** *Gorm. reg.*, p. 152.

delights of the marriage bed were believed to have, in consequence, insatiable sexual appetites. Widowhood was an ambiguous state. It could, as many believed, either give widows the opportunity to devote their lives to God or indulge their sexual appetites. Beautiful young widows were seen as the worst offenders. Widows were, in many ways, outside society. Their personal freedom was openly satirized and thus acknowledged, as one can see here in this sixteenth-century comment:

> Me thynke I lead a metely mery lyfe
> Which I should not yf that I whre a wyfe
> To bed I go and ryse whan I wyll
> All that I do is reason and skyll
> I commande others but none commandeth me
> And like I stand at mine own liberte.[49]

A wealthy, fairly young widow with a sizeable dower was a valuable commodity, which many lords sought to utilise in the marriage market of medieval society. Lords were often reluctant to leave wealthy widows alone after their bereavement; such a woman was a valuable prize from which the lord could benefit by bestowing her on a favourite or a political ally. A widow needed her lord's permission both to remarry and not to remarry; if she did not obtain it, then the repercussions could be serious. When in 1299 Margaret, the widow of Thomas Fitz Maurice, married Reginald Russel without the king's knowledge her lands in Waterford, Cork and Kerry were seized until she paid a substantial fine to the king by four instalments over two years. Only then was she to be replevied of her own lands and her dower.[50] A widow, then, like any landholder had first to respect her duties towards her lord in the matter of remarriage.

A widow had a number of options on entering widowhood. If she was able, she could make a fine not to marry again or to have her own choice of future husband. She could refuse a marriage partner provided for her by her lord if it meant disparagement, which was usually meant in the financial and not the social sense.[51] Practically speaking, however, many kinds of pressures may have been applied to widows, especially the wealthier ones, to force them into remarriage or force them to abandon remarriage plans. Despite her new and, in many ways more independent status, a widow who was the recipient of a substantial and important dower could often find herself manipulated and pressurised because of it.

Widows were also often subject to pressure urging them not to remarry, purely to benefit their lord it appears in many cases. In 1299 Robert Ufford, tenant in chief of the king, died, and the king's first concern was to have his

---

49 Robert Copeland, *The seven sorrowes that women have when theyr husbandes be deade* (London 1568). Printed in Mary Prior (ed.), *Women in English society, 1500–1800* (London 1985). **50** *Just. rolls*, 1295–1303, 27 Ed. I., m. 21, m. 5. **51** *E.H.D.*, 1042–1189, p. 401.

widow, Joan, swear that she would not marry again without licence.[52] At this stage, Joan had not been dowered and to decide what she was to be dowered with, the justiciar, John Wogan, was ordered to make an extent of her husband's lands, which the king had automatically taken into his own hand. After a survey was made of Robert's landed assets, the escheator gave his report. Robert held nothing except one hundred marks of rent, so a third part of the rents was offered to Joan as her dower provided the king approved, which he did. The control exerted over widows with regard to their subsequent marriage was of great importance, especially when referring to the widows of great tenants in chief. In 1248, after Margaret, widow of Theobald Butler, had given security that she would not marry without the king's licence, he arranged for her dower to be assigned to her.[53] She could have made a fine not to marry again or to choose her own second husband and could refuse a marriage partner, if it meant disparagement; theoretically, a widow was not to be forced into remarriage provided she gave security not to marry again without her lord's consent, as Margaret did in this case.[54]

Throughout the thirteenth century there were numerous examples of women who paid fines in court to have the right to choose their next marriage partner for themselves. Alternatively, they could simply take out a fine so as to avoid having to remarry at all. When Joan de la Rokele decided in 1233 that she either wanted to marry a man of her own choice or none at all, she obtained a licence from the king for that right, provided she did not marry one of the king's enemies.[55] In 1237, for example, Margery le Bigot undertook to pay the king a fine of one hundred marks to enable her to marry Geoffrey de Camera, the king's yeoman.[56] Even when licence to marry again was obtained, it was not always a smooth process. In 1300, Lucy, the widow of Nicholas Aylward, was to marry Henry de la Roche, who gave security for the marriage. The escheator was ordered to let the marriage go ahead, but problems arose when Henry failed to make satisfaction with the escheator for Lucy's dower lands. The sheriff was immediately ordered to take the dower lands, which Lucy had held of the king. Henry was then forced to pay 100s. to retrieve them.[57] If a widow married without a licence from her lord, whether it was the king or not, then the repercussions could be disagreeable. As a woman, a widow was still vulnerable, despite the measure of legal protection.

CONCLUSION

Despite the difficulties which procuring their dowers could bring, widows knew their dower to be a valuable part of their lives. It gave them a measure of security,

52 *C.C.R.*, 1296–1302, 27 Ed. I., m. 11; *Just. Rolls* 1295–1303, 27 Ed. I., m. 39d.
53 *C.D.I.*, i, 1171–1251, no. 2958. 54 *E.H.D.*, 1189–1327, p. 22. 55 *C.P.R.*, 1232–47, 17 Hen. III, m. 6. 56 Ibid. 21 Hen. III. m. 1. 57 *Just. rolls*, 1295–1303, p. 330.

freedom and power, although this was dependent, of course, on the size and wealth of the dower involved. A widow could enter into legal contracts and sue if they disappointed her. She could administer her lands freely and take the necessary legal measures to safeguard them. In 1295 Matilda, described as the widow of William de Freynes, put William Dunston in court in Dublin against Roesia, the widow of Alex de Alton.[58] There are dozens of other examples of widows actively engaging in the legal process over perceived threats to their interests. Agnes de Valence was one such woman, an heiress and also a widow dowered twice over. She was a woman of some consequence in Ireland and monitored her Irish lands carefully. In 1276 when newly widowed for the second time she was busy appointing attorneys in Ireland[59] As the mistress of fairly large estates in Ireland, Agnes had to be watchful especially as, like many of the widows of Anglo-Norman Ireland, she spent most of her time in England.

The importance for women of a dower in Irish medieval society cannot be underestimated. It provided in most cases a land-based safety net for their post-marital lives. It gave many of them financial security and bargaining power. A dower enabled widows to transform piety into actuality through donations, gifts and charitable bequests to the Church. Becoming a widow must have meant that, for many women, their perspective on their lives changed. The permanent absence of a husband meant that, more than ever, they needed to rely on their own sense and resources. In order to gain maximum profits and enjoyment from their dower lands an aggressive policy towards a possible denial of this right to them by any party was often required. Many noble women, in particular, had plentiful experience of administering lands as wives. However, as widows they could themselves pursue the actions in court against transgressors that before they could only recommend their husbands to take.

Of course not all women seized the opportunities of widowhood. There are many reasons why widows remarried; loneliness, fear, and inability to administer land. There are enough examples of capable and resourceful widows guarding their lands and rights, however, to indicate that perhaps many women did embrace this new stage in their lives and the benefits and liabilities that accompanied the award of a dower. Developing from being simply the legal inferior of a husband, wives, as they became widows, took over the role of the husband, to a large extent, in the local community and much more so, in the life of the Church. This necessitated a change in both the attitudes and behaviour of the women themselves, their families and of their contemporaries, all of whom had to accustom themselves to a subtle but demonstrable shift of power in outlook and in localised power.

58 Ibid. p. 75. 59 *C.D.I.*, ii, 1252–84, no. 1308; *C.D.I.*, iii, 1285–6, nos., 195, 277, 339, 319. See also C. Ó Cléirigh, 'The absentee landlady and the sturdy robbers: Agnes de Valence', in C.E. Meek and M.K. Simms (eds.), '*The fragility of her sex*'? *Medieval Irish women in their European context* (Dublin, 1996), pp. 101–18.

Freedom of movement? Women travellers in the Middle Ages

Diana Webb

In July 1447 a group of pilgrims from Hungary came to Aachen to witness the exhibition of the major relics which took place there once every seven years.[1] While they were there it came to be known that they spoke the dialect of Liège, not very far away from Aachen; they said that their ancestors had gone from there to Hungary to escape starvation. They went on from Aachen to Liège, where they told their story and it was agreed that they did indeed speak the local Walloon dialect. At the command of the bishop the archives were searched and the story confirmed. The visitors explained how they had preserved their language. Once they were settled in the places allotted to them in the diocese of Eztergom, the men had travelled about in pursuit of business and learnt to speak the Hungarian *idioma*; the women, by contrast, never went anywhere, but remained at home attending to the care of the children. They preserved their language in all its purity and taught it to the rising generations, among whom the girls, it is perhaps implied, never spoke anything else.

We are not, of course, to suppose that the male members or descendants of the original party of emigrants all routinely made journeys of comparable length thereafter. Social status and occupation determined how mobile different men were, or were permitted or compelled to be. Trade, warfare, litigation and political business impinged differently on men of different ranks, but relatively slightly on most women. The division of labour between the sexes allocated to men most of the more-or-less routine return journeys that were undertaken by way of business; but this division of labour itself was to a degree predicated on perceptions of the physical and not infrequently also the moral vulnerability of women, which made it undesirable for them to travel far afield.

---

[1] *Rerum Leodiensium sub Johanne Heinsbergio et Ludovico Borbonio episcopis, opus Adriani de Veteri Busco*, in E. Martène and U. Durand, *Veterum scriptorum et monumentorum amplissima collectio* (9 vols. Paris 1724–33), 4, cols 1216–17; Cornelius Zantfleet, *Chronicon*, ibid., 5, cols. 455–6. Oddly the two chroniclers give very different dates for the original emigration to Hungary. Adrianus dates it precisely to 1052, in the episcopate of Bishop Wazo, while Cornelius locates it 'about a hundred and thirty years ago'. The latter date

Of course, medieval women travelled. Like men, they did so as vagrants and social marginals, as beggars, camp followers and strolling players. Unusual circumstances, such as exile, persecution, or the threat of starvation which had prompted the emigration from Liège, might promote unusual types of female mobility. Our present concern, however, is primarily with the journeys which formed the stuff of ordinary travel by respectable people. Women, especially women of rank, frequently undertook quite lengthy journeys on a pretext which was both normal and unimpeachably respectable: marriage. We might take as one example of hundreds the journey that Anne of Bohemia had to make to become the wife of Richard II of England. For Anne, as for many others, her marriage ended with her own death and she found burial in her adopted country. While for some widows the option of returning to their native land was open, many stayed with their children, as Henry V's French wife Katherine did after his premature death in 1422. Similar scenarios were enacted by women of lowlier social standing who joined or accompanied globetrotting husbands on overseas postings.

Many of the longer journeys undertaken by medieval women were similarly one-way, leading once and for all to a new life. We might instance some of the Englishwomen mentioned in Margaret Harvey's recent study of English expatriates in Rome.[2] The emigration from Liège was such a journey. The women involved, in face of an emergency which threatened their very existence, had with their menfolk traversed a distance of some six hundred and fifty miles. Wives accompanied their husbands, daughters their parents, doubtless widowed mothers their sons. They and their female descendants after them then settled to a life which in all probability resembled the one they had left behind, in that their mobility was by common consent restricted.

This pattern must have been repeated many times at defining moments in the history of medieval Europe. From the days of the so-called barbarian migrations into the territory of the Roman Empire, to the Latin settlements in the eastern Mediterranean or the Christian recolonisation of Spain, women in varying numbers participated in significant shifts of population from place to place. The distances they travelled, in exceptional circumstances, in order to make possible the creation or recreation of societies in new settings, were not usually repeated and did not generate new patterns of mobility in their normal lives. They also exemplified the basic truth that women travelled to further the interests of the group to which they belonged. For the most part, the same was also true of journeys performed by men; travel undertaken on an individual whim or purely for purposes of recreation was more of a rarity than it is for us.

might have in its favour that 1317 fell in a period of dire famine in much of northern Europe. 2 M. Harvey, *The English in Rome, 1362–1420: portrait of an expatriate community* (Cambridge, 1999), especially pp. 120–31.

The pattern observable in individual lives varied, of course, with the circumstances of the society to which the individual, male or female, belonged. Few medieval women known to us led such adventurous lives as some of the characters in the Icelandic sagas which tell the story of the tenth-century Vinland expeditions, that is, *Graenlendinga Saga* and *Eirik's Saga*.[3] Three of these women are worthy of particular remark. First in time was the splendidly-named (in the translation used here) Aud the Deep-Minded, the Norwegian wife of Olaf the White, who made himself king of Dublin and the adjacent territory. After his death she went with her son Thorstein the Red to the Hebrides. She was in Caithness when she heard of Thorstein's death, whereupon 'she had a ship built secretly in a forest' and sailed away to Orkney. This was but a stepping-stone to Iceland, whither she set out 'with twenty free-born men in her ship'. Bereft of husband and son, she was, it seems, aiming to join her brother Bjorn, who was already in Iceland, but having spent her first winter there with him, she established her own dominion over an extensive district, allocating land to her male followers.

The other two women were Icelandic-born and both participated in the voyages to Vinland on the American coast. Freydis, perhaps the illegitimate daughter of Eirik the Red, was an unappetising but undeniably formidable personage, described as an 'arrogant, overbearing woman'. She took the initiative in organising a commercial voyage to Vinland with two brothers called Helgi and Finnbogi. It is almost as an afterthought that the presence of her husband Thorvard on this voyage is mentioned; he acted as her catspaw in the cold-blooded murder of her business partners, which Freydis completed, herself slaughtering their womenfolk with an axe. When the Skraelings, the indigenous people of Vinland, attacked the Viking settlement and the pregnant Freydis found herself surrounded by them, she seized a sword from a dead man, pulled one of her breasts out of her bodice and slapped it with the sword. The Skraelings, perhaps unsurprisingly, turned and fled.

If Freydis was pregnant in Vinland, was she the first European woman to bear a child on the American continent? That honour is usually accorded to another, perhaps more attractive character, Gudrid, daughter of Thorborn Vifilsson. 'Very beautiful and a most exceptional woman in every respect', she left her Icelandic homeland first with her parents, when her father fell on hard times and decided to try his luck in Greenland. At some point she was married to a Norwegian called Thorir and with him was shipwrecked on a reef near Greenland, whence they were luckily rescued thanks to the sharp eyesight of Leif Eriksson. Thorir then died in an epidemic and Gudrid was married second time around to Leif's brother Thorstein Eriksson. She set out once with

---

[3] The quotations here are taken from the translations by M. Magnusson and H. Pálsson, *The Vinland sagas: the Norse discovery of America* (London, 1965).

Thorstein from Greenland to Vinland, but they were driven back to the Western Settlement on Greenland, and here another epidemic carried Thorstein off. Rather alarmingly he came back to life for just long enough to impart to Gudrid a detailed prophecy of her future, including her extensive travels. Her third husband was the Icelander Karlsefni and she was foremost among those who urged him to undertake a voyage to Vinland, where she gave birth to her son Snorri. Thorstein Eriksson's prophecy had included the detail that she would go with her next husband to Norway, and she probably did, but this journey is not specifically mentioned in either of the sagas. She did however return to Iceland with Karlsefni and their son, where they settled to an agricultural existence. Gudrid and Snorri managed the farm after Karlsefni's death, but when Snorri married, Gudrid betook herself on a pilgrimage to Rome. On her return to Iceland she settled at a church Snorri had built at Glaumby and lived the rest of her life as an anchoress.

Although Gudrid's travels, like those of some other Icelandic and Norse women, were by European standards unusually frequent and extensive, they still fit the conventional pattern in that she accompanied either her parents or her husband, and she ended her life, implicitly, under the protection of her son. The pattern is similar with Aud the Deep-Minded and the ferocious Freydis, but all, as married women and as widows, are described as exerting decisive influence in the setting up of overseas ventures. The last of Gudrid's journeys, furthermore, her pilgrimage to Rome, was apparently undertaken of her own volition and not in the company of husband or son. She was one of thousands of widows in medieval European history who undertook long-distance pilgrimages.

Pilgrimage in fact accounts for a disproportionate number of the medieval women travellers about whom we have any information. For men and women alike, pilgrimages were among the few voluntarily undertaken journeys for which there was no strictly practical necessity; the individual chose to go on pilgrimage and made it a priority which was planned for and invested in. There were also of course involuntary pilgrimages, imposed by way of punishment or penance; the fact that women were sometimes sent on them (although they were often only short-distance) is itself testimony to the acceptability of pilgrimage as a form of female mobility. When the voluntary female pilgrim took the initative in embarking on her travels, did this meet with the approval of society, meaning (as it usually does) men ?

'Do you not realise you are a woman and cannot just go anywhere?' These discouraging words were uttered, somewhere around the year 400, by Abba Arsenius, a Roman patrician, once tutor to the sons of the emperor Theodosius, but now a holy man in the east. They were addressed to a woman of his own rank and city, a 'pious virgin', who had dared to seek him out for her edification.[4] It is

---

[4] Translation by Benedicta Ward, *The sayings of the Desert Fathers* (London and Oxford,

tempting to suspect that the real nub of his objection was that she was annoying him, and that like men in all ages and climes he sought to justify his personal displeasure on general principles. These general principles, rooted in centuries of social practice in the Mediterranean world, were available for adoption or adaptation by medieval Christians, and for centuries to come they would be invoked to control the Roman virgin's spiritual descendants. Arsenius himself had turned his back on the norms of life that had hitherto governed Roman males (marriage and family and cultural, civic and political involvement); it rapidly came to be felt that when women made a comparably radical choice they must preserve a strict and honourable seclusion.[5]

Such sentiments, strengthened and articulated in ecclesiastical legislation, came to bear heavily on nuns. In the 790s the assembled fathers at a synod held at Friuli stated as a truth universally acknowledged that women could not travel without coming into contact with men. For women vowed to religion, this was obviously impermissible; therefore nuns must abstain from pilgrimage.[6] The problem of escort and protection during travel affected ordinary laywomen as well as nuns, but it did not have the same implications for them; it was their business, after all, to have contact with men as wives and mothers. The religious woman was supposed to be acutely aware of her interwoven weaknesses, physical and spiritual, and to internalise and accept the resultant constraints. An Irish recluse whom St Columbanus consulted in the late sixth century had apparently done so: she would have sought out a more fitting place of pilgrimage outside Ireland 'had it not been for the frailty of my sex'.[7]

The *de facto* mobility of women on the road to Rome in the eighth century clearly sharpened these anxieties. Bede is witness to the popularity of the Roman journey with Englishwomen as well as men by 700. In a much-quoted letter written in 747 Boniface of Wessex urged Archbishop Cuthbert of Canterbury to take steps to prevent 'veiled women and matrons' from going to Rome. There was not a town between Rome and the channel but boasted a harlot of English stock, who had evidently, like Marie Lloyd somewhat later, dillied and dallied on the way.[8] Other letters, however, show Boniface advising and even encouraging pious women in their Roman pilgrimages. In 745 the cardinal deacon Gemmulus referred to 'reverend sisters and handmaids of God' who had arrived in Rome with introductions from Boniface, and the saintly

---

1975), pp. 13–14.   5 Cf. S. Elm, *'Virgins of God': the making of asceticism in Late Antiquity* (Oxford, 1994), especially, in respect of pilgrimage, pp. 272–81.   6 J.D. Mansi, *Sacrorum conciliorum nova et amplissima collectio* (31 vols., Florence, 1759–98), 13, cols. 850–1; D.M. Webb, *Pilgrims and pilgrimage in the medieval West* (London, 1999), p. 31. 7 *Vitae Columbani abbatis discipulorumque eius libri duo auctore Iona*, ed. B. Krusch, *MGH, Scriptorum Rerum Merovingicarum* 4, p. 68.   8 *S. Bonifatii et Lulli epistolae*, ed E. Dümmler, *MGH Epistolae*, 3, n. 78 ; translated by E. Emerton, *The letters of Saint Boniface* (New York, 1940), pp. 136–41.

Eadburga of Minster in Thanet not only made the pilgrimage after consulting him, but met with Boniface himself at Rome, not all that long before he wrote his disapproving letter to the archbishop.[9] Furthermore, the mere fact of being kin to Boniface, male or female, seems to have carried with it a real risk of bodily removal to join his missionising in Germany. The nun Leoba was hauled from the blameless seclusion of her convent at Wimborne in Dorset to preside over a community of nuns at Bischofsheim on the Tauber. We are told by her biographer, Rudolf of Fulda, that she went about visiting other convents for which she was responsible and that she was many times summoned to Charlemagne's court; she was also, by Boniface's own special permission, enabled to visit his burial place at Fulda to pray, and here eventually she too was buried and worked miracles.[10] The brothers Willibald and Winnebald, kinsmen of Boniface, died and were venerated as saints in southern Germany, and they brought with them not only their sister Walburga (incongruously commemorated in Walpurgisnacht) but another female relative, who as a nun at Heidenheim wrote their *Lives* around the year 780.[11]

This was obviously a very special form of female mobility, serving a higher purpose which ceased to exist in the later medieval centuries. When it was no longer possible to advance comparable justifications for religious women to breach the *cordon sanitaire* of their enclosure, anxiety about their seclusion reached fever pitch. In 1298 Pope Boniface VIII crowned a series of legislative efforts to enforce strict enclosure on nuns when he issued the significantly entitled bull *Periculoso*, identifying litigation and general convent business as the most likely causes of breach of enclosure.[12] It is interesting to note that very early in his pontificate, in 1295, he had asserted the general undesirability of women acting as witnesses in lawsuits: 'It is not befitting for them to wander abroad, nor to be involved in assemblies of men.'[13] The underlying principle that a woman's proper sphere was the private one prevailed, with all its implications for their freedom of movement.

The nun was subject simultaneously to this social imperative, to the known fragility of corrupted female nature and also to the special requirements of the

---

9 *Epistolae*, nn. 62, 27; *Letters*, pp. 113–14, 56–7. A later letter to Boniface from Aethelberht of Kent relates that Eadburga made the pilgrimage and returned to England (*Epistolae*, n. 105; *Letters*, pp. 177–9). 10 *Vitae Leobae abbatissae Biscofesheimensis*, ed. G. Waitz, *MGH Scriptores*, 15, pp. 118–31; translation by C.H. Talbot, *The Anglo-Saxon missionaries in Germany* (London, 1954), reprinted in T. Noble and T. Head, *Soldiers of Christ: saints and saints' lives from Late Antiquity and the early Middle Ages* (London, 1995), pp. 257–77. 11 Hugeberc's Lives of Willibald and Winnebald are in *MGH Scriptores*, 15, pp. 86–117; the *Life* of Willibald (the *Hodoepericon*) was translated by C.H. Talbot, *Anglo-Saxon missionaries*, reprinted in Noble and Head, *Soldiers of Christ*, pp. 143–64. 12 Text and translation in E. Makowski, *Canon law and cloistered women: Periculoso and its commentators, 1298–1545* (Washington, D.C., 1997), pp. 133–6. 13 In the bull *Mulieres quas vagari*, ibid., p. 221.

religious life, which theoretically demanded enclosure of male and female religious alike. One of St Boniface's early correspondents, in fact, grounded her doubts as to whether she and her daughter should go to Rome not on their gender but on the demands of *stabilitas*, that all should fulfil their vows where they had taken them.¹⁴ That the principle was in fact generally accepted is indicated by the request unsuccessfully made by Philip VI of France to Pope Clement VI that he should make the benefits of the 1350 Jubilee indulgence available to certain categories of person who could not make the journey to Rome, among them cloistered nuns.¹⁵

Perhaps Chaucer's prioress should not strictly have been on the road to Canterbury, but eyebrows were probably not raised very high on account of her and her like if they confined themselves to local pilgrimages. It may well have been the case that most of the pilgrimages undertaken even by laywomen were in fact short-range, for much of the evidence suggests that men far outnumbered women as long-distance pilgrims. The Opera of San Jacopo in the cathedral church of Pistoia in Tuscany gave alms to pilgrims, principally to Compostela, from the mid-fourteenth century onwards, and its records reveal humble females, like Giovanna who laundered vestments and altar cloths for the Opera, among those who made the long journey to Santiago. Women, however, constituted less than 6 per cent of the total number of pilgrims whose gender is ascertainable, that is, about 200 out of over 3100 who received alms between *c.*1360 and *c.*1480.¹⁶

It seems probable that many male pilgrims from the extremities of Europe to Jerusalem, Rome or Compostela were seeking spiritual benefits not only for themselves but for parents, wives, children and other kin and friends. However, when men who in their lifetimes may have travelled extensively by way of business, citizens of places like Hamburg and Lübeck, approached death and made their wills, they sometimes commissioned their wives and female kin to carry out pilgrimages on their behalf. In 1363, for example, Johann Schof of Lübeck said that his sister Geseke had promised to go to Rome and also to Aachen for him. Heinrich Sasse of Hamburg in 1360 left 40 marks and all his household moveables to his niece Beke, in recognition of the eleven years she had served him, probably as housekeeper, but stipulated also that for the salvation of his soul she was to make one pilgrimage to Trier and another to Aachen. She was not expected to pay for these trips herself, but to receive her necessary expenses from the estate, in addition to the bequests that had been made to her.¹⁷ Such testamentary dispositions reinforce the perception that for

---

14 *Epistolae*, n. 14; *Letters*, pp. 36–40.   15 Clement VI, *Lettres se rapportant à la France*, ed. E. Déprez and G. Mollat (3 vols., Paris, 1901–1961), n.4426; partial translation in Webb, *Pilgrims and pilgrimage*, pp. 78–9.   16 D. Webb, 'St James in Tuscany: the Opera di San Jacopo of Pistoia and pilgrimage to Compostela', *Journal of Ecclesiastical History* 50 (1999), pp. 207–34.   17 For these and other examples see Webb, *Pilgrims and*

both women and men travel served the purposes, economic or spiritual, of the family or larger society to which they belonged. The normal division of labour allocated the burdens of travel to men, the guardianship of the domestic hearth to women, but in special circumstances, even if only temporarily, a reallocation could take place. While Henrich Sasse lived, his niece's place was at home, serving him; when his posthumous well-being required it, she would undertake the journey from Lübeck to Trier and Aachen. While the normal division of labour clearly itself rested on deeply engrained assumptions about the undesirability of female mobility, equally clearly these assumptions did not always and everywhere amount to a rigid and unbreakable code. Such testamentary bequests did not involve only women who were related by blood or marriage to a male testator. Gerhard Hardenacke of Lübeck in 1358 left money, described as 'alms', to enable women to go to Trier, Rocamadour, Cologne and Aachen on pilgrimage; his son had to go to Compostela before he was permitted to enter into his inheritance. This bequest, and others like it, looks like an extended form of the practice of giving alms to poor persons in exchange for their prayers; it is interesting that female pilgrims should be specified.

Male or female, such hireling pilgrims were probably most often people of lowly social status, and here there is a further consideration of some importance. All travellers were vulnerable to physical assault, but the vulnerability of women, then as now, was understood to be the greater because of their relative physical feebleness and inability to defend themselves. The risk was not merely of physical injury but of rape, and this threat was greatest to women who were deemed to possess social honour. In addition, the obviously prosperous, male or female, were attractive to robbers. All of these considerations meant that wealthy and respectable women had to be sedulously guarded on the road. Whether or not women of low status and little wealth were in fact at less risk, they created less anxiety in that, like their menfolk, they had less honour to protect. The biographer of the 'servant-saint' Zita of Lucca (d. 1278) would have us believe that she went on her little local pilgrimages entirely unaccompanied. Zita may not have possessed social honour, but as an aspirant saint she possessed virginity, which had to be shown to be inviolate. On one occasion she was left to return to Lucca from San Piero a Grado near Pisa alone, on foot and in large part by night, but she was not totally bereft, for the Virgin Mary kept her company.[18] Similar solutions were found to this vexed problem by other Italian saints: for example, Bona of Pisa (d. 1207) was frequently accompanied to Compostela and back by St James himself.[19]

The woman of rank to some degree shared the mobility of her menfolk and was able to pay for the protection she needed to guard person, property and

pilgrimage, pp. 137–40.   18 *Acta Sanctorum*, Aprilis 3, p. 502.   19 *Vita* in *Acta Sanctorum*, Maii 7, pp. 142–60.

honour when in transit. In 1355, Joan of Bar le Duc, countess of Warenne, informed the pope that when at sea between England and France she had vowed not to return to England until she had visited Santiago de Compostela. Hearing afterwards of her husband's death, she had returned to England to look after his property and now sought prorogation of her vow for a period of three years. Whether Santiago had always been Joan's destination, and what the precise circumstances were in which she made her vow, we are not informed; perhaps her ship had been in danger and that prompted a vow of pilgrimage, as it often did. A picture emerges from her petition of a woman for whom a degree of mobility was an attribute of rank, and wherever she went, she would have been able to ensure a fitting escort.[20]

Many women of course travelled, as pilgrims and otherwise, with their husbands or sons. Birgitta of Sweden went to Santiago with her husband; another saint, the Prussian Dorothea of Montau, similarly went more than once with her husband from Danzig to Aachen and Einsiedeln. On their last journey to Einseideln, he was ageing, and the rigours and dangers of travel through what at the time was a war zone, as the Swiss fought the Hapsburgs, were scarcely diminished by his presence. Because of his infirmity, Dorothea went to Rome without him in 1389–90; he died while she was away, while she herself was ill for eight weeks in Rome.[21] Many of the problems Dorothea experienced, whether created by human or natural agencies, were not specific to pilgrimage; they were the hazards of travel. That most famous of medieval English female travellers, Margery Kempe, tended to compound these inevitable difficulties. Resolutely pursuing her religious vocation in pilgrimages both at home and abroad, and intensely desirous that this vocation should be recognised and respected, she displayed a veritable genius for alienating her companions. Her earliest pilgrimages were undertaken with her husband, but he soon succumbed to the considerable embarrassment involved in being seen with her and on one occasion at Canterbury shamefully pretended that he did not know her.[22] It may have been more usual for the husband to go to Jerusalem and the wife to mind the shop, but in this case the roles were reversed and Margery embarked, with her husband's permission but without his company, on a lengthy and exceedingly eventful journey which took her via Venice to Jerusalem and back and then to Assisi and Rome. Both in Italy on her way back from Jerusalem, and later in her life in Germany, she often found herself alone and uncomfortably dependant on the charity and forbearance of strangers. Her cherished self-image was badly compromised if she was alone or escorted, as sometimes happened, only by a solitary male.

20 *Calendar of entries in the papal registers relating to Great Britain and Ireland, Petitions*, I, p. 287; Webb, *Pilgrims and pilgrimage*, p. 183.   21 *Vita Dorotheae Montoviensis Magistri Johannis Marienwerder*, ed. H. Westpfahl (Cologne-Graz, 1964), pp. 110–11, 125–9, 144.   22 *The book of Margery Kempe*, ed. B. Windeatt (London, 2000), pp. 92–3.

This uncomfortable isolation was highlighted by the contrasting situation of women of standing whom she encountered on the road. At Assisi, for example, she met Dame Margaret Florentyne, who had come from Rome for the Indulgence of the Portiuncula at the beginning of August; she 'had with her many Knights of Rhodes, many gentlewomen and mickle good carriage'.[23] At Aachen, on her way back from Wilsnack some years later, Margery was for a while hospitably treated by 'a worshipful woman' of London who had 'much many with her', but, having had a little of Margery, she gave her the slip and left town without her. A poor friar bore her company for a while thereafter, but when they paused for refreshment at a tavern the good wife of the house 'counselled that she should take a wain with other pilgrims and not go so with a man alone'. Margery knew that perfectly well; her problem was keeping suitable company when she had it.[24]

On her English pilgrimages she encountered more mundane irritations, most notably at York where a senior clergyman subjected her to close questioning. Ascertaining that she had a husband, he wanted to know whether she had with her a letter recording his permission for her travels. If Margery was factually correct in asserting that other women present had no such letter with them, she may have attracted particular scrutiny by her conspicuous dress and behaviour and by lingering at the shrine for a prolonged period of time.[25] Wives (and for that matter, all married persons) were undoubtedly supposed to get the permission of their spouses before undertaking a long-distance pilgrimage, as Margery evidently did when she went to Jerusalem, and it was commonly held that husbands should control their wives' pious junketings. The reformer Hugh Latimer in the 1530s strongly urged that husbands and priests should exercise a veto over vows of pilgrimage made by women.[26] Sometimes they did so, and a wife might find that different husbands took different views. In 1391, Margaret, now the wife of Sir George Frung, and dwelling in London, had to be dispensed from a vow to visit Santiago which she had taken 'at the command and with the consent' of her previous husband, Sir Thomas Naunton. Sir George now did not consent, although Margaret also adduced her age and the number of her children as excuses for her failure to perform her vow.[27] Margery Kempe incurred her confessor's indignation when she returned from Germany, because she had undertaken what turned out to be a marathon trip without his permission.[28] The journey had not in fact originated as a pilgrimage. After the death of her son, Margery had agreed to escort her widowed German daughter-in-law home and took ship with her from Ipswich to Danzig. The opportunity to go to Wilsnack grew out of this journey, and Margery then visited Aachen on her painful way back from Prussia to Calais.

23 Ibid., p. 181.   24 Ibid., pp. 408–10.   25 Ibid., p. 246.   26 *Selected sermons of Hugh Latimer*, ed. A. Chester (Charlottesville, Virginia, 1968), pp. 23–5.   27 *Calendar of entries in the papal registers*, 4, pp. 188–9.   28 *The book of Margery Kempe*, p. 420.

However we evaluate the strictures of observers like Latimer, who was anyway hostile to pilgrimage, it is hard to avoid the conclusion that, with or without their husbands, women were in fact reasonably successful in laying claim to a certain freedom of movement in the cause of devotion and perhaps also of recreation. The censorious clearly believed that women used vows as an excuse to get away from the domestic sphere to which they properly belonged and the supervision which it was the duty of men – husbands and priests – to impose on them. Once well away, because of their well-known giddiness of character, they exemplified all that was wrong with both themselves and pilgrimage: superstition, frivolity, extravagance, and worse. Thomas More, writing towards 1530, reported the advice of a contemporary preacher that if wives wanted to visit Our Lady of Willesden, one of a number of shrines around London which had no good reputation as places of resort, their husbands should either keep them at home or go with them.[29] Widows had greater disposal over both their persons and their property, and to an extent were freer to band together in congenial company, to get a change of scene and indulge a taste for devotion. Sometimes, at least, a widow's intention must have been to offer prayers for the soul of the departed husband, perhaps in consequence of a promise made to him or of a testamentary disposition on his part, or both. Such women not only travelled themselves, but were the cause of travel in other women, because of their need for female servants.

Even though only a tiny proportion of pilgrimages, whether by men or women, have left documented traces, they are widely scattered in records of different kinds. Among these, *The Book of Margery Kempe* is sadly untypical. We could do with more such eccentric autobiographies, and of course we could also do with the letters and diaries of a later age; but failing these we are bound to prize the glimpses we are afforded by, for example, the permissions to travel issued by the English kings to overseas travellers male and female, including pilgrims. One incidental virtue of some of these licences, thanks to royal concerns about the movements of money, horses and men at arms, is that we learn about the escorts which the nominated leader of the party was authorised to take with her (and of course him). These licences do not seem always to have enumerated every member of the party, but concentrated on the able-bodied males and also members of the clergy, whose movements the monarchy was particularly concerned to monitor. In March 1348, for example, Elizabeth Ashton, widow of Sir Robert Ashton, set off to the Holy Land with a chaplain and two yeomen.[30] It seems unlikely that she had no maidservant with her, or that she can have intended to perform the whole journey in so small a party, but probably she expected to join up with other pilgrims.

29 *A dialogue concerning heresies*, in *Complete Works*, ed. T. Lawler, G. Marc'hadour and M. Marius, 6, pt ii (New Haven, 1981), p. 99.   30 *Calendar of close rolls, Edward III*, 8, p. 501.

Such licences were especially numerous in the early autumn of 1350, because this was the year of the second Roman Jubilee, and there were several women (although again they were in a minority) among the pilgrims.[31] Ida lady Neville of Essex was permitted to travel with 'damsels and grooms to the number of twenty persons and twenty horses'. Elizabeth, late the wife of Bartholomew de Lisle, was accompanied by a chaplain, a damsel, two yeomen, three grooms and five horses, and Beatrice Luttrell by a damsel, a chaplain, a yeoman and a groom. Agnes, the widow of Jordan Sheppey of Coventry, was taking four men and two horses, but she must surely have had a maid. Women are sometimes listed by their name alone, without any accompanying party, and here it is to be presumed that, although they were individually licensed, they were in fact travelling in a larger group. Half a century later, there is an unusually detailed description of the preparations made by Agnes Bardolf, widow of Thomas Mortimer knight, for her pilgrimage to Rome, Cologne and 'other foreign parts' in 1403. She was licensed to take with her twelve men and twelve horses, with her goods and harness, and also to pay £300 for her expenses to merchants of Genoa and other persons who would give her letters of exchange to their fellows in foreign parts.[32] Women of substance, like their male counterparts, appointed attorneys to deal with their legal affairs while they were abroad.

Sometimes, however, the sources portray women as adjuncts, and sometimes merely anonymous adjuncts, to male principals. In 1383 Richard II licensed a couple of Bretons to pass through his jurisdiction to Rocamadour and Santiago; the men, a knight and a clerk, were named, but their party included an unnamed 'lady' and two maids.[33] An English party which received royal permission to go to Rome in 1378 was headed by one Ralph Fleshhewer of Chesterfield; going with him were not only Sara his wife and Henry his son, but no fewer than six other women, who (unless they were all servants) were perhaps neighbours, friends or kinsfolk who were taking the opportunity to join the family party. In 1393, a Lombard dwelling in London was paid 48 marks, payable to three named men and five unnamed women who were going on pilgrimage to the Holy Land in their company.[34]

The contemporaneous records of the Opera di San Jacopo of Pistoia, mentioned above, convey a similar impression of the varieties of female travel. Wives travelled with their husbands and sometimes also with their children; women, sometimes but not invariably described as widows, were given alms as individuals; and there were parties of women travelling together, which we may surmise consisted of or at least included widows. Women, both named and unnamed, who were described as 'poor' also sometimes received alms; were they

---

[31] The lists are in Thomas Rymer, *Foedera* (10 vols., The Hague, 1739–45), 3, pt i, pp. 56–7, supplemented by *Calendar of close rolls, Edward III*, 9, pp. 267–8, 271–2.
[32] *Calendar of patent rolls, Henry IV*, 1, p. 214. [33] Rymer, *Foedera*, 3, pt i, p. 157.
[34] *Calendar of close rolls, Richard II*, 1, p. 530; 5, p. 523.

going on pilgrimage on their own account or someone else's, or were they perhaps little more or less than vagrants? One of the more striking entries concerns the pilgrim who gave birth to a boy in the hospital of San Jacopo in 1370.[35] How many pregnant women were to be found on the road, or indeed became pregnant on the road? The childbearing years were not, for most women, the best time for long-distance travel. Papal dispensations granted because of failure or inability to perform pilgrimages indicate that repeated pregnancies sometimes in fact prevented women from carrying out their pious intentions.

The fictional Wife of Bath, we are left in no doubt, dined out on the stories of her many travels. Occasionally real-life women had remarkable tales to tell and did not scruple to tell them. One of the more egregious was Isolda Parewastel of Bridgwater in Somerset, who in 1366 informed the pope that 'for three years she has daily visited the Lord's Sepulchre and other holy places of the Holy Land, and has there been stripped and placed head downwards on a rack and beaten; then, half dead, she miraculously escaped from the Saracens and now proposes to build a chapel at Bridgwater in honour of the Blessed Virgin ...' What she had done to annoy the Saracens is not specified; but she was clearly determined to occupy a prominent place in her local society on the strength of it.[36] More pathetically, Matilda de Brionie, of the diocese of London, related in April 1330 that she had been on her way to visit the Holy Sepulchre, Santiago and Assisi when the boat she was in on the Rhone capsized, some of her companions were drowned, and she lost her money so that she could not continue.[37] Matilda had a near miss; but often pilgrims, female as well as male, did not live to tell their stories. An inquisition taken in Dorset in June 1376 heard that Elizabeth de Keynes, who would have been the heir to a property left by her niece, had set out for the Holy Land with some neighbours in Christmas week of 1373; the neighbours had returned a year ago bearing news of her death.[38]

Long-distance travel on the scale of Roman, Santiago or Holy Land pilgrimage was not of course the typical form of female mobility. The Paston and Stonor letters shed a little light on the movements of women of modest rank in fifteenth-century England. Once again it can be deduced that while family needs established the overall framework within which women operated, personal circumstances and attributes were not without significance. This is demonstrated by the case of Elizabeth Riche, daughter of one London merchant and first married to another. In the summer of 1475 she became the wife of William, later Sir William, Stonor of Oxfordshire. During the four years

---

35 Webb, 'St James in Tuscany', p. 228.   36 *Calendar of entries in the papal registers, Petitions*, 1, pp. 512–13; A. Luttrell, 'English women as pilgrims to Jerusalem: Isolda Parewastell, 1365', in J.B. Holloway, J. Beehtold and C.S. Wright (eds.), *Equally in God's image* (New York, 1990), pp. 184–97.   37 *Calendar of entries in the papal registers*, 3, p. 318.   38 *Calendar of inquisitions post mortem*, 14, n. 234.

of this second marriage Elizabeth spent substantial periods of time in London, even while her children by her first husband resided with Sir William at Stonor. She went to London to commemorate her former husband and later her father, to visit her mother and also her son-in-law Thomas Betson, and she conducted business there on William Stonor's behalf. She was sometimes able to take advantage of already-established connections with the duchess of Suffolk, Joan de la Pole, sister of Edward IV, and in October 1476 she reported witnessing the king's meeting with his mother, Cicely duchess of York, at Greenwich.[39]

Stonor was forty miles or more from London, a distance which it seems that Elizabeth thought she could cover in one day on horseback. An epidemic which had cleared London was still raging in Oxfordshire in the autumn of 1476; Elizabeth was concerned both for her husband and for her children. If William could or would not send the children to London for their greater safety and indeed come there himself, she would go to him at Stonor, and asked him to send horses to make this possible.[40] Elizabeth may have made decisions about her own movements, but we can assume that she would always have been fitly accompanied. In March 1478 Thomas Betson came from London to meet her at Windsor, and, as he wrote to William Stonor, 'from thence to London to my simple power I helped to convey her'. In April, perhaps significantly, he further told William that Elizabeth had had her way in the matter of some capons, 'as she doth in all other'. By October, however, she was weary of London and told Sir William that she once she had done her pilgrimages (what they were is unclear) she cared not how soon she was at Stonor with him, and asked him to send her horses by the following Saturday at the latest.[41] It is clear from the sketchy record left by her correspondence that, as we might expect, both her husband and her son-in-law were more frequently mobile in the cause of business.

Margaret Paston did not see so much of London. We know of only one visit she made to the capital, with her daughter Margery, in September 1465, when her husband John was imprisoned there. Her younger son John earnestly recommended that they should take the opportunity to visit the Cross at the North Door of St Paul's and St Saviour at Bermondsey, to help Margery to secure a good husband, thus showing off a knowledge of the sights which his mother and sister presumably lacked.[42] Norwich, where Margaret spent much of her time until in old age she retired to the countryside, was further from London than Stonor, and she lacked the independent London interests and connections which Elizabeth Stonor possessed. In addition, the prolonged absences of first her husband and then her sons, in London and elsewhere, while enemies swarmed around the Paston properties in Norfolk, made her continued presence and vigilance the more essential. Pilgrimages, to Ipswich or

39 *The Stonor letters and papers, 1290–1483*, ed. C.L. Kingsford (2 vols., Camden Third Series 30, London, 1919), 2, p. 14.   40 Ibid., pp. 10–11.   41 Ibid., pp. 42–3, 44, 69.
42 *The Paston letters*, ed. J. Gairdner (6 vols., London 1904; reprinted in one volume,

Walsingham, must have been welcome diversions. The mobility of these two women was very obviously conditioned by the differing circumstances in which they found themselves.

Occasional reflections are cast in both the Paston and the Stonor letters by the movements of greater ladies, such as the countess of Norfolk and the countess of Suffolk, sometimes in the company of their husbands and sometimes not. When Elizabeth Stonor wanted to speak to the countess of Suffolk in London in 1476, she found her too busy with preparations for a trip to Canterbury – perhaps a pilgrimage – to talk.[43] Royal and noble women, especially widows, are not infrequently recorded undertaking pilgrimage tours. Joan Beaufort, countess of Westmoreland (who once met Margery Kempe) arrived at St Albans in the summer of 1428 as a widow of three years' standing who was undertaking a tour of holy places.[44] Such ladies enjoyed both a relative abundance of leisure and abundant means, great facilitators of travel then as now.

For respectable women, less likely than their menfolk to be taken from home by the demands of politics, warfare, business or litigation, pilgrimage was of special significance as a pretext for travel. It offered them opportunities at least for modest journeys which they might not otherwise have enjoyed. With the opportunity to see the world and to obtain spiritual fulfilment, came the hazards which were inseparable from all travel: mishaps by land and sea, robbery with violence, and for some, like Elizabeth Keynes of Dorset, death a thousand miles from her native land.

Gloucester 1983), 4, p. 186.   43 *Stonor letters*, 2, p. 14.   44 *Annales monasterii S. Albani a Johanne Amundesham monaco, ut videtur, conscripto A.D. 1421–1440* ed. H.T. Riley (2 vols., Rolls Series 28 pt 5, London, 1870–1) 1, p. 24.

The gender of lordly women: the case of Adela of Blois

Kimberly A. LoPrete

The groundswell of scholarly responses to Joan Scott's eloquent plea for gender to be taken as a fundamental category of historical analysis has greatly enriched our understanding of the interrelations amongst political powers, social structures and cultural concepts in past and present times alike.[1] However – and not without a certain irony – analysis of women's signal contributions to their wider worlds has been less well served by gazing at women primarily through the prism of gender. There is a double risk in such a perspective: on one hand, to downplay the importance of other categories constitutive of women's social identity – such as status, rank or class, age-range, or life-stage – when analysing the typical spheres of their activities and the value accorded them; on the other, to confuse human beings with that congeries of gendered traits and attributes prevailing in cultural constructs – a form of 'idealising essentialism' by which individual women are ahistorically reduced to what men thought all females were (or ought to have been).[2]

When pre-modern women are viewed largely in the light of gender there is the additional danger of anachronism in two key conceptual domains. First, in insufficiently grasping the differences in how gendered concepts were construed and mapped onto men and women as then understood in physiological terms.[3] Second, when mapping how the spheres of men's and women's activities related to the structures governing access to authorised power as wielded within

---

[1] Joan W. Scott, 'Gender: a useful category of historical analysis', *American Historical Review* 91 (1986), pp. 1053–75. [2] See, for example, the perceptive comments of Susan M. Stuard, 'Fashion's captives: medieval women in French historiography', in S.M. Stuard (ed.), *Women in medieval history and historiography* (Philadelphia, 1987), pp. 68–76, at pp. 71–5. [3] Now fundamental on the interrelations of gender and 'sex' (that is, biogenetic understandings of women), is Joan Cadden's comprehensive *Meanings of sex difference in the Middle Ages* (Cambridge, 1993); Alcuin Blamires, *The case for women in medieval culture* (Oxford, 1997), discusses perhaps the most comprehensive range of medieval 'defences' of women, though many of the arguments presented were either elaborated significantly earlier or invoked more frequently than he often implies; note in

society as a whole.⁴ While it is widely acknowledged that even those pre-modern writers who stressed complementarity over hierarchy in discussions of gendered relations and properties still tipped the scale to some degree in favour of maleness as the normative or superior gender, less often appreciated is the extent to which pre-modern aristocratic or elite women's routine domestic roles placed them at the hub of the circles of power spiralling outward from dynastic noble lords and patrician household heads.

This disjunction in the pre-modern world between apparently normative cultural concepts and social practices, combined with the risk of employing anachronistic categorical maps when studying it, has had two important consequences on prevailing assessments of medieval noblewomen's socio-political status and powers. First, the number of, and frequency with which, women exercised authoritative lordly powers as they played out their gendered social roles has been unjustly minimised. Second, how male contemporaries perceived and valued the lordly women in their midst has been largely misconstrued.

If it assumed that medieval women, as females of the human species, were always deemed inferior and incompetent compared to all men and thus prevented from exercising political authority directly, the women whose attested powerful deeds cannot be ignored create interpretive problems. In much recent writing about such women, the difficulties are eliminated with one of two main rhetorical sleights of hand. Either the woman under discussion is cast as the singular exception who proves the rule of every other woman's powerlessness or she is said to have been perceived and treated by her contemporaries as an honorary man; that is, she was not taken for a woman at all.⁵ In other words, if, at the limit,

particular pp. 234–7. **4** Trail-blazing discussions of the links between aristocratic women's 'public' powers and the domestic base of all noble power include Marion Facinger, 'A study of medieval queenship: Capetian France, 987–1237', *Studies in Medieval and Renaissance History* 5 (1968), pp. 3–48; Jo Ann McNamara and Suzanne Wemple, 'The power of women through the family in medieval Europe, 500–1100', rev. ed. in Mary Erler and Maryanne Kowaleski (eds.), *Women and power in the Middle Ages* (Athens, Georgia, 1988), pp. 83–101 (first published in 1973); Pauline Stafford, *Queens, concubines, and dowagers: the king's wife in the early Middle Ages* (Athens, Georgia, 1983) – elaborating upon ideas published in an article in 1978; and Megan McLaughlin, 'The woman warrior: gender, warfare, and society in medieval Europe', *Women's Studies* 17 (1990), pp. 193–209. Though the authors argue that women's public-political powers diminished significantly over the course of the eleventh and twelfth centuries, in part because of the growing elaboration of the apparatus of state, the steady stream of research into the lives of numerous individual women suggests that the effects of such broader socio-political transformations on the powers of noblewomen – especially those below the rank of queen – have been exaggerated (see Kimberly A. LoPrete and Theodore Evergates, 'Introduction', in Theodore Evergates (ed.), *Aristocratic women in medieval France* (Philadelphia, 1999), pp. 1–5, 179–80). **5** Such has been the approach popularised by Georges Duby in, for example, 'Women and power', in Thomas N.

her deeds are admitted to have been of public-political consequence during her lifetime, she and her accomplishments are excluded from the general history of women and the gendering of socio-political domains over the *longue durée*.

By analysing the full range of contemporary representations of one politically prominent woman, the countess Adela of Blois – widely, but inaccurately, held to have been without peer in her day – this essay reveals the anachronism involved in categorising powerful female lords as exceptional women and as honorary men alike.[6] It will be shown, on one hand, that such labeling depends on the uncritical importation to the central middle ages of distinctly modern conceptions of sexuality, love, power and their interrelations; on the other, that it deflects attention from the dynamic interplay between the life-cycles of aristocratic families and the domestic base of their power that routinely produced a significant number of women who exercised lordly authority within their traditional social roles.

Bisson (ed.), *Cultures of power: lordship, status, and process in twelfth-century Europe* (Philadelphia, 1995), pp. 69–85, as at p. 78: 'To assume this command a woman must cease to be a woman, must take on masculinity, must change in gender'; and his *Women of the twelfth century, vol. 2: remembering the dead*, trans. Jean Birrell (Chicago, 1997), pp. 105–49; and in contradistinction to Marc Bloch, *Feudal society*, trans. L.A. Manyon, 2 vols. (Chicago, 1961), e.g., pp. 200–1; Duby also argues that such strong women were most often castigated as 'abnormal' for acting against their prescribed roles, usurping powers nature had assigned to men.   6 Among Adela's contemporaries were the politically-active countesses Ermengard of Anjou/Brittany (see Therese Latzke, 'Robert von Arbrissel, Ermengard und Eva', *Mittellateinisches Jahrbuch* 19 (1984), pp. 116–54); Richilde of Hainaut and Flanders (see Megan McLaughlin, 'The woman warrior', pp. 194, 200; and Karen S. Nicholas, 'Countesses as rulers in Flanders', in *Aristocratic women*, pp. 111–37, 220–5, at pp. 115–17, 221); Clementia of Flanders (see Penelope Adair, 'Countess Clemence: her power and its foundation', in Theresa M. Vann (ed.), *Queens, regents and potentates* (Dallas, Texas, 1993), pp. 63–72); Ida of Boulogne (see Renée Nip, 'Godelieve of Gistel and Ida of Boulogne', in Anneke B. Mulder-Bakker (ed.), *Sanctity and motherhood: essays on holy mothers in the Middle Ages* (New York, 1995), pp. 191–223, esp. pp. 209–18); Mathilda of Tuscany (see now Elke Goez and Werner Goez (eds.), *Die Urkunden und Briefe der Markgräfin Mathilde von Tuszien*, MGH, Laienfürsten- und Dynasten-Urkunden der Kaiserzeit, no. 2 (Hannover, 1998), and the literature cited therein); the countess-queen Bertrada of Montfort (still awaiting a study based on documentary sources; an overview and guide to narrative sources can be found in Jean Dhondt, 'Sept femmes et un trio de rois', *Contributions à l'histoire économique et sociale* 3 (1964–65), pp. 35–70, at 62–9); the active queens Adelaide of Maurienne (see Facinger, 'Medieval queenship', pp. 28–31), and Matilda II of England (see Lois L. Huneycutt, 'The idea of the perfect princess: the *life* of St Margaret in the reign of Matilda II (1100–1118)', *Anglo-Norman Studies* 12 (1989), pp. 81–97); as well as Heloise, another Latin-literate married woman educated at a nunnery. The list could be lengthened significantly by adding lower-ranking politically-active lordly women, several of whom are discussed in the works cited in the next note, as well as by Amy Livingstone, 'Aristocratic women in the Chartrain', in *Aristocratic Women*, pp. 44–73, 200–7.

Adela, daughter of William the Conqueror, by marriage countess of Blois, Chartres and Meaux, and mother of count Thibaud (Theobald) 'the Great' of Blois-Champagne (d. 1152), king Stephen of England (d. 1154), and bishop Henry of Winchester (d. 1172), has long attracted the attention of historians, though more for her cultural patronage than for her political activities, the full extent and impact of which have been revealed only recently.[7] Conceived shortly after her father's consecration as king, she was William and Matilda's youngest daughter, their only girl born with royal blood from both parents. Fully literate in Latin, she evidently received instruction in letters and religion prior to her marriage, most likely alongside her professed sister, Cecilia, at their parents' pre-conquest foundation of Holy Trinity in Caen. In *c*.1083, after an engagement of one to two years, Adela wed Stephen-Henry, the eldest son and primary heir-designate to count Thibaud III of Blois, Chartres, Meaux and Troyes, one of the leading princes of northern France. The young countess was about fifteen, her husband, an experienced co-count in his mid-thirties. Her dowry appears to have been in the form of liquid wealth; the full extent of her dower lands is unknowable, but included property ranging from uncultivated forest to castles in all regions of her husband's far-flung domains. During the approximately fifteen years the couple lived together, Adela bore at least six, and perhaps eight, children, including five sons.

Stephen-Henry became count of Blois, Chartres and Meaux in his own right on his father's death in 1089; his step-mother joined her sons in Troyes, leaving Adela to manage the comital household without interference from a female in-law. During the nine years her husband ruled as count in France, Adela accompanied him on major administrative perambulations, while routinely and publicly participating in the exercise of all non-military aspects of comital lordship. Whether alongside or apart from her husband, Adela is attested in those years alienating lands and rights to make pious bequests or reform monasteries, serving as an advocate or otherwise protecting churchmen and religious communities, granting privileges, adjudicating property disputes at the comital court and authorizing donations or sales by comital followers. She was thus well-placed to serve as regent-guardian when Stephen departed with the first crusaders. Contemporaries praised Adela's proficient exercise of full comital authority during his almost three year absence, powers she would wield again when Stephen returned to the Holy Land late in 1100. After his martyr's death at Ramla in 1102, Adela continued to rule as countess until her monastic retirement in 1120, though, like her male peers, she associated her eldest sons in comital lordship as they came of age.

---

7 For an overview and reference to further literature, see Kimberly A. LoPrete, 'Adela of Blois: familial alliances and female lordship', in *Aristocratic Women*, pp. 7–43, 180–200, which also contains the sources for, and further discussion of, points mentioned in this essay; note also LoPrete, *Adela of Blois. ... c.1067–1137* (Dublin, forthcoming).

Because she was of higher status than her crusader husband, belonged to two of the most powerful princely families of northern France and was widowed with young sons when in her mid-thirties, Adela was well placed – regardless of personal proclivities – to intervene in the power politics of her day. She did so incisively when opportunities arose and circumstances demanded, even though her chief weapon was diplomatic acuity rather than the sword. In 1105 her ability to orchestrate a reconciliation between her brother, king Henry I, and his exiled archbishop of Canterbury, Anselm, paved the way for the English king's takeover of Normandy and the renewal of the Anglo-Norman-Thibaudian alliance that had been sealed with her marriage. Two years later she provided cash and generous hospitality at the extensive network of comital castle-towns to support pope Paschal II's French tour and delicate negotiations with the emperor Henry V. Consolidating her husband's earlier reacquisition of Sully by arranging her eldest son's marriage in 1104, in 1107 she named her second son as Stephen-Henry's primary heir in order best to assure the continued defence and firm rule of her affinal family's extensive and far-flung domains. As the next decade turned she rallied powerful neighbours – including the king of France – to defend with force of arms the lands of border castellans and churchmen alike.

When negotiations between the kings Louis VI and Henry I over the status of Normandy broke down and warfare loomed, Adela directed the Thibaudian family's response. During a decade that was punctuated by two major conflicts, she continued her relentless circuits of the comital domains, making timely visits to neighbouring lords and liberally bestowing bribes, brides and other favours on border castellans with multiple allegiances. Such behind-the-lines diplomacy helped secure the military victories of her brother and sons that drew the principal antagonists back to the bargaining table. Adela's participation in the multi-party negotiations resulted in a peace that strengthened the comital family's extensive frontiers when hostilities ceased. At that point (spring 1120) the countess, aged about fifty, retired from the active life, but even in her final seventeen years as a nun she put her political skills to good use, whether in preserving Marcigny's lands or in resolving disputes in the domains she had ruled as countess.

Adela's multifarious activities left their trace in an array of contemporary and near-contemporary sources extant today, the number and variety of which are perhaps unequalled for a French countess of her generation.[8] They include about ninety-five documents (overwhelmingly ecclesiastical charters drafted by the beneficiary); nineteen necrologies (listings of the dead for whom prayers were offered, sometimes recording gifts made to endow the anniversaries);

8 For comparative purposes note the new edition of Mathilda of Tuscany's charters, as cited in n. 6; and those of her mother Beatrice, c.1013x1026–1076, calendared in Elke Goez, *Beatrix von Canossa und Tuszien: eine Untersuchung zur Geschichte des 11. Jahrhunderts* (Sigmaringen, 1995), pp. 195–235.

thirty-three letters either to or about the countess sent by seven high-ranking churchmen, three letters to her from laymen (including two by her husband), and three written by Adela herself; six poems, including three verse epistles by literary-minded prelates; five hagiographical narratives composed between 1095 and the mid-twelfth century to record the lives of potential new saints or new miracles performed by long-dead ones; and eleven historical or chronicle texts from the early twelfth to early thirteenth centuries written by French or English churchmen, five of whom may well have met Adela on more than one occasion.[9] In addition to documenting the events outlined above, these sources show that Adela patronised about forty religious houses (though only two communities of women), both within and beyond the domains she ruled as countess, and that she treated directly with fifteen different bishops and archbishops, as well as two popes. Adela clearly was well known to leading ecclesiastical and lay lords alike and the surviving sources provide important insight into how elite men viewed this generous patron and powerful countess in their midst.

Close examination of a sample of available evidence, drawn from each of the main categories, confirms what is manifest from looking at it all: her male contemporaries viewed Adela primarily as a woman who was also a lord. As a woman, they portrayed her in the same general terms typically used to represent any lay woman: with particular reference to her sexuality and relationships to men. As a lord, they depicted her wielding the same lordly powers as her male peers. Though those powers were often construed as 'male' and Adela was herself occasionally portrayed as acting 'with manly strength' (*viriliter*), such manly actions in 'male' domains did not make her any less of a woman in the eyes of her male contemporaries, who expected her to conform to standards of behaviour applicable to any woman active in the world. In an age when 'public' and 'private' powers as distinguished by modern analysts tended to be conflated in noble households, the notion of lordly women or female lordship entailed no contradiction in the gendered logic of separate 'male' and 'female' spheres: noblewomen need cross neither conceptual nor tangible thresholds to exercise their domestically-rooted lordly powers. Nor did politically-active women consistently generate anxiety in men, in large part because such *dominæ* usually exercised their lordly powers within the bounds of their traditional women's roles.

The commonplace acknowledgment of Adela's place as a sexually-active female in a world dominated by men is shown when all types of evidence are considered. She is most frequently described as the daughter of king William, the wife of count Stephen-Henry, the sister of king Henry I, the mother of count Thibaud or king Stephen, or some combination thereof.[10] Exceptions

---

9 Of the historians, the two who certainly had met Adela were Eadmer of Canterbury and Hugh the Chanter of York; Orderic Vitalis most likely had, as had perhaps Suger of St Denis and Guibert of Nogent (based on inconclusive circumstantial evidence).
10 Two documents stand out from the rest – largely written by the ecclesiastical

exist in two readily explicable contexts: necrology entries referring simply to 'countess Adela' for whose personal salvation anniversary prayers were offered and a couple of dozen charters and letters from her widowhood recording her official acts as countess: in those documents, her name and title sufficed to designate the individual actor and the legal authority empowering her deeds. Yet throughout her widowhood Adela continued to be identified in terms of her relationship to men and even formal documents reveal that she most often acted at the request, or to the benefit, of male relatives. Thus, while Adela had a lifelong personal, and a sometime legal, identity of her own, it should come as no surprise to see that her relationships to men mattered more to her male contemporaries; indeed, they were a fundamental source of her social powers.

As a daughter, wife, and mother Adela's sexuality was also central to men's conception of her social roles and the behaviour deemed appropriate as she acted them out. Only rarely remarked upon in documents and little developed in the often sparse passages in prose narratives, her 'femininity' in conventional sexual terms is developed most fully in poems and letters.[11] The earliest extant reference to Adela – a verse epistle written about the time of her betrothal – introduces her as a beautifully elegant royal virgin, even as she is set apart from other young girls because of her ultimate responsibility for her father's conquest of England: the Fates had arranged William's victory so that Adela would be born to a crowned king instead of to a mere count.[12] Notwithstanding the poet's conceit to underscore her high status, he presents the future countess as a sensual young maiden, poised to be passed from the hand of her father to that of a husband. The authors of later letters and poems likewise used stereotyped images of bodily beauty, gracious elegance and pleasing charm to praise this married mother. Still, three stressed that those potentially seductive assets were matched by such modesty that Adela's sexual fidelity to her husband, even when widowed, was beyond reproach.[13] Such emphasis on physical beauty

---

beneficiary – by identifying Adela as the daughter of king William and queen Matilda [I]; they were written by a cleric trained in the English royal chancery and Adela's chaplain (see *Cartulaire de l'abbaye de Conques en Rouergue*, ed. Gustave Desjardins, Paris, 1879, pp. 340–2, 352–3, nos. 470, 485: the latter of which must be corrected against a near contemporary copy unknown to the editor, Archives Départementales de Seine-et-Marne, H.824; hereafter cited as *Conques*); nor are her daughters mentioned by name in any family document. In narrative sources, Adela's activities are most often reported in digressions motivated by reference to one of the men in her life.   11 Note, however, the exceptional – if oft-cited – document referenced in n. 37 below, and the narrative vignette in n. 21.   12 Godfrey of Rheims to Archdeacon Ingelrannus of Soissons, ll. 127–56, ed. André Boutemy, 'Trois oeuvres inédites de Godefroid de Reims', *Revue du Moyen Âge Latin* 3 (1947), pp. 335–66, at 340–4.   13 Note in particular Hugh of Fleury, in the dedicatory epistle and epilogue to the first recension (1109) of his so-called *Historia ecclesiastica*, ed. *PL*, 163:824b, 829a; chroniclers who employed such stereotyped imagery are Guibert of Nogent (*c.*1108–11), *Gesta Dei per*

combined with chaste behavior leaves no doubt that the countess was perceived as a fully-fledged woman – though perhaps not a typical one, unless the authors, two of whom knew her personally and benefited from her patronage, were actually protesting her chastity too much(!).

Such routine evocation of Adela as a sexually-charged female in a male-dominated world, however, does not exhaust the complexity of contemporaries' representations of the countess. Analysis of the works of individual authors reveals how the categories of 'the female' and 'the lordly' – or, the discourses of 'gender' and 'power' – interacted when men depicted Adela in a range of activities and real-life situations. A good place to begin is with the *Ecclesiastical history* her contemporary, Orderic Vitalis, composed in the first instance for a monastic audience. Adela makes eight cameo appearances in his lengthy narrative; though not described as fully as some other women better known to that Anglo-Norman chronicler, she is among those he consistently portrays in a positive light.[14]

Her first appearance is as the bride who will confirm an alliance between her father and the Thibaudian counts; Adela is duly engaged, married and becomes the mother of several sons.[15] In recounting five further episodes from her years as wife and mother, Orderic accords her her title, 'countess Adela': when, acting for her absent husband and minor sons, she sends a contingent of knights to fight for the young co-king Louis;[16] when she receives Agnes of Ponthieu, who

---

Francos, 2.15, ed. in *Recueil des historiens des croisades, historiens occidentaux*, 5 vols. (Paris, 1841–1906), 4:148 (who paired beauty with prudence, as well emphasising her wisdom, wealth and generosity); Hugh the Chanter, see n. 47, below; and Orderic Vitalis, see n. 21. For the pairing of beauty and chastity, see Hildebert of Lavardin, bishop of Le Mans, ep. 13, as cited in n. 53, below; the anonymous poem cited in n. 50; and Baudry of Bourgueil, ep. 134, lines 1–88; 1,354–66, ed. Karlheinz Hilbert, *Baldricus Burgulianus, Carmina* (Heidelberg, 1979), pp. 145, 149 (I have discussed Baudry's representations of Adela more thoroughly in the paper cited in n. 53). For further discussion of poetic representations of women see Therese Latzke, 'Die Fürstinnenpreis', *Mittellateinisches Jahrbuch* 14 (1979), pp. 22–65; E.M.C. van Houts, 'Latin poetry and the Anglo-Norman court, 1066–1135: the *Carmen de Hastingae Proelio*', *Journal of Medieval History* 15 (1989), pp. 39–62; and the interesting – if not always convincing – discussion of representations of Adela by Gerald A. Bond in his *The loving subject: desire, eloquence, and power in romanesque France* (Philadelphia, 1995), pp. 129–57, 194–201, 251–62, which also includes translations of some key texts; in particular, his proposed chronology of Hildebert's letters will not withstand careful scrutiny. 14 Adela appears in sections Orderic wrote *c*.1127–29 and *c*.1135–37 (after she had retired to a convent); Marjorie Chibnall, 'Women in Orderic Vitalis', *Haskins Society Journal* 2 (1990), pp. 105–121, discusses his portrayal of several other women, as well as his approach to representing women in general. 15 Orderic Vitalis, *The ecclesiastical history of Orderic Vitalis*, 13 books in 6 vols., ed. Majorie Chibnall (Oxford, 1969–80), 5.11, ed. 3:116 (hereafter cited as OV); Orderic omits one son who died young and does not mention her daughter(s), only one of whom appears by name elsewhere in his text. 16 OV 11.35, ed. Chibnall, 6:156/8 (events datable to 1101).

had escaped from imprisonment at the hands of her husband, a castellan in revolt against Henry I;[17] when she hosts the French royal entourage at Chartres, organising honourable and abundant festivities to accompany the wedding of king Philip's daughter to the crusader hero Bohemond of Antioch (celebrations Orderic may well have attended and which he describes twice);[18] and, finally, when she receives pope Paschal on his 1107 tour and makes generous donations to his mission, obtaining a papal blessing for her family in return. Orderic expanded his comments in that episode, praising Adela as a 'mistress' (using the classical *hera*) who 'honourably governed her husband's county after his pilgrimage and assiduously educated her young sons to protect holy church'.[19] Proceeding to discuss her four adult sons, he rounded off his sketch of this 'noble mother' and '*genitrix*' of such powerful offspring with her even more praiseworthy decision to renounce the sensual pleasures of the world to fight for God as a nun. In yet another walk-on role, Adela, alongside her son count Thibaud and another mother-son pair of comital followers, is praised by Orderic for the devout and generous support she accorded Bernard of Tiron and his new community of hermits.[20]

The range of activities recorded in those seven passages has been emphasised because they are overshadowed in the modern imagination by Orderic's remaining invocation of Adela. In that oft-cited vignette, he transforms a particular countess into 'a wise and spirited everywoman (*mulier*)'. Capitalising on her sexual charms, she, 'between conjugal caresses', persuades her aging but valiant husband to return to the Holy Land in order to secure the Christians' triumph at the expense of 'the heathen'.[21] The perennial popularity of this uncharacteristic passage speaks more to enduring stereotypes of womanly wiles and peculiarly feminine forms of influence than to careful source criticism: the bedroom setting and words voiced by Adela are the products of the chronicler's own rhetorical art.[22]

---

[17] OV 8.24, ed. Chibnall, 4:300 (events datable to 1101–2).   [18] OV 5.19, ed. Chibnall, 3:182, together with OV 11.12, ed. Chibnall 6:70 (spring 1106); Chibnall, ed. OV 1:26, plausibly suggests that Orderic either himself attended the wedding or that his source was an eye-witness. Constance was Adela's former sister-in-law, though Orderic does not allude to that connection, mentioned in other accounts of these events.   [19] OV 11.5, ed. Chibnall, 6:42/44, (1120); other sources stating Adela ruled are discussed in LoPrete, 'Adela of Blois', pp. 20, 25–6.   [20] OV 18.27, ed. Chibnall, 4:330.   [21] OV 10.20, ed. Chibnall, 5.324, the only passage in which Orderic called Adela a *mulier*.   [22] The psychological acuity in Adela's alleged appeal to a fifty-year-old's lost youth and the special glory reserved for those who fight for Christ are overlooked by commentators who focus on the shame Stephen-Henry suffered for his departure from the siege of Antioch; several chapters earlier Orderic wrote that the threat of sanctions for 'failed crusaders' was sufficient to cause Stephen to return to the Holy Land and that he successfully recruited a large host of knights to accompany him (OV 10.12, ed. Chibnall, 5:268).

The seductive charm of his recourse to romantic *topoi* – even as it highlights Adela's 'essential femininity' – must be resisted and Orderic's universalising representation read in the context of his other depictions of the countess. She then emerges as a high-born daughter, dutiful wife and loving mother whose traditional household roles lead to her wielding a count's lordly powers both as a regent and as a widow until she renounces the world to serve the Lord of Hosts as a nun. Adela is praised for the intelligent and generous ways she fulfilled her duties to male relations, her king, the pope and the church. Sexually active within the confines of Christian marriage and perfectly able to govern as countess, a 'manly woman' she is not: in Orderic's history the hundred or so people who act *viriliter* are all men and the one praiseworthy but nameless virago slips in through a miracle story he copied from an English colleague.[23]

Letters written by high-ranking churchmen also confirm that Adela was perceived by male contemporaries primarily as a woman who wielded lordly powers in the performance of her routine household duties. The bishop best known to the countess was Ivo of Chartres and that pair of lordly neighbours enjoyed largely amicable relations during his twenty-five years in office (1090–1115). His letters are of particular significance on two counts. At one level they reveal the range of authoritative powers subsumed in Adela's *principatus*, or princely lordship, as he termed it when writing to advance the commonplace, if sometimes hotly-contested, affairs of public import in which they both became involved, most often during her regencies or widowhood.[24] At the same time, his matter-of-fact reference to the exercise of such powers by a woman – whose husband, sons, and brothers also appear in his correspondence playing out their appropriate political roles – is worthy of note. However great their occasional differences – most notably, when the extent of episcopal and comital jurisdictions was in dispute – Ivo nowhere hinted that the countess had ever overstepped the bounds because it was a woman who had done what he was

---

23 Orderic's virile men – both lay and religious – can be found via Chibnall's word index, s.v. *viriliter* and *virilis robur*; for the nameless wife of one Bricstan speaking out in court to defend her unjustly-accused husband see OV 6.10, ed. Chibnall, 3:346/52 at 352; although her speech did not save him from wrongful imprisonment, saintly intervention freed him.   24 Ivo's relations with Adela are discussed in greater detail in Kimberly A. LoPrete, 'Adela of Blois and Ivo of Chartres: piety, politics, and the peace in the diocese of Chartres', *Anglo-Norman Studies* 14 (1991), pp. 131–52; eighteen of his almost three hundred letters are either addressed to Adela or explicitly mention her, while another four are directly related to events discussed therein; for reference to Adela's *principatus*, see his eps. 101, 121, ed. *PL*, 162:120, 134–5; and Jean-François Niermeyer, *Mediae latinitatis lexicon minus* (Leiden, 1976) p. 851, s.v. *principatus*, for the range of contemporary meanings of the term; note also his evocations of Adela's *potestas*, a near synonym (eps. 133, 179, ed. *PL*, 162:143, 180–1). Adela's domains lay in twelve different dioceses and she had documented dealings with most of the resident bishops, though evidence is less plentiful than for her interactions with Ivo; indeed, his

complaining about. Whether Ivo wrote about the oaths she swore to defend the bishop or to keep the peace, the jurisdictional rights she held over monasteries, the safe-conducts she granted to travelling ecclesiastics, the judgements she pronounced as a feudal lord in land disputes or the executive orders (*præcepta*) she issued to her 'sergeants' and other officials, he never paused to remark that such commonplace lordly powers were in any way extraordinary when wielded by a woman.[25] Indeed, the very lack of comment in his routine, official correspondence suggests that female lordship was far from unusual in his day.[26]

At the same time the bishop's letters reveal the lordly wrath Adela directed at religious communities with whom she sometimes disputed over rights, though Ivo – like most authors who criticised the actions of a powerful lay lord – blamed her 'evil counsellors' more than the countess herself for such recourse to force.[27] When urging her to desist from violence and follow established juridical procedures to resolve disputes, he appealed to her probity (*probitas*), honour (*honestas*), earthly reputation (*fama*) and desire to avoid ignominy (*ignominia*) as much as to her desire to attain eternal salvation.[28] Ivo once presented Adela with a choice of gender-specific scriptural *exempla*: he urged her to moderate her rash judgements and life-threatening edicts so that she would be praised like the strong woman (*mulier fortis*) commended by Wisdom (in Proverbs 31.10–31) rather than be condemned publicly for cruelty like perverse women such as Herodias; writing in the midst of one of the countess's two violent disputes with his canons he nonetheless refrained from placing the diocese under the interdict his chapter wanted to impose 'because of his love' (*pro amore*) for her.[29] In all the letters Ivo addressed to Adela, his arguments

---

letter collection is a key source for many of those relations. **25** Oaths: see Ivo, ep .17, ed. J. Leclercq, *Yves de Chartres: Correspondance* (Paris, 1949), p. 17, and Ivo ep. 179, ed. *PL*, 162:180–1; jurisdiction: eps. 91, 187, ed. *PL*, 162:112, 190; safe-conducts: ep. 141, *PL*, 162:148; feudal lordship: eps. 168, 173, *PL*, 162:171–2; 175–7; precepts: eps.121, 179, ed. *PL*, 162:134–5, 180–1. **26** The episcopal advocate, or *vicedomina*, for much of his tenure was also a woman, namely Helisende (cp. his ep. 91, ed. *PL*, 162:112) and in the early years of his episcopate, viscomital powers were in the hands of the viscountess Alice of Montlhéry/LePuiset (cp. eps. 76–77, 111–12, 114, 124, ed. *PL*, 162: 97–8, 128–31, 136); a thorough study of all the women in Ivo's letters has yet to be undertaken. **27** Ivo, eps. 116, 121, ed. *PL*, 162:132, 134–5; see also his ep. 136, ed. *PL*, 162:145 (for the 'evil counsellors' of her son William) and the related passages in eps. 126, 133 (to archbishop Daimbert), ed. *PL*, 162:138, 143. **28** Note in particular his ep. 5, ed. Leclercq, pp. 14/16; and eps. 121, 136, 179, 187, ed. *PL*, 162:134–5, 145, 180–1, 190. **29** Ivo, ep. 179, ed. *PL*, 162:180–1: 'Nos enim pro amore vestro sententiam nostram quamvis justam et judicio diffinitam temperavimus ... Ita ergo vos habetote, ut laus fortis mulieris quam Sapientia commendat, de vobis praedicetur, non crudelitas perversae mulieris (quam in Herodiade Chrysostomus detestatur) per omnes nostras provincias publicetur'; note in particular Proverbs 31.27, stressing a good woman's wise and clement pronouncements; Ivo also evoked his political 'love' (*amor*) for the countess

based on scripture and canon law, together with appeals to her inner self and the spirit of wise counsel, testify to the bishop's conviction that this lordly woman was capable of ruling reasonably and well, even if she occasionally stumbled on the path of moral rectitude.[30]

Hildebert, the bishop of Le Mans, also portrayed Adela as a lordly woman (*domina*) in a letter asking the countess to exercise her protective power (*patrocinium*) by granting him an armed escort to attend a church council.[31] Asserting that successful ruling depended more on intellectual than bodily endowments, he appealed both to Adela's powers of discernment (she would know he was worthy of such a benefit) and her broad early education (by citing a classical author). But when Hildebert then declared he was certain Adela would grant his request because she embodied 'service to honourable conduct' and was 'both an example and an instrument of virtue (*virtus*)', he artfully raised the mundane level of comital rule to the exalted plane of political morality: it was the duty of all Christian lords – irrespective of gender – to use their power (*virtus*) to protect bishops. He thus elevated the virtuous countess to the status of an exemplary lord, who both glorified the entire feminine sex (*sexus*) and acted with the dignity of her ruling (male) ancestors. Hildebert's *domina* was both a woman and a lord, but her female body did not prevent her from applying her mind to the task of wielding authoritative comital powers in a morally responsible way.

Authors of hagiographic texts, most often eye-witnesses or near contemporaries of the events reported, also struck a balance between Adela's social roles as a woman and her powers in the wider world when depicting her actions. At the

in ep. 136, ed. *PL*, 162:145, likewise in the context of a dispute in which he chose to show some mercy before applying the full force of legal sanctions. 30 Note in particular his ep. 5, ed. Leclercq, pp. 14/16, and eps. 91, 101, 116, 179, 187, ed. *PL*, 162:112, 120, 132, 180–1, 190; in ep. 91, ed. *PL*, 162:112, Ivo's use of the term *interior homo* for Adela's inner self reflects Augustine and traditional conceptualising of the rational soul as male, while his appeal to his female addressee to apply hers to the problem at hand underscores his conviction that at least she and the other *domina* implicated in those events had one. 31 Hildebert, ep. 3^8, ed. *PL*, 171:288–9: 'Absentia mariti, laboriosior tibi cura consulatus incubuit. Ea enim magis animo quam corpore ad diversa te demigrare compellit. Incertus igitur ubi locorum invenirem te, certus autem quod honestatis obsequia ubique invenirem apud te, domi residens ad dominam litteras dedi, quarum summa haec est: "Episcopo Carnotensi conductum, sicut fertur, providisti ad concilium profecturo. Quod si ita est, praefata gratiae beneficium mihi communices exoro". Symmachus dicit: "Ex usu venit, ut opem desiderantes ad suffragia probata confugiant". Eapropter ad tuum patrocinium transvolavi, quae tota super feminam, et exemplum virtutis es et instrumentum. Vivunt in te boni saeculi reliquiae, per quam et sexus respirat ad gloriam, et genus elabentem retinet dignitatem. Arguerer mendacii, nisi cujusque optimi mecum in hoc judicium conveniret'; see also Ivo, ep. 141, ed. *PL*, 162:148. For the range of meanings current in key terms Hildebert was playing upon, see Niermeyer, s.v. *beneficium, conductus, patrocinium* and *virtus*.

translation of the relics of the empress Helena, her husband and his brothers are described as taking the lead in establishing a market for the saint's monastic guardians at Hautvillers, but it was the literate countess who participated with the officiating bishops in the ceremony honouring the monks' powerful female patron. Joining them on the purpose-built platform, the daughter of king William and wife of count Stephen read out to the assembled multitude the label identifying the empress' relics as they were transferred to a new and precious reliquary – most likely provided by the comital couple themselves.[32] Recalling how Adela, identified as the mother of the current count, was once cured of high fevers by the relics of the monks' patron at Rebais, the anonymous recorder of that miracle noted how it was fitting for such a woman (*tanta femina*) to be surrounded by physicians from Normandy, Gaul and 'overseas', even though they were unable to heal her on this occasion. To express her thanks the countess gave the monks at this long-established community a *pallium* reflecting her status and wealth, which they display behind their crucifix on major feast days, and, as a later charter reveals, on the eve of her retirement she granted Rebais an annuity from her fair revenues at Sézanne. Yet the countess could be a taxing lord as well, for it was she who convened and presided over the special ecclesiastical tribunal that quashed the monks' long-contested claims to a priory in Coulommiers – events the hagiographer perhaps chose to gloss over in silence.[33]

Such equilibrium between the woman and the lord appears most clearly in the life of Bernard, the saintly founder of Tiron, written by the house's chancellor in the decade after Adela's death. According to the author, when the countess, 'a matron of royal stock', offered Bernard new lands on which to reestablish his community, he 'refused them, preferring to place the site of his house under the protection of the virgin Mary rather than under the guardianship (*advocatio*) of any secular person whatsoever'.[34] The community's

---

[32] Notcher of Hautvillers, 'Miracula sanctae Helenae apud Altumvillare', ed. Jean Mabillon, *Acta sanctorum ordinis Sancti Benedicti in saeculorum classes distributa* (Paris, 1680), 4^2:156 (a passage often deleted in later published extracts made from this set of excerpts from a manuscript since lost). Adela's sister-in-law, Constance, is treated in similar fashion by Notcher; twice identified as the daughter of king Philip and wife of count Hugh of Troyes (Stephen-Henry's half-brother), she is presented as acting for her absent husband when Stephen consulted about the market.   [33] See the additions to the eleventh-century anonymous *vita* of St Aile, 1.19, ed. J. Mabillon, *Acta sanctorum ordinis Sancti Benedicti*, 2:331 (rpt. in *Acta sanctorum*, Aug. 6:591), an event that cannot be dated but was perhaps linked to her documented illness in 1101–02; for Adela's grant in 1119 of a 60 *sous* annuity, see *Cartulaire de l'abbaye de Molesme, ancien diocèse de Langres, 916–1215*, ed. Jacques Laurent (Paris, 1907–11), 2:440, no. 524; the tribunal met in January 1101 to resolve a dispute festering for over twenty years, as described in *Conques*, pp. 340–2, no. 470.   [34] Geoffrey Grossus (writing 1137–49) in his *Vita Bernardi*, ch. 9, ed. *PL*, 172:1413b: 'Porro quaedam matrona regali stirpe progenita, Adela videlicet Blesensium comitissa, eo tempore S. Bernardo latiores terrae amplitudines, ad

charters suggest she would have been willing to forego her advocacy rights as the new hermitage's patron, but the chancellor was writing for posterity. He presented Bernard's relentless struggles for reform as proof of his saintliness and did not pass up this opportunity to use the royal-born (and recently-deceased) countess to exemplify the contrast between strict reformers' principles and traditional lay lords' practices. In the event, Bernard and his successor readily received lands from the countess for two new priories, and in one case Adela explicitly renounced her lordship (*totum dominium*) over the land granted.[35] Orderic Vitalis was thus not off the mark when he praised Adela as a generous benefactor of Bernard's new community.[36]

Not all religious were as concerned as the chancellor of Tiron to deny lay patrons their traditional guardianship rights. In their charters, the monks of Marmoutier, outside Tours, St Père in Chartres, St Florentin in Bonneval, St Satur-sous-Sancerre, Ste. Foi in Coulommiers and St Germain in Auxerre explicitly acknowledged Adela's lordly powers as their advocate.[37] The monks of Marmoutier in particular waxed eloquent about their numerous princely patrons, especially in third-person notifications they drafted to record important settlements and bequests. In 1096 they recounted how countess Adela, introduced as the daughter of king William and wife of the crusading count Stephen, renounced customs at the monks' oven in Chartres. They cast her renunciation as a gift of alms that the countess, 'acting as a good patron (*bene*

---

monasterium suum construendum, et loca multo utiliora offerebat; quae tamen refutabat, malens coenobii sui sedem locare sub protectione beatae Mariae semper virginis, quam sub advocatione qualiscunque saecularis personae': events datable to *c*.1114; note that the bequest was not refused because the potential donor was female, but because it was feared she would claim a lord's advocacy rights over the land granted. 35 For her establishment of a new priory at Montrion, with explicit renunciation of all her lordly rights, see *Cartulaire de l'abbaye de la Sainte-Trinité de Tiron*, ed. Lucien Merlet (Chartres, 1883), 1:41–2, no. 24: a grant that may well have been made in 1116 during Bernard's visit to Chartres a few months prior to his death (see *Vita altera beati Roberti de Arbrissello*, 4.17, ed. *PL*, 162:1065–6); in *c*.1119 she confirmed in writing for abbot Hugh, Bernard's successor, her initial land grants at what became the priory of St Andrew, Ecoman (*Tiron*, 1:28–9, no. 14); her earliest documented support for the community dates to 1114–15 and concerns the hermits' cell at Bouche d'Aigre (*Tiron*, 1:14–16, nos. 3–4), but the current damaged state of the original charters makes it impossible to determine Adela's precise role in that priory's foundation. 36 See n. 20, above. 37 Marmoutier: *Cartulaire de Marmoutier pour le Dunois*, ed. Emile Mabille (Châteaudun, 1874), pp. 146–7, no. 156 (hereafter *MD*), and *Marmoutier cartulaire blésois*, ed. Charles Métais (Blois, 1889–91), pp. 114–16, no. 118 (hereafter *MB*); St Père: *Cartulaire de l'abbaye de Saint-Père de Chartres*, ed. Benjamin E.C. Guérard, 2 vols. (Paris, 1840), 2:408–9 no. 10 (hereafter *SPC*); Bonneval: Archives Départementales d'Eure-et-Loire, H.613; St Satur: Archives Départementales du Cher, 13.H.36; Ste Foi: Archives Départementales de Seine-et-Marne, H.824; St Germain, Auxerre: *Recueil des chartes de l'abbaye de Cluny*, ed. Auguste Bernard and Alexandre Bruel, 6 vols. (Paris,

patrizans) [granted to us, the monks of Marmoutier], who had received many benefits and generous donations from her father and were especially beloved by him; [she made the grant] because she wanted to emulate her father's love (*amor*) for us'.[38] Adela, the woman, is a praiseworthy patron; the monks are the beloved (*amati*) of her father, the generous lover. The love binding William to the monks was not primarily erotic – any more than was the love that stopped bishop Ivo from placing an interdict on Adela's lands;[39] a female lord who renounced comital customs was as worthy a patron as any man. Five years later at the comital court Adela negotiated a settlement in a dispute involving Marmoutier monks and canons from Blois. In the two notifications the monks drafted to document the ceremonies by which its terms were implemented, they depicted their female lord (*domina*) and founder of a major new priory as their 'most fervent lover' (*amatrix ferventissima*) in one, and as a 'virago' in the other; in each case the context is laudatory as well as lordly.[40]

Those three Marmoutier charters are of particular importance because they point to how medieval discourses of love, gender and power intersect in ways that may surprise the unwary modern interpreter. Monks who routinely looked to Adela's court for patronage and protection were well aware of her lordly powers (the countess heard pleas in at least nine disputes concerning Marmoutier). Nor did they doubt that she was a woman, whose standing in the world stemmed in part from her birth to a king, and whose authoritative powers were integrally linked to the activities subsumed in her prescribed role as a count's wife. To them, as to their contemporaries, love was the universal force that bound society together: parents to children, lords to their followers and dependents, lay lords to ecclesiastical lords, all in imitation of God's boundless love for his human creatures. 'Amor' was not reducible to the erotic charge between two individuals, however much that most human of feelings could be tapped to kindle heartfelt love for those to whom one was less potently attracted.[41]

1876–1903), 5:63–4, no. 3717 (hereafter *Cluny*).   38 Paris, BNF, MS latin 12776, pp. 247–9: 'Ne res temporibus nostris gestae per vetustatem oblivione qualibet ignorentur, maiorem sequentes instituta posteris nostris intimare, praesentis paginae indicio curavimus qualiter Adela comitissa, regis Anglorum Guillelmi filia Stephanique comitis uxor, bene patrizans erga nos, Maioris scilicet monasterii monachos, beneficia multa et largitationes a patre ipsius assecutos et ab eodem specialiter amatos, fecerit eleemosynam quandam B. Martino Maioris monasterii atque nobis eius monachis, cum ipsa patris sui erga nos amorem vellet imitari, quantumque poterat opibus adimpleret, anno dedicationis basilicae nostri monasterii ab Urbano secundo Romano papa factae [1096], cum vir eius Stephanus comes isset in Jerusalem cum exercitu Christianorum contra paganos eunte, dimisit Deo et Beato Martino atque nobis eius monachis consuetudinem quandam vir eius et ipsa habebant in quodam furno nostro apud Carnotium sito ...'   39 See n. 29, above.   40 See *MD*, pp. 60–2, no. 67: 'illustrissima comitissa Adila, Guillelmi senioris Anglorum regis filia, conjunx autem Stephani incliti comitis palatini, et Majoris Monasterii amatrix ferventissima' and Adela as 'domina et soror nostra'; and no. 68: Adela as a virago.   41 See also Paris, BNF, MS latin 12878, fol. 306r, no. 352,

If women could be lords of men and monks the beloved of kingly lovers, what then was Adela the virago to these churchmen? A woman most certainly, and in this instance a praiseworthy female lord who used her powers in the world to further the monks' earthly well-being. As a woman 'performing the duties or office of a man', she conformed perfectly to Isidore of Seville's popular definition of viragos. Framing his discussion with definitions of *mulier* and *femina*, Isidore, quoting Servius' popular *Aeneid* commentary while differentiating himself from Augustine, clearly distinguished viragos – namely, women (*mulieres*) who act as men do, performing virile works with masculine vigour – from virgins, that is, those who are physically intact and innocent of female passions. Continuing to blend classical and Christian exegetical traditions, he also called viragos 'strong women' (*fortes feminæ*), acknowledging like many writing before and after that some persons of the feminine sex – who are generally weaker and softer in body than men – can nonetheless act with masculine strength to perform deeds more usually done by men.[42]

What made such 'manly women' a small but normal subset of the feminine sex can be explained by ancient and medieval notions of men's and women's natures. As Thomas Laqueur intimated and Joan Cadden comprehensively explained, widespread medieval understandings of the psycho-physical constitution of men and women are quite different from modern ones that presuppose two incommensurable and sexed natures, primordially and teleologically distinguished by reproductive function. The earlier approach posited a single set of gendered physiological properties and psychological traits that would be distributed in varying proportions to individual persons through the processes of sexual reproduction – in which women, as well as men, were deemed to have

another Marmoutier notice claiming that the 'dominus de celo' inspired countess Adela to be 'prudent, wise and provident on the monks' behalf' as she worked to resolve a dispute between her provost and the Marmoutier monks in Meaux; and the diploma of Ivo confirming Adela's privileges for the canons of Bourgmoyen, Blois, describing her as 'burning with the flame of divine love (*amor*) and inflamed with the desire to augment religion' (Ivo, *diplomata* no. 1, ed. *PL*, 162:289–90). For further development of this theme see LoPrete, 'Adela of Blois', pp. 28–9, and Frederic L. Cheyette, 'Women, poets, and politics in Occitania', in *Aristocratic women*, pp. 138–77, 225–33, and the literature cited therein.   42 Isidore, *Etymologiarum sive originum, libri* xx, 11.2, ed. W.M. Lindsay, 2 vols. (Oxford, 1911), 2:11.ii, 18–24: 'Alias [virgo] ab incorruptione, quasi virago, quod ignoret femineam passionem. Virago vocata, quia virum agit, hoc est opera virilia facit et masculini vigoris est. Antiqui enim fortes feminas ita vocabant. Virgo autem non recte virago dicitur, si non viri officio fungitur. Mulier vero si virilia facit, recte virago dicitur, ut Amazona'. For Augustine, Jerome, Ambrose and other fathers who stress virgin viragos, note Augustine, *De Genesi contra Manichaeos*, 2:13, ed. *PL*, 34:206, and, among the growing literature, the discussion by Barbara Newman, *From virile woman to WomanChrist: studies in medieval religion and literature* (Philadelphia, 1995), pp. 3–6, 22–8; and comments by Joan M. Ferrante, *To the glory of her sex: women's roles in the composition of medieval texts* (Bloomington, Indiana, 1997), pp. 14–18, 94–6, 113–14, 159–70.

an active role to play. In other words, that some women, in anatomical terms, would be born with attributes enabling them to perform in some capacities as well as, or even better than, some men, was built into the order of things -or, 'only natural'.[43] Indeed, as many medieval readers of scripture were well aware, the *Ur*-virago was none other than the first woman, created by God in paradise from the rib of Adam.[44] However great that *Wo-man's* subsequent fall, a virago was a divinely created female who could use her God-given attributes to act with masculine strength and perform men's social roles when circumstances dicated that she do so. 'Virago' was thus a fitting term of praise for women, who, in the natural course of a noble family's life-cycle, played out their prescribed lordly roles as vigorously and intelligently as worthy men.

It was a term only rarely evoked, however. In the approximately one hundred and seventy-five sources in 'the Adela dossier', the countess was praised as a virago merely four times. Like the Marmoutier monks, the other three authors who dubbed Adela a virago never lost sight of her femininity, traditional female roles and powers in the world. William of Malmesbury devoted one sentence to Adela when discussing William the Conqueror's offspring. She was the 'wife of count Stephen of Blois, a virago of praiseworthy power in the world who recently has taken a nun's habit at Marcigny'. Writing a history of the kings of England, William did not elaborate on Adela's lordly deeds in France, merely noting in passing her diplomatic contribution to the settlement of 1120.[45] Hugh

---

[43] Thomas Laqueur's widely-read *Making sex: body and gender from the Greeks to Freud* (Cambridge, Mass., 1990), oversimplifies the complex skeins of medieval medical thought, though his insight about fundamental ancient ideas that endured is useful; Cadden, *Sex differences*, in particular pp. 93–7, 117–30, 201–8, is essential for explicating the complexity and co-existence of various views, whereby, for example, so-called 'two-seed' theories of conception continued in mitigated form with 'one-seed' theories, even after the reintroduction of Aristotlean texts in western Europe in the thirteenth century; John W. Baldwin, *The language of sex: five voices from Northern France around 1200* (Chicago, 1994), pp. 43–8, 173–210, confirms that theories of conception stressing women's participation were not fully displaced by 'newer' Aristotlean notions. [44] Genesis 2.23: 'Dixitque Adam ... : haec vocabitur Virago, quoniam de viro sumpta est'; the feminine pronoun should be noted. Even though some medieval bibles substituted 'mulier' for Jerome's 'virago', his term was well-known through commentaries on a host of biblical books; I have discussed, as part of an on-going study of medieval viragos, aspects of the commentary tradition – in particular, eleventh- and twelfth-century churchmen who equated 'viragos' with 'good wives', capable of using the strength of their original rib to moderate the lusty desires of their 'feminine' flesh, even as they remained obedient to their husbands – in an unpublished paper, 'Regendering viragos: sexuality and social identity in lordly women', delivered to the Medieval Academy of America, April, 2000. [45] William of Malmesbury, *Gesta regum Anglorum* 3.276, ed. R.A.B. Mynors, R.M. Thomson and M. Winterbottom (Oxford, 1998), 1:504: 'Adala, Stephani Blesensis comitis uxor, laudatae in seculo potentiae virago nouiter apud Marcenniacum sanctimonialis habitum sumpsit' (my translation);

the Chanter of York, travelling with his archbishop, Thurstan, had been honourably received by the countess and her son when that exiled prelate was shuttling between Adela's court, the papal entourage in France, and the French royal court during those complex negotiations. He introduced Adela to his English audience as the sister of their lord (*dominus*), king Henry, who loved Thurstan as if she were his lord (*domina*).[46] Hugh later described how the archbishop accompanied the countess to Marcigny, where, renouncing the riches and pomp of the world, she became a nun. Hugh's concluding assessment: 'by the testimony of king Louis and the princes of all France, there had been no more prudent, better formed (*melius composita*), or more virile virago in all Gaul for many an age'.[47] A fitting tribute to the woman who helped reconcile Thurstan to her brother, as she had instigated the reconciliation of Henry and Anselm of Canterbury fifteen years before.

Writing to Adela's youngest son, Henry, the bishop of Winchester, Osbert, the prior of Westminster abbey, turned to flattery to coax support from that prelate and his brother, king Stephen. Osbert's fawning took the form of praise for their illustrious ancestors, most notably Adela, the daughter of the 'most victorious' king William. She was 'a splendid and distinguished virago who, with her husband count Stephen, bore sons, producing in the light of time pontiffs, kings, and counts. Laying aside ostentatious displays of prideful flesh and renouncing the purple of secular glory, she conquered both the world and her sex at Marcigny, just as the queen of Sheba did when she approached Solomon' (cp. 3 Kings, 10.1–10).[48] Osbert's resort to 'virago' in this passage taps the doubled sense of the term, conjuring up images both of powerful women in the world and the perpetual virgins who totally renounced sexuality to win their

---

William's praise of this virago should be contrasted with his comments on her sister in the same passage, whom he erroneously claims was poisoned because of her strict application of justice. For 1120 see *Gesta regum* 5.419, ed. Mynors and others, 1:758.
46 Hugh the Chanter, *The history of the Church of York, 1066–1127*, ed. Charles Johnson, rev. by M. Brett, C.N.L. Brooke and M. Winterbottom (Oxford, 1990), pp. 152–54 [1120]: 'In Franciam perueniens, ad Blesensem comitissam, corde eciam quam genere nobiliorem, et ad filium suum comitem Teobaldum diuertit. A quibus hilariter et acurate suscepto, quamdiu in terra eorum uel transeundo uel perhendinando esse placuit, nichil ei defuit. Sororem domini sui regis et nepotem quasi dominam et dominum habebat, et ipsi eum ualde diligebant, et de eius exilio fratri et auunculo suo minime fauebant. Que fecerat, que deferebat, non omnia eos celauit'; the meetings probably took place at Meaux or Château-Thierry.   **47** Hugh the Chanter, rev. ed., p. 54 [1120]: 'Archiepiscopus ad comitissam reuersus, eam cum aliis episcopis et abbatibus usque ad Ma[r]ciniacum produxit. Que, spretis seculi diuiciis et pompis, ibi monialis effecta est. Qua quidem, testimonio regis Ludouici et principum tocius Francie, nulla prudencior, nec melius composita, nec magis uirilis uirago, ex multa retro etate in tota Gallia extiterat'; my translation.   **48** Osbert of Clare, ep. 15, ed. E.W. Williamson, *The letters of Osbert of Clare* (Oxford, 1929), pp. 83–5, at 84–5 (datable to early 1139); my translation.

heavenly crowns.⁴⁹ But the praise is clear – for Adela's worldly achievements as well as for her choice to renounce her powers – and both were linked to her traditional female roles as a high-status daughter, sexually-active wife, and mother of famous sons.

An anonymous poem in praise of the countess makes a fitting end to this discussion because the conceptual antitheses its author harnessed to represent this lordly woman come closest to turning Adela into an honorary man.⁵⁰ Overwhelmed with choice as to which qualities to praise in a woman (*femina*) surpassing all others of his day, the poet focuses on Adela's family (*genus*), personal status, dignity and wealth. She is the sister and daughter of kings whose religiosity brings her merit; her rank and station are determined by her roles as the mother and wife of counts, while her household is abundantly well-endowed with riches. Thus far, there is nothing to surprise in this praise of a laywoman. Next, however, the poet turns to assess Adela's character; fortune generously bestowed material goods upon her and nature endowed her with beautiful grace, yet wealth does not make her arrogant nor does such elegance bring dishonour. Indeed, the greater her wealth, the less haughtily she acts and such great beauty makes her even more modest: her behaviour has never been shameful, her comeliness never corrupted her modesty. Most noteworthy in this paragon of virtue is that rare combination of beauty and modesty, because 'Woman (*femina*) is such a light-weight thing: Adela, though a woman, is not a Woman because she lacks every feminine trifle. A *mulier* by sex, she is a man (*uir*) by acting *uiriliter*; with her ruling as duke (*qua duce*), the glory of the realm stands affirmed and flourishes. Here in the fragile sex is strength and a virile spirit'.⁵¹

To this poet, a ruling female lord is a woman by sex and a man by deeds; however much she may be distinguished from ordinary females, the countess is praised as a woman whose lordly powers are grounded in women's traditional social roles as daughters, wives and mothers, while her wordly honour and reputation are assessed in terms of traditionally feminine virtues (piety, attractiveness, and a fitting sense of shame). Indeed, the poet's emphasis on modesty in beauty makes one wonder whether Adela would have been able to preserve the glory of the realm if she *had* slipped from the path of marital chastity, for in their world politically-active female lords were not exempted from the norms of sexual morality regulating the behaviour of all women.

---

49 See n. 42, above.   **50** See the edition by André Boutemy, from a copy made in the first half of the thirteenth century, in 'Deux pièces inédites du manuscrit 749 de Douai', *Latomus* 2 (1938), pp. 123–30, at 126–7; and his discussion of the manuscript in 'Notice sur le manuscrit 749 ... de Douai, *Latomus* 3 (1939), pp. 183–206, 264–98, at p. 184; the last line of text is missing.   **51** Boutemy, 'Deux pièces', p. 127, ll. 18–23: 'Rara tamen res est forma pudorque simul. / Femina res leuis est; haec, cum sit femina, non est / Femina, feminae nil leuitatis habens! / Est mulier sexu, sed agendo uiriliter uir, / Qua duce stat regni gloria et usque uiget, / In fragili sexu uigor est animusque virilis'; my

Not all authors relished in such conceptual antitheses when depicting lordly women. As noted above, Orderic Vitalis, a sharp critic of effeminate men, did not cast female lords in his history as virile women.[52] Nonetheless, he repeatedly described the powers women exercised in the life-course of lordly families: a natural progression which routinely produced heiresses, wives acting for absent husbands and widow-regents. Ivo of Chartres and other churchmen treated with the countess in the same ways as they did male lords while also acknowledging that she was a woman. Like hagiographers, the bishop Hildebert, in the letter discussed in this essay, balanced the female and the lordly when describing the *domina* Adela. In a long letter urging her to cultivate clemency when exercising her princely power to punish others, Hildebert praised Adela as an able administrator who embodied all that was required for governing. In this instance he played on the conceptual antithesis between nature and grace, which he joined to that between the feminine as personal and the masculine as public, to portray Adela as a female lord who ruled both self and others through the exercise of reason. With such a carefully-crafted and sustained display of rhetorical art, the bishop thus set the countess forth as an exemplary prince to be emulated by lords of both genders.[53]

However, it is a serious interpretive error to move from such rhetorical delight in antithesis, occasionally deployed to represent seeming paradoxes in human society, to the conclusion that medieval men treated female lords as honorary men. When the evidence is read *in toto* rather than selectively, such a conclusion is not only patently unsustainable, but it also reveals fundamental misapprehensions about the ideological structures that comprehended the proportionally modest yet consistently significant number of publicly active and politically powerful women produced by medieval socio-political structures. It is in large part the erroneous result of reading medieval texts anachronistically, through the lenses of modern dichotomised and polarised analytical categories, in particular those concerning gender, love and power. The medieval discourses of sexual difference and the physiology of reproduction may be complex and arcane, but together they write a place for 'manly women' into the divinely-ordained nature of things. That medieval and modern typologies of 'love' differ significantly, especially on where any lines should be drawn between 'profane'

---

translation varies from that by Bond in *Loving subject*, p. 134.   **52** See n. 23, above, and Henry Platelle, 'Le problème du scandale: les nouvelles modes masculines aux XIe et XIIe siècles', *Revue Belge de Philologie et d'Histoire* 53 (1975), pp. 1071–96.   **53** Hildebert, ep. 1^3, ed. *PL*, 171:144–5 (rpt. in Peter von Moos, *Hildebert von Lavardin, 1056–1133: Humanitas an der Schwelle des höfischen Zeitalters*, Pariser historische Studien, no. 3 (Stuttgart, 1965), pp. 341–3); his use of antitheses in a way that acknowledges the 'natural' ruling powers of lordly women is analysed in my 'The *domina* Adela: female lord or courtly lady', unpublished paper presented to the Early Medieval Seminar, Institute of Historical Research, London, November, 1996.

or 'physical' forms and 'religious' or 'spiritual' ones, undoubtedly underlies the lack of scholarly consensus on the nature of 'courtly love', even amongst those who believe it existed in the middle ages.[54] Yet modern scholars who take such pains to differentiate the fundamentally 'private' powers of medieval lords from the truly 'public' powers of the authorised agents of modern states and then deny medieval women the exercise of acknowledged authoritative powers are blinded by their own dichotomies. The powers of medieval noblewomen were those of lords. The extent to which lordly powers had a private domestic core as well as a public political face is the extent to which women as females could be viewed as legitimately wielding powers of command over others and intervening in public events without sinning against either the socio-political or the gender logic of their day.

To remove lordly women from the history of women by casting them as honorary men thus occludes the social dynamics inherent in a political system grounded in the demographics of lordly families that regularly and routinely produced some women whose traditional activities as daughters, wives and widows placed them at the centre of public affairs. Perhaps more significantly, it minimises our appreciation of the political skills of these lordly women in a misogynistic society, who exercised authority over men in predominately male arenas while still having to act in conformity with restrictive behavioural norms laid down for all women. Adela appears to have been a master in that regard. If she was an exceptional woman, it is more for the fact that no gender-based criticism of her lordly deeds survives than for the lordly powers she wielded and how she acquired them.

---

[54] See, for an orienation to the vast literature and range of views, John F. Benton, 'Clio and Venus: an historical view of medieval love', in F.X. Newman (ed.), *The meaning of courtly love* (Albany, New York, 1968), pp. 19–42; and Frederick Goldin, 'The array of perspectives in the early courtly love lyric', in *In pursuit of perfection, courtly love in medieval literature*, ed. Joan M. Ferrante and George D. Economou (Port Washington, New York, 1975), pp. 51–100.

Women on the margins: the 'beloved' and the 'mistress' in Renaissance Florence

Catherine Lawless

INTRODUCTION

I record that on July 31, 1383, there died the ill-famed Letta, daughter of Federigo di Pierozzo Sassetti, in the house of Giovanni di Noldo Porcellini, in the Borgo Ogni Santi. She was buried by the friars of the church of Ogni Santi at the hour of vespers. May the devil take her soul, for she has brought shame and dishonor to our family. May it please God to pay whoever was blameworthy. And this is sufficient to describe this evil memory, which has dishonored us all. But man cannot change that which God, for our sins, has willed. But we are contemplating a vendetta which will bring some balm to our feelings.[1]

This quotation concerns a woman from the wealthy Sassetti house, Letta di Federigo di Pierozzo, who died in 1383 while in the house of Giovanni di Noldo Porcellini. The reaction of the Sassetti family is typical of attitudes concerning women who placed themselves (or were placed) outside the sanctioned family structure. Letta is described as ill-famed due to her presence in the house of a man who was neither her husband nor her relative. She was the bearer of dishonour to the family; her sin tainted all. Most of all, the Porcellini family had transgressed against the property of the Sassetti family, a transgression which would be avenged. The report points out that Letta was buried in the church of Ognissanti, which was not the burial place of the Sassetti. She was thus excluded from family memory and ritual for ever.

This article will discuss women who found themselves in irregular relationships in late medieval and Renaissance Florence. It will look both at women who were idealised as love objects and women who were in fact involved in pre- or extra-marital sexual relationships. Numerous histories of women have been

[1] Gene Brucker, *The society of Renaissance Florence: a documentary study* (New York, 1971), p. 42. The case is rendered even more interesting by the record, also reported by Brucker, which showed that in 1379 Porcellini had been injured by an intruder who had

written in the last thirty years or more. Social history has examined the roles of women in the family, the convent, in urban trades and as peasants. Woman as wife, mother, homemaker has been studied with regard to the formation of the early modern ideology of the state, where the home or family can be seen as a microcosm of the state. Historians of art and literature have shown how images were gendered and also how male artists and writers mediated female forms or types. The space of the Italian city state has been studied in terms of public ritual and display by Richard Trexler[2] and Edwin Muir,[3] and in terms of its relationship with gender by Robert Davis,[4] Sharon Strocchia,[5] Patricia Simons and others.[6] Renaissance historians now know a great deal about wives, widows, mothers, nuns, tertiaries, anchoresses, even, although to a much lesser degree, about women who were poets and artists. However, despite histories of *mentalité* and feminist scholarship, women who did not fit into such clearly sanctioned, or perhaps it is more true to say, clearly defined, roles have received little attention. If gender 'has been the most important factor in shaping the lives of European women' and 'women have traditionally been viewed first as women, a separate category of being', then how much more difficult is it to look at the life of an 'Other Woman' than the life of 'Woman as Other'?[7] This is partially due to the difficulty in accessing source material. The term 'mistress' is unsatisfactory and gendered, as neatly encapsulated in the title of Pollock and Parker's work on feminism and art history, *Old Mistresses*.[8] Nevertheless, due to the lack of a suitable alternative – the word 'lover' is equally problematic, implying a reciprocity and depth of affection that cannot be shown in the majority of cases – the word mistress will be used to indicate women who were sexually active outside wedlock. The lives of women who were mistresses and not wives have been approached, like their more regular sisters, through the lives of the men they were involved with or the children they mothered. This article is a short enquiry into the reality of the lives these women led; it is based on primary sources such as *ricordanze*, letters, baptismal registers, and on secondary literature on subjects such as Renaissance love, illegitimacy and slavery. It will contrast the platonic/chivalric ideal of the Beloved with the mistress. For the most part it will look at sexual unions outside marriage but will not address the related area of prostitution.

raped his wife, Anastasia (Brucker, *Society of Renaissance Florence*, p. 97). **2** Richard Trexler, *Public life in Renaissance Florence* (New York, 1980). **3** Edwin Muir, *Civic ritual in Renaissance Venice* (Princeton, 1981). **4** Robert C. Davis, 'The geography of gender in the Renaissance', in Judith C. Brown and Robert C. Davis (eds.), *Gender and society in Renaissance Italy* (London, 1996), pp. 19–38. **5** Sharon Strocchia, 'Gender and the rites of honour in Italian Renaissance cities', in Brown and Davis, *Gender and society*, pp. 39–60. **6** Patricia Simons, 'Women in frames: the gaze, the eye, the profile in Renaissance portraiture', *History Workshop Journal* 25 (1988), pp. 2–29. **7** Bonnie S. Anderson, and Judith P. Zinsser, *A history of their own: women in Europe from prehistory to the present*, vol. 1 (London, 1988), xv. **8** Roszika Parker and Griselda Pollock, *Old*

However difficult it is to retrieve information on women who lived socially approved lives, it seems almost impossible in the case of those who suffered exclusion from that world. Helen Ettlinger addressed the topic in an important article on mistresses in the Italian Renaissance courts.[9] A view of the Renaissance court mistress can be found in the literature (and occasionally, the painting) of the courts. Studies of illicit relationships, liminal groups and sexuality have been undertaken in recent years. Thomas Kuehn has examined the legal status of illegitimate children in the Florentine city state.[10] As in many cases the identity of the mothers was disclosed in legitimation petitions, their names are available through his detailed work. The names of women can be retrieved from the criminal records which were used by Serena Mazzi and Richard Trexler in their examinations of prostitution in Florence.[11] Michael Rocke used similar records in his analysis of the large number of prosecutions for sodomy, again, in Florence, while Guido Ruggiero has examined questions of sexuality, criminality, marriage and concubinage in Venice.[12] Studies of slavery by Iris Origo and A. Zanelli have shown that slaves were usually female and vulnerable to the sexual appetites of their masters and others.[13] The relationship of women and criminality has been examined by Samuel K. Cohn Jr[14] and presented in a range of documents by Gene Brucker.[15] Brucker has also presented a micro-history of Giovanni della Casa and his disputed betrothed, Lusanna, in which the validity of a marriage is discussed through a Renaissance court case.[16] Ideas of perfect female beauty and portraiture were the subject of a recent exhibition in Washington.[17] The intersection of the poetic construct of the ideal love and the

---

mistresses: women, art and ideology (London, 1987). **9** Helen S. Ettlinger, '*Visibilis et invisibilis*: The mistress in Italian Renaissance court society', *Renaissance Quarterly*, 47 (1994), pp. 770–92. See also Chad Coerver, '*Donna/Dono*: chivalry and adulterous exchange in the Quattrocento', in Geraldine A. Johnson and Sara F. Matthews Grieco (eds.), *Picturing women in Renaissance and Baroque Italy* (Cambridge, 1997), pp. 196–221. **10** Thomas Kuehn, *Illegitimacy in Renaissance Florence*, (Ann Arbor, 2002). **11** Maria Serena Mazzi, *Prostitute e lenoni nella Firenze del Quattrocento* (Milan, 1991); Richard C. Trexler, *The women of Renaissance Florence, power and dependence in Renaissance Florence*, vol. 2 (Asheville, 1998). **12** Michael Rocke, *Forbidden friendships: homosexuality and male culture in Renaissance Florence* (Chicago, 1997); Guido Ruggiero, *The Boundaries of Eros: sex crime and sexuality in Renaissance Venice* (Oxford, 1985). **13** Iris Origo, 'The domestic enemy: eastern slaves in Tuscany in the fourteenth and fifteenth centuries', *Speculum*, 30 (1955), pp. 321–66; A. Zanelli, *Le schiave orientali a Firenze nei secoli XIV e XV* (Florence, 1885). **14** Samuel K. Cohn Jr., *Women in the street: essays on sex and power in Renaissance Italy* (Baltimore and London, 1996). **15** Brucker, *Society of Renaissance Florence*. **16** Gene Brucker, *Giovanni and Lusanna: love and marriage in Renaissance Florence* (Berkeley, 1986). **17** David Alan Brown, *Virtue and beauty: Leonardo's Ginevra de' Benci and Renaissance portraits of women* (Princeton and Oxford, 2001). Also important for Renaissance ideals of beauty is Francis Ames-Lewis and Mary Rogers (eds.), *Concepts of beauty in Renaissance art* (Aldershot, 1998).

reality of women's lives was examined in the seminal article by Joan Kelly, 'Did women have a Renaissance?'[18]

THE BELOVED

These poetic constructs were frequently composed around a lady celebrated for her chastity and beauty, often married, and hence unavailable. The lady would symbolise a courtly, or, depending upon the period and the poet, a neo-platonic, ideal of perfect goodness and her virtue would have a salutary effect upon the man, although he was tormented by the pangs of love. Dante's Beatrice and Petrarch's Laura were frequently the models for these courtly affairs. The ideal courtly love was rarely consummated, thus enabling it to be celebrated in public without, in theory, endangering the virtue of the lady. Medicean Florence, with its large number of public festivals, jousts, processions and pageants, had a number of women who were venerated as love objects. The contradictions inherent in chivalric romances are of course seen in the story of Guinevere, which was the downfall of Dante's Francesca da Rimini.

Platonic love could be overt as it was little more than a poetic game, perhaps epitomised in the medal presented to Giovanna degli Albizzi, wife of Lorenzo Tornabuoni. In the medal there is an image of the Three Graces designed after a medal owned by Pico della Mirandola. Her medal answers his by reversing the emblem: instead of Pico's PULCHRITUDO-AMOR-VOLUPTAS, it reads CASTITAS PULCHRITUDO-AMOR. Therefore, according to Wind, in place of the platonic male definition of love: 'Love is Passion aroused by "Beauty", we have a female response "Beauty is Love Combined with Chastity".'[19] These elaborate rituals confined women within a paradigm of male desire and female chastity: women were the object of the male gaze but could not return the gaze; their desirability was only possible if they resisted the pleadings of the poetic lovers. 'It is not, in fact, Beauty that arouses desires; but the justification of lasciviousness proposed by the platonic theory of love is hypocritical ... "The nude is chaste," declare those old gentlemen who collect obscene photographs under the name of "artistic nudes".'[20]

In Florence, the high-born ladies that were the objects of affection for individuals such as Lorenzo and Giuliano de' Medici and their friends are similarly shown as objects in art. If the work forms part of the literary or artistic

---

18 Joan Kelly, 'Did women have a Renaissance?', *Women, history and theory: the essays of Joan Kelly* (Chicago and London, 1977), pp. 19–50.   19 Edgar Wind, *Pagan mysteries in the Renaissance* (Oxford, 1980), pp. 73–4.   20 Simone de Beauvoir, *The second sex* (London, 1980), p. 579. It is worth quoting de Beauvoir's views of the mistress as object, or hetaira, 'In the hetaira men's myths find their most seductive embodiment; she is beyond all others flesh and spirit, idol, inspiration, muse; painters and sculptors will want her as model; she will feed the dreams of poets; in her the intellectual will explore

canon, as in the case of the poetry of Lorenzo de' Medici or the painting of Botticelli, the identity of the women concerned forms part of a search for biographical information on the author. The courtly nature of the love affair can be fleshed out by the letters and *ricordanze* of contemporaries, as in the case of Lucrezia Donati, the love of Lorenzo de' Medici. Lucrezia, along with Simonetta Vespucci and others form the subject of Charles Dempsey's *The portrayal of love: Botticelli's 'Primavera'*.[21]

As Dempsey demonstrates, contemporary views of Lucrezia Donati show tensions between the poetic ideal and the reality of chastity and marital fidelity. The story of Lorenzo de' Medici's pledge to Lucrezia Donati is related in Pulci's *La giostra*. At the wedding of Braccio Martelli to Costanza de' Pazzi, Lucrezia wove a garland of flowers for Lorenzo de' Medici and asked that he wear them in the joust out of love for her.[22] Martelli was one of Lorenzo's youthful *brigata*. Lucrezia's sister, Costanza, is also referred to in Pulci's *Giostra*. She had been wooed by Braccio Martelli but was rejected in favour of Costanza de' Pazzi.[23] At the joust, which was held in 1468, Lorenzo carried a banner with Lucrezia's image, painted by Verrocchio.[24] By this time Lucrezia had been married for three years to the merchant Niccolò Ardinghelli.[25] Although the relationship between Lucrezia and Lorenzo appears, from literary evidence, to have been a courtly ideal, a letter of Ardinghelli's relative by marriage, the widow Alessandra Strozzi, makes the caustic remark that as Lucrezia hardly sees her husband due to his absence she diverts herself with balls and feasts.[26] While Lorenzo was in Milan, his *brigata* wrote letters in which the activities of Lucrezia and her friends were described. One letter tells of Ardinghelli's absence and implores Lorenzo to return to Florence so as not to leave 'sweet terrain unplowed'. Another, this time from Braccio Martelli, describes how a friend has spied on Lucrezia's wedding night and makes fun of Ardinghelli's physical endowments. Pulci and Bernardo Rucellai wrote of how pale Lucrezia had become, attributing this condition to remorse. The poem *Da che'l lauro* reminds the reader that Lucrezia is of the same blood as a Piccarda, presumably the Piccarda Donati that Dante met in Paradise, a woman who had been torn

the treasures of feminine "intuition"' (p. 581). 21 Charles Dempsey, *The portrayal of love: Botticelli's 'Primavera'* (Princeton, 1992). 22 Ibid., p. 82. 23 Ibid., p. 88. 24 Ibid., p. 83. 25 Ibid., p. 85. 26 Alessandra Macinghi negli Strozzi, *Lettere di una gentildonna fiorentina del secolo XV*, ed. C. Guasti (Florence, 1877), p. 385. Bartolomea Nasi was, according to Guicciardini, the lost love of Lorenzo de' Medici. His affections had lasted many years 'benché non fussi formosa, ma maniera e gentile.' ('She was not comely, but refined and noble'). He considered her marriage to Donato Benci to be a 'mad thing in considering that one was of such grandeur and reputation and prudence, aged forty, thus to be taken by a woman not beautiful and already full of years' ('cosa pazza a considerare che uno di tanta grandezza e riputazione e prudenzia, di età anni quaranta, fussi sì preso di una donna non bella e già piena di anni'), Francesco Guicciardini, *Storie Fiorentine*, ed. Alessandro Montevecchi (Milan, 1988), pp. 178–9.

from a convent and forced into marriage.[27] This imagery recalls the violated chastity of Piccarda Donati and perhaps equates the marriage of Lucrezia to Ardinghelli with that of Piccarda.

Other women were idealised in a similar fashion. Ginevra de' Benci (1457–1521) was known as a beauty in Florence; she was depicted in Ghirlandaio's *Visitation* in the Tornabuoni chapel, S. Maria Novella as well as in the famous portrait by Leonardo da Vinci.[28] Ginevra, the daughter of a Medicean banker, inspired two sonnets from Lorenzo de' Medici and another two from Bernardo Bembo.[29] She was a poet in her own right, although only one line of her poetry survives. In 1474 she married Luigi di Bernardo di Lapo Niccolini, and at some time between then and 1481, had her portrait painted by Leonardo. The portrait shows Ginevra with a frame or halo of juniper, a device which plays on the Italian for juniper, *ginevra*. As Mary Garrard has shown, the historiography of the portrait has downplayed Ginevra's identity in its celebration of Ginevra as the platonic or romantic love of Bernardo Bembo and the subject of poetry by Braccesi and Landino. Garrard redresses this balance and shows that the individuality of Ginevra herself both as a poet and as a person is portrayed by Leonardo.[30] Ginevra's very name may have contributed to this mythology; it is worth noting that the less chaste but courtly ideal of King Arthur's wife, Guinevere, is known in Italian as *Ginevra*.[31] This portrait shows Ginevra as the ideal lady, pure, desired but chaste, and framed by a secular reminder of the Virgin Mary's halo.

Botticelli frames the head of Venus in *Primavera* with a similar halo of foliage. The arguments concerning the identity of Botticelli's Venus are irrelevant here. What matters are the ideals of beauty and love created by the Medici brothers, Poliziano, Ficino and others, to which Botticelli gave pictorial form. One of the most celebrated of their muse-like women was Simonetta Cattani – the love of Giuliano de' Medici. The legend of the beautiful Simonetta was linked to the paintings of Botticelli by Vasari by 1555 and attracted much literary comment in the nineteenth century. Simonetta was born in Genoa and had moved to Florence upon her marriage to Marco Vespucci.[32] As with Lorenzo and Lucrezia in 1469, Giuliano's love for Simonetta was celebrated in a joust in 1475, which was commemorated by Poliziano's *Stanze per la giostra*, completed in 1478. Simonetta fell ill in 1476 and her father in law,

27 Dante, Par.iii. **28** Vincenzo Fineschi, *Memorie storiche degli uomini illustri del Convento di S. Maria Novella* (Florence, 1787; reprint Rome, 1977), p. 26. **29** Paola Tinagli, *Women in Italian Renaissance art: gender, representation, identity* (Manchester, 1997) pp. 88–9. **30** Mary Garrard, 'Leonardo da Vinci: female portraits, female nature,' in Norma Broude and Mary Garrard (eds.), *The expanding discourse: feminism and art history* (New York, 1992), pp. 58–85. **31** Ginevra herself was probably named after her grandmother, Ginevra Peruzzi. For Peruzzi's marriage with Giovanni Benci see *Dizionario Biografico degli Italiani*, 8, pp. 194–6. **32** Tinagli, *Women in Italian*

Piero, solicited Lorenzo for his help in shouldering the medical expenses. Lorenzo was informed of Simonetta's death and alluded to it in his poetry. Although the relationship between Giuliano and Simonetta clearly fell into the typical courtly ritual of Medicean Florence and was unlikely to have been consummated, it gave rise to at least one speculation that it was one of the causes of Vespucci involvement in the Pazzi conspiracy of 1478.[33]

The tension between being a celebrated object of beauty and public display and the demure behaviour expected of a virtuous woman is exemplified by Filippa di Nofri Bischeri. Bryce cites a letter of Rosselli that describes Bischeri dancing while he and others awaited the arrival of galleys.[34] Like Lucrezia Donati, she failed to escape the criticism of Alessandra Macinghi Strozzi who described her as flighty.[35] The tensions can also be seen in the life of Marietta Strozzi. She was the daughter of the exiled Lorenzo Strozzi and Alessandra Bardi. Her mother was celebrated by Vespasiano da Bisticci in his lives, and like Filippa Bischeri, was a woman who was used by the commune to entertain ambassadors and visitors. Like Bischeri, she had to manage a balance of beauty and virtue in an image presented for public display. Marietta's father died while she was young, thus rendering her an orphan in fifteenth-century terms. She attracted the attention of another member of Lorenzo's *brigata*, Bartolomeo Benci. In 1464 Filippo Corsini wrote to Lorenzo de' Medici about a snowfight between Bartolomeo Benci and others that had occurred outside Marietta's house.[36] A festa, or tournament, was held in her honour later in 1464 and was written about by Benci.[37] The situation of Marietta, however, was different from that of Lucrezia Donati and Simonetta Cattani. By the time of the jousts held in their honour, Lucrezia and Simonetta were already married, thus rendering them, in the tradition of chivalric love, unassailable. Marietta was not only unmarried, but was without a father, which meant that she was without a protector of the family honour. Further, she was the daughter of the exiled Lorenzo di Palla Strozzi, a fact which made a good marriage even harder to achieve. In the late 1460s Marietta attracted the notice of her cousin, Lorenzo di Matteo Strozzi, another exile who spent most of his adult life in Bruges and Naples. Lorenzo had caused much distress to his mother, the above-mentioned Alessandra Macinghi Strozzi, by delaying in his choice of a wife. In 1469, Filippo di Matteo Strozzi, in order to dissuade his brother Lorenzo from marrying Marietta, referred to her as being likely to have a 'stained' reputation because of her beauty, her lack of parents and her unmarried state.[38] Lorenzo

---

Renaissance art, p. 73.   33 Luca Landucci, *Diario fiorentino dal 1450 al 1516*, ed. Iodoco del Badia (Florence, 1883), p. 22.   34 Judith Bryce, 'Performing for strangers: women, dance and music in Quattrocento Florence', *Renaissance Quarterly*, 54 (2001), pp. 1074–1107 at p. 1076.   35 Bryce, 'Performing for strangers', p. 1077; Strozzi, *Lettere*, p. 470.   36 Isidoro Del Lungo, *Women of Florence*, trans. by Mary C. Steegman (New York, 1908), p. 206.   37 Del Lungo, *Women of Florence*, p. 200.   38 Strozzi, *Lettere*, p. 595.

did not persist and Marietta married Messer Theophilo Calcagnini from Ferrara, while her admirer Bartolomeo Benci married Lisabetta Tornabuoni.[39]

MISTRESSES

Marietta's suitor, Lorenzo di Matteo Strozzi, like many prosperous Florentines, had a mistress. What was more unusual about his situation was that the mistress does not appear to have been a slave or servant. We know nothing about his mistress, Caterina di Chimenti da Sommaia, apart from her bearing two children of Lorenzo's and her marriage to a Neapolitan in 1467.[40] However, in an entry into his records, Giovanni Rucellai noted how a certain Chimenti da Sommaia had lost his wife and two children in the 1456 earthquake in Naples.[41] This Chimenti da Sommaia appears as a Florentine who lived in Naples, a merchant who was in contact with the top tier of Florentine society personified by figures such as Giovanni Rucellai and Giovannozzo Manetti. It is tempting to think that this Chimenti da Sommaia was Caterina's father, but, although the name da Sommaia is used in this period as a family name, it could also simply mean Chimenti from Sommaia, a village near Florence.

The quintessential 'Renaissance man', Leon Battista Alberti was illegitimate. Although we know a great deal about Alberti's views on family life and about his own illegitimacy, we know little about his mother, Bianca di Carlo Fieschi, who bore the name of an illustrious Genoese family and who was the widow of a Grimaldi. Leon Battista was born in 1404; his father was Lorenzo Alberti, an exiled Florentine patrician. The reasons why Fieschi and Alberti did not marry are obscure. Bianca gave birth to another son, Carlo (who appears to have been named after her father) and she died in the plague of 1406.[42] Lorenzo Alberti then married a Florentine.[43]

Bartolomea Bagnesi (c.1336–1416) had an illegitimate son according to the *ricordanze* of her legitimate son, Lapo di Giovanni Niccolini.[44] Bartolomea was the daughter of a Filippo di Rosso Bagnesi who had served as a prior,[45] and the

---

39 Heather Gregory, 'Daughters, dowries and the family in fifteenth-century Florence,' *Rinascimento*, ser. 2, 27 (1987), pp. 215–37 (at p. 235); Del Lungo, *Women*, p. 205. 40 Strozzi, *Lettere*, p. 586. See also Lorenzo Fabbri, *Alleanza matrimoniale e patriziato nella Firenze del '400: studio sulla famiglia Strozzi* (Florence, 1991), p. 48. 41 Giovanni Rucellai, *Giovanni Rucellai ed il suo Zibaldone – I. Il Zibaldone Quaresimale*', ed. Alessandro Perosa, Studies of the Warburg Institute, 24 (London,1960), p. 57. 42 Thomas Kuehn, *Law, family and women: toward a legal anthropology of Renaissance Italy* (Chicago and London, 1991), p. 161. 43 Susannah Foster Baxendale, 'Exile in practice. The Alberti family in and out of Florence 1401–28', *Renaissance Quarterly*, 44 (1991), pp. 720–56 at p. 746. 44 G. Niccolini di Camugliano, *The chronicles of a Florentine family, 1200–1470* (London, 1933), p. 68. 45 Marchionne di Coppo Stefani,

wife of Giovanni Niccolini, a prosperous wool merchant and a prior many times. Again, the sparseness of the records leaves questions of how a woman with a prominent family name became involved in an illicit relationship, and how she then married into another prosperous family. The compiler of the Niccolini *ricordanze* remarks on the generosity shown by Lapo di Giovanni Niccolini in his bequest to his illegitimate half-brother.

The travels of Florentine merchants kept them away from the city for long periods of time. Many had mistresses in foreign cities. Serena Berotti de Cimegne of Avignon was the mistress of Messer Tome Soderini. In 1406, their son, Lorenzotto, was convicted of faking documents in an attempt to prove that his parents were legally married and that he was entitled to inherit.[46] He had been brought to Florence and raised there, and although legitimated by the Signoria in 1390, he had been left out of his father's will in 1400.[47] Maria Rendi was the daughter of a Greek notary. She became the lover of Neri di Jacopo Acciaiuoli and the mother of Antonio, who inherited his father's kingdom in Thebes.[48] Agnola Velluti's mother was the proprietress of a lasagne shop in Trapani and her father a Florentine merchant. After the death of her father, although illegitimate, her uncle Donato took her in, and, after some difficulty, married her off to a Florentine factor, Piero Talenti.[49]

WOMEN MARRIED TO SOMEONE OTHER THAN THEIR LOVER

Some of the mistresses uncovered by Kuehn in his book on illegitimacy were the wives of others, such as Piera di Nuto di Grazia Cingatti, wife of Vanni di Dino of San Clemente and the mistress of Niccolò di Jacopo del Palagio. She had two children with del Palagio and remained in his house as a servant and wet nurse. He declared that he owed her money but specified that it was not to go to her husband.[50] Tessa, the mistress of Damiano d'Antonio di Santi, was the wife of messer Nigio Alfani, but claimed the marriage had not been consummated. Her son Niccolò brought suit to the Podestà stating that he was legitimate and had been slandered by an uncle, Cosimo.[51] The wife of Fascello Petriboni asserted the legitimacy of her son, but did not deny adultery. Lena di Giovanni di ser Benedetto di Neri was the wife of Benedetto di Piero and mistress of Francesco di Bartolo Bischeri.[52] These cases are interesting, as Nigio Alfani is titled messer, indicating that he was either a knight or a doctor of law,

---

Cronica Fiorentina, ed. Niccolò Rodolico, Rerum Italicum Scriptores, 30.i. (Città di Castello, 1903), p. 228.   **46** Brucker, *Society of Renaissance Florence*, pp. 163–6. See also Kuehn, *Illegitimacy*, pp. 99–100.   **47** Kuehn, *Illegitimacy*, pp. 99–100.   **48** *Dizionario Biografico degli Italiani*, I, pp. 77 and 86.   **49** Donato Velluti, *Cronica domestica di messer Donato Velluti*, ed. Isidoro del Lungo and Guglielmo Volpi (Florence, 1914), pp. 147–50. **50** Kuehn, *Illegitimacy*, p. 179.   **51** Ibid., p. 101.   **52** Ibid., p. 149.

Petriboni is a family name, and Lena di Giovanni di ser Benedetto di Neri would appear, from the names, to have come from a notarial family.

NUNS

A number of illicit relationships were conducted from convents.[53] As early as the thirteenth century, Diana, the abbess of the Monastero delle Scalze, was the mistress of Giovanni Angelini Machiavelli and bore him a son. When the case was heard, it emerged that other nuns of the convent had also been involved with Machiavelli.[54] In 1441 a certain Michele di Piero Mangioni was convicted of having sexual relations with a nun,[55] while in 1446 Gimignano Moronti was convicted of having entered the convent of S. Jacopo in Via Ghibellina and of sleeping with a nun.[56] In 1452 Pope Nicholas V wrote to the Florentine archbishop, Antoninus, asking that he enquire into the conditions of the convent of Santa Caterina in Cafaggio as two of its nuns had borne children the previous year.[57] By 1490 the convent had become branded as little more than a brothel.[58] The prestigious Franciscan convent of Monticelli was reformed in 1434 and strict enclosure enforced due to scandals. Although the Convento delle Convertite had been set up primarily for reformed prostitutes and 'fallen women', it was the subject of scandal in the fifteenth century.[59] In 1448 Giovanni di Bartolo was convicted of having been with some nuns of S. Agata. More seriously, he was also convicted of the abduction and rape of the abbess of S. Anna. Cecilia, a nun of San Giovannino, had a relationship with a Sante di Bartolo. They ran away together but were found in 1447–8. A Suor Caterina, a nun of S. Margherita, had a relationship with Nofri, a dyer.[60] Twins brought to the Hospital of San Gallo in 1437 were said to be the children of Suor Nanna of San Baldassare.[61] The most famous renegade nun was Lucrezia di Francesco Buti, the lover of Fra Filippo Lippi and mother of Filippino Lippi. Lucrezia and her sister Spinetta were both nuns in the Pratese convent of Santa Margherita, having been placed there by their brother Antonio in 1451.[62] In around 1456,

---

[53] See Trexler, *Florentine women*; and for Venice, Ruggiero, *Boundaries of Eros* and Mary Laven, *Virgins of Venice* (London, 2002). [54] Robert Davidsohn, *Storia di Firenze*, 8 vols. (Florence, 1957–73) IV, pp. iii, 33. [55] Brucker, *Society of Renaissance Florence*, p. 209. [56] Mazzi, *Prostitute*, p. 133. See also the case of ser Piero di Lippo Puccetti who was convicted in 1434 of having gone to the monastery of S. Maria della Neve in via San Gallo and there having had sexual relations with the nuns and of having committed many nefarious acts. (Mazzi, *Prostitute*, p. 136). [57] Brucker, *Society of Renaissance Florence*, p. 192. [58] Trexler, *Women*, p. 64. [59] Mazzi, *Prostitute*, p. 401. [60] Mazzi, *Prostitute*, p. 136. [61] Trexler, *The children of Renaissance Florence: power and dependence in Renaissance Florence*, vol. 1 (Asheville, 1998), p. 20. [62] Megan Holmes, *Fra Filippo Lippi, the Carmelite painter* (London and New Haven, 1999) pp. 106, 264. Giorgio

Lucrezia, Spinetta, and three other women including the noblewoman Brigida Peruzzi, left the convent after being accused of having illicit relations with men. However, in 1459, all five women renewed their vows in an elaborate ceremony. Although Lucrezia was one of these, Lippi clearly continued to visit as, in 1461, an anonymous complaint brought to the Ufficiali di Notte e Monasteri accused Lippi and another of having sexual relations with nuns in the convent and stated that Lippi had a son, Filippino, already by one of the nuns.[63] That same year, on 8 May, through the intercession of Cosimo de' Medici, Pope Pius II conceded to Filippo Lippi the right to hold Lucrezia as his legitimate wife, and both parties were relieved of their monastic vows.[64] Four years later Filippo and Lucrezia had another child, Alessandra.[65]

Some of these scandals can be explained by the use of convents as a dumping ground for daughters who had no chance of marriage. The role of the convent in Renaissance society was not only its explicit one, that of a house of women dedicated to God, but it was also as a repository for women who otherwise would be unmarried and therefore, uncontrolled.[66] Giovanna di messer Ugo Altoviti was forcibly put into the convent of San Domenico by her brothers at the age of twelve. The nuns initially refused her permission to take the habit due to her age, but sometime between 1347 and 1350 they conceded it to her under pressure from the papal legate.[67] In the fifteenth century the high dowries required for marriage in the city resulted in the less marriageable female members of a family being sent into convents, where the dowries required were lower; for example, in 1466 Tommaso Deti wrote to the Dowry Fund asking that his payment for his daughter Marietta be transferred to another daughter, as Marietta suffered from a physical infirmity and would thus be better off in a convent.[68] Ginevra di Piero Parenti was born in 1500 and had a dowry account in the Dowry Fund opened for her in the same year, but by 1510 her father had decided to put her in a convent.[69] Ippolita Minerbetti, born in 1497, caught rubella which blinded her in one eye. In 1502 she was placed in the convent of S. Maria Montughi where she remained for the rest of her life.[70] Caterina di Paolo Niccolini,

Vasari, *Vite de'più eccellenti pittori, scultori ed architettori*, ed. G. Milanesi, 9 vols. (Florence, 1878–85) (cited as Milanesi-Vasari) , II, p. 634.   63 Holmes, *Fra Filippo Lippi*, p. 106.   64 Maria Pia Mannini and Marco Fagioli (eds.), *Filippo Lippi: catalogo completo* (Florence, 1997), p. 148. However, Geoffrey Ruda states that although they were no longer living under religious vows there is little evidence to suggest that they married. Geoffrey Ruda, *Fra Filippo Lippi* (London, 1993), p. 40. Milanesi states that they were released from their vows by Pius II. Milanesi-Vasari, II, p. 638.   65 Holmes, *Fra Filippo Lippi*, 106, 265. Filippino Lippi's will, dated 21 September 1488, identifies his mother as Lucrezia (the anonymous complaint had named her as Spinetta) and his sister as Alessandra. Milanesi-Vasari, II, 638.   66 For the situation in Venice, see Laven, *Virgins of Venice*, pp. 23 ff.   67 Luigi Passerini, *Genealogia e storia della famiglia Altoviti* (Florence, 1871), pp. 30–1.   68 Anthony Molho, *Marriage alliance in late medieval Florence* (Cambridge, Mass., and London, 1994) p. 68.   69 Ibid., p. 171.   70 Ibid., pp. 173–5.

born in 1434, 'made herself a nun in the convent of the Murate in Via Ghibellina on the 29th February 1440, and she took the vows in May 1448, with the name of Agostina. The said Agostina died in the said convent on 24 Oct. 1451'.[71]

MISTRESSES OF THE CLERGY

The sexual proclivities of priests and the clergy formed a *topos* in late medieval literature.[72] Although this is a literary *topos* which cannot be used as evidence of fact, and perhaps not even of contemporary attitudes to the clergy, historical evidence can be found that priests and friars also had mistresses, not surprisingly, given the notoriety of Renaissance popes. Between 1550 and 1650 priests and friars made up 58 of the 263 criminal and disciplinary trials in Venice.[73] Laurence Stone reports that an English penitential tract gave more penance to a priest for sodomy with a woman than for the adultery which was part of the same activity.[74] Giorgio Dati, a canon of Florence cathedral, was convicted of having entered the convent of S. Caterina illegally at night. Sandra of Ponte Carraia had a child by a friar of Santo Spirito.[75] Boccaccio, who received holy orders by 1360[76] and was himself illegitimate, had five illegitimate children.[77] Margherita, a freed slave, had a child by Ser Andrea, a priest. The child was brought to the foundling hospital of the Innocenti with a note in an identifying almond shape stating: 'So that the said child may be found when her mother wishes to do her some good. I have discovered that the child is called Elisabetta and her mother Margherita; she is a slave, though free, and the father who is a priest is called Ser Andrea, and he has taken this child from her mother and sent her to the hospital, and has made the slave give suck to the child of a fellow townsman, telling her that her own child has been put out to nurse; and he does not wish her to know that she has come to the hospital.' In this case, Margherita was later reunited with her child.[78]

WOMEN FROM THE RANKS OF THE LOWER GUILDS AND PEASANTS

Florentine men found some mistresses in the ranks of the lower guilds. The mistress of Fruosino d'Ugolino Ciucci was the daughter of a dyer, and that of

---

[71] Niccolini di Camugliano, *Chronicles*, p. 130. [72] Christopher Kleinhenz, 'Texts, naked and thinly veiled: erotic elements in medieval Italian literature,' in Joyce E. Salisbury (ed.), *Sex in the Middle Ages: a book of essays* (New York, 1991), p. 102. [73] Laven, *Virgins of Venice*, p. 166. [74] Lawrence Stone, *The past and present revisited* (London, 1987), p. 351. [75] Mazzi, *Prostitute*, p. 136. [76] A. Barigozzi Bini and P. Lavagetto Ceschi, 'Boccaccio' in *Dizionario Biografico degli Italiani*, 10, pp. 838–57, at p. 842. [77] Vittore Branca, *Boccaccio:the man and his works* (New York, 1976), p. 71. [78] Origo, 'Domestic Enemy',

Uberto di Giovanni Albizzi the daughter of a blacksmith from Cortona.[79] Caterina d'Antonio di Tome was the daughter of a weaver and the mistress of Ser Jacopo di ser Paolo della Camera.[80] Mea di Angelo was daughter of a *pizzicagnolo* and the *femmina* of Bartolomeo di Barone.[81] The mother of Pope Clement VII remains an enigmatic figure. The woman is identified in a record of the Pazzi conspiracy by Antonio da San Gallo as 'a woman of the Gorini.'[82] Another version, however, says 'Giulio son of Messer Giuliano de' Medici was born on 6 March 1478 (s.f.), who was later pope Clement VII. Giuliano the aforesaid was killed in the Pazzi conspiracy. Antonio da Sangallo, who lived in the Pinti, gave the news to the Magnifico Lorenzo of this baby born of Monna Antonia del Cittadino, a free woman, which baby was held at baptism by the said Antonio as a favour to Giuliano. Lorenzo recommended him to the said Antonio up to his seventh year ...'[83] Cambi stated that Antonia was the daughter of Antonio di Michele del Ciptadino, a member of the minor guilds. A certain Andrea Maddalena di Antonio di Michele del Cittadino was baptized on 18 August 1463, making her fifteen in 1478 and thus fourteen at the conception in 1477.[84] Seraccini is cited as stating that she was Fioretta di Antonio di Michele di Jacopo del Ciptadino *corazzaio*. Pieraccini, however, states that the mother's name was certainly 'Fioretta', but that all else is unknown.[85] An unpleasant paragraph then follows outlining the importance of knowing who the mother was, since with the laws of hereditary biology, the knowledge of whether Fioretta was daughter of nobles or plebs must be important, for example, to recognise the inheritance of particular refined talents or dispositions (such as the aesthetic taste), which were presumably more developed in the Florentine upper classes than in the lower ones.[86] Giulio had

---

p. 347. 79 Kuehn, *Illegitimacy*, pp. 145–6. 80 Ibid., p. 188. 81 Mazzi, *Prostitute*, p. 218. 82 Gaetano Pieraccini, *Le Stirpe de' Medici di Cafaggiolo*, 3 vols. (Florence, 1924–5), vol. 1, p. 309. 'una donna de' Gorini sua amica. Il detto Lorenzo lo andò a vedere e diede poi alla cura del medesimo Antonio, dove stette fino al settimo anno. Detto figlio aveva nome Giulio ...' 83 'Giulio figliolo del M.co Giuliano de' Medici nato addì 6 di marzo 1478 (s.f.) che fu poi papa Clemente VII. Giuliano sopra detto fu morto nella Congiura dei Pazzi. Antonio da Sangallo, che stava nei Pinti, dette notizie al Magnifico Lorenzo di questo bambino nato da M.a. Ant.a del Cittadino, donna libera, il qual bambino fu tenuto a battesimo da detto Ant.o per far cosa grata a Giuliano. Lorenzo lo raccomandò a detto Antonio da Sangallo fino a sette anni ...' s.f. or Florentine style refers to the Florentine dating system, where the year began on 25 March, so that 6 March 1378 Florentine style was 6 March 1379. 84 Opera di S. Maria del Fiore, Registri Battesimali, Reg.2 (fg.161) f.80. 85 Gene Brucker, *Florence: the Golden Age: 1138–1737* (Berkeley, Los Angeles and London, 1996), 264; Pieraccini, *La stirpe de' Medici*, I, p. 309. 86 'sulle leggi della ereditarietà biologica; il sapere se la Fioretta era figlia di nobili o di plebei può avere importanza, ad esempio, per riconoscere la eredità di particolari raffinati talenti o disposizioni (come il gusto estetico), presumabilmente più sviluppati nelle classi superiori fiorentine che nelle inferiori.' Pieraccini, *La stirpe de'*

himself declared legitimate during the cardinalate of Giovanni de' Medici, saying that his mother had been secretly married to Giuliano.[87] The eighteenth-century Jesuit antiquarian, Giuseppe Richa, in an attempt to ensure the Medici pope's legitimacy to the throne of St Peter, repeated this claim of a secret marriage.[88] Hibbert follows the Gorini reference, and identifies her as Fioretta Gorini. 'This boy, whose mother soon afterwards died, was adopted by Lorenzo.'[89] Young identifies her as Antonia Gorini.[90] Zaccaria's archival research shows that a certain Antonio di Michele del Cittadino had several children (including the above-mentioned Andrea Maddalena), but none of them were named either Antonia or Fioretta. She discounts the Gorini name as unlikely given its scarcity as a surname in the period.[91]

Other women were daughters of peasants, such as Domenica, *contadina*, the mistress of Niccolò Baldovinetti,[92] Apollonia d'Antonio of Impruneta, who bore an illegitimate child,[93] as did Tana di Pagolo di Giovanni da San Casciano, Gemma di Marchionne di Castel Nuovo, Mea d'Agnolo da Casentino, and Mea da Quarantola.[94] Women of lower rank were more obviously available to men of higher rank. According to Vern L. Bullough: 'If a nobleman desired a peasant-woman so strongly that he could not resist the temptation, he was free to rape her on the spot since a courteous approach would only be wasted on a woman who could not possibly feel love.'[95] The ideology of romantic love posed a serious threat, it seems, only to those who were not expected to feel it.

SLAVES AND SERVANTS

The easiest mistresses for a Florentine male were, naturally, the most socially vulnerable, slaves and servants. The mistress of Pongano Baldi was his servant, Margareta,[96] while Nencia was the servant and mistress of Francesco di Cambio da Siena. Camilla, a servant, had a child with Ruberto Migliorati. The child was legitimated and studied canon law.[97] Cilia di Vittorio, a servant, had a daughter, Cornelia, by her employer, Giovanni di Francesco Soderini.[98] A famous

Medici, I, p. 309.   87 Pieraccini, *La stripe de' Medici*, I, p. 310.   88 Giuseppe Richa, *Notizie istoriche delle chiese fiorentine divise ne' suoi quartieri*, 10 vols (Florence, 1754–62), VI, pp. 142, 294. Mirella Levi d'Ancona suggests that Giuliano was in fact secretly married to Oretta de' Pazzi. *Due quadri del Botticelli eseguite per nascite in casa Medici* (Florence, 1999).   89 Christopher Hibbert, *The rise and fall of the house of Medici* (London, 1974), p. 144.   90 G.F. Young, *The Medici* (New York, 1910), p. 775.   91 Raffaella Maria Zaccaria, 'Documenti e ipotesi sulla madre di Giulio de' Medici', *Interpres: Rivista di Studi Quattrocenteschi*, 18 (1999), pp. 234–43.   92 Kuehn, *Illegitimacy*, p. 162.   93 Mazzi, *Prostitute*, p. 345.   94 Kuehn, *Illegitimacy*, p. 145.   95 Vern L. Bullough, 'Prostitution in the later Middle Ages,' in Vern L. Bullough and James Brundage (eds.), *Sexual practices and the medieval church* (Buffalo, 1982), pp. 176–86 at p. 185.   96 Kuehn, *Illegitimacy*, p. 193.   97 Ibid., p. 142.   98 Molho,

example of a slave as mistress cited by Origo and Niccolini da Camugliano is Lucia, the slave of Paolo Niccolini, who bore him two children and remained in his household throughout his marriage to Cosa Guasconi.[99] Otto Niccolini's son, Giuliano, was the child of Otto's slave, Nastagia.[100] Carlo, the provost of S. Stefano in Prato, was the son of Cosimo de' Medici and a Circassian slave, Maddalena.[101] Other examples include Lucia, the slave and mistress of Jacopo Tani, the slave of Tommaso di Piero Giovanni,[102] the slave of Giovenco di Giuliano de' Medici,[103] Gianna, the slave of Bernardo Salviati,[104] Maddalena, the slave of Giovanni di Luca Ubertini,[105] Caterina, the slave of Andrea della Stufa,[106] and Caterina, the slave of Piero di Jacopo Rinuccini.[107]

There are numerous examples in the city's baptismal records of children identified as the child of a slave, for instance, 'Francesco della schiava di Jacopo degli Agli', baptized on 5 February 1451 (Florentine style).[108] When a slave is baptized herself, the entry gives evidence of the estimated age of the slave and her child, as in the case of 'Francesca and Maria slave of Amerigo di Simone Carnesecchi, aged 14 or thereabouts'.[109] Sometimes the slave's name is given, as with 'Leonardo e Domenico della Chaterina schiava', baptized 16 November 1462.[110] Although the records rarely state that these children are illegitimate,[111]

Marriage, p. 244.   **99** Holmes, *Fra Filippo Lippi*, p. 283.   **100** Niccolini da Camugliano, *Chronicles*, p. 181.   **101** André Rochon, *La jeunesse de Laurent de Médicis (1449–1478)* (Paris, 1963), p. 26.   **102** Kuehn, *Illegitimacy*, p. 144.   **103** Ibid., p. 148.   **104** Ibid., p. 118.   **105** Molho, *Marriage*, p. 96.   **106** Ibid., p. 93.   **107** Ibid., p. 245.   **108** Opera di S. Maria del Fiore, Registri Battesimali, Reg.1, f.33. The Registers have been scanned (not transcribed) onto the internet at http://www.operadelduomo.it. The relevant opening is indicated by 'fg'. In this case f.33 is found at fg.65. Other examples include Anna 'della schiava di messer Piero da Iesi', baptized 9 March 1451, s.f. (Reg.1, f.35v (fg.71).   **109** 'Francesca e Maria schiava di Amerigo di Simone Carnesecchi d'età d'anni 14 o circha', Opera di S. Maria del Fiore, Registri Battesimali, Reg.2, f.63v (fg.128). See also 'Anna e Maria schiava di Bongianni Gianfigliazzi d'età d'anni 22 o circha', ibid., f.69v (fg.140); 'Maria e Jacopa schiava di Lionardo di Michele Pescioni d'età d'anni 20 o circha', ibid., f.70v (fg.142); 'Horetta e Maria schiava di Dietisalvi Neroni d'età d'anni 19 o circha', ibid., f.71 (fg.143); 'Domenico della schiava di Bernardo Mellini', Reg.1, f.41v (fg.82); 'Antonio della schiava di Ser Gherardo', ibid., f.44v (fg.88).   **110** Opera di S. Maria del Fiore, Registri Battesimali, Reg.2, f.59 (fg.119). See also 'Giovanni e Ambrogio della Maddalena schiava fu di Piero Bonaguisi', ibid., f.76 (fg.153); 'Margherita e Benedetta dell'Anastasia schiava di Piero di Simone dello Sarto', ibid., f.78 (fg.157); 'Bartolomeo e Giovanni della Chaterina schiava di Gerozzo de Pilli', ibid., f.80v (fg.162).   **111** The records do frequently state that a child is illegitimate, but in those cases the mother's name is not given, for example 'Nofri di Piero di Nofri non legittimo', baptized on 9 April, 1452. Opera di S. Maria del Fiore, Registri Battesimali, Reg.1, f.38v (fg.76); see also, 'Pulisena e Lisabetta di ser Benedetto di Agnolo di Stagio non legittima', ibid., Reg.2, f.71v (fg.144); 'Piero e Bernardino di Giorgio di Piero di Riccio non legittimo', and 'Zanobi e Bernardino di Miniato di Giovanni non legittimo', ibid., f.74 (fg.149); 'Zanobia d'Andrea di Cresci non legittima', Reg.1, f.42 (fg.83); 'Maria e

the lack of a father's name would seem to indicate it. The same can be said where children are identified as the offspring of a 'serva' or a 'balia', as in the case of 'Jacopo di mona Mattea di Andrea Visdomini balia',[112] or 'Alessandra e Apollonia della Nastasia serva di di Salvestro Spini.'[113] We yet again find ourselves having to trace the lives of women through the records of their children or partners. What, for instance, is the story behind the record of 'Cristofano di mona Giuliana in S. Gallo', baptized on 14 March 1451 (s.f.),[114] or Bartolomeo di mona Lisa of Monte Lupo, baptized on 25 March 1452?[115] The alterity of some of these women is seen in their identification as foreign, as can be seen in the baptism of 'Bianca e Domenica della Caterina Tartara'.[116] Slaves were frequently described as Tartars and it seems likely that Caterina was a freed slave. Another entry reads 'Sforzo e Giovanni di Mona Caterina d'Arezzo delle Stinche'.[117] Again, one can only speculate about Mona Caterina, and about whether Sforzo Giovanni was illegitimate, whether she was in the Stinche, a

Caterina di Bartolomeo Serragli non legiptima', Reg.1, f.39 (fg.77); 'Francesco e Girolamo di Marco degli Asini non legittimo', Reg.2, f.64 (fg.129); 'Lucretia e Antonia di Bernardo di Cristofano Bonaguisi non legittima', ibid., f.66 (fg.133); 'Filippo e Bartolomeo di Agnolo di messer Giannozzo Manetti non legittimo', ibid., f.80v (fg.162); 'Caterina di Giovanni Sapiti non legittima', Reg.1, f.46 (fg.91); 'Galeotto di Giuliano Gondi non legittimo', ibid., f.45v (fg.90); 'Lionardo di Uguccione de' Pazzi non legittimo', ibid., f.34 (fg.68); however, Carlo di Giovanni di ser Lodovico della Casa, born illegitimate in 1453 (Brucker, *Giovanni and Lusanna*, p. 78) is not listed as illegitimate at his baptism, 3 February, 1453 (Reg.1, f.10 (fg.16). There are frequent entries where the registrar states that he does not know the child's parents, for example, 'Virgilio non si sa di chi si sia', baptized on 14 April 1452. Opera di S. Maria del Fiore, Registri Battesimali, Reg.1, f.39 (fg.77). See also 'Maddalena e Giovanna no so di chi', baptized 19 November 1462, Opera di S. Maria del Fiore, Registri Battesimali, Reg.2, f.59 (fg.119), 'Bartolomeo e Giovanni non so di chi', ibid., f.61 (fg.123); 'Maddalena e Maria non so di chi', ibid., f.62v (fg.126); 'Caterina e Giovanna non so di chi', ibid., f.67 (fg.135); 'Girigoro e Domenico non so di chi', ibid., f.68 (fg.137); 'Maria e Jacopa non so di chi', and 'Gerardo e Francesco non so di chi', ibid., f.74v (fg.150); 'Francesco e Domenico non so di chi', ibid., f.75 (fg.151); and others at f.78v (fg.158); f.79 (fg.159); Reg.1, f.45 (fg.89).   112 Opera di S. Maria del Fiore, Registri Battesimali, Reg.1, f.38v (fg.76). See also 'Bartolomeo e Benedetto della Giuliana balia di Michele del Grasso Capponi', Reg.2, f.81v (fg.164).   113 Opera di S. Maria del Fiore, Registri Battesimali, Reg.2, f.65v (fg.131). See also 'Domenico e Giovanni dell'Anna serva di Giovanni del Rosso galigaio', ibid., f.76 (fg.153).   114 Opera di S. Maria del Fiore, Registri Battesimali, Reg.1, f.36 (fg.72).   115 Opera di S. Maria del Fiore, Registri Battesimali, Reg.1, f.36v (fg.73). See also 'Domenica e Bartolomea di Mona Fiore', baptized 9 January 1462 (s.f.), Opera di S. Maria del Fiore, Registri Battesimali, Reg.2, f.63 (fg.127); 'Maria e Caterina di mona Nanna d'Anversa' ibid., f.69v (fg.140). If Nanna was from Antwerp she was foreign, and could possibly have been a prostitute. On the tradition of foreign women working as prostitutes in Florence, see Mazzi, *Prostitute*.   116 Opera di S. Maria del Fiore, Registri Battesimali, Reg.2, f.64 (fg.129). See also `Lionarda e Agnoletta della Chaterina Raugia', ibid., f.77 (fg.155).   117 Opera di S. Maria del Fiore,

notorious Florentine prison, or whether she simply happened to live near the Stinche and be so identified in the register. Her place of origin according to her name is Arezzo; women who worked as prostitutes rarely did so in their own town, perhaps her profession brought her to Florence, and indeed, the Stinche.[118] Some entries in the records list a child of a woman who 'stays' with an identified man, as in the case of 'Ventura e Benedetto della Chaterina che sta con Cipriano saponaio',[119] and 'Caterina e Madalena della Margherita che sta con Bernardo Chanbini'.[120] These cases can be compared with mona Antonia, the mother of a child by Giuliano di Agnolo Benciatti, described by him in his tax return as one who 'sta mecho in casa',[121] and Maria, the mistress of Belfredello dello Strinato and mother of two of his children, as a 'foristiera la quale è in chasa meco mia' (a foreigner who is in my house with me).[122]

Slaves were easy prey not only to their masters but to others. Caterina, the slave of Andrea della Stufa (possibly the same woman as the above-mentioned) was attacked by a certain Francesco in 1453.[123] Della Stufa registered dowries for two illegitimate children in the Dowry Fund, one by a Maddalena from Raugia, the other from Caterina 'mia schiava', and may have seen an attack on his slave as not only an attack on his property, but also as a problem in identifying paternity.[124] Della Stufa was particularly unfortunate in protecting his slaves; a slave of his had a child by Vieri di Antonio Davanzati.[125] The slave of Giovanozzo Biliotti married Tommaso Biliotti. The slave of Pagolo da Diacceto had a child by Lionardo di Zanobi del Recha.[126] A certain Tommaso da Asti was convicted of impregnating a slave of Nerone di Nigi's in 1435. Tommaso was forced to pay her full worth to her owner in case her childbirth went wrong.[127] The slave of Otto Niccolini, himself the father of illegitimate children conceived with slaves, had a child with Vieri di Tommaso Corbinelli.[128] Francesco Strozzi fathered two children by other people's slaves.[129] Anna, the slave of Lorenzo Barducci, was the mother of Damiano, an illegitimate child by Giovanni d'Amerigo Benci.[130] Caterina, the slave of Giovanni Rucellai, bore a

---

Registri Battesimali, Reg.2, f.66 (fg.133). **118** See also the baptism of Maddalena e Lucia 'della Margherita da Pistoia', 23 July, 1463, Opera di S. Maria del Fiore, Registri Battesimali, Reg.2, f.78 (fg.157). 'Giovanni e Felice della Maddalena Raugia', ibid., f.79 (fg.159). **119** Baptized on 22 March 1462 (s.f.), Opera di S. Maria del Fiore, Registri Battesimali, Reg.2, f.69 (fg.139). **120** Ibid., f.70 (fg.141). Baptized 4 April 1463; See also 'Lazaro e Giovanni dell'Anastasia che sta con Tommaso Soderini', ibid., f.72v (fg.146); 'Alessandra e Domenica della Margherita che sta con Braccio Guicciardini', ibid., f.75 (fg.151); 'Lorenza e Domenica di mona Piera con Francesco Inghirami', ibid., f.79v (fg.160); 'Giannozzo e Chimenti della Marta sta con messer Bernardo d'Aglione', ibid., f.81v (fg.164). **121** Kuehn, *Illegitimacy*, p. 142. **122** Ibid., p. 93. **123** Mazzi, *Prostitute*, p. 119. **124** Molho, *Marriage*, p. 93. **125** Kuehn, *Illegitimacy*, p. 143. The child was raised with Davanzati. **126** Ibid., p. 143. The child was raised with Del Recha. **127** Mazzi, *Prostitute*, p. 119. **128** Trexler, *Children*, p. 23. **129** Kuehn, *Illegitimacy*, p. 143. **130** Holmes, *Fra Filippo Lippi*, p. 283.

child of Pagolo Ottavanti.[131] The slave of Giuliano di Cattaneo di messer Cristiano had a child by Filippo d'Ardingo Ricci.[132] In 1474 Jacopo Niccolini had a child by the servant of the Baldovinetti house.[133]

Although a servant was technically a free person, slaves had no control over their fate or their children. Ruggieri Crucci had a child by his brother's slave; the child, Lisa, was kept, the slave sold. Ruggieri's other child, Francesco, was also illegitimate. In his tax declaration of 1458 Ruggieri named the child's mother, Mona Papera di Cienni Cenini, but declined to name her husband due to reasons of honour.[134] Goro Dati had a child by a Tartar slave, Margherita, whom he owned while he was in Valenza. The child was sent to be educated in Florence.[135] The slave of Giovanni di Luca Ubertini bore him a child in 1449, was manumitted in 1452, yet bore him a second child in 1454.[136] Bernardo Morelli had no legitimate children with his wife, Simona, but plenty of illegitimate ones: 'he had many illegitimate ones, partly from a woman quite well off, and partly from a slave of his, quite beautiful, and later he married her off in the Mugello: I do not want to name [them], because a [family] line so made is not honest, and they are of quite good condition, according to their type'.[137] Antonio Ricci petititoned to have his child by his slave Caterina legitimated; she was separated from her child.[138] Lucia, the slave and mistress of Jacopo Tani, was freed 1458 but she remained in his house, having given birth to a son, Filippo, in 1440.[139] The foundling hospitals of Renaissance Florence were filled with children, many of them the children of slaves.[140] Their higher-born counterparts, however, also had few rights over their children in a society where a legal wife was not the automatic guardian of her children in the event of her husband's death.

---

131 Origo, 'Domestic enemy', p. 346.   **132** Kuehn, *Illegitimacy*, p. 142.   **133** Christiane Klapisch-Zuber, *Women, family and ritual in Renaissance Italy*, trans. Lydia Cochrane (London and Chicago, 1985), p. 141.   **134** Kuehn, *Illegitimacy*, p. 148.   **135** Mazzi, *Prostituti*, p. 53.   **136** Kuehn, *Illegitimacy*, p. 144.   **137** 'ebbene molti non ligitimmi, parte d'una donna assai da bene, e parte d'una ischiava era sua, assai bella, e di poi la maritò in Mugello: non gli vo'nominare, perché non è onesto sì fatta ischiatta, come ch'e' sieno di buona condizione assai, secondo loro essere', Giovanni Morelli, 'Ricordi' in Vittore Branca (ed.), *Mercanti Scrittori: Ricordi nella Firenze tra Medioevo e Rinascimento – Paolo da Certaldo, Giovanni Morelli, Bonaccorso Pitti, e Domenico Lenzi, Donato Velluti, Goro Dati, Francesco Datini, Lapo Niccolini, Bernardo Machiavelli* (Milan, 1986), p. 145.   **138** Origo, 'Domestic enemy', p. 345.   **139** Kuehn, *Illegitimacy*, p. 144. **140** The wife of Nerone di Nigi Dietisalvi came to the Spedale degli Innocenti admitting that a child left there anonymously was the child of her slave. Giovanna, the wife of Jacopo Ardinghelli similarly came to the Spedale of San Gallo and claimed that a child there was the son of her husband and their slave (Trexler, *Children*, p. 23). Giovanni Cerretani's slave had a child named Agata; the child was left in the Innocenti in 1445 (Origo, 'Domestic enemy', p. 349; Molho, *Marriage*, p. 106). Vieri di Tommaso Corbinelli was identified as the father of a child belonging to a slave and deposited in the

LIFE AFTER BEING A MISTRESS

As is shown above, mothers were frequently parted from their children, although sometimes they were retained in the home in a type of parallel family, as is the case of Lucia, the slave of Paolo Niccolini. Former mistresses were sometimes married off to others, as in the case of Caterina da Sommaia who was married to a Neapolitan merchant.[141] The mistress of Francesco di messer Arnaldo Mannelli was married off to another man,[142] as was Lorenza di Lazzerino, the servant of Bernardo Machiavelli and mistress of Niccolò Machiavelli.[143]

Illicit relationships did, however, sometimes end in marriage to the lover concerned. Verdiana, the mistress of Rosso del Boneca Rossi was first listed as the wife of Martino di Pietro da Ulignano and then listed as Rossi's wife.[144] Caterina di Filippo del Buono was married on her lover's deathbed in a clear attempt to legitimise their children. Those who contested his will accused her of being a nun.[145] Giovanna di messer Jacopo del Panna married Giovanni Casciatelli in a similar attempt to legitimise children.[146] Guidantonio di messer Domenico di ser Mino married his mistress.[147] Tommaso Biliotti married the slave of Giovanozzo Biliotti, but the matter was not to be discussed for the sake of honour.[148] Marsilia di Bartolomeo di Luca, mother of the sculptor, Lorenzo Ghiberti, lived with the goldsmith Bartolo di Michele while still married to Cione Ghiberti. It was only after Cione's death that she married Bartolo di Michele.[149]

Some cases show affection between the parties although not marriage. Marchione di ser Marchione Donati freed Maddalena, slave of Stoldo Frescobaldi. He had a child with her and called her his *donna*, although there is no record of a marriage in this case.[150] Andrea Rucellai presented a petition to the Signoria in 1388–9 to legitimise his son Santi, saying of his mistress that: 'for some twenty years, she has lived with him in his house as his concubine, and since he has never had a wife, he loves her as though she were his legitimate spouse'.[151]

The marginality of these women is defined by their exclusion from marriage. The chivalric ideal of chaste love existed side by side with the reality of clandestine affairs, foundlings deposited in the middle of the night at the gate

---

Spedale di S. Gallo in 1447 (Trexler, *Children*, p. 23). 141 Strozzi, *Lettere*, p. 368. Fabbri quotes ASF, Carte Strozziane III, 82, p.348, 'Maritai Caterina detta, 1467, 23 ottobre, a Giovanello Rosso di napoli, et dote f.200'. Fabbri, *Alleanza matrimoniale*, p. 48n. 142 Kuehn, *Illegitimacy*, p. 180. 143 Brucker, *Society of Renaissance Florence*, pp. 218–22. 144 Kuehn, *Illegitimacy*, pp. 99, 178. 145 Ibid., pp. 170, 196–7. 146 Ibid., p. 170. 147 Ibid., p. 159. 148 Ibid., p. 144. 149 R. Krautheimer, *Lorenzo Ghiberti* (Princeton, 1956), 3. On Ghiberti's use of a dual identity to his advantage, and ultimately his disadvantage, when accused of illegitimacy in 1444, see Krautheimer, pp. 3–5. 150 Kuehn, *Illegitimacy*, pp. 143–4. 151 Brucker, *Society of Renaissance Florence*, p. 59.

of the Foundling hospital and the separation of mothers from children. Woman's virtue lay in her virginity or chastity; without these, other roles such as wife, mother, widow, daughter, sister, all defined in relationship to male others, were worthless. Husband, father, widower, son, brother, these roles were arguably secondary to merchant, banker, prior, rentier; a man's virtue was never, except sometimes in hagiography, dependent upon sexual continence. The family in Renaissance Florence can be seen as a building block of the state. Those who lived outside the family (with the exception of the religious, who themselves used the language of the family to create hierarchies: brother, sister, mother, father) were marginal and by creating parallel families or structures, were also subversive. However, both men and women were offered numerous alternative narratives in *novelle*, romances, painting, even hagiography. These fictional constructs were in direct opposition to the lives women had to lead in order to be socially accepted. Some women, such as Lucrezia Donati, Simonetta Vespucci, Ginevra de' Benci could flirt with romantic love outside marriage without serious peril to their status; for others, however, sexual involvement brought marginality and life-long exclusion from social normalcy. The Florentine Renaissance city state is hardly historically unique in this, but the contrast of socially accepted, even lauded, poetic constructs with lived illicit relationships, of courtly narratives with bourgeois family structures is particularly acute here. The lives of some of these women who formed a liminal social group in Florence can be reconstructed; it is time do so.

Women and violence in late medieval Ireland

Dianne Hall

... the aforesaid abbess attacked the nuns, Elicia Gall and Anne Cleri, causing blood to be shed, and attacked Katerine Mothing without bloodshed. When the nuns were asked whether she did this through the desire to correct them, the nuns said no, she attacked them through anger and quarrelling ...[1]

On the evidence of these nuns on this and other charges, Elicia Butler, abbess of Kilculliheen, was deposed from office in 1531 in the court of Milo de Baron, bishop of Ossory.[2] Violence perpetrated by women is a subject that has been neglected in the historiography of medieval women. Historians understandably have given more attention to women who were the victims of violent crime and warfare in medieval societies. Women were not however always victims; they resorted to violence in many different circumstances. In Ireland there are fewer sources for women than elsewhere in medieval Europe, so the accusation of unjustifiable violence that was made against Elicia Butler offers a rare chance to analyse aspects of women's violence in later medieval Ireland. The most serious accusations made against Elicia were her alleged mismanagement of monastic resources and dilapidation of the fabric of the buildings. There were also accusations, however, that she used excessive violence towards her nuns, violence that her nuns thought was out of the ordinary and motivated by 'quarrelsomeness' and not from the 'desire to correct'. She was also accused of

---

[1] *Irish monastic and episcopal deeds, 1200–1600*, ed. N.B. White (Dublin, 1932) p. 182.
[2] The deposition was recorded by Milo de Baron, bishop of Ossory, and the document was preserved in the Ormond archives (National Archives of Ireland, MS D 2247). A partial translation was published by John Mulholland, 'The trial of Alice Butler, abbess of Kilculliheen', *Decies* 25 (1984) pp. 45–6. For a discussion of the trial see D. Hall, 'Immoral and contemptuous: The trial of Elicia Butler, abbess of Kilculliheen, in sixteenth-century Kilkenny', in *Deviance and textual control: new perspectives in medieval studies*, ed. M. Cassidy, H. Hickey and M. Street (Melbourne, 1997), pp. 17–33, and B. Bradshaw, *The dissolution of the monastic orders in Ireland by Henry VIII* (Cambridge, 1974), pp. 18–19. For a discussion of Elicia and her family connections see D. Hall,

assaulting John McOdo, a servant of Magnus Fusc. Elicia did not attend the hearings so her version of events is not recorded and she was convicted in her absence. These accusations raise questions about both the nature of violence and discipline among women in late medieval Ireland and how medieval authorities viewed women who used violence against men. Scholars of medieval war and crime recognise that descriptions of violence are subjective, that medieval people viewed violence in different ways depending on the context, purpose and meaning of violence, its perpetrators and victims.[3] These varied subjective contexts then need to be explored in order to understand the contemporary meaning for those hearing the accusations.

The world in which Elicia Butler moved was the upper strata of lay and religious society in the Butler lordship. She was almost certainly the older sister of Piers Butler, who finally succeeded in gaining crown recognition of his claim to the earldom of Ormond in 1537.[4] If she was his sister, she and two other sons were born before their parents, Sadhbh Kavanagh and James Butler, received papal dispensation allowing their marriage within the prohibited degrees of kinship in 1467. Piers' claim to succeed to his cousin's earldom was based on his birth after this date.[5] Elicia had probably been in the convent since her irregular profession as a nun in 1469, and so by the time of the deposition in 1531 she may have been in her seventies.[6] She must have either always enjoyed patronage from her powerful brother or regained it by the time of her death, because there is an expensive tomb that almost certainly was built for her under the patronage of Piers and his wife Margaret in St Canice's Cathedral.[7] The motives of her accusers are not fully known, though there are many possibilities, including internal jealousies or anger at financial mismanagement as well as the influence

---

Women and the church in medieval Ireland (Dublin, 2003), pp. 191–200.   **3** S. Amussen, 'Punishment, discipline and power: the social meanings of violence in early modern England', *Journal of British Studies* 34 (1995), pp. 1–34 and P. Maddern, *Violence and social order: East Anglia, 1422–1442*. (Oxford, 1992) pp. 1–26.   **4** Piers Butler succeeded to the title of earl of Ormond after the death of his cousin, Thomas the 7th earl. The succession was complex and its outcome deeply embroiled in contemporary politics in both Ireland and England. For a discussion of this see G. Butler, 'Red Piers Butler of Ormond', *Journal of the Butler Society* 1 (1968), pp. 37–44, 113–19.   **5** *Calendar of Ormond deeds, 1172–1603*, ed. E. Curtis (Dublin, 1932–43), iii, p. 298.   **6** This calculation of her age is based on identifying the Elicia Butler of the 1531 deposition with Elina Butler who was granted a papal dispensation for bearing illegitimate children and irregular profession as a nun at Kilculliheen in 1469. *Calendar of entries in the papal registers relating to Great Britain and Ireland, 1458–71*, pp. 687–8 (hereafter cited as *Calendar of papal letters*) and Hall, 'The trial of Elicia Butler' pp. 20–1. It is also possible that Elina and Elicia were two different women of the Butler family who both entered the abbey under very similar circumstances.   **7** M. Phelan, 'An unidentified tomb in St Canice's cathedral, Kilkenny', *Old Kilkenny Review* 48 (1996), pp. 40–4. I am grateful to Mrs Phelan for correspondence and discussions of the connections between Elicia

of prominent rival local families in convent affairs. Whatever their motivations, one of the accusing nuns, Katherine Mothing, was the abbess at the dissolution of the nunnery nine years later, so the accusations were successful in bringing about change. Since Elicia herself was also still resident at this time and received a pension, some sort of harmony must have been re-established after the turbulent period of the trial.

Deposition of a monastic superior was serious and could only be done by the bishop of the diocese. It was not common in either England or Ireland, although it did occur. The case of Elicia Butler is the only known case of a religious woman being deposed by a bishop in Ireland. The accusations aired at Elicia's trial have many features in common with those raised in episcopal visitations of English convents and monasteries in the same area of Ireland. In both episcopal visitations and depositions there were usually many accusations made with the most important frequently being the financial mismanagement of the resources of the monastic house and the refusal of the accused to obey directions given by the bishop. This is also the case with Elicia. The accusations of dilapidation of the conventual estate, buildings and resources were described first and were also given in most detail. Her alleged disregard of excommunication and disobedience of episcopal direction were also matters of importance to Milo de Baron's court. Some of the other accusations, including fornication, were mentioned almost more briefly. For all the importance placed on the mismanagement charges though, the charges of violence were given considerable attention and were also among the few charges for which witnesses were called and questioned, so they were evidently considered to be important in composing the case against Elicia.

RELIGIOUS DISCIPLINE

Diarmait Mac Murchada founded Kilculliheen in about 1150 under the Augustinian rule. Although its patrons changed over the centuries, as far as can be established it remained an Augustinian convent until its dissolution in 1540.[8] The Augustinian Rule for nuns was popular in medieval Europe from about the eleventh century and was based on the writings of St Augustine of Hippo.[9] Although similar in many ways to the basic principles of the Benedictine Rule, it was a simpler text that allowed for more individual interpretation, which may explain its ready acceptance and popularity in Ireland. Like other monastic rules one of its principal premises is that women should 'live harmoniously' together,

Butler and St Canice's Cathedral.   8 A. Gwynn and R.N. Hadcock, *Medieval religious houses: Ireland* (Dublin, 1970), p. 319 and Hall, *Women and the church*, p. 81.   9 For discussion of the textual and intellectual origins of the Augustinian Rule see G. Lawless, *Augustine of Hippo and his monastic rule* (Oxford, 1987).

although it is not specific about how this was to be achieved.[10] One avenue for ensuring harmony was for the superior to discipline malcontents and those who disobeyed the rule. Discipline by superiors was a subject that concerned the writers of both the Benedictine and Augustinian rules. Both rules stated that quarrels should be ended quickly, and that superiors had special duties to punish and correct infractions of the rules impartially, and the Benedictine rule states clearly that physical correction should be used when necessary.[11] Clearly superiors were expected to discipline members of their communities. How this was done would have differed according to the local and cultural contexts in which the communities operated, as well as how closely they followed the monastic rules.

The extent of individual communities' adherence to monastic rules and familiarity with their contents is not known. The monastic rule was supposed to be read regularly to members of communities to ensure all knew and could follow it. This was usually when the monks or nuns were gathered together in the refectory or chapter house.[12] In late fifteenth- and sixteenth-century Ireland, however, there were widespread complaints about the failure of religious communities to live together as stated in the rules. The Cistercian monastery of Holy Cross (Co. Tipperary) was the subject of investigation by its order in 1536 with accusations of general decline in discipline as well as of monks living outside the cloister.[13] Other accusations were made against monastic houses in the area based on evidence of local juries. James Butler, abbot of Inishlonaght, was accused of being a man of 'odyous lif', keeping women, not following divine service and wasting the material resources of his monastery.[14] There were also suggestions that monks of this abbey were setting up separate individual households.[15] This would presumably have meant that the regular reading of the rule in the refectory would no longer occur, if the monks and their superior were living separately. Details of community life for nuns at this time are fewer than even the scanty evidence available for monks. What evidence there is suggests that by the end of the fifteenth century the number of nuns was small

---

10 'Regula Sancti Augustini' ed. and tr. G. Lawless in *Augustine of Hippo*, p. 110. 11 Ibid., p. 117 for Augustinian Rule for women and for the Benedictine Rule see T. Fry and others (eds), *The rule of St Benedict: in Latin and English with notes* (Collegeville, Minnesota, 1981), p. 25. See also F. Lifshitz, 'Is mother superior?: towards a history of feminine *Amtscharisma*', in J.C. Parsons and B. Wheeler (eds), *Medieval mothering* (New York and London, 1996) pp. 117–23 for a discussion of gender in the Benedictine and other rules.   12 The Augustinian rule states that it should be read to the community once a week, 'Regula Sancti Augustini', p. 118, while the Benedictine rule should be read 'often' Fry, p. 137.   13 *Irish monastic and episcopal deeds*, pp. 81–3 and discussed by Bradshaw, *Dissolution*, p. 20.   14 Herbert J. Hore, and James Graves (eds), *The social state of the southern and eastern counties of Ireland in the sixteenth century* (Dublin, 1870), p. 202.   15 Bradshaw, *Dissolution*, pp. 22–3.

and, although there were breaches of conventual discipline among some, there is not evidence for the same sort of separate living arrangements as in the male houses. The nuns of Kilculliheen did publicly state their adherence to their rule, particularly the requirements of enclosure, when they were facing judicial censure for non-attendance at a court case over a property dispute in 1506.[16] This suggests that they were aware of at least some of the elements of the monastic rule to which they had made vows, so the provisions on discipline and living together in harmony were probably also known to the nuns. Another of the accusations made against Elicia was that the nuns were forced to leave the convent to seek material aid from local lay people. This coupled with Elicia's own absence during the trial suggests that one of the underlying reasons for her deposition was her inability to participate in and maintain the religious community.[17]

Strict discipline by the abbess was not necessarily the reason for the complaints by the nuns of Kilculliheen. They alleged two other crucial elements – that Elicia had drawn blood and that she had been motivated by anger and quarrelsomeness. In underlining the seriousness of the violence, it is also suggested that she was prompted in her actions by the devil. Although the supernatural intervention is not brought up again in the record of the accusations against her, her motivations are explored to some extent in the questioning of the nuns by the bishop. He asked two of the nuns if the violence was used while Elicia was carrying out her duties as an abbess. Their reply indicates that they were aware of the different value placed on the motivations for violence. The distinction that they (or the scribe who recorded their replies) made was between striking as a part of discipline and through anger. The three nuns clearly stated that Elicia was motivated by 'rixam et iniuriam' or quarrels and anger rather than the desire to correct. This is a vital distinction in proving inappropriate use of force by a superior of a religious community. According to the Benedictine rule, physical force was justified if the superior of a monastic house used it in the course of discipline. There are examples of nuns using physical force for disciplinary purposes throughout medieval Europe, and it is clear that force was not judged by the extent of the violence or even the evidence of bloodshed, but by the motivation behind the actions. One of the most shocking examples of this to modern readers is the episode from the 1160s of the nuns in the Gilbertine double monastery at Watton as told by Aelred of Rievaulx. This story is significant for its explication by a noted monastic writer of justifiable violence by religious women. While Aelred reports that he did not approve of either the bloodshed or the castration ordered by the nuns of a young cleric who had had a sexual relationship with a nun of the house, he also expresses his praise of the 'zeal' behind the deed.[18] The distinction is clear that while

16 *Calendar of papal letters, 1503–16*, p. 424. 17 *Irish monastic and episcopal deeds*, p. 179 and *Letters and papers of the reign of Henry VIII*, vol. 14, pt 2, p. 11. 18 'De

shedding of blood by religious women is wrong, motivation is the crucial factor in determining how such actions should be viewed. If this motivation is thought to be pure or justifiable then this could excuse violence and even bloodshed.

Male ecclesiastical authorities passed judgement on the motivation of the nuns in complaints about discipline and individual nuns were admonished for using discipline that was too severe. The main criteria for judging severity seems to have been trivial motivation along with physical signs of violence, such as bloodshed, as proof of its unwarranted nature. The cases that have been reported are those where the outside authority of the bishop has been sought, and while his judgement is presented as final, it is given on the evidence of the nuns and they provide him with the motivation as they viewed it. The prioress of Catesby in Lincolnshire was accused in 1442 of many irregularities, including being bad tempered and tearing off the veils of nuns who angered her and dragging them around by their hair.[19] Her sisters supplied evidence of both the motivation and the examples of her bad temper to the bishop, who admonished the prioress to improve her relationships with them. During an episcopal visitation of Redlingfeld convent in the diocese of Norwich in 1514, one of the nuns accused the subprioress of using her disciplinary powers inappropriately and of drawing blood during punishment.[20] In both these English cases the accused nuns had reputations for vexatious anger and were considered by their community to have used their positions of power inappropriately.

This gives an ecclesiastical context to the charges laid against Elicia by her nuns and the meanings that they were given by the authority of Bishop Milo. The nuns of Kilculliheen diagnosed the motivations behind Elicia's forceful actions as anger rather than discipline, and it was this coupled with the resulting bloodshed that was presented to the bishop as another convincing piece of evidence that Elicia was unfit to continue to manage their convent. There are, however, other contexts in the secular world within which Elicia's actions should also be viewed.

PARENTAL DISCIPLINE

Both the complaints by nuns about excessive discipline and the injunctions by bishops for the tempering of such discipline are similar to discussions of parental discipline. This is not surprising given that the rule of the superior of

---

sanctimoniali de Wattun', *Patrologia Latina* ed. J-P. Migne, vol. 195 (Paris, 1855), col. 197A-B. This episode has been much discussed by modern scholars; for a summary of this see E. Freeman, 'The medieval nuns of Watton: reading female agency from male-authored didactic texts', *Magistra* 6 (2000) pp. 5–8. **19** Cited in E. Power, *Medieval English nunneries, c.1275–1535* (Cambridge, 1922), pp. 82–3. **20** *Visitations of the diocese of Norwich, 1492–1532*, ed. A. Jessopp (London, 1888), pp. 138–40.

a medieval monastery was likened to that of a parent, with the Augustinian rule explicitly stating 'Obey your superior like a mother'.[21] Within medieval society parents generally had a responsibility to ensure obedience. There is evidence of parents using what was considered by many contemporaries to be reasonable force to compel their children to obey their wishes, in what were assumed to be the children's best interests.[22] Parents were expected to be motivated by their responsibility to teach and discipline their children. There were instances though where parents were considered to have crossed the line between discipline and unjustifiable force, although there were few avenues for children to redress their wrongs. Catherine Mckesky's parents had to beat her severely in order to compel her to marry John Cusack in fifteenth-century Armagh. This display of parental will seemed to have attracted a sort of fascinated disapproval within the local community, as there was no shortage of witnesses who had stood by during the attacks to testify to the violence when Catherine later sued for divorce on the grounds that she was compelled against her will to marry.[23] In this case again, it is the motivation behind the force that was considered to be crucial. The church did not permit marriage without consent, and the force needed to compel Catherine to marry was an indisputable marker of withheld consent. The force was considerable, her mother struck her with a 'bepoke' so hard that the 'bepoke' broke in two and her father beat her to the ground. So physical force by mothers in disciplining their daughters was recognisable in medieval Irish communities – as it was in other medieval societies. That Catherine knew to allege that her parents used extreme force to compel her to marry indicates both that the episcopal court she applied to was willing to accept this accusation as evidence of withheld consent and also that Catherine was aware of the likely reception her accusation would receive. This suggests that there were different standards between lay and ecclesiastical communities on the correct levels of force that were justified between parents and their children. Both communities did seem to recognise that even in a violent society, there were written and unwritten limits on violence and the degree of force that was permissible.

LAYWOMEN AND VIOLENCE

Nuns were part of both the secular and ecclesiastical worlds. Elicia Butler's actions in using physical force against her nuns and in assaulting a member of a

---

[21] 'Regula Sancti Augustini' p. 117. See however the discussion problematising the equation of abbesses with mothers, and arguing that abbesses were 'female fathers' instead. Lifshitz, 'Is mother superior', pp. 120–5.   [22] B. Hanawalt, *Growing up in medieval London: the experience of childhood in history* (Oxford, 1993), p. 72.   [23] *The register of John Swayne, archbishop of Armagh and primate of Ireland, 1418–1439*, ed. D.A. Chart (Belfast, 1935) pp. 165–6. There are other examples cited by K. Simms, 'Women

neighbour's household must be seen within a wider context of how women used violence in medieval secular society in Ireland as well as how violence was regarded within religious communities. That medieval Ireland was a violent society is something of an historical truism. Certainly the communities of late medieval Ireland were involved in many local acts of war and conflict between and among the different groups vying for power and influence in a politically unstable age. Contemporaries described Ireland as a 'land of war'.[24] How women were affected by and participated in this 'land of war' has not been extensively studied by historians as yet, although the admittedly scanty evidence does indicate that women were involved in many aspects of the violence, warfare and crime that plagued communities in medieval Ireland. A few were in positions of power that involved control of troops, such as Dearbhfhorgaill, the daughter of Maghnus O Conor who led a troop of galloglass against the churches of Drumcliffe in 1315.[25] Others were popularly known to have been the force behind men who fought, one famous example occurring during the rebellion of the earl of Kildare in the 1530s. Janet Eustace, the earl's aunt, was thought by many to have been the 'chief counsellor' of the rebellion.[26] These acts of war were explicable to commentators given the class and social position of the women. They, like their male relatives, directed others to fight using their resources.

Unlike these overt acts of war, women who used indirect violence were more likely to be described as treacherous and deceitful. In 1305 the wife of Piers Bermingham stood on the battlements and directed her husband's troops to where Irish guests were hiding. Her actions were credited with ensuring that the death toll among the Irish was particularly high. This attack was viewed by the Irish as extremely treacherous because Bermingham had invited the Ó Conchobháir Failghe to his house.[27] There is an implication in the annalists' version of this episode that the motivations behind the woman's actions were not justifiable, as she was not engaged in recognisable conflict with the Irish guests, so her actions were particularly deceitful. It follows then that her actions in directing the English to the hiding places of the Irish were considered additional evidence of Bermingham's duplicity and treachery.

---

in Norman Ireland', in Margaret MacCurtain and Donncha Ó Corráin (eds.), *Women in Irish society* (Dublin, 1978), p. 17. **24** J. Lydon used the term 'Land of War' as the title for his chapter in *New History of Ireland*, vol. 2, *Medieval Ireland* ed. A. Cosgrove (Oxford, 1987), p. 240. He finds the first reference to this term in 1272 in a document calendared in *Calendars of documents relating to Ireland, 1252–84*, ed. H.S. Sweetman and G.F. Handcock (London, 1886), no. 930. **25** *Annála Connacht*, ed. A. Martin Freeman (Dublin, 1944), 1315. **26** The various reports are cited and discussed by W. Palmer in 'Gender, violence and rebellion in Tudor and early Stuart Ireland', *Sixteenth Century Journal* 22 (1992) pp. 700–1. **27** *Annals of Innisfallen* ed. S. Mac Airt (Dublin, 1951), p. 395 and see Cormac Ó Cléirigh, 'The problems of defence: a regional case study', in J. Lydon (ed.), *Law and disorder in thirteenth-century Ireland: the Dublin parliament of 1297* (Dublin, 1997), pp. 46–55.

Some women were effective enemies within castles whose actions either directly or indirectly led to the capture or destruction of military strongholds. Such actions were probably behind the laconic reports of the capture of the castle at Athlone in 1455 when it was 'taken by the English having been betrayed a woman who was in it' and when Limerick 'both stone and wood was burned by one woman in 1413'.[28] One interpretation of these events is that annalists may have had little information about the downfall of the these heavily fortified places and could imagine no other way for such huge stone defences to be defeated except by inside treachery, which in Irish annals was often caused by women. When women were behind violence indirectly or out of sight, it was often taken by the annalists as an indicator that the motivations were treacherous. These women were seen to have used unwarrior-like tactics such as poison or spying to achieve what 'honest' fighting could not.

Other women were excused behaviour that resulted in violence, perhaps on the grounds that they were not as responsible for their actions as men. Two women, Agnes, widow of John Moyl, and Nevok Inyn Oconoyl were accused in 1297 of collaborating with many men in the murder of Walter Sweyn, a crown official in Kildare.[29] Agnes was accused of assisting the men with the murder that occurred in Nevok's house. Agnes was then accused of concealing Nevok in a church until she was rescued. The women seem to have been part of a premeditated attack, but they were not outlawed, as were the men with whom they conspired, although Nevok's goods were taken. As women they may have been viewed as less dangerous than the men and so not liable to the same punishments and the local jurors may also have been more aware of the circumstances than the rather short surviving record attests. As the women were accused of facilitating the murder rather than taking up arms, this may also have affected how the jurors viewed their involvement.

The little that is known of other women in Elicia Butler's family suggest that they acted within the complex weave of local networks and influence just as the men from their families did. There are strong suggestions that these women used force, or the threat of force, to ensure that their wishes were carried out. Piers Butler's wife, Margaret Fitzgerald, was legendary for her forceful pursuit of her husband's interests, and her unwomanly abilities. Holinshed wrote that she was 'manlike, tall of stature; very rich and bountifull; a bitter enimie'.[30] Later historians collected tales of her hanging prisoners in her castles, and her name being used to frighten children.[31] Katherine Butler, Elicia's niece, was married to Richard le Poer, lord of Curroughmore, and was another formidable

28 *Annals of the Four Masters*, 1455, 1413. 29 *Calendar of justiciary rolls of Ireland, 1295–1307*, p. 187. 30 *Holinshed's Irish chronicle*, ed. L. Miller and E. Power (Dublin, 1979), p. 256. 31 Walter Fitzgerald, 'Notes on Lady Margaret Fitzgerald who married Pierce, 8th Earl of Ormonde in 1485', *Kildare Archaeological Society Journal* 8 (1915–17), p. 510.

woman well known for exercising her powers in her husband's lands and ordering political assassinations. During the investigations by the English crown into conditions in Waterford and the surrounding countryside in the sixteenth century, many complaints were made against her management including that her men had robbed and murdered several people at her instigation.[32] Their contemporary and later enemies made much of their forceful, 'unwomanly' natures, but there is little evidence to suggest that these Butler women acted outside the bounds of behaviour expected of strong women of their class.

Violence perpetrated by women in medieval Ireland was viewed in different ways depending on the perceived motivations behind the use of force and the contexts in which it was reported. Murder, directing troops in conflict and assassinations were part of life in the violent and unstable communities of medieval Ireland and some women engaged in these conflicts in much the same way as their male relatives did. There is some implication that women may have been less likely to have been convicted of violent crimes, perhaps due to jurors' reluctance to admit that women could be as violent as men. Women were, however, often suspected of using particular treachery or underhanded means when they perpetrated violence. Their motivations were implicitly less pure than men who fought directly with their enemies. What is interesting in all the examples cited is that they involve violence used or ordered by women against male enemies, either individually or collectively. Elicia's alleged assault against John McOdo may have been seen within this context. It is not clear from the deposition what prompted Elicia's assault on John, and when witnesses were called this accusation was silently dropped, suggesting it may not have been able to be proved conclusively. It is significant that this assault is given less prominence in the accusations against her than the other accusations and the complaint appears to be less that Elicia used force against him but that she was not absolved of the crime by the ecclesiastical authorities.[33] The implication is that this may have been a violent episode but that force used against servants or social inferiors was not seen as significant as that against peers.

The accusations against Elicia highlight different perceptions of violence perpetrated by women within medieval Irish society. By condemning the force Elicia used against her fellow nuns Milo de Baron and his court emphasised that it was the context of violence that was significant. Unlike other acts of force by women, Elicia used her own hands, she assaulted her social peers and her motivations were not justifiable. Other women, who ordered men in battle or plotted to ensure that their interests were protected, received a much less hostile reception by annals and authorities. Elicia's case demonstrates that in a society well known for its violence and lawlessness, there were societally accepted constraints on violence. Violence perpetrated by women that occurred outside of certain boundaries was not acceptable.

32 *The social state of the southern and eastern counties*, pp. 189, 207.   33 *Irish monastic and episcopal deeds*, pp. 180–1.

Theory in the absence of fact: Irish women and the Catholic Reformation

Tadhg Ó hAnnracháin

The extension of the Catholic Reformation to Ireland in the closing decades of the sixteenth and the first half of the seventeenth centuries was one of the most significant processes in Irish history. Both in the short and the long term the political implications of this development were extraordinarily profound. The consolidation of a Catholic identity throughout the island, the gradual alienation of Catholics from the political structures of the state, their mass participation in rebellion in 1641, and the ferocious repression of that rebellion by the Interregnum government were the essential components in a highly visible chain of events leading to the formation of a minority Protestant ascendancy and a politically marginalised Catholic majority during the eighteenth century.

Yet the Catholic Reformation in Ireland was not exclusively or even principally a political phenomenon. Nevertheless, through lack of records the social and cultural dimensions of this process are infinitely less amenable to historical analysis, particularly in the pivotal decades under discussion in the present essay. And, amid the general dearth of sources, the situation relating to women is particularly pitiful. Scattered and impressionistic fragments, looted from odd locations, are the basic materials which offer themselves.

Despite this paucity of material, several theories relating to women and the spread of the Counter-Reformation have been put forward by a variety of historians, mostly men. The best supported of these relates to the important role played by women in the first establishment of Catholic reform within the Old English community of the Pale and the towns. Because the Elizabethan state was chiefly concerned with the religious conformity of male heads of households, women were freer to remain absent from the services of the established church. This in turn, Nicholas Canny has suggested, allowed them to become particular targets for the missionary priests of the Counter-Reformation, who were thus able to consolidate the Catholic allegiance of the women of the older colonial community.[1] The daughters, in particular, of that

---

[1] Nicholas Canny, *From Reformation to Restoration: Ireland, 1534–1660* (Dublin, 1987), pp. 153–4.

first generation of religiously convinced women, in their marital transfers to new households, have been taken as important agents of cultural change.

Such a model of the diffusion of the Counter-Reformation conforms quite closely to that posited for English Catholicism by John Bossy.[2] It possibly overestimates the significance of the daughters of the second as opposed to the first generation; their brothers after all, in contrast to their fathers, had already begun to demonstrate a more rigid demeanour in religious matters. It can also be noted that the priests who supposedly helped to confirm the first generation of women in their Catholicism were themselves already the product of hardening religious convictions. Nevertheless there is sufficient evidence relating to women such as Margaret Ball, prosecuted by her own son for recusancy, Margaret Bermingham, who died in prison after arrest on religious grounds, Anastasia Strong, the mother of the future archbishop of Cashel and receiver of priests, and Joan Roche, the intensely pious mother of the future bishop of Ferns to make it clear that the convinced adherence of Old English women to Catholicism was a development of real significance within the older colonial community.[3]

That Protestant authors were bitterly aware of the influential relationship between Catholic clergy and Irish women is indicated by the stridency of their allegations concerning its sexual impropriety. With dripping sarcasm Barnaby Rich recorded how

> Our holy holy brood of Iesuites, Seminaries, Fryers and such other, do performe strange thinges, but specially for the increase and propagation of children, not a barren woman in a house where they be lodged.[4]

In similar vein Fynes Moryson's discussion of Irish women's 'immoderate drinking' led him to note:

> you may well judge that incontinency is not rare among them ... but how their priests triumph in this luxurious field, lett them tell who haue seen their practise.[5]

Parr Lane also echoed this theme declaring that Catholic priests 'whom well you fathers call' could make 'more children without wives/than all our married churchmen for their lives'.[6]

2 John Bossy, *The English Catholic community, 1570–1850* (London, 1975), p. 153. 3 Patrick Corish, 'Women and religious practice', in Margaret MacCurtain and Mary O'Dowd (eds.), *Women in early modern Ireland* (Dublin, 1991), p. 215; Colm Lennon, *The lords of Dublin in the age of reformation* (Dublin, 1989), pp. 213–14. 4 Barnaby Rich, *A new description of Ireland* (London, 1610), p. 47. I am deeply indebted to Clodagh Tait for this reference and also for the references in footnotes 6, 9, 25 and 26. 5 Graham Kew (ed.), *The Irish sections of Fynes Moryson's unpublished Itinerary* (Dublin, 1998), p. 68. 6 Quoted in Alan Ford 'Reforming the Holy Isle: Parr Lane and the conversion of the

This relationship between women and priests was in a sense a comfortable target for Protestant observers because it offered no disturbance to the notion that the threat of Catholicism lay in its seductive attractiveness to the basest elements of humanity, both within individuals and within the reservoir of such human weakness represented by the female gender.[7] At least on an unconscious level, comments of this nature can be read as the mobilisation of the vast metaphorical power of the story of Adam's fall to explain the degenerate condition of Irish religion. But the depth of hostility also reflected a realisation of the importance of the problem from an evangelical perspective. Female adherence to the Church of Rome was to have significant implications for the failure of the Protestant Reformation. Fynes Moryson was acutely aware of this, describing a situation in which:

> Iesuites and Roman Priests swarmed in all places, filling the houses of lordes, gentlemen, and espetially Cittisens and dominering in them, as they might well doe, for howsoever the men grewe weary of them, they had the wemen on theire sydes.[8]

The familial pressure exerted by women whose consciences had been activated by Counter-Reformation clergy undoubtedly acted as a growing barrier to the continued conformity of many male heads of households. As one contemporary Protestant observer noted: 'Romish priests so persuade the women that they declare that they will as soon bring their husbands to the gallows as to our church.'[9] Men who were excommunicated by the Catholic clergy for attendance at Protestant worship could find that their wives would not only refuse to share their beds but even their dinner tables.[10] Religion may also have played a part in forming the surprising female hostility to the English language which Fynes Moryson noted in Cork and Waterford:

> Common experience shewed, and my self and others often observed, the cittizens of Watterford and Corcke hauing wyues that could speak English as well as wee, bitterly to chyde them when they speak English with us.[11]

Even if husbands proved immune to wifely persuasion, they often proved unwilling or unable to prevent their wives from transmitting their religious

---

Irish', in T.C. Barnard, Daibhí Ó Cróinín, and Katherine Simms (eds.), *'A miracle of learning': studies in manuscripts and Irish learning. Essays in honour of William O'Sullivan* (Aldershot, 1998), p. 144.   7 I am grateful to Robert Armstrong for a stimulating discussion of this point.   8 Kew, *The Irish sections of Fynes Moryson's Itinerary*, pp. 50–1.   9 William Dennehy, 'Irish Catholics in the Seventeenth Century', *Irish Ecclesiastical Record* 4th series, 18 (1905), p. 419.   10 Raymond Gillespie, *Devoted people: belief and religion in early modern Ireland* (Manchester, 1997), p. 30.   11 Kew, *The*

culture to their children and the tightly linked marriage patterns of the Old English community resulted in its rapid diffusion.[12] As a result, conforming male Protestants could end their lives religiously isolated within their own households and on their death beds it was reported that their families:

> denyed them relief or rest, keeping meate and all thinges they desyred from them, and the wemen and children continually pinching and disquieting them when they would take rest, that they might thereby force them to turne Papists agayne.[13]

Naturally, it was not easy for such men to gain access to Protestant clergy, thereby increasing the pressure upon them to make their peace with the Church of Rome. The best documented example of such behaviour dates from the 1630s and involved the Sexton family of Limerick. Edmund Sexton the elder, who was in a gravely sick condition, was eager to be attended by Protestant clergymen but his family closed ranks in a concerted attempt, first to prevent their access to the house and, when this failed, to disrupt by noise and the threat of violence any attempts to minister to him. Although his son, Edmund the younger, played a prominent role in this resistance, the other principal figures were women, namely Joan Sexton, the sick man's wife, Mary and Alison, his presumably unmarried daughters, and Catherine Lysaght.[14]

The principal 'delinquents' in the Sexton case, both women and men, were ultimately punished by the imposition of massive fines and sentenced to confinement in the stocks for three days, but the entire incident served as a sharper reminder of the state Church's impotence than its power. The critical role of the home, and in particular of women, in the transmission of religious faith in early modern Ireland[15] meant that female abandonment of the established religion represented a potentially fatal wound to the Irish Reformation.

Backed by rather more slender evidence is a second general theory concerning Irish women and Catholicism, which argues that the anomalous development of Irish Catholicism helped create a domestic religion heavily influenced by women and particularly by wives, largely because the post-Tridentine norm of religious practice centred on the parish church was impossible to achieve in Irish conditions.[16] This in a sense is a positive outgrowth from the commonly received notion that the evolution of relatively distinct spheres of the public and private in seventeenth-century Europe trapped women in domesticity.[17] If Catholicism in Ireland became essentially domestic

---

Irish sections of Fynes Moryson's Itinerary, pp. 50–1.   **12** Ibid., pp. 49–50, 67, 107.
13 Ibid., p. 92.   **14** London, Public Record Office, State papers Ireland 257, 45, ff. 130–5 (microfilm p. 2699 in National Library of Ireland).   **15** Gillespie, *Devoted people*, p. 12.   **16** Corish, 'Women and Religious Practice', pp. 213–14.   **17** Margaret MacCurtain, 'Women, education and learning in early modern Ireland' in MacCurtain

then the implication follows that in this dimension of life Irish women avoided marginalisation to a greater extent than their continental counterparts. This point may be true but it is intensely difficult to prove, certainly for the seventeenth century.

Indeed, rather than a quiet, feminine colonisation of religion in domesticity, there is relatively more evidence extant concerning a surprising level of public and collective organisation by women, which seems to have been based on the notion of a strong reciprocal relationship with the Catholic clergy. In this regard a series of riots is of particular interest. The best documented of these occurred in Cook Street in Dublin on St Stephen's day in 1629. On that morning the Protestant archbishop of Dublin, Launcelot Bulkley, and the mayor and recorder of the city together with a party of soldiers broke into the Franciscan chapel in Cook Street which was then full in preparation for mass. They proceeded to dismantle the pulpit and to pull down pictures and most importantly captured two young friars. These, however, were rapidly liberated by an avenging posse of women under the leadership of the widow Nugent of Winetavern Street, aided by some youths and, eventually, by some pilgrims from the countryside.[18] Another account indicates that these women were a devout group who had been assembled in the oratory.[19] The details of this incident bear a close resemblance to a similar occurrence in Drogheda a decade earlier where another friar, Francis Healy, was captured while saying mass. Once again it was the women of the town who staged an attack on the soldiers with sticks and stones and eventually liberated him from custody.[20]

The involvement of women in these disturbances in itself is little cause of surprise. Even women from the most privileged socio-economic groupings in seventeenth-century Ireland appear to have been quite prepared to participate in physical conflict when the need arose. The example of the formidable Lady Dowdall and her defence of Kilfenny castle springs to mind,[21] or the even more redoubtable Mrs Briver, the wife of the mayor of Waterford in 1642 who, hearing that her husband had become involved in an unwise confrontation against sixteen angry townsmen, ran from her house 'without either hatt or mantle' and taking him by the neck dragged him back to their house 'whether he wud or no'.[22] Nevertheless, in the two riots mentioned above women were clearly the principal and leading actors, with the adult men of the cities conspicuous by their absence from the confrontation with the forces of the state. In this regard the lesser likelihood of women facing prosecution for

and O'Dowd, *Women in early modern Ireland*, p. 175. **18** Brendan Jennings (ed.), *Wadding papers* (Dublin, 1953). pp. 330–1. **19** John Roche to Luke Wadding, Jan. (?) 1630 (ibid., p. 333). **20** Brendan Jennings, 'Brussels Ms. 3947: Donatus Moneyus Provincia Hiberniae S. Francisci' in *Analecta Hibernica* 6 (1934), p. 33. **21** J.T. Gilbert, *History of the confederation and war in Ireland* (7 vols., Dublin, 1882–91), ii, pp. 69–73. **22** Ibid., p. 10.

participation in such disturbances may have been a factor of some importance. It can be noted, for instance, that the Drogheda incident took place some years after the prosecution of a group of local men who had intervened violently to prevent a Franciscan friar from harassment.[23] Following the Cook Street incident, although one women was subsequently arrested, it is significant that the chief ire of the state was directed against the Catholic aldermen of the city, eight of whom were imprisoned for their inactivity in the face of the riot.[24] Women may thus have represented the shock troops of popular sentiment because they were less liable to be held criminally responsible. Certainly this was the contemporary Protestant analysis of another female riot in 1623 which occurred at the funeral of the Protestant Lady Killeen, Suzanna Plunkett, née Brabazon. At the service apparently,

> Fowre women being the captainesses and two of these being sisters to the Lord Killeen with about fowre score other women, imagining that sex to be lawless did without the church dore assault the minister coming forth to meete the corpse, rent his surplis, toare a leaf of the Communion booke and with blowes did offer him such violence that the better disposed people were inforced to rescue him.[25]

O'Sullivan Beare relates a very similar incident at another funeral. In this case an English minister attempted to take over the burial service. No men were present 'for fear of the English' but the women present attacked the minister and placing him in the open grave began to bury him until he promised to trouble them no more.[26]

This would suggest that the illegal character of the Catholic Church in Ireland actually facilitated an occasional public role for women as leaders in the expression of the Old English community's resentment of the religious policy of the state. A similar pattern has been detected with regard to female violence in other contemporary European societies. Olwen Hufton has noted that some Dutch riots in the seventeenth century saw women enjoining their menfolk to stay away to avoid the possibility of prosecution.[27] Natalie Zemon Davis has

---

23 Reginald Walsh (ed.), 'Miscellaneous documents', *Archivium Hibernicum* 6 (1917), p. 65. 24 Jennings, *Wadding papers*, pp. 330–1; the constables of Cook Street, High Street and Corn Market were also imprisoned. 25 J. Brady, 'Funeral customs of the past', *Irish Ecclesiastical Record* 78 (1952), pp. 330–2; *Cal. S. P. Ire.* 1615–25, 429–30. 26 M.J. Byrne (ed.), *Ireland under Elizabeth ... being a portion of The History of Catholic Ireland by Don Philip O'Sullivan Beare* (Dublin, 1903), pp. 45–6; for a wider discussion of the occurrence and significance of such violence at burials see Clodagh Tait, *Death, burial and commemoration in Ireland, 1550–1650* (forthcoming Dublin, 2002), chapter three. 27 Olwen Hufton, *The prospect before her: a history of women in Western Europe. Volume One, 1500–1800* (London, 1995), p. 463.

observed corresponding developments in early modern France and interestingly has suggested that organised group violence by women in France during the early modern period was the particular province of Catholics, involving such behaviour as stone throwing at Protestant women, mud throwing at Protestant clergy and in one case the hanging of the wife of a Protestant bookseller by a group of Catholic female butchers.[28]

The possibility also exists, nonetheless, that the action of the women in the first two incidents discussed testified to a particularly strong bond between them and the local clergy. In this regard the reference to the devout women of the oratory is of particular interest. And the theory that women may have acted to protect those to whom they believed they had special and reciprocal responsibilities is strengthened by parallel evidence from within Gaelic Ireland, which was recorded during the 1640s by the Italian party who arrived in the island in the company of the papal nuncio, GianBattista Rinuccini.

Rinuccini landed in Kenmare Bay in October 1645 after a terrifying ordeal at sea involving a prolonged pursuit by a Protestant privateer. Despite his relief at a safe landfall, the archbishop may in fact have found the assembly of the local female population to greet him almost as frightening as the sea passage. As word went out of his arrival, the 'most noble women of the region gathered from all the villages' came to where he was staying. The highest in rank among them then attempted to kiss the prelate who apparently 'drew himself back as if she was a dragon'.[29] He was haunted apparently by the thought that if he submitted to the kiss of one he might be expected to accommodate all the others as well. Rinuccini's secretary's recording of this encounter concentrated quite strongly on the attempted kiss presumably because of its surprising novelty. Outside observers in early modern Ireland, but particularly those from Latin cultures, found the osculatory lack of inhibition of Irish women in offering a greeting somewhat shocking. The clerics of the Italian party certainly found it particularly inappropriate. But the incidental detail of the account, preserved almost by accident, that an organised and hierarchically arranged group of noble and gentry women immediately assembled to greet the nuncio, is of much greater interest. Why was the group exclusively female? Was this a normal gesture of respect which would have been accorded any distinguished visitor to the locality or was it related more narrowly to Rinuccini's ecclesiastical status? That it was the latter is suggested quite strongly by two companion incidents of the 1640s in another predominantly Gaelic area of the island, namely mid Ulster.

28 Natalie Zemon Davis, 'City women and religious change', and 'Women on top' in her, *Society and culture in early modern France* (Stanford, 1975), pp. 92–3, 146.   29 'donne nobilissime congregate da tutti quei villaggi'; 'egli ritiratosi in dietro come se fosse stato un drago', Lettera di Alessandro Neroni sul viaggio in Irlanda del Nuncio Apostolico, 1645 (Archivio di Stato, Firenze, Mis. Medicea, 436 ins 19).

Rinuccini's most important subordinate on the Irish mission was the dean of Fermo, Dionysio Massari, another of the group who fended off a series of greeting kisses from women in Kerry with some difficulty. In the summer of 1646, Massari was dispatched to Ulster by his superior with a minimum of advertisement. His purpose was flatly political, to liaise covertly with the general of the Ulster army, Owen Roe O'Neill, about a pre-emptive strike on Dublin later that year. In the course of his visit to the Ulster army's camp, however, Massari was forced to abandon political negotiations for several hours while he was visited by a group of women with whom he performed a number of devotions and to whom he offered lunch because, he recorded, this was the usage of the country.[30] Within a few days, while lodging in a fortified crannog he underwent a similar experience. The chief women of the area rowed over to visit him, he provided them with lunch and took part in their devotions and they then left greatly satisfied.[31] It is evident that the women in question were claiming a privilege of secluded and uninterrupted contact with an important ecclesiastical figure who had come to their vicinity as a direct representative of the pope.

The parallels between these incidents and the encounter which so discomforted the nuncio himself on his first landfall in Kerry are quite striking. On each occasion the arrival of the distinguished Italian cleric was largely unexpected and unheralded. And yet, with remarkable swiftness, on three occasions local gentlewomen appear to have assembled to meet and interact with the visitor in a disciplined and ordered fashion. Taken together, these incidents, and in particular the manner in which Massari stressed his own conformity with established custom in meeting with these groups, are strongly indicative of some type of corporate and exclusively female organisation based upon religious practice.

To what extent it is possible to extrapolate from this apparently Gaelic custom concerning more Anglicised areas of the island is difficult to determine. It is certainly suggestive that this cultural pattern existed in areas as geographically distant as Cavan and Kerry and it is possible that women of the Old English population were also accustomed to organize in this fashion. In this regard, it is germane to note that although Rinuccini and his subordinates tended to distinguish between the Gaelic Irish and Old English populations in a variety of memorials to Rome, this tendency is not evident in their remarks concerning Irish women. And those remarks, particularly in the early years of the mission, tended to be highly positive. To the secretary of the party, Alessandro Neroni, they seemed 'more angels than women', while Massari was also struck by the beauty, purity and frankness of mind and conversation, decorum and fecundity of the women of Gaelic Munster.[32] Rinuccini was also

---

30 Archivio della Sacra Congregatio de Propaganda Fide, Miscellaneae Varie, ix, 133.
31 Ibid., 140.   32 'parevano piu toste angele che(?) esser femine', Lettera di Alessandro Neroni sul viaggio in Irlanda del Nuncio Apostolico (A.S.F., Mis. Medicea, 456 ins 19);

extravagant in his praise of the Irish as mothers,[33] while he considered the nuns of the island a shining example to the male and, from his perspective, distressingly lax regular clergy.[34] This last was noteworthy praise. Due to the Counter-Reformation Church's preoccupation with cloistering, it was more difficult for women to fulfil a vocation as nuns in Ireland than almost anywhere else in Catholic Europe.[35] One of the nuncio's most stringent instructions on his departure from Italy had concerned the urgent necessity to attend to the secure cloistering of female religious in the island.[36] The exacting archbishop's fulsome commendation of Irish nuns, therefore, is another indication of a strongly established tradition of female Catholic devotion.

Rinuccini's high opinion of Irish women was, however, strained to the uttermost by two incidents in April and December of 1647. On both occasions, his house was surrounded by a mob of keening women, proclaiming the wrongs which they had suffered at the hands of the Ulster soldiers. O'Neill's solders had been billeted in the province of Leinster since the winter of 1646–7 and having been largely starved of supplies had effectively mutinied and begun to pillage large tracts of the south of the province. The details of the complaints which were being made were hidden from Rinuccini by a linguistic barrier but, given the exclusively female nature of the group, rape was almost certainly among their woes, something which evidently created acute embarrassment and anger for the nuncio.[37] It is tempting to view these incidents as similar in character to those previously analysed and it is certainly interesting that once again a body of women directly focused their collective attention on a prominent ecclesiastic. Nevertheless, a number of points tend to suggest at least an added secular dimension to these demonstrations. Rinuccini himself certainly believed that the sieges of his house reflected political concerns. The Ulster army styled itself as the army of the pope and it was for this reason that he believed that he was credited with responsibility for its excesses.[38] Moreover, he was convinced, although not necessarily correctly, that both demonstrations had been orchestrated by his male political enemies, by Viscount Mountgarrett in April and by the peace party on the Supreme Council of the confederates in December.[39] And on each occasion, Rinuccini was not the exclusive target of these protests: in April the Supreme Council was also harangued from the street, while in December O'Neill too became the target of the female protesters.

Massari to Tomasso Rinuccini, 31 Oct. 1645 (Stanislaus Kavanagh (ed.), *Commentarius Rinuccianus, de sedis apostolicae legatione ad foederatos Hiberniae catholicos per annos 1645–9* (6 vols., Dublin, 1932–49), ii, pp. 19–20).   **33** Rinuccini to Alesio Celli (?), Nov. 1646 (A.A.F., iii C/10).   **34** Kavanagh, *Comment. Rinucc.*, ii, p. 177.   **35** Phil Kilroy, 'Women and the Reformation', in MacCurtain and O'Dowd, *Women in early modern Ireland*, pp. 188–92.   **36** Kavanagh, *Comment. Rinucc.*, i, p. 617.   **37** *Comment. Rinucc.*, ii, pp. 539–40.   **38** See the report on the proceedings of O'Neill (Aiazzi, *Nunziatura*, p. 224).   **39** *Comment. Rinucc.*, ii, p. 807.

Thus neither incident can be portrayed as deriving exclusively from a tradition of female interaction in a collective manner with prominent ecclesiastics, although it remains noteworthy that Catholic women were prepared to make public complaint about a topic of some sensitivity[40] to a cleric. Certainly here, the openness and frankness of disposition, which the Italians had previously come to find praiseworthy and indicative of unaffected innocence in Irish women, crossed the line into what they perceived as an embarrassing lack of modesty and deference.

It is certainly important not to over-interpret these impressionistic fragments but taken together they do offer evidence of public and collective activity by exclusively female groups in the first half of the seventeenth century and in each instance Catholicism seems to have acted as a focus for the group, whether such groups were directed towards the liberation of captured friars, or expressing public resentment of Protestant ministers presiding at funerals, or seeking access to important foreign clerics or in presenting collective complaints to high ecclesiastical authority. And Italian Catholic observers in particular evidently found Irish women unusually and occasionally embarrassingly frank and assertive, although they were consistently impressed by their religious zeal and devotion.

However assertive female groups of this kind may have been, it nonetheless seems probable that the strengthening movement of clerical reform in the seventeenth century often impacted on a restrictive fashion on women. By 1630 a resident Catholic hierarchy which had been exclusively seminary trained, indeed in some ways the very template of a post-Tridentine episcopate, had been re-instituted in Ireland.[41] In common with their continental counterparts, these bishops exerted themselves strenuously to control what they perceived as sinful and licentious behaviour. Clerical concubinage was certainly one of their prime targets, although it is seldom mentioned explicitly in reports to Rome. Nevertheless the generalised castigations of scandalous behaviour and excesses are probably in part coded references to sexual irregularities.[42] Women involved in liaisons with priests must inevitably have come under pressure at this time although little direct evidence occurs in the sources. The thrust of reform, however, was almost certainly not confined to the clergy. Malachy O'Queely, for instance, in his stint as vicar apostolic of Killaloe was credited with effecting a

---

40 There is startlingly little reference to rape by Protestant gentlewomen in the contemporary depositions for instance. In this regard see Mary O'Dowd, 'Women and war in Ireland in the 1640s', in MacCurtain and O'Dowd, *Women in early modern Ireland*, p. 101.   41 D. Cregan, 'The social and cultural background of a Counter-Reformation episcopate, 1618–60', in A. Cosgrove and D. MacCartney (eds.), *Studies in Irish history presented to R. Dudley Edwards* (Dublin, 1979), pp. 85–117; *Wadding papers*, p. 581.   42 See for example A.P.F., 'S.O.C.G.', 140, ff. 169r-171v, 308r-309r; see also Ross MacGeoghegan to John Colgan, 4 Oct. 1638 (*Analecta Hibernica*, 6 (1934), pp. 229–30).

dramatic transformation in the mores and morals of the general population of his diocese.⁴³ His impact was certainly over-estimated in these reports but the solid moral authority which the clergy demonstrated during the crisis of the 1640s is an indication that some degree of alteration had been made. The effect on women of a strengthened and more intrusive clerical authority must have varied. In general, it seems probable that women who were seen as transgressive, particularly in sexual terms, such as harlots, adulteresses and clerical concubines would have become the target of ecclesiastical reformers. On the other hand, the clergy's increased preoccupation with social control may have operated to provide a protective framework in other instances. In the aftermath of the 1641 rebellion, clerical support was an integral factor in the repression of looting, pillage and rapine, or at least in the curtailment of its spread to the Catholic segment of the community. Given that women were generally the greatest victims of the upheavals of war,⁴⁴ they were also probably the greatest beneficiaries of the clergy's support for order. Some women may also have benefited from the clergy's increased preoccupation and authority concerning sexual irregularity. It seems probable that the bishop of Ossory was acting in defence of a gentlewoman's honour in 1630 when he wrote:

> And because your lordship in your last ... moved of wrong done to a Catholic gentlewoman by some that liveth within my walke, I have sent for the gentleman and questioned with him at large about the matter; whose answer as it came from itself written I thought fit to insert herewith for your lordship's satisfaction, wishing it may be a contentment to the gentlewoman to know his full mynd and declaration of himself.⁴⁵

The almost casual sense of social authority evident in this letter is certainly noteworthy and evidently could have positive as well as negative implications for some women within his diocese.

The extension of the Counter-Reformation in Ireland, however, did not relate merely to the tightening of social control by an educated clerical elite. Critical processes of moral internalization also occurred. How did this affect women and the relationships between men and women? As with all other important questions of this nature, it is practically impossible to say anything definitively, but the series of letters preserved in the Lynch Blosse correspondence does provide a series of often revealing snap-shots of marital relationships in at least one family deeply influenced by the Catholic Reformation.⁴⁶ Both Roebuck Lynch, the mayor of Galway in 1638 and a prominent confederate Catholic politician during the 1640s, and his son Henry were highly

43 In this regard see *Wadding papers*, pp. 77–83. 44 O'Dowd, 'Women and war', pp. 100–1. 45 *Wadding papers*, p. 430. 46 K.W. Nicholls (ed.), 'The Lynch Blosse Papers', *Analecta Hibernica*, 29 (1980), pp. 115–30.

educated and devout men[47] and in their letters to their wives demonstrated a strong sense of moral responsibility which operated simultaneously both to underpin and to soften patriarchal authority. In a letter of 14 April 1635, for instance, Roebuck wrote to his wife Ellis:

> Sweet Heart,
> I find my brothers Darcy and Martin[48] stronglie inclined to sell theire interest in Bourshule for 2000 pound wherein I will not joine without your consent having had that fortune by you and believeing that your advise (though a woman's) will prove successful unto me in this and all my othere occasions that concerne my own particular for your prayer be to God I finde the comfort of your virtue and judgement.
> If it be sould my mother-in-law is to have a hundred marke a year during her life and after her decease ... she need not desire more than what love, gratitude conscience and honour doe a most high degree bind us unto. I pray you commend me unto her most heavelie and tell her that we expect by your convenience her resolution in this business. Deare love and most worthy to be my dearest, let no melancholy thoughts come neere your heart and put your onelie trust in Him that can bless yowe with plentie without abatement of His store ... I rest your loving husband,[49]

Noteworthy here is the expressed determination not to exercise his legal right to sell the property which she brought to their marriage without her consent, the framework of values, namely love, honour, gratitude and conscience which define and underpin his relationship with his mother-in-law and, it can be surmised, with others, the loving injunction to trust in God, and his acceptance, based on experience, that her advice, although a woman's, will prove useful to him. The letter conveys a strong sense of a reasoned and confident morality, grounded in a conviction of masculine superiority and responsibility.

Although similarly pious his wife's letters are far less measured and more apparently spiky. One can note the missive during the troubled times of 1656 which opened: 'Sweet heart I am afeard I am with child and I am not so well pleased with you for mistrusting your son Henry':[50] the pointed juxtaposition of the news of her pregnancy (she already had been married for over twenty years at this juncture and had grown children) and her displeasure concerning his attitude to Henry is hardly without significance. Ellis's irritation with what she saw as her husband's economic improvidence, probably compounded by the

---

[47] For details of the Lynch family see Aoife Duignan, 'For the preservation of religion and the safety of the nation: the Connacht Group, 1625–42' (unpublished M.A. thesis, National University of Ireland, 2000), esp. pp. 5–11. [48] Richard Martin, Patrick Darcy and Roebuck Lynch all married sisters. In addition, Darcy and Lynch were half brothers: see ibid., p. 8. [49] 'Lynch Blosse Papers', p. 118. [50] Ibid., p. 120.

apparently fleeting conjugal visit which had left her inconveniently pregnant, is very evident in her letters. Nor was she meekly obedient. But the moral framework of their religious faith evidently loaded the guns in Roebuck's favour; only as a co-parent insisting on their duty to their children did Ellis find the opportunity to base her resistance to Roebuck's authority on moral grounds, declaring:

> Seing wy are not able to help our poor children wy should rather comfort them than give them cause of grife. I am sure he is verie naturall and dutifull to his parens.[51]

This discrepancy is even more evident in the apparently more troubled relationship between their son Henry and his wife Mary. Like his father's, Henry's private relationships were informed by a strong sense of moral responsibility. While quarrelling with Mary he wrote: 'God direct you and give you and me the Grace to be governed by our reasons and not by our passions.'[52] Eager for his children to be sent to school in Galway he invoked their shared moral obligation: 'we are not worthy of such children that doe not give ordinary education to them.'[53] But even more clearly than his father's, Henry's conscience, while it dictated respect and consideration for his wife, also reinforced his conviction of his right to obedience. Indeed the entire notion of moral obligation which the Lynch men demonstrate operated apparently to reinforce patriarchal authority because it strengthened their claim to female obedience in return for their honourable and responsible concern. So Henry, disappointed when his wife did not comply with what he saw as his reasonable wishes, was able to threaten coercion with a formidable sense of moral centredness:

> Therefore I pray faile not to observe my instructions in this particular, and let us carrye ourselves so towards each other that there may be a good correspondence between us, for if you go thwarting me in this I have resolved, after I had done what laye in me in order to receive you here … I must frame my thought to new resolutions which I am sure will not please you nor myself but yet must be done to avoyde disgrace.[54]

The Lynch Blosse correspondence is itself fragmentary and disappointingly close to unique. Again the temptation is to over-interpret such fragments. Yet it offers a certain window on an important process. From it I would very tentatively suggest that the domestic culture of the Counter-Reformation could operate to strengthen patriarchal structures in two principal ways. First the framework of the conjugal relationship was itself weighted against wives

51 Ibid. 52 Ibid., p. 125. 53 Ibid. 54 Ibid. p. 124.

because the religiously reinforced notion of marital responsibility meant that wifely obedience was an unquestioned bed-rock of personal relationships. The end result may in fact have been both a kindlier and a stronger patriarchy. Secondly, this process was probably intensified by the differential in education between men and women; the type of carefully constructed conscience exemplified by Roebuck and Henry was suited to men of considerable education. Their wives, although unquestionably pious, were considerably less educated. It seems possible, in fact, that women may have been socialised by the movement of Catholic Reform towards a less reflective and more devotional morality of the kind demonstrated by Roebuck Lynch's mother, Mary French, who, evidently when nearing death, wrote in 1639:

> +Jesus
> Dear Daughter remember my son Harry Lynch that I leaft hime your good father's dyemount to be, God willing, his wearing Ring and meamorye of his parents, my black beadge which is called the Crowne of Jesus, which I do daily saye and praye unto the most Holy Trinity that my sonne Sir Robert Linch, yourselfe and your sisters may hav the longe life and Godly condition of our great-grant-father Stivine Linch ... Good knows at this tim I can do no more but praying God to keepe them and increase (?) them and the fruit of woumbe in vertue and good life. It is an old proverb that the blessing of the departed given to them that come mylyons of blessings.[55]

This last, however, remains little more than a hypothesis. As such, it is a fittingly emblematic note on which to conclude a discussion of a topic of unquestionable importance but one where fragmentary evidence means that every conclusion must necessarily be tentative and hedged with qualifications.

---

55 Ibid. p. 119.

'What will my sister think of me now': the role of sisterhood in sustaining resistance by the Port-Royal community

Carol Baxter

In 1710, Sr Anne de Sainte-Cécile Boiscervoise signed a declaration acquiescing in the Catholic Church's condemnation of Cornelius Jansen's *Augustinus*. Her signature marked the end of her involvement in Port-Royal's opposition to the condemnation of *Augustinus*. By 1710, Port-Royal's lengthy resistance had resulted in the dispersal of its nuns and the destruction of its monastery. By that stage, the remaining elderly resisters had been prohibited from receiving the sacraments. Indeed, Sr Anne de Sainte-Cécile ended her resistance only so that she might be allowed to receive the sacraments on her death-bed. However, what is remarkable about her submission is that she did not lament either the destruction of her monastery or the price paid for resistance. Instead, what was recorded was her anxiety that her submission would attract the disapproval of a fellow-nun. As she said to the confessor appointed to oversee her signature: 'what shall my sister at the Visitation convent say of this great volte-face? She will not be happy when she hears what I have just done.'[1]

That a fellow-nun's poor opinion might be more important than an act of submission to the legitimate authority of pope and king has brought into focus the role of sisterhood in sustaining the Port-Royal resistance. Could individual nuns have been prevented from submitting to the commands of the church authorities out of loyalty to their community? To what extent did fear of breaking ranks or of being isolated within the community shape the actions of individual sisters? Would the Port-Royal resistance have ended more quickly had communal solidarity been less cohesive? If this is the case, how important was the reform established at Port-Royal from 1609 onwards in forging strong ties of sisterhood within the community and in creating a communal predisposition towards resistance?

---

1 'que dira ma Sœur qui est à la Visitation, d'un si grand changement, elle ne sera gueres contente d'apprendre ce que je viens de faire.' *Recueil de pièces concernant les religieuses de Port-Royal des Champs qui se sont soumises à l'Eglise* (Paris, Imprimerie Royale, 1710),

This article intends to argue that the strong bonds of sisterhood between the Port-Royal nuns became critical in maintaining resistance. Furthermore, the article will also argue that the communal dynamic, placing emphasis on unity and on the pursuit of collective interests over those of the individual, prevented many nuns from considering the alternative possibility of submission. Even nuns who initially submitted were soon prompted to retract their submission out of guilt and from an acute sense of having betrayed their fellow-nuns. While this article intends to demonstrate how the potency of collective bonds of sisterhood enabled individual women to undertake radical actions, it will also suggest that these ties enforced a collective mental rigidity which forced some members of the community to resist even when they might have preferred to submit.

Research by sociologists such as Rebecca Adams or Graham Allan on the dynamics of relationships of kinship and friendship has suggested that such bonds tend to be moulded by societal structures and cultural norms.[2] Does the converse also apply – can it be argued that strong ties of solidarity and common purpose influence collective actions and choices?[3] Research on nineteenth-century women has found that they received the greatest emotional support from other women, creating support networks which linked their political and social lives.[4] What is interesting in the Port-Royal case is that the shared experience of living within an enclosed religious community would have added an extra dimension to the nuns' relationships, since these women would have spent their lives together in a confined geographical space, with limited

---

pp. 24–5. All translations are the author's own.   2 See Rebecca G. Adams and Graham Allan (eds.), *Placing friendship in context* (Cambridge, 1998), and Graham A. Allen, *A sociology of friendship and kinship* (London, 1979). The impact of social and cultural factors on female friendships is given particular importance in *Placing friendship in context*. Kaeren Harrison, one of the contributors to the collection makes this explicit in the introduction to her own article, outlining the reasons for her decision to focus on the friendship networks of a specific social group: 'By focusing on a specific socio-economic group, one of the central themes of this book – that different structural features influence personal ties and organise informal relationships – can be made explicit here.' Kaeren Harrison, 'Rich friendships, affluent friends: middle-class practices of friendship', in Adams and Allan, *Placing friendship in context*, pp. 92–116 at p. 92. This view is shared by Pat O'Connor who stresses the social homogeneity of female friendship networks in Pat O'Connor, 'Women's friendships in a post-modern world', in Adams and Allan, *Placing friendship in context*, pp. 117–35.   3 While focusing on the societal and cultural conditioning of relationships, Allan does, however, refer in his introduction to studies which have been carried out on the reverse phenomenon, showing how networks of neighbourhood and work relationships influence the way people interpret and experience their worlds, and are thus of consequence in shaping political and economic aspirations See Allan, *Sociology of friendship*, p. 3.   4 June Hannam, 'Women, history and protest', in Victoria Robinson and Diane Richardson, *Introducing women's studies: feminist theory and practice* (2nd ed., London, 1997), 1st ed.,

opportunities for friendships outside the abbey. Furthermore, many nuns including the principal resistance leaders such as Sr Eustoquie de Flécelles de Brégy[5] had lived at Port-Royal since childhood, having been educated within the abbey. So the experience of communal sisterhood would have been stronger for those women who had not had an opportunity to cultivate alternative relationships outside the community.

The sociologist Pat O'Connor[6] in her study of friendships between contemporary women presents a complex picture of such relationships which nuances our often idealised notion of female interaction. She has found that female friendships are often ineffectual, for instance, in providing assistance, particularly in times of crisis. Furthermore, she argues that there is a tendency for female friendships to perform a conservative function by providing a safety valve which dilutes the pressure which might otherwise force the woman to challenge repressive structures. This article advances the argument that, contrary to O'Connor's thesis, the pattern of female relationships at Port-Royal demonstrates evidence of a level of solidarity which persisted throughout the period of resistance, in particular during the 1660s, enabling the community to maintain a united stance of opposition for almost half a century.

In approaching the task of analysing the Port-Royal relationships, one must be conscious of the difficulty in arriving at a definition of sisterhood which fully conveys its complex, difficult and above all dynamic quality. The concept of sisterhood used includes two broad categories: firstly, the category of siblings linked by a blood relationship, and secondly (and principally for this article), sisterhoods of women who have taken certain vows and live together under conventual rule, or who are otherwise devoted to religious life. The close relationships between women associated with Port-Royal were not unique – there is abundant evidence pointing to supportive bonds within other female religious orders of the period, such as the Ursulines, but such relationships were not tested by religious controversy.

The pattern of sororial relationships can be best represented conceptually as a series of concentric circles at the centre of which were situated three key members of the Arnauld family who dominated the community for much of its history – Mère Angélique Arnauld, her sister, Mère Agnès, and their niece, Mère Angélique de Saint-Jean Arnauld d'Andilly. Mère Angélique occupied the post of abbess from 1602 until 1629 and again from 1642 until 1654, Mère

---

1993, pp. 77–97 at p. 90.   **5** Pierre Leclerc (ed.), *Histoire des persecutions des religieuses de Port-Royal, écrite par elles-mêmes* (Villefranche, 1753), p. 131, 140.   **6** Pat O'Connor, *Friendships between women* (Hemel Hempstead, 1992). She confirms this view in her article in Adams and Allan, *Placing friendship in context* when she states: 'It has increasingly been recognised that intimate confiding between women, which has been seen as the epitome of closeness, is simply a kind of shared victimisation and that a stronger and more enduring solidarity must be based on shared strengths and resources.'

Agnès was abbess from 1636 until 1642 and from 1658 to 1661 while Mère Angélique de Saint-Jean held the abbatial position from 1678 until her death in 1684. The second circle of relationships is formed by the remaining members of the Arnauld family[7] and the third by the wider community of sisters whose unconditional submission and obedience, with a few exceptions, defined the nature of their interaction with the leadership figures.

The theological controversy which moved the Port-Royal community into a position of suspected heresy within the Roman Catholic Church had, at its heart, a fundamental dispute over differing conceptions of the role of divine grace in human salvation.[8] The controversy was triggered by the publication of Cornelius Jansen's synthesis of Augustinian theology, the *Augustinus* in 1640, which allegedly argued that human salvation was solely due to divine grace, removing a role for free will in the person's salvation.[9] Following the condemnation of the *Augustinus* in 1653,[10] reiterated in 1656,[11] the French Catholic Church attempted to eliminate support for what it viewed as a heretical interpretation of Augustinianism by demanding that all clergy and religious orders

Pat O'Connor, 'Women's friendships', p. 122.   [7] Three other sisters of Mère Angélique entered Port-Royal – Anne Eugénie (1592–1653), Marie-Claire (1600–42) and Madeleine (1608–49). In addition, four of her nieces, all sisters of Mère Angélique de Saint-Jean and daughers of Robert Arnauld d'Andilly, entered Port-Royal – Catherine (1614–43), Marie-Charlotte (1627–78), Marie-Angélique de Sainte Thérèse (1630–1700) and Anne-Marie (1631–60). Finally, two of Angélique de Saint-Jean's nieces, daughters of the marquis de Pomponne, became *pensionnaires* at Port-Royal – Marie-Emmanuelle (1663–86) and Charlotte (1668–1746). Both were forced to leave when Louis XIV ordered the removal of all *pensionnaires* in 1679. See Alexander Sedgwick, *The travails of conscience: the Arnauld family and the ancien régime* (Cambridge, Mass. and London, 1998).   [8] For an overview of Jansenism's position within the religious and philosophical beliefs of the seventeenth and eighteenth centuries see Monique Cottret, *Jansénismes et lumières: pour un autre XVIII*e *siècle* (Paris, 1998). Jean Delumeau and Monique Cottret analyse Jansenism's role within the French Catholic Church of the period in *Le Catholicisme entre Luther et Voltaire* (Paris, 1971, 6th ed., 1996).   [9] For a general history of the evolution of Jansenism during the seventeenth century, see Antoine Adam, *Du mysticisme à la révolte: les jansénistes du XVII*e *siècle*, (Paris, 1968). Marie-José Michel analyses both seventeenth- and eighteenth-century Jansenism in *Jansénisme et Paris, 1640–1730* (Paris, 2000).   [10] *Cum occasione*, the bull issued by Pope Innocent X on 31 May 1653, condemned the five propositions as heretical, prohibiting any further defence of these propositions and calling on the secular authorities to take measures against anyone seeking to contest this judgement. *Bulle ou Constitution de Nostre S. Pere le Pape Innocent X. Par laquelle sont declarées & definies cinq propositions en matiere de foy. Avec le Bref de sa Sainteté aux Archevesques & Evesques de ce Royaume. Et le Mandement de Monseigneur l'Archevesque de Paris, pour la publication & observance de ladite Constitution* (Paris, Pierre Targa, 1653).   [11] Cardinal Mazarin placed successful pressure on the Sorbonne to accept the papal bull, *Ad sacram Petri sedem*, issued in 1656, which explicitly condemned the *Augustinus*. For a history of the crystallisation of opposition to Jansenism during the 1650s, see Jacques Gres-Gayer, *Le jansénisme en Sorbonne*,

should sign a Formulary or declaration condemning five heretical propositions allegedly drawn from the *Augustinus*. The Port-Royal nuns became enmeshed in the controversy for a number of reasons, including, most notably, their sympathy for Augustinian theology and their links with defenders of the *Augustinus*.[12] While this article is devoted to the Port-Royal community, its focus is not intended to suggest that the nuns were the only actors in what was an exceptionally multi-faceted controversy involving theologians, philosophers and parliamentarians as well as the secular and religious authorities for almost 150 years.[13] Furthermore, the preceding statements, summarising Jansenism in a few sentences result necessarily in a certain simplification of what was a highly complex theological controversy.

In 1661, the Port-Royal nuns were ordered by the vicars-general of the archdiocese of Paris to sign the Formulary condemning Jansen's *Augustinus*.[14] The nuns tried to avoid condemning Jansen by drawing on an argument devised by Antoine Arnauld which involved agreeing that the five propositions were heretical while refusing to agree to what Arnauld termed the issue of fact (or *fait*), namely whether or not these propositions were to be found in the *Augustinus*.[15] They continued to refuse to sign the Formulary without pre-conditions, notwithstanding escalating pressure against them from the religious and secular authorities. King Louis XIV first attempted to force them to submit by having all students and postulants removed in April 1661 and by prohibiting them from admitting any new nuns. Three years later, the newly-appointed archbishop of Paris, Hardouin de Péréfixe, instituted the most severe measures against them, placing 12 of the community's leading nuns in captivity in other communities on 26 August 1664, removing further nuns in November 1664, prohibiting the remaining nuns from receiving the sacraments and imposing members of the Visitandine order in positions of authority at the community's Paris house, Port-Royal de Paris. When captivity failed to break the majority's continued resistance, the archbishop had all resisters removed to the community's smaller house, Port-Royal des Champs, in July 1665, giving Port-Royal de Paris to

---

1643–1656 (Paris, 1996). 12 For an analysis of Port-Royal's progressively deepening involvement in the Jansenist controversy from the 1650s onwards, see F. Ellen Weaver, *The evolution of the reform of Port-Royal, from the rule of Cîteaux to Jansenism* (Paris, 1978). 13 Recent works on eighteenth-century Jansenism include Monique Cottret, *Jansénismes et lumières*, Dale K. Van Kley, *The religious origins of the French Revolution: from Calvin to the Civil Constitution, 1560–1791* (New Haven and London, 1996) and Catherine Maire, *De la cause de Dieu à la cause de la nation: le jansénisme au XVIIIe siècle* (Paris, 1998). 14 The most comprehensive history of the Port-Royal community was undertaken in the nineteenth century by Sainte-Beuve. See Charles Augustin Sainte-Beuve, *Port-Royal*, edited by Maxime Leroy, 3 vols. (Paris, 1955). 15 See for instance the *acte* of 10 July 1664 in *Divers actes des religieuses de Port-Royal du Saint Sacrement. Touchant l'Ordonnance de Monseigneur l'Archevesque de Paris, par laquelle il exige la foy humaine du fait de Jansenius. Et les étrange violences qui leur ont esté faites en consequence de*

9 nuns who had signed the Formulary.[16] The nuns remained under house-arrest at Port-Royal des Champs and were denied the sacraments until 1669 when they acceded to a compromise wrought as part of the *Paix de l'Église* (Peace of the Church) in which 'Jansenists' were reconciled to the Catholic Church. However, this compromise ended in 1679 with the renewal of pressure by King Louis XIV to force Port-Royal's full submission – postulants and novices were removed and the community was subsequently prevented from accepting any new members. The king's final response to the nuns' resistance occurred a generation later when in 1709, as stated above, the monastery was declared extinct and the nuns were removed to other communities.

The evolution of the Port-Royal history of resistance which resulted in the community's eventual destruction, raises two fundamental questions – why did the nuns resist and why did they maintain their resistance in the face of serious pressure to conform? The nuns of Port-Royal would certainly have been sympathetic to a theology which foregrounded the role of divine grace in salvation, since they viewed salvation as uncertain and impossible to attain without divine assistance. Furthermore, their religious beliefs emphasised humanity's inherent sinfulness and its overwhelming need for divine mercy. The nuns also believed that by resisting the condemnation of the *Augustinus*, they were defending the theology of St Augustine.[17] In addition, their spiritual directors and key interlocutors were deeply involved in the struggle to protest against the condemnation of the *Augustinus*.[18] However, it should not be assumed that the nuns engaged in resistance simply as an act of blind obedience to their male spiritual directors – what is interesting about the Port-Royal resistance is that the nuns maintained their stance of opposition long after the deaths of their most significant spiritual directors. One of the leading resistance figures, Sr Christine Briquet, emphasised to Gaston Chamillard in 1664 that her stance was formed by God and not by the views of her superiors:

ce commandement (no date or place indicated [1664]), p. 4. **16** William Ritchey Newton undertakes a sociological analysis of the backgrounds of the 9 signatories to whom Port-Royal de Paris was given in 1669. See William Ritchey Newton, *Sociologie de la communauté de Port-Royal: histoire, économie* (Paris, 1999), pp. 107–11. **17** The view that the resistance in which the community was engaged was in fact a defence of Augustinianism can be seen in the spiritual reflections prepared by Mère Angélique de Saint-Jean Arnauld d'Andilly to maintain her community's resistance in the 1680s, where she explicitly describes her community as disciples of St Augustine who are being sacrificed by those who wish to attack all followers of St Augustine and the cause of Augustinianism. Angélique de Saint Jean Arnauld d'Andilly, *Reflexions de la R. Mere Angelique de S. Jean Arnaud, Abbesse de P.R. des Champs, pour préparer ses Soeurs à la persecution, conformément aux Avis que la R. Mere Agnès avoit laissés sur cette matiere aux Religieuses de ce Monastere* (no place indicated, 1737), p. 7. **18** A text dated 28 August 1665 reveals their belief that their signature would make them complicit in condemning their own directors since the latter were most closely involved in defending the

Monseigneur, I honour Mr Arnauld greatly and I am his humble servant. But he can sign when he pleases – I do not look to him or to our mothers on this point but to God alone.[19]

Certainly, the nuns' conviction that they were a spiritual elite intended to defend God's truth in a world where the majority succumbed to the temptation of laxity and compromise helped to convince them that their resistance was part of their divinely-appointed mission. They believed that persecution was a sign of God's favour and martyrdom the confirmation that they had been chosen to share in Christ's sufferings. As early as 1661, for instance, Sr Jacqueline de Sainte-Euphémie Pascal pronounced herself ready to become a martyr, 'it is up to us to die for the Truth',[20] viewing her potential sacrifice as a heroic act, 'will that not be our glory?'[21] Similarly, Sr Christine Briquet, writing in 1665 of her period in captivity, perceived her ordeal as proof that Christ had chosen her as one of His disciples – it represented the fulfilment of Christ's promise that His chosen ones would share His suffering:

> I was so happy to see accomplished in me Christ's promise to His disciples that they would share in His sufferings and that they would be permitted to receive on their bodies some of the indignities inflicted on Him.[22]

As a consequence, the strategy pursued by the authorities of imposing harsh punishments on the community was counter-productive as each act of pressure was interpreted by the nuns as a sign that they were being offered the most prized privilege of sharing in Christ's martyrdom. When combined with the collective unifying dynamic of strong sisterly relationships, it is possible to see how a dynamic was created, enabling the Port-Royal nuns to resist against the combined hierarchies of church and state over such a long period.

Augustinus. To condemn the position of their directors in this way would be 'tremper nos mains dans le sang de l'honneur de ceux qui sont nos peres en Jesus-Christ ...' ('to soak our hands in the blood of the honour of those who are our fathers in Jesus-Christ ...'). *Acte des religieuses de Port-Royal. Du 28. Aoust 1665, contenant leur disposition à la vie & à la mort touchant la signature du Formulaire, & leurs sentimens en cas de refus des sacremens à la mort* (no place indicated, 1722), p. 5.   19 'Mgr. J'honore beaucoup Mr. Arnaud, je suis sa trés-humble servante; mais il peut signer quand il lui plaira, je ne tiens ni à lui ni à nos Meres sur ce point, mais à Dieu seul.' *Relation contenant les lettres que les religieuses de Port-Royal ont écrites, pendant les dix mois qu'elles furent renfermées sous l'autorité de la Mere Eugenie,* p. 82 in *Divers actes, lettres et relations des religieuses de Port-Royal du Saint Sacrement touchant la persecution & les violences qui leur ont été faites au sujet de la signature du Formulaire,* (no place or date indicated [1724]).   20 'c'est à nous à mourir pour la vérité'.   21 'n'est-ce pas notre gloire?' Victor Cousin, *Jacqueline Pascal: premières études sur les femmes illustres et la société du XVIIe siècle* (Paris, 1856, 3rd ed.), p. xvii.   22 'j'etois si heureuse que de voir accomplir en moy la promesse que J.C. à faite

The nuns' sense of solidarity was greatly enhanced by some of the key reforms established at the monastery. One of the fundamental elements of Mère Angélique's reform of Port-Royal from 1609 onwards was to re-institute full observance of the rule of St Benedict. Return to the rule of St Benedict involved the abolition of individual property and the institution of the principle of communal ownership, contrary to the practice in many monasteries of the period where wealthy nuns had their own personal quarters, coming together perhaps only for religious ceremonies.[23] There is a reference, for instance, in the pre-reform period, to a certain Dame Motelle who had a private garden at Port-Royal to which she alone had right of access.[24] Communal ownership of property abolished separate privileges and reinforced the importance of community through the practice of meals in common and communal work duties. Furthermore, with the imposition of the cloister[25] preventing nuns from moving outside the monastery in accordance with the requirements of the Benedictine Rule (reiterated by the Council of Trent), the Port-Royal sisters had little possibility of leaving the confines of the abbey and so spent their lives with their community. It is also likely that solidarity was enhanced by Mère Angélique's decision to end the practice, common in almost all convents of the period, of demanding a large dowry[26] from women seeking to join the order.[27] Women who demonstrated the requisite commitment to the religious life were

à ses disciples de leur donner part à ses opprobres en permettant qu'ils receussent en leur personnes quelqu'un des reproches qui lui ont été faits.' PR 66 – *Relation de ma Sr de Ste Christine Briquet* [A manuscript held at the Bibliothèque de Port-Royal in Paris], p. 89 [pagination added later]. **23** See Jérôme Besoigne, *Histoire de l'abbaye de Port-Royal*, 6 vols. (Cologne [Amsterdam], 1752–3), vol. I for a description of the reform undertaken by Mère Angélique Arnauld at Port-Royal from 1609 onwards. Perle Bugnion-Secretan, in her biography of Mère Angélique, confirms that the process of reform at Port-Royal began essentially with the introduction of communal ownership of property as well as the imposition of the cloister. Perle Bugnion-Secretan, *La Mère Angélique Arnauld, 1591–1661 d'après ses écrits abbesse et réformatrice de Port-Royal* (Paris, 1991), p. 27. **24** Besoigne, *Histoire*, vol. I, p. 18. **25** idem, Vol. I, p. 18. See also M.A. Schimmelpennick, *Select memoirs of Port Royal* (5th ed., London, 1858, 3 vols.), vol. I, p. 90. **26** In contrast, the prevailing customs within other monasteries was to demand considerable dowries. The dowries demanded varied according to the standing of the community and its location. A fashionable monastery like the Benedictine abbey of Gif (which Mère Angélique was invited to reform in 1626) was able to demand a dowry of almost 8,000 *livres* from Eusèbe Renaudot to secure a place there for his daughter in 1667–8. Similarly, the convent of Saint-Pierre at Lyon, which admitted only titled ladies, set its dowry at 30,000 *francs* during the same period. See Wendy Gibson, *Women in seventeenth-century France* (Basingstoke, 1989), p. 212. **27** Besoigne, *Histoire*, vol. I, p. 26. See also Fabian Gastellier, *Angélique Arnauld* (Paris, 1998), pp. 106–7 for a description of Mère Angélique's strong distaste for the practice to 'marchander les filles' ('treat girls like merchandise') and of her determination to accept suitable candidates regardless of dowry considerations.

accepted regardless of income.[28] This ensured that the Port-Royal nuns were bound by a shared commitment to the religious life.

It is notable that Port-Royal's reform was rooted in an act of resistance which signalled the priority attached to sisterhood over that of family. The Port-Royal reform was consolidated on 25 September 1609 in an event known as the *Journée du Guichet* when Mère Angélique Arnauld refused her parents entry into the monastery's cloister. She was supported in her action by her two sisters, Agnès and Marie-Claire, who had already joined her as nuns at Port-Royal. Accounts of the *Journée du Guichet*, most notably by Mère Angélique de Saint-Jean, depict her aunt's act of rebellion as 'the resistance she was obliged to make to Monsieur her father'[29] so that she might fully observe the requirements of the Council of Trent that nuns should be enclosed. Maurice Halbwachs specifically cites this event in his work on collective memory to highlight how religious belief supports the individual to undertake the process of separation from family which is necessary when the person enters a convent: 'When a member of a family separates from it in order to embrace another group that is not a family, for example when one decides to enter a convent, the person finds the power to do so through a religious belief that is opposed to the spirit of the family.'[30]

What is implicit in Halbwachs' comment and is borne out in Port-Royal's history is that the individual who entered the convent became bound by the obligations of sisterhood rather than those of the family. What Mère Angélique's resistance during the *Journée du Guichet* signalled was that nuns would be required to forge new ties of loyalty based on the criteria of shared religious goals rather than on blood relationships. A nun entering Port-Royal severed her links with her family in the secular world to join the new family of the religious sisterhood.

At Port-Royal, emphasis was placed on fostering close bonds between the community as a whole while the development of particular friendships between individual nuns was discouraged. The aim of the community, as reflected in the *Constitutions de Port-Royal* was that all nuns should treat each other equally, without favouritism.[31] The *Constitutions* recommended:

---

28 Some of the nuns accepted without a dowry included Sr Jeanne Radegonde de Sainte-Fare Lombard and Sr Catherine de Sainte Ildegarde Fontaine. See Pierre Leclerc (ed.), *Histoire des persecutions*, pp. 137, 144.   29 'la resistance qu'elle fut obligée de faire à Monsieur son pere', Angélique de Saint-Jean Arnauld d'Andilly, *Memoires pour servir à l'histoire de Port-Royal, et à la vie de la Reverende Mere Marie Angelique de Sainte Magdeleine Arnauld Reformatrice de ce Monastere* (2 vols. Utrecht, Aux depens de la Compagnie, 1742), vol. I, p. 53.   30 Maurice Halbwachs, *On collective memory*, edited, translated and with an introduction by Lewis A. Coser, *The heritage of sociology* (Chicago and London, 1992, originally published as *Les cadres sociaux de la mémoire*, Paris, 1952), p. 79.   31 The *Constitutions de Port-Royal* were drafted by Mère Agnès Arnauld and Sr Jacqueline de Sainte-Euphemie Pascal (Blaise Pascal's sister), following Mère

> That they examine their hearts carefully to see if they have a similar feeling of love for each member of the community, that they do not have strong affection for certain nuns and feelings of coldness towards others ...[32]

Furthermore, the *Constitutions* reminded nuns that before criticising their fellow-sisters, they should remember the Christian maxim that one was not to comment on the chip in a sister's eye while being unaware of the block of wood impeding one's own vision. They were commanded to guard against any tendency to criticise fellow-sisters unjustly but rather to approach their relationships with humility and charity.[33] While they should not burden their fellow-sisters with inappropriate confidences, neither should they make a practice of having unnecessary secrets.[34] The *Constitutions*' provisions might be interpreted as an attempt to guard against inappropriate friendships or lesbian relationships. However, if observed as specified, it is possible to see how they could have helped to avoid divisions and to foster instead a strong sense of communal sisterhood.

The reform at Port-Royal may have encouraged an atmosphere of solidarity among nuns but it often did so at the expense of the individual. Priority was accorded to self-abnegation in the belief that the conquest of individual desires and preferences could assist the process of spiritual development. The encouragement of self-abnegation may have fostered consideration for others but the methods used to encourage this sense of self-abasement often provided the occasion for what appears today as bullying and cruelty by the leading figures of the community. Jérôme Besoigne's description of the priority given by Mère Agnès, the novice-mistress, to the elimination of 'amour-propre' among the nuns appears rather chilling, notwithstanding the hagiographic nature of his account: 'She strove particularly to destroy the smallest particle of self-love and egotism both in herself and in others.'[35]

It was the experience of persecution which, by throwing existing structures within the community into disarray, served to highlight the importance of sisterhood. When the principal officers of the community were imprisoned by the archbishop of Paris in August 1664, the community became leaderless and

---

Angélique's directions, and with the assistance of Mère Angélique de Saint-Jean Arnauld. See F. Ellen Weaver, *The evolution of the reform of Port-Royal from the rule of Cîteaux to Jansenism*.   **32** 'Qu'elles sondent humblement le fond de leur cœur au regard de la charité en considerant si elles l'ont égale & universelle envers leurs Sœurs, si elles n'ont point une affection trop sensible pour les unes & de la froideur pour les autres ...' Mère Agnès de Saint-Paul Arnauld, *Les constitutions du monastère de Port-Royal du Saint-Sacrement* (Mons, 1665), p. 36.   **33** Idem, p. 26.   **34** Ibid., p. 54.   **35** 'Car elle n'avoit rien tant à coeur que de détruire & dans elle & dans les autres jusqu'aux plus petites fibres de l'amour propre & de la recherche de soi-même.' Besoigne, *Histoire*, vol.

ordinary sisters were forced to make personal decisions as to whether or not they should sign the Formulary. It was at this point that the particular conception of sisterhood fostered at Port-Royal came to be more significant than the experience of operating within a hierarchical power model. A tradition of privileging the community at the expense of the individual, of creating communal rather than individual bonds, of eliminating self-love ensured that the community essentially acted as a collective unit, despite the removal of its leaders. The archbishop of Paris had been convinced that when the principal officers were removed, the ordinary nuns would cease, as he considered it, to be duped by the manipulation of their female superiors[36] and would submit to his orders. He was amazed when only 7 of the 75 nuns agreed to sign by September 1664.[37] His surprise was shared by Mère Angélique de Saint-Jean who later wrote that she was less surprised by the number of nuns who signed the Formulary than by the fact that the majority did not: 'I found it much less strange that some should succumb than that a great number should remain firm.'[38]

I would argue that resistance was maintained because of the strength of the emotional bonds linking the nuns, not out of obedience to their leaders. Certain key figures, gifted with the ability to inspire and motivate others, such as Christine Briquet or Eustoquie de Flécelles de Brégy, did become prominent within the community in 1664. However, their role remained motivational in nature as they did not appropriate for themselves more conventional leadership positions. Christine Briquet saw her role more as one of offering support to her fellow-sisters. As she indicated in a letter written in 1664:

> all my time has been spent talking to one nun and then to another, trying to foster mutual support and strength. I could not possibly deny this support to those sisters who seek it from me, no matter how incapable I feel of satisfying their needs. Leaderless as we are, and exposed to all sorts of dangers, we will only be able to maintain our stance if we preserve the unity that God has established between us.[39]

I, p. 120.   36 Gaston Chamillard, the Sorbonne theologian imposed as their spiritual director, also firmly believed that the nuns resisted simply because they had been brainwashed by their leaders. See Gaston Chamillard, *Response aux raisons que les religieuses de Port-Royal proposent contre la signature du Formulaire avec leurs maximes et leur esprit* (Paris, F. Muguet, 1665), pp. 29–30.   37 These seven signed on 12 September 1664. See Jean Orcibal, *Port-Royal entre le miracle et l'obéissance: Flavie Passart et Angélique Arnauld d'Andilly*, Desclée de Brouwer, no place indicated, 1957, p. 61. While further nuns signed the Formulary and later retracted their signatures, only 9 nuns maintained their submission permanently.   38 'je trouvois bien moins étrange qu'il y en eût quelques-unes qui y succombassent, que non pas qu'il y en eût un si grand nombre, qui demeurassent fermes.' Angélique de Saint-Jean Arnauld d'Andilly, *Relation de la captivité de la M. Angélique de St-Jean* (no place indicated, 1711), p. 59.   39 'tout mon loisir à été employé à parler aux unes & aux autres, pour nous entr'aider & fortifier. Je

The available evidence suggests that both she and Eustoquie were acutely conscious of the collective nature of the Port-Royal resistance, of the necessity for unity rather than personal ambition and it is interesting that once pressure against the community ended, neither sought formal leadership positions within the monastery. The collective nature of the nuns' resistance was demonstrated concretely in their practice of gaining collective approval for resistance texts such as their various appeals to the Parlement de Paris, their public protests against the archbishop's actions and affidavits.[40] While Gaston Chamillard, the spiritual director appointed by the archbishop, sought to prove that most nuns were being duped into resistance by their leaders, Christine Briquet was careful to stress that the resistance had the community's full support. When he accused her of drawing up an affidavit without consulting her fellow-sisters, she responded that, in fact, the affidavit had been released only after it had been agreed by the community as a whole: 'I assure you that this was prepared in consultation with all of the community and that each nun signed the document only after having agreed that it was truly accurate.'[41]

Evidence suggests that nuns were routinely consulted on documents issued in the name of the community – Sr Elisabeth-Agnès mentions, for instance, in one letter that some elements of an agreed declaration had been softened to take into account the concerns of certain sisters and to ensure that they could support the text.[42] The importance of consultative practices during that period is underlined by the request made by the nuns in an appeal to *Monseigneurs de Parlement de Paris* in 1664 to be granted the right to private parlours within their monastery where they could consult one another freely without interference from the Visitation nuns imposed by the archbishop of Paris. That texts

---

n'oserois refuser cela aux Sœurs qui le désirent de moi, quelque incapable que je sois de les satisfaire; car étant délaissées & exposées à toutes sortes de périls comme nous sommes, nous ne pouvant plus nous maintenir qu'en conservant l'union que Dieu a établie parmi nous …' *Relation contenant les lettres*, p. 57 in *Divers actes*.   40 Documents which were collectively prepared included a daily journal, recording the measures taken against the community and justifying their resistance. The journal of the period from 1665 until 1669, for instance, was subsequently printed as *Journaux de ce qui s'est passé a Port-Royal, depuis que la Communauté fut transferée à Port-Royal des Champs, jusques à la paix qui leur fut renduë en 1669*. The printed version of this text is to be found in *Divers actes*. Other collective records of this type include the *Relation de ce qui s'est passé à Port-Royal depuis le commencement d'Avril 1661. jusqu'au 27. du même mois de l'année suivante 1663. où l'on rapporte les dispositions de la Communauté au sujet des deux Mandemens de Messieurs les Grand-Vicaires de Monseigneur le Cardinal de Rets* which is also to be found in *Divers actes*.   41 'je vous assure qu'il a été bien concerté avec toute la Communauté, & qu'on ne l'a point signé qu'après être demeurées d'accord qu'il n'y avoit rien que de très-veritable.' *Relation contenant les lettres*, p. 36 in *Divers actes*.   42 As she said in her letter : 'il a fallu adoucir quelques mots … afin d'ôter les scrupules de quelques unes de nos Sœurs.' 'it has been necessary to soften some words … in order to meet the concerns

prepared through this consultative process were intended to represent the views of the community as a whole rather than those of individual nuns is confirmed by the practice which they developed of collectively signing almost all of the public documents drafted at Port-Royal during the period.[43] This practice was adopted once again by the nuns during the final years of pressure from 1706 until 1709 when they published pamphlets attempting to appeal to public opinion to prevent the destruction of the monastery.[44]

While emphasis was placed on communal solidarity, it is interesting that the key resistance figures were bound by close relationships with one another. An intense emotional bond was evident between Christine Briquet and Angélique de Saint-Jean. At the end of her captivity Christine Briquet was informed in July 1665 that she was to be transferred to the convent of St Marie du Faubourg, where she would join the other Port-Royal nuns who had been released from captivity so that they might all be removed together to Port-Royal des Champs. As she was escorted to the gate, she was told that another nun was waiting in the carriage. Her account tells of how she longed that the nun in the carriage would be Angélique de Saint-Jean. Her description of the joy which she experienced on discovering that her prayers had been answered reveals a notion of an inspirational sisterhood in which Angélique de Saint-Jean lovingly coached her fellow-sister along the path to salvation:

> My strong desire that it should be one of the people to whom I am closest, with the exception of God, convinced me that I was going to find Sr Angélique in the carriage and I was not disappointed as it was she, and if the darkness of the night prevented me from seeing her face and obliged me to ask if it was truly she, I had no sooner heard her voice, which I easily recognised, than the infinite mercy of God bestowed its grace on me and I felt that the eternal sun was returning to me the person who had been given to me to guide my steps and to teach me to walk along the path of His commandments and His truth.[45]

---

of some of our nuns'. She went on to stress that all had signed freely. Idem, p. 53. **43** Examples of texts collectively signed include *Declaration des Religieuses de Port-Royal, touchant leurs actes qui ont été imprimez* (no place indicated, 1664). **44** Documents which were signed collectively and printed during the final years of the community include *Requeste presentée au Roy par les Religieuses du Port-Royal des Champs en mars 1707*, (no place indicated, 1707) and *Requeste presentée à son Eminence Monseigneur le Cardinal de Noailles Archevêque de Paris, par les Religieuses du Port-Royal des Champs au mois d'octobre 1707* (no place indicated, 1707). **45** 'Le desir que j'avois que ce fut une des personnes qui m'est tout apres Dieu me fit croire que j'y allois trouver ma Sr Angelique, et je ne m'y trompay pas, elle y étoit en effet, et si les tenebres de la nuit m'empecherent de voir son visage, et mobligerent de lui demander si cétoit elle, je n'eus pas plutost entendu sa voix quil me fut facile de reconnoitre, que la misericorde infinie de Dieu me visitoit par sa grace, et que ce soleil éternel me rendoit celle qu'il ma donnée pour eclairer mes pas,

The respect felt by the community for Angélique de Saint-Jean and her inspirational qualities of leadership is reflected in a comment by Sr Geneviève Pineau in 1664, which confirms the close emotional bonds between Angélique de Saint-Jean and the other resistance figures: 'few have a love like hers which is of burning gold, fearing nothing and surmounting everything.'[46]

The strong emotional bond binding Geneviève and Christine to Angélique de Saint-Jean is also evident in wider community relationships. These persisted not only among choir-sisters but also among the *Sœurs Converses* (lay sisters) who, according to Sr Eustoquie, offered unwavering support to the resisters and declared themselves ready to leave the monastery rather than assist the signatories or the Visitation nuns then in control.[47] Loyalty prevented nuns from considering possible submission. However, if resistance was seen as much as a sign of loyalty as the outcome of the individual's personal choice, then those who signed were perceived as traitors who gained personally from their capitulation. Divisions between the first 7 signatories and the resisting majority became particularly acute when the archbishop chose to appoint some of those who had signed to positions made vacant by those who were now in captivity.[48] Loyalty to those sisters who had been legitimately elected by the community can be seen in the determination of resisters to try to prevent those who had signed from occupying these offices. In an appeal to the Parlement de Paris in 1664, for example, they protested strongly against the removal of their fellow-sisters by the archbishop on 26 August and against his decision to depose officers legitimately appointed under canon law and to substitute in their place nuns from the Visitation order 'who exercise a tyrannical domination in their monastery, without any legitimate authority'.[49] Stressing that there was 'no act more criminal than to remove the existing office-holders and to substitute others in their place',[50] referring in particular to the assumption of official posts by those who had been 'gagnées' (won to the opposing side), the appeal requested furthermore that the seven signatories specifically named in the appeal – 'Flavie, Dorothée, Euphromie, Philiberte, Catherine, Pelagie et Isabelle des Anges' – be removed from these charges pending the outcome of the various appeals lodged by the resisters.[51] The bitterness felt against them by

---

et m'apprendre à marcher dans la voye de ses commandemens et de la verité.' PR 66 – *Relation de ma Sr de Ste. Christine Briquet*, p. 96.   **46** 'tout le monde n'a pas comme elle cet or brulant de la charité qui ne craint rien & qui surmonte tout.' *Relation contenant les lettres*, p. 63 in *Divers actes*.   **47** Idem, p. 46.   **48** Sr Flavie Passart, for instance, was given the post of *sous-prieure* or deputy-prioress on 24 September 1664. See Jean Orcibal, *Port-Royal*, p. 61.   **49** 'qui exercent dans leur Maison une domination tirannique, sans aucun pouvoir legitime', *A Monseigneurs de Parlement*, no place indicated, [1664], [an unpaginated manuscript held at the Bibliothèque Sainte-Geneviève in Paris].   **50** 'rien de plus abusif que cette deposition et substitution de ces officieres'.   **51** It is interesting that even as late as August 1717, when it was proposed

resisters is reflected in a remark by Sr Marguerite de Sainte Thècle Racine, an aunt of the playwright, Jean Racine, and a future abbess of Port-Royal, who stated that of all the crimes perpetuated against Port-Royal, that of the betrayal by fellow-sisters was the worst. As she said: 'God may pardon them but their crime is appalling.'[52]

That the decision to sign was regarded as an act of betrayal rather than the product of reasoned, independent choice confirms the importance of communal solidarity for the nuns' continued resistance. However, the communal dynamic could operate in both directions. If the strong bonds between sisters helped to maintain a united stance of communal resistance, the sisterhood ties might also persuade nuns to sign the Formulary if led by nuns to whom they were close. Sr Geneviève Pineau recounted how Sr Magdeleine de Sainte-Melthide's signature, for instance, was perceived to have the potential to persuade waverers to abandon their resistance. 'Her fall has inspired dread in the minds of our sisters ... we have reason to fear that the weakest will be further weakened by this example.'[53]

Since the collective resistance stance was built upon the close emotional bonds between sisters and since key resistance figures saw the potential danger of even one additional signature, it was inevitable that the nuns who played a key role in trying to persuade others to sign would be viewed as a particular threat. The nun who acted as a spy for the archbishop and who sought most actively to get others to sign the Formulary was Sr Flavie Passart. When she saw, for instance, that Sr Marie-Angélique de Sainte-Thérèse Arnauld d'Andilly was reluctant to engage in resistance, she attempted to convince her to sign the Formulary by saying on 3 August 1664 that she had received a vision in which Jansenius had exhorted her, through a process of quasi automatic writings, to transcribe a message, exhorting the nuns to humility.[54] Flavie Passart's actions ensured that she was generally portrayed as a 'traîtresse' in the nuns' writings.[55]

The level of bitterness occasioned by her actions can be seen in two manuscript texts written by Angélique de Saint-Jean which lift the veil on the

---

that Sr Marie de Sainte Anne Le Couturier, Sr Françoise de Sainte Agathe Le Juge and Denise de Sainte Basilisse Noiseux, who had recently been transferred to Malnouë, should be brought back to Port-Royal de Paris where the abbess, Mère de Monperoux, was anxious to incorporate them into the community, they refused to return to Port-Royal because this would involve recognising what they still regarded as the original usurpation of their convent in 1665. *Suplément au Nécrologe de l'Abbaïe de Notre-Dame de Port-Roïal des Champs, Ordre de Cîteaux, Institut du St-Sacrement* (no place indicated, 1735), p. 269.   **52** 'Dieu leur pardonne, mais le crime est épouvantable', *Relation contenant les lettres*, p. 44 in *Divers actes.*   **53** 'Cette chûte a repandu une frayeur dans tous les esprits de nos Sœurs ... Nous avons sujet de craindre que les plus foibles ne s'affoiblissent encore d'avantage par cet exemple.' idem, p. 62.   **54** Orcibal, *Port-Royal*, p. 24.   **55** Ibid., p. 24.

inner tensions within the community. Both texts – a *Relation de quelques circonstances de la vie des srs Flavie et Dorothée* and a *Recit fidelle des miracles et visions de la Soeur Flavie* written in 1666 – present, as can be expected, rather caricatural depictions of Flavie and demonstrate the anger of Angélique de Saint-Jean towards the woman who had broken communal solidarity. She is characterised as a woman who sinned more out of ambition than ignorance.[56] She was accused of having insinuated her way deviously into the post of mistress of boarders by bullying the previous incumbent, Anne-Eugénie Arnauld, Angélique de Saint-Jean's aunt.[57] Once in a position of responsibility, she had then instituted a tyrannical regime bullying the children in her care.[58] That Angélique de Saint-Jean's bitterness towards Flavie Passart was shared by other nuns is reflected in the admission by Sr Elisabeth Agnès Le Féron that she could not bear even to look at Flavie: 'I have to admit to you that I cannot look at her without feeling upset'.[59] Given the level of hostility towards Flavie Passart, it is understandable if others were prevented from submitting to the archbishop's authority out of fear that their emotional bonds with their fellow-sisters might be severed as a consequence.

While the nuns were much less bitter towards another signatory, Sr Magdelaine de Sainte-Melthide Thomas du Fossé, who was probably unique in vacillating between non-signature, signature, retraction, signature and retraction once more, they also saw her signature as a sign of sinfulness rather than as the outcome of a personal choice. Sr Geneviève Pineau viewed Magdelaine de Sainte-Melthide's signature, for instance, as a sign of the community's unworthiness, revealing the presence of a notion of collective culpability which was the corollary of the communal solidarity binding sisters together: 'we used all means given to us by God to support her but this was futile since we were not worthy of gaining this grace from God for her or for us.'[60]

---

56 PR 38 – Angélique de Saint-Jean Arnauld d'Andilly, *Relation de quelques circonstances de la vie des srs Flavie et Dorothée, et de ce que la premiere a été capable de faire un an devant leur enlevement, ou se trouve la refutation de quelques endroits d'un livre qui a paru pendant leur captivité avec privilege rempli de calomies ou il paroit que cette Sr y avoit une grande part*, no place indicated |1666| [A manuscript in the handwriting of Angélique de Saint-Jean and held at the Bibliothèque de Port-Royal], p. 13 [pagination added later]. **57** Angélique de Saint-Jean Arnauld d'Andilly, *Suite des precedentes relations ou l'on rapporte dautres circonstances omises de la vie de ma soeur Anne-Eugenie de lincarnation Arnauld et sa mort* [PR 20 – a collection of miscellaneous manuscript accounts of the lives of some of the Port-Royal nuns held at the Bibliothèque de Port-Royal], pp. 175–6. **58** 'cette fille changea la Conduite si chrestienne et si charitable que l'on avoit tenue jusqu'a lors a Port Royal dans leducation des Enfans en un gouvernement qu'on peut appeler tirannique, …'. 'this sister changed the very Christian and charitable conduct that had hitherto characterised the education offered to children at Port-Royal into a regime that might be described as tyrannical', idem, pp. 176–7. **59** 'je vous avouë que je ne la puis voir sans grande peine …', *Relation contenant les lettres*, p. 42 in *Divers actes*. **60** 'nous avons employé tout ce que

Sr Magdelaine de Sainte-Melthide felt herself that she was viewed as a traitor by the community once she signed the Formulary. She revealed how she was considered by the others as dead to the community once she had signed the Formulary and was accordingly shunned. As she indicated in a letter to the archbishop published in January 1665 when she had decided to sign once again, her fellow-sisters' hostile treatment was partially responsible for the retraction of her original signature as her misery at capitulation was exacerbated by feelings of separation and isolation from the community.[61] When she retracted her signature for the first time, the resisters seized on this retraction as a potential propaganda tool and had her letter of retraction printed publicly in 1664. While the printed text, the *Lettre de la Sœur Magdelaine de Ste Melthide, R. de P.R. a Monseigneur l'Archevesque de Paris. Au sujet de la retractation de sa signature du Formulaire*,[62] emphasised how she had freely arrived at the decision to retract her signature, it is evident that the primary motivating factor was that of her relationship with the community. In this document, she described how the evident happiness felt by her fellow-sisters who had maintained their resistance had convinced her to retract her submission while their prayers and affection now strengthened her resolve.[63] The degree to which her affection for her fellow-sisters influenced Sr Magdelaine de Sainte-Melthide can be gauged by the fact that she described herself as in tears at the thought that she had permission to go to communion at a time when her sisters were deprived of it.[64] The influence of communal relationships is reiterated again and again in her text. Though fear of dying while being denied the sacraments had prompted her signature, only a factor as strong as the terror of eternal damnation could overcome her latent desire to be a part of her community and to follow its example. She stressed how she would have:

> very much wished to follow the community perfectly, and, in particular, the admirable example of firmness and constancy demonstrated by our

Dieu nous a donné, pour la soûtenir, mais inutilement, car nous n'avons pas été dignes d'obtenir cette grace de Dieu pour elle & pour nous.' *Relation contenant les lettres*, p. 61 in *Divers actes*. 61 Magdelaine de Ste Melthide Thomas du Fossé, *Lettres de la Sœur Magdeleine de Sainte Melthide, religieuse de Port-Royal, a Monseigneur l'Archevesque de Paris et aux religieuses de Port-Royal ses sœurs. Par lesquelles, elle témoigne la douleur qu'elle a d'avoir retracté sa premiere signature, & la disposition où elle est de signer tout de nouveau, sans jamais estre capable de retomber en sa premiere faute* (Paris, F. Muguet, 1665), p. 5. 62 Magdelaine de Ste Melthide Thomas du Fossé, *Lettre de la Sœur Magdelaine de Ste Melthide, R. de P.R. A Monseigneur l'Archevesque de Paris. Au sujet de la retractation de sa signature du Formulaire* (no place indicated [1664]). A date of 22 November 1664 is given at the end of this text. 63 As she says in the pamphlet: 'j'ay toûjours crû que mes Sœurs qui estoient demeurées fermes estoient bien plus heureuses que moy ...'. 'I always believed that my sisters who had remained firm were much happier than me' idem, pp. 4–5. 64 Ibid., p. 6.

dear mothers and sisters who, both within and outside the community, suffered so willingly for the Truth.[65]

The importance of her community's example in influencing her first retraction was explicitly underlined in her subsequent letter to the archbishop on the occasion of her second signature in which she attributed her first retraction to the communal dynamic:

> I do not lie, my Lord, when I say that it was a great temptation to me to find myself among my sisters whose firm resistance was unshakeable, particularly as I was convinced of their sincerity and considered myself through the act of signature to be separated in a certain manner from them.'[66]

That she too saw her signature as a betrayal of her community is confirmed in her statement that she felt it necessary to make a public retraction of her signature, recognising that she had committed a sin against all of her fellow-sisters: 'I feel obliged to prostrate myself before His Divine Majesty to acknowledge to all of my sisters and to the Church the sin which I committed ...'[67]

The final confirmation of the community's influence on individual decisions is provided by the fact that Magdelaine de Sainte-Melthide signed the Formulary on the second occasion only when the archbishop of Paris removed her from the community's control and sent her to the Visitation order where she was placed under severe pressure to submit. Those who were forcibly separated from the community were most at risk of submitting, since isolation and fear broke their resistance, confirming the importance of communal support in sustaining an individual's resistance. Sr Marie-Angélique de Sainte-Thérèse Arnauld d'Andilly is an example of one of those who signed when in captivity, although she retracted very quickly thereafter. Like Sr Magdelaine de Sainte-Melthide, Sr Marie-Angélique de Sainte-Thérèse submitted primarily because she was afraid that without the grace offered to her in the sacraments, her own human weakness would not be enough on its own to bring her to salvation.[68]

---

[65] 'bien desiré de suivre en tout la communauté, & l'exemple loüable de la fermeté & de la constance de nos tres-cheres Meres & Sœurs, qui dedans & dehors souffrent si genereusement pour la verité', Magdelaine de Sainte Melthide Thomas du Fossé, *Lettre de la Sœur Magdelaine de Ste Melthide*, [1664], p. 2. [66] 'Mais sans mentir, MONSEIGNEUR, ce m'estoit une grande tentation de me voir au milieu de toutes mes Sœurs, qui estoient dans une fermeté inébranlable, sur tout estant persuadée de leur bonne conscience, & me voyant par ma Signature en quelque façon separée d'elles.' Magdelaine de Sainte Melthide Thomas du Fossé, *Lettres de la Sœur Magdeleine de Sainte Melthide* (1665), p. 5. [67] 'Je me sens obligée de me prosterner devant la Majesté Divine pour reconnoistre devant toutes mes sœurs et à la face de l'Eglise, la faute que j'ay faite & commise ...', *Lettre de la Sœur Magdelaine de Ste Melthide*, [1664], p. 7. [68] Marie-Angélique de Sainte-Thérèse Arnauld d'Andilly, *Relation de la Sœur Marie*

While Marie-Angélique de Sainte-Thérèse signed the Formulary only so that she could receive the sacraments, she was immediately paralysed by guilt. If she felt that she did not have the confidence to continue as an 'outcast' within the Catholic Church, neither could she ignore the reality that her signature separated her from her community. She became unable to receive communion because of her guilt (like that of Sr Magdeleine de Sainte-Melthide) at being accorded a privilege denied to her sisters.[69] As her reaction demonstrates, she was horrified by her action not only because it signaled her consent to Jansen's condemnation but also because it was a source of pain for the Port-Royal circle, particularly for her fellow-nuns:

> The declaration seemed like a real trap to me while my *acquiescence in the condemnation* appalled me ... together with the scandal that I had given to all friends of the Truth, and, in particular to my very dear sisters, [it] made me see the abyss into which I had fallen.'[70]

That her sense of devastation at causing her community pain could have caused her to rethink her signature, notwithstanding her fear of damnation, shows how important group solidarity remained for the Port-Royal nuns in maintaining their capacity for resistance. Sr Marie-Angélique de Sainte-Thérèse's account confirms the linkage between sisterhood and resistance particularly her description of her return to Port-Royal des Champs in July 1665. What emerges from her account is her acute sense of guilt at having 'failed' her community (in spite of the fact that she had by that stage retracted her signature) and her intense need for affirmation from her fellow-sisters, her wish to be enfolded once again in the sisterhood of Port-Royal. As in Magdelaine de Sainte-Melthide's account, what is stressed is the strong example provided by those who never wavered in their resistance, the influence of that example on those who submitted and their fear of being rejected by the community. Marie-Angélique de Sainte-Thérèse described her emotional response to her return journey as follows:

> The happiness of my companions who had remained faithful seemed so great that it re-opened my wound, especially when I saw our dear sisters in the carriages: I considered them to be saints, seeing myself as a poor sinner. I was delighted to return with them, although I was also somewhat

Angelique de Sainte Therese Arnauld d'Andilly, sur l'enlevement & la captivité de la Mere Catherine Agnés de Saint Paul Arnauld sa tante, avec laquelle elle fut mise au Monastere de Sainte Marie du Faubourg Saint Jacques à Paris, p. 36 in *Divers actes*.   **69** Idem, pp. 46–7, 49.   **70** 'La Déclaration me parut un veritable piege, *l'acquiescement à la condamnation* me faisoit une frayeur horrible, [...] joint au scandale que j'avois donné à tous les amis de la verité, & en particulier à mes très-cheres Sœurs, me firent voir l'abîme où j'étois

apprehensive, fearing that they would be distant with me because of what I had done; … but instead they received me with so much love and friendship that my gratitude will last, please God, until my final breath. I threw myself at our dear mothers' and sisters' feet, demanding pardon from them very humbly for having scandalised and hurt them.[71]

Not only did the nuns themselves recognise the importance of their sisterhood ties in influencing their actions, the authorities also regarded the bonds of solidarity between the nuns as an important element in their resistance. Accordingly, they consistently sought to persuade resisters to sign the Formulary by trying to persuade them of their isolation from the community. News of any possible future submission was relayed, particularly to those in captivity, to undermine their resolve. Like others in captivity, Sr Christine Briquet was given news of submission of other sisters – for example, she was forced to read a letter from Sr Elisabeth Agnès Le Féron in favour of signature.[72] Similarly, a false rumour was circulated to Port-Royal de Paris in 1664 that Mère Agnès Arnauld, one of the original reformers of Port-Royal taken into captivity with other leaders of the community, had signed the Formulary. This rumour appears to have been circulated in order to weaken the nuns' resistance and it certainly affected them acutely, although, in the end, it did not weaken their resistance permanently. The shock of the news is reflected in a letter written by Sr Eustoquie de Flécelles de Brégy:

> Who would not tremble? Who would not fear when one sees the fall of someone from the race from which one would have hoped for the salvation of Israel. It is the most acute pain in the world.[73]

This strategy was not unique to the 1660s resistance. Conscious of the impact that capitulation by senior figures or by the majority of the community might have on resisters, Archbishop Hardouin de Péréfixe's successors repeatedly adopted a similar strategy two generations later of focusing on communal resistance and seeking to convince recalcitrant nuns of the isolation of their

tombée,' ibid., p. 45. 71 'Le bonheur de celles avec qui j'étois & qui étoient demeurées fidelles, me sembloit si grand, que cela rouvrit ma plaie, sur tout qand je vis nos cheres Sœurs dans les carrosses: je les considerois comme des saintes, au lieu que je me voyois une pauvre pecheresse: j'étois ravie de retourner avec elles, & je l'apprehendois un peu, craignant que ce que j'avois fait ne leur donnât de l'éloignement pour moi; … mais elles me reçurent avec tant de charité & d'amitié, que j'en ai une reconnoissance qui durera, s'il plait à Dieu, jusqu'au dernier soupir de ma vie. Je me jettai aux pieds de nos cheres Meres & de nos cheres Sœurs, & leur demandai trés-humblement pardon de les avoir scandalisées & affligées.' ibid., p. 45. 72 *Relation de la Soeur Madeleine de Ste Christine Briquet, religieuse de Port-Royal, sur sa captivité*, p. 110 in *Divers actes*. 73 'Qui ne tremblera? Qui ne craindra, lors que l'on voit ceux de la race par laquelle on esperoit le salut d'Israël tomber. C'est une douleur la plus sensible au monde.' *Relation contenant les*

position. Sr Anne de Sainte-Cécile Boiscervoise's submission has already been mentioned at the beginning of this article. The profound shock occasioned by the suppression of the Port-Royal community, the physical destruction of its monastic buildings and the dispersal of its nuns into other communities did trigger a number of submissions in 1710. Once again, as with the previous generation of resisters, nuns kept apart from their fellow-sisters in captivity in hostile communities, found it difficult to maintain their resistance. However, it should be noted that many of the nuns who signed the Formulary such as Sr Marie de Sainte Anne Cousturier,[74] Sr Marie-Madeleine de Sainte Sophie de Flécelles,[75] Sr Françoise de Sainte Agathe Le Juge[76] and Sr Denise de Sainte Basilisse Noiseux[77] almost immediately regretted their submission and prepared written acts of retraction.

In what could be interpreted as a recognition of the link between communal solidarity and resistance, the ecclesiastical authorities took the decision to communicate news of these submissions to the remaining recalcitrants, probably in the hope that an acceleration in the momentum of submission would convince the final resisters of the futility of their cause. The strategy of using the submissions of other sisters as a lever to force the signature of remaining resisters was explicitly employed to break down Sr Marie-Magdelaine de Sainte-Cécile Bertrand's resistance. Sr Marie-Magdelaine, who had been sent to the monastery of the Visitation at Amiens, refused firmly for five months. In response, M. de Pontchartrain made the bishop of Amiens aware of the submission of the other exiled nuns in the hope that these examples would influence her. The tactic was successful and she submitted on 27 March 1710.[78] One of the remaining non-signatories, Mère Louise de Sainte Anastasie du Mesnil, for instance, was told on her death-bed in 1716 that, as the majority of her sisters had now returned to the church, she would alone carry the penalty before God for having inspired resistance to the commandments of the church.

> Most of your sisters have returned to the bosom of the church: you are the only one on whom the terrible punishment will fall, the person who alone will bear God's punishment for having inspired their disobedience and stubborn pride.[79]

lettres, p. 23 in *Divers actes*.   **74** A manuscript copy (PR 241) of an 'acte de rétractation' by Sr Marie de Sainte Anne Cousturier, dated 1717 is still extant in the *Ancien Fonds d'Amersfoort – Collection 'Port-Royal et Unigenitus'*, a collection of Jansenist material held at the Rijksarchief in Utrecht.   **75** The retraction of her signature which she made in writing on 8 September 1714 is contained in *Suplément au Nécrologe*, pp. 152–6.   **76** Part of a manuscript confirming her retraction of her signature as early as 20 May 1710 is extant in the *Ancien Fonds d'Amersfoort* (PR 259).   **77** Evidence of the latter nun's retractions is to be found in the *Suplément au Nécrologe*, pp. 270–1.   **78** J. Corblet, *Notice sur quatre religieuses de Port-Royal-des-Champs exilées dans divers monastères d'Amiens* (Amiens, 1861), pp. 13–14.   **79** 'La plûpart de vos Sœurs son rentrées dans son

It is not the aim of this article to suggest that bonds of sisterhood were the only factor in Port-Royal's resistance. However, as this causal factor has been largely overlooked, it seems appropriate to devote some attention to the connections linking communal solidarity with the maintenance of resistance. While this article has focused on 1664 and 1665, the importance of sisterly loyalty in pursuit of a common aim remained one of the characteristics of the Port-Royal resistance in subsequent years. Similarly, in subsequent decades, the community became aware of the importance of creating a record of their collective resistance, both to underline the injustice of their persecution but also possibly to demonstrate the strength of a sisterhood united in a common purpose. The available evidence would appear to suggest that close emotional ties, combined with a tradition of communal solidarity, created a sisterhood capable of sustaining a campaign of resistance which served in a certain sense to empower those involved. Notwithstanding their difficulties, the women of Port-Royal seem to have developed a notion of active sisterhood which transcended the tests of external pressure, internal rivalry and hierarchical structures and can be viewed as the triumph of solidarity over adversity.

---

sein: il n'y aura donc que vous sur qui le mauvais sort tombera, & qui porterez seule devant Dieu la peine de leur avoir inspiré votre désobéïssance & votre entêtement.' *Relation de la vie et de la mort de la Reverende Mere de Ste Anastasie, derniere prieure de P.R. des Champs* (no place or date indicated), pp. 12–14.

'Hyr wombe insaciate': the iconography of the feminised monster

Samantha J.E. Riches

In 1552 the German engraver Peter Gottland created a piece of visual propaganda based on the battle between St George and the dragon as a commentary on the Reformation (figure 1). In this image the role of St George is played by the infant Christ, who rescues the True, or Reformed, Church (the princess) from an evil many-headed monster.[1] The dragon wears a papal tiara on one of its heads; this clearly identifies the creature as a figure of both the Roman Church in general and the pope in particular. However, Gottland's characterisation of the dragon is more complex than a simplistic identification with the 'false' Church of Rome, and plays on several well-established *topoi* within late medieval and early modern popular understandings of monsters and the monstrous.

Most obviously, Gottland's dragon is a composite beast. The combination of a human head (or, as here, heads) and the body of an animal is a standard formula in the presentation of monsters; this image goes rather further by endowing the dragon with humanised hands as well. The serpentine necks are also a borrowing from one type of creature into another: most significantly, it plays on the Biblical association of snakes with evil and underlines the extent to which conceptions of dragons were based on fears of snakes.[2] Meanwhile, the creature's position (on its back, with the horse's hooves poised threateningly above), indicates complete subjection; again this is an important visual trope, particularly in treatments of St George and the dragon. However, for our purposes here the most salient factor in the presentation of the dragon is its possession of a clearly-defined breast, and hence its identification as a female

---

[1] The allegory plays, perhaps unconsciously, on the iconography of St George in the early Greek Church where the saint was a form of Christ, rescuing the princess Ecclesia (the Church) from the clutches of the Devil.   [2] Bartholomew Anglicus' statement that dragons are the 'the most greatest of all serpents' seems to have been typical. Robert Steele (ed.), *Medieval lore: an epitome of the science, geography, animal and plant folk-lore and myth of the Middle Age: being classified gleanings from the encyclopaedia of Bartholomew Anglicus on the properties of things* (London, 1893), pp. 124–5.

1 Peter Gottland, St George and the Dragon – *Allegory of the Triumph of the New Faith over the Old* (1552)

beast and also, arguably, a sexualised creature. The *topos* of the feminised and/or sexualised beast is by no means the most commonly-occurring feature of the iconography of the monstrous, but it occurs with sufficient frequency that we should perhaps think of it as one of a number of options available to the image-maker, and one that is potentially freighted with significance.

The earliest use of the trope of the feminised monster is unclear, but it is notable that the creation epic of the Babylonian civilisation, which flourished between 1750 BC and 539 BC, featured Tiāmat, a dragon-like female spirit of salt water who was associated with primeval chaos.[3] The narrative related that at the

---

[3] A simplified version of the Babylonian creation epic is related in the context of other early dragon narratives in Peter Hogarth with Val Clery, *Dragons* (London, 1979), pp. 15–19. For a more detailed analysis see the entry 'Tiāmat' by B. Alster in K. van der Torn, B. Becking and P.W. van der Horst, *Dictionary of deities and demons in the Bible*

beginning of time two elemental forces existed: Tiāmat and her counterpart Apsu, who was a male spirit of fresh water. The coupling of these two entities produced a vast and ill-assorted brood of gods, some of whom grew up to antagonise their father so much that he threatened to kill them. One of the young gods then murdered Apsu in a pre-emptive strike, whereupon the enraged Tiāmat turned upon her offspring. To aid her vengeful fight she spawned a group of monsters – serpents, dragons and composite beasts such as the centaur and the scorpion-man – in preparation for a great battle. A descendant of one of Tiāmat's first brood, Marduk, emerged as a champion prepared to fight his progenitor in single combat, on condition that he should be made king of the universe if he triumphed. An epic struggle ensued, and Marduk emerged as the victor. He killed the matriarch and all her monsters, then created heaven and earth before fashioning the first people from the blood of a god.

The combat between Marduk and Tiāmat seems to be the original *topos* on which many subsequent tales of heroes and dragons were modelled, although the motif of dragon-as-mother, and specifically mother-of-hero, was generally abandoned as the format changed from creation myth to a simple discourse of good against evil. Later versions of the dragon combat narrative tend to present the iconic monster as unsexed, or male-by-default,[4] rather than specifically gendering the monster male or female, but gender is highlighted in a small but significant number of visual and literary treatments.[5] However, the sexuality

(Leiden, New York, Cologne, 1995), cols 1634–9.   **4** The male-by-default category tends to arise in literary retellings: in visual treatments of dragons the genital area is often obscured or unmarked so that the gender of the beast is neither obvious nor, it would seem, significant. Meanwhile, in both British and Latin medieval narratives of St George (with one notable exception, discussed below in note 5) the dragon is consistently referred to as either 'it' or 'he' without any appreciable differences in the meanings attached to the animals: none of the dragons seems to behave in ways which can be obviously designated male (such as making a sexual threat towards the princess, for example), which tends to imply that the dragon has been designated as 'he' without any particular meaning being attached to this male gender. Medieval lives of St George in English, Scottish and Latin are listed in Charlotte D'Evelyn and Frances A. Foster, *A manual of the writings in Middle English*, general ed. J. Burke-Severs (Hamden, Ct., 1970), vol. 2, p. 589.   **5** My research so far has only uncovered one medieval text where the dragon is referred to as female, a version of the narrative of St George by Alexander Barclay dated 1515 which is a translation of a slightly earlier Latin version; the earlier work seems to make no mention of the gender of the dragon. Interestingly, Barclay's dragon is female-by-default: although the creature is consistently referred to as 'she' there seems to be no particular meaning associated with this gender – there are no sexual references in this work, and no mention of the dragon's breasts, dugs, offspring or genitalia, but it is definitely referred to as female. The quotation in the title of this paper is taken from line 528, but we should be aware that the *Middle English Dictionary* glosses the word 'wombe' as 'stomach' in addition to the more obvious 'womb': the dragon is

encoded within the trope of the mother-dragon does emerge in later accounts of dragons more generally: our (post-)modern readings of dragon imagery and dragon legends tend to stress allegories of heresy (as in Gottland's image) and generalised evil which we see encoded in these monsters, but we must not overlook the simple fact that many of our forebears believed that dragons were literal creatures of flesh and blood with real powers to spread pestilence, to threaten life and limb and, most significantly in this context, to contaminate water supplies through their sexual activity. As late as 1725, Henry Bourne, a Newcastle curate, wrote that the custom of lighting bonfires on Midsummer Eve was derived from the desire to frighten dragons away, because the monsters, 'being incited to lust through the Heat of the Season, did frequently, as they flew through the Air, Spermatize in the Wells and Fountains.'[6]

This sexualised agenda was by no means restricted to understandings of dragons, however, for it seems to inform the imagery of the monster who almost certainly enjoyed the widest recognition in the medieval and early modern era: the serpent in the Garden of Eden. Despite the fact that this character is strongly identified with a conventionally male devil, it was commonly presented as female in visual imagery of the narrative of the Fall. As with Gottland's treatment of St George's dragon, one of the most important aspects of the medieval understanding of the serpent is its presentation as a composite creature, very often in the form of a snake with a human head.[7] Furthermore, this human head frequently has a woman's face. This may well derive from, or at least have a common root with, the concept of Lilith. This character, who was probably based on a Babylonian storm demon, is named as Adam's first wife in the Talmud, a woman who was created equal with her husband rather than fashioned on a rib taken from his side. She is envisaged as a snake with a woman's head, and from the High Middle Ages was sometimes directly identified as the creature who gave Eve forbidden knowledge and thereby gained revenge on both her husband and God himself.[8]

---

perhaps constructed as a creature of insatiable physical hunger, as well as, or even instead of, the insatiable sexual appetite which the line seems on first reading to indicate. See R.E. Lewis and others (eds.), *Middle English Dictionary* part W.7 (Ann Arbor, 2000). Barclay's narrative is published in W. Nelson (ed.), *The life of St George by Alexander Barclay* (Early English Text Society, Original Series 230, London 1955). 6 John Brand, *Observations on popular antiquities* (Newcastle, 1777), cited in Beryl Rowland, *Animals with human faces: a guide to animal symbolism* (Knoxville, 1973) p. 69. 7 This treatment cannot be derived from the Biblical description of the episode, for, although the tempter is clearly endowed with human speech, it is never said to be anything other than a serpent. One variation on this form is the so-called 'pre-Lapsarian serpent', a lizard-like creature with (usually four) short legs and, in general, a human face: this is thought to be a visual reference to God's subsequent curse that the creature should crawl in the dust on its belly (Genesis 3: 14), which tends to imply that it would lose the use of any legs which it may have had. 8 Lilith is a fascinating character for those with an interest

Figure 2 shows a typical visual treatment of the Fall from the end of the fifteenth century, by the German artist Lucas Cranach the Elder. The serpent is represented with the head of a woman but is also endowed with a voluptuous torso, belly and hips which merge into a gently tapering tail, rather like a land-bound equivalent of a mermaid. Eve hands an apple to Adam, whose modesty is already protected by a carefully-positioned small branch growing from the main trunk of the tree. Eve herself is turned towards her husband in a pose which highlights the similarities between her own body and that of the serpent, another common artistic device which seems to relate to the concept that Eve, as the first to fall, was particularly guilty. Cranach's version takes a slightly different approach, however, for he has underlined both the feminine and sexual elements of the composition by placing the apple very close to the breasts of the serpent: the similarity of shape and size is unmistakable. St Michael, who approaches on the left to warn of God's impending judgement, is something of a bit-part player in this image: the focus is clearly on the sensual group on the right.

It is very common for the serpent to be represented as female in late medieval images of the Temptation. She is often gendered by obvious breasts and long hair, but occasionally she will wear a wimple or ornate headdress. This type of presentation is probably a reference to the idea that sexually-experienced women are dangerous and untrustworthy: the serpent's covered hair forms a strong contrast to Eve's long, loose hair, a visual motif which often signifies a state of feminine innocence. However, Cranach's treatment seems to present the serpent as a form, or even a mirror-image, of Eve herself: it is arguable that this imagery not only relates to the idea of woman as the culpable sex, but also plays on the idea of Eve's sexuality as auto-erotic or lesbian. Eve used her feminine wiles to cause Adam to fall, and, even worse, she was more interested in pursuing a sexual

---

in the evolution of women's rights. The Talmud maintains that she fled from Paradise when her demand to be considered equal with Adam was denied, refused to return to live with him, and subsequently married Samael, the king of the demons. She was envisaged as a long-haired demon night-visitor, who brought about miscarriage in pregnant women, stole male babies less than a week old and forced nocturnal emissions from men, using their semen to conceive demon children. She would also seduce and kill men, and is closely connected with Lamia, another female demon who is known as a blood-sucking child killer and derives from classical mythology. Lilith is also able to fly (she is sometimes understood as the night hag, or night mare). A ninth-century Irish gloss on the Old Testament explicitly equates the Lamia with the Celtic Morrígan, another flying female death-dealing demon (who could be singular or plural). This name is derived from the Irish meaning 'queen of ghosts', and her appearance presaged bloody battles. For further on these characters generally see Diane Apostolos-Cappadona, *Dictionary of women in religious art* (Oxford, 1998), pp. 219–20, 214–15, 258, and relevant entries in Van der Torn et al., *Dictionary of deities and demons*; on Lilith, Lamia and the Morrígan in an Irish context see Jacqueline Borsje, 'Omens, ordeals and oracles: on demons and weapons in Early Irish texts', *Peritia* 13 (1999), 224–48, at pp. 243–4.

2 Lucas Cranach, *The Fall of Man* (late fifteenth century)

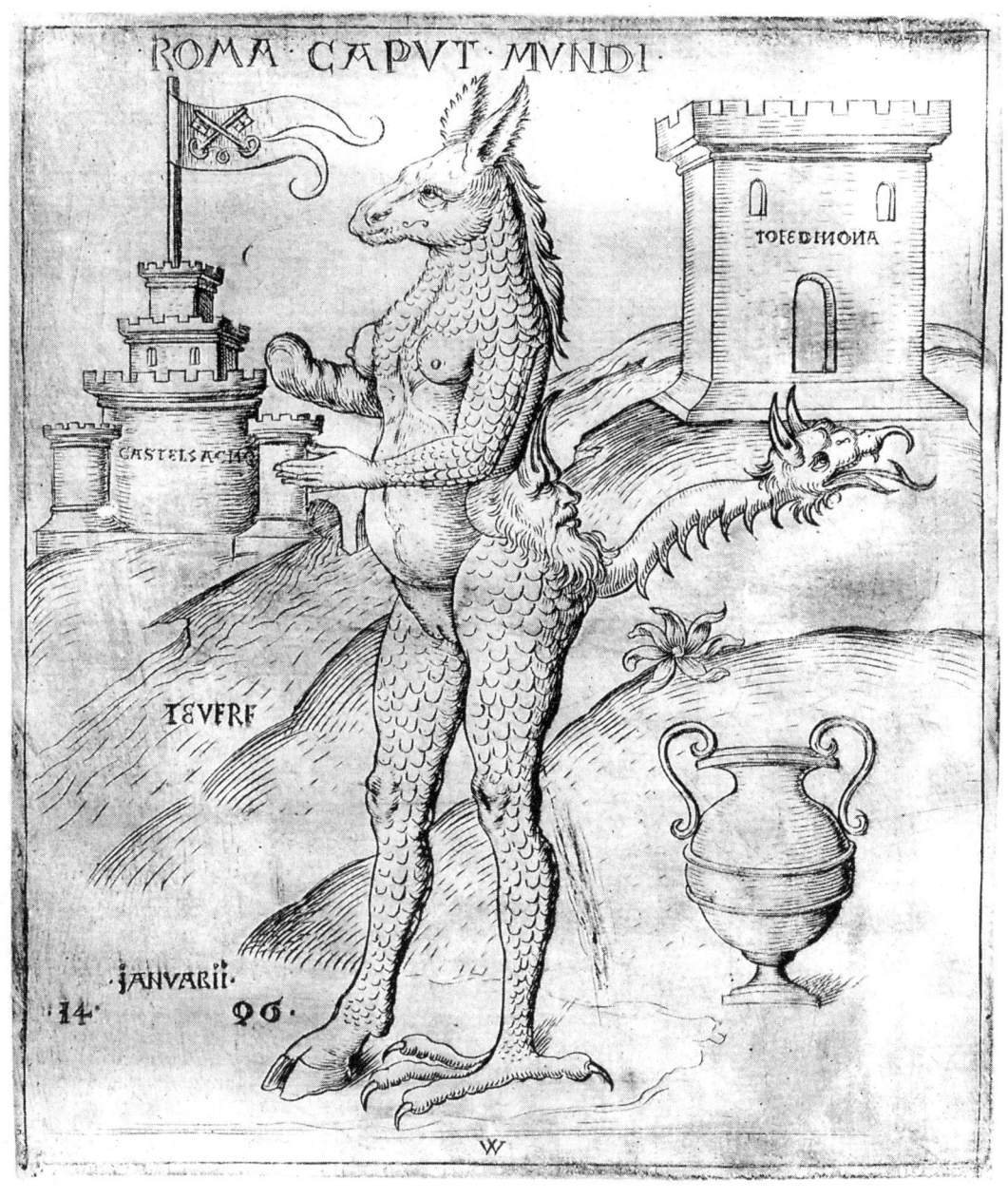

3 Wenzel of Olmutz, *The Papal Ass* (c. 1500).

agenda that could never lead to procreation. Eve is thus damned on all counts, as a weak woman who fell, as a temptress who beguiled an innocent man, and as a sexualised creature in pursuit of inappropriate, hedonistic pleasure.[9]

The Papal Ass (figure 3) is another significant late-medieval version of the sexualised, feminised monster, but it goes even further than Cranach's serpent in depicting the link between female sexuality and depravity. The beast itself was believed to be real, and was said to have been dragged from the River Tiber in 1496 and was depicted the following year in relief on the north door of the cathedral at Como. It seems that the Papal Ass was originally conceived as an allegory of the faults of the city of Rome,[10] but once it had been engraved on copper by the Bohemian goldsmith Wenzel of Olmutz it became widely accepted as emblematic of the hierarchy of the Roman Church and all its associated problems. The monster was a feature of pamphleteering by both sides during the Reformation and was invoked in political polemic in Italy as well as Germany from the end of the fifteenth century, but it is perhaps most associated with Reformers' pamphlets produced in the workshop of Lucas Cranach the elder. In 1523 the German reformer Philip Melanchthon interpreted the Papal Ass in terms which are deeply indicative of the revulsion with which semi-human sexualised monsters were viewed.[11] The whole creature was an allegory of the institution of the papacy, he claimed, whilst the ass head stood for the pope himself.[12] The Church should not have a mortal at its head, and the ass head was thus as fitting as the pope as head of the Church. The right hand, which is an elephant's foot, signifies the spiritual power of the pope, which he uses to crush all consciences; the right hand usually signifies the soul, and it should be ruled by Christ, not an ass's head. The humanised left hand signifies the secular power of the pope, something acquired only by human means. The right foot is the hoof of an ox; this signifies the servants of the pope's spiritual powers who oppress the souls of all people in the Church, the preachers, confessors and theologians. The left foot is an eagle's or griffin's claw; this signifies the servants of the pope's secular power, the canon lawyers. The female belly and breasts signify the cardinals, bishops, priests and monks who lead whorish lives, just as the Papal Ass stands in its shaming nakedness.[13]

---

9 Again, ancient Jewish tradition appears to inform this medieval Christian understanding: the Talmud states that the serpent had sexual intercourse with Eve. Apostolos-Cappadona, *Dictionary of women in religious art*, p. 335.   10 It has also been claimed that the original target was Alexander VI, who held the papacy from 1492 to 1503: R.W. Scribner, *For the sake of simple folk: popular propaganda for the German Reformation* (Cambridge, 1981), p. 131.   11 Scribner, *For the sake of simple folk*, pp. 131–2.   12 Martin Luther's own commentary on the image relates the entirety of the monster to the head of the Church of Rome: '... what God himself holds of the papacy is shown by this terrible picture. Everyone should therefore shudder as he takes it to heart.' *Depiction of the papacy* (1545), cited in Scribner, *For the sake of simple folk*, p. 132.   13 Melanchthon does not

For our purposes, the salient aspect of the Papal Ass is this female gendering, which is achieved by the inclusion of breasts, a rounded belly and genital labia. As the figure was used by Reformers to stand for everything which was wrong with the Church, this feminisation of the monster is deeply meaningful: femaleness, and specifically a depraved, sexualised femaleness, is cast as a wicked state of existence. Comparison with figure 4 demonstrates the extent to which this iconography could be employed to make specific, and easily-recognised, arguments – surely a vital component of successful propaganda. Here we see an image of Hercules at the crossroads used to illustrate a Parisian edition of Sebastian Brant's tract *Narrenschiff* [*The Ship of Fools*] (1498). The hero has reached a junction in his path, and has to choose between the hard, rocky road of righteousness, beset with thistles and thorns, and the broad, easy path to damnation, with its beguiling flowers and promises of lasciviousness. A female figure stands at the end of each route, and the iconography of each makes the contrast between the two very clear. A modestly-attired spinster, distaff in hand, is labelled 'Virtus'; an immodest, whorish creature, her hair piled high or perhaps decked out in an ornate headdress, is labelled 'Voluptas'. She is accompanied by a grinning, skeletal figure of death, but the display of her pronounced breasts and belly, so similar to the treatment of the Papal Ass, are clear indicators of her status as a sexual, dangerous female. Figure 5 shows an image from an anti-Reformation polemic, *Luther's Game of Heresy* (1535), which again uses the display of breasts or dugs both to feminise and to sexualise malevolent characters, here a group of demons. The creature in the left foreground is particularly clear. She is another monstrous confection, with avian talons and beak, a reptilian tongue, a pig's tail and the fur and horns of what may be a cow, but the breasts are perhaps her strongest characteristic: they are positioned rather awkwardly to one side of the chest so that both are clearly visible despite the torsion in her pose. In this class of imagery it is evident that womanhood, and specifically sexualised womanhood, is cast as the unfavoured state, and the possession of the attributes of sexualised womanhood is strongly associated with negative, monstrous conditions. The connection is clearly made in figure 6, another German image, this time pro-Reformation. Albrecht Altdorfer's treatment of the story of St George and the dragon is similar to the approach taken by Gottland some 40 years later, in that this dragon too has a visible breast or dug, although here there is less obvious use of analogy overlaying the conventional narrative.[14] Again, the display of the breast genders

---

comment on the demon face on the Papal Ass' back, nor her dragon-headed tail, although these motifs are standard in most, if not all, treatments of the subject. It is likely that the implications of this presentation are related to a desire to underline her monstrous and evil qualities. Additionally, we should note that Wenzel's version of the Papal Ass shows the creature defecating, an act which clearly establishes her base nature.
14 The presence of nipples, breasts or dugs is relatively uncommon in medieval

Uoluptas.   **Uirtus.**

4   *Hercules at the Crossroads*, from Sebastian Brant's *Narrenschiff* (1498)

5 Luther's Game of Heresy (1535)

6   Albrecht Altdorfer, *St George and the Dragon* (1511)

the animal female whilst also playing on the idea of sexualised femininity. The treatment of the dragon in both these images is very reminiscent of the feminised serpents in the Garden of Eden, but another factor which may be significant is the physical function which breasts had, according to medieval lore. It is known that infants were thought to ingest spiritual values along with physical nutrition when they were suckled:[15] the moral virtues of a wetnurse were as important as a generous supply of milk for families who had both the means and the desire to pay for their children to be fed by someone other than the mother herself. The breasts or dugs of a female dragon can thus be interpreted as emblems of the evil traits that she will inevitably pass on to her brood of dragonlets.

Medieval depictions of dragons with offspring are rare (figure 7 is one example),[16] but enough examples are known for us to conclude that this trope was available as an option to the image-maker. It is arguable that this is a less clear-cut, and ultimately less successful, means to gender a dragon as female. There seem to be two main reasons for this. Firstly, it is possible for the dragon to be interpreted as a father rather than a mother, although the acknowledged propensity for most male animals to leave as fast as possible once procreation has occurred and ideas about the fierceness of female animals defending their young – the tigress with her cubs, for example – make this quite unlikely. The second problem is that baby animals tend to have an inherent appeal, even baby monsters, and the danger is that the viewer identifies with the wrong protagonist in this combat. In fact the dragon seems to be almost justified in her predation on humans, for she obviously has a family to support. An alternative reading of the imagery would propose that the artist has made an effort to push the viewer to categorise the mother dragon as the worst type, because she is bringing yet more

depictions of dragons, but given the vast quantity of dragon imagery which has never been adequately researched or catalogued it is likely that further examples are yet to be discovered. One intriguing version of St George with a feminised dragon, a creature with numerous dugs, hangs in the National Gallery in Dublin. It is attributed to the Venetian artist Paris Bordone (1500–71), and will surely repay further investigation. I am very grateful to Dr Catherine Lawless for drawing my attention to this image.
15 Clarissa W. Atkinson, '"Your servant, my mother": the figure of St Monica in the ideology of Christian motherhood', in C.W. Atkinson, C.H. Buchanan and M.R. Miles (eds.), *Immaculate and powerful: the female in sacred image and social reality* (Boston, 1985), p.150.   16 Four examples of images of 'parental monsters' are known to me, all versions of the fight between St George and the dragon. Figure 7, which is discussed further below, is by the German artist Leonard Beck, and dated to 1515. A mid-to-late fifteenth-century engraving by a Dutch artist known as 'Master Zwolle' (often identified as Jan van den Mijnnesten, c.1440–1504) also includes a single dragonlet. However, a miniature from the *Belles Heures*, a French book of hours created c.1408, and a fifteenth-century wall painting in St Gregory's Pottergate, Norwich, both feature an adult dragon with two dragonlets (possibly more in the latter example, which is in need of

evil into the world with her terrible spawn. This is reminiscent of the role played by Grendel's mother in *Beowulf*: her awfulness is made all the more terrifying by the fact that she has been able to reproduce, to make more wickedness.[17] However, this interpretation carries the implication that the dragon may have other progeny elsewhere, which clearly undermines the analogy between St George killing the dragon and Christ's ultimate overthrow of the devil or Antichrist, as found in Gottland's image (figure 1), for example.

The problems associated with the identification of monsters as mothers may have contributed to the apparent unpopularity of this iconographic form, but it is notable that a much larger group of images employ a different method of marking the beast as female, by presenting a gendering orifice at the base of the tail.[18] There is a wide variety of depictions of the orifice itself: some are almond-shaped, some are more rounded, whilst others are slit-shaped, whether placed across the base of the tail or orientated to lie along the line of the tail. It

---

conservation). 17 It is arguable that the implications of the monster-as-mother were not fully developed in early medieval texts. Christine Rauer has observed that the gender of dragons does not seem to be an issue in *Beowulf* and its analogues (personal communication, April 2002); the only reference she has noted of a dragon as a parent does not comment on the gender of the adult monster: Rauer, *Beowulf and the dragon: parallels and analogues* (Cambridge, 2000), p. 85, n. 52. By contrast, the Error Monster in Edmund Spenser's *Faerie Queene* (1589) may well provide an example of the fully developed trope. This creature is explicitly described as the mother of a spawn of a thousand serpents and monsters (Book I, canto 1, verse 15), who suckle upon her. It is notable that Alexander Barclay's *Life of St George* (discussed above, in note 5), or its own source, may well have influenced Spenser. 18 To date, I have collected some fifty examples of medieval images of dragons with 'female' genitalia. All but one relate to St George (the other is an image of St Michael and the dragon), but it is likely that this group of images, which are all chance discoveries, represent only the tip of the iceberg. However, it is important to clarify just how unusual the presentation of the dragon as a gendered or sexualised creature actually is. There are hundreds, possibly thousands, of images of St George and the dragon extant from the medieval period, and those which appear to show genitalia constitute a tiny fraction of that number. The overwhelming majority of dragons are either shown in an attitude that obscures this area of their anatomy or they are depicted with the genital region visible but unmarked, in a way that is reminiscent of a doll's complete absence of genitalia. Yet the group of images which seem to depict a dragon with an orifice are sufficiently numerous to allow us to infer that they have not arisen by chance. We should note that German and Netherlandish artists active around the time of the Reformation were particularly interested in this treatment of the dragon: Albrecht Dürer, Martin Schongauer, Israhel van Meckenem and the anonymous Master of the Calvary were all important artists and engravers who elected to make use of this motif in some of their depictions of St George, and it seems reasonable to suggest that they may have been drawn to the idea because it was widely accepted that femaleness, especially sexualised femaleness, was often a concomitant of evil and depraved creatures. An extended discussion of this visual topos forms the basis of a paper to be published in *Studies in Iconography*.

is difficult to decode these images with real confidence, and although several factors point to the identification of the dragons as female we should also consider two other possibilities. The first consideration is that the 'orifice' is actually intended to be read as a wound, the site of a piercing made by St George's lance or spear. This idea must not be ruled out altogether, but the overwhelming body of evidence suggests that the iconography of the combat demands that the dragon is wounded in the mouth or, less frequently, in the throat. Indeed, this very group of 'gendered' dragons are all depicted being stabbed in the mouth or throat, or else display clear signs of a wound to this area. I have yet to discover a medieval image which shows the dragon being attacked by St George in any other part of the body, but, given the vast numbers of treatments of the subject of the combat, we should not overlook the possibility that somewhere a depiction does exist of the saint stabbing the dragon in the genital region. However, such an image would undoubtedly be highly suggestive of a sexualised discourse. We must also bear in mind the contemporary medieval idea, as expressed in bestiaries, for example, that the dragon's power lies in its tail rather than its teeth:[19] the mouth is by no means the most dangerous part of the creature. It is notable that the only other dragon-slayers who direct their attention to the mouth tend to kill their monstrous enemy by feeding it explosive or corrosive matter,[20] so the consistent presentation of St George as a hero who stabs a dragon in the mouth is surely indicative of some underlying meaning. St George's fixation with attacking the dragon's mouth may well be related to the long-established popular connection made between the mouth and the female genitals:[21] wounding in the mouth, perhaps particularly by means of a rather phallic lance, is likely to be sexually suggestive.

A second interpretation of the orifice is that it represents an anus. This argument does have rather more merit than the contention that a wound is

---

19 Rowland, *Animals with human faces*, p. 68.   20 A wide range of techniques is employed by literary and pseudo-historical dragon slayers. According to a non-canonical legend, related in the Biblical Apocrypha, the prophet Daniel caused a fire-breathing dragon to expire by means of feeding it cakes made of pitch, fat and hair: Daniel, Bel and the Dragon 1: 27. This method later proved popular with dragon slayers in many parts of Europe, but alternative strategies could involve persuading the creature to swallow a heavily armed man, sometimes equipped with spiked armour, who would then fight his way out. There is often a focus on a vulnerable spot, such as a wart on the leg or the creature's eyes (a trope which seems to be derived from the approved method of killing crocodiles), whilst others try to wound the beast in the belly. One example of this latter strategy is the northern European hero Sigurd the Vulsung, who killed a dragon by hiding in a pit and stabbing the creature's underside as it walked overhead. On methods of killing dragons, see Jacqueline Simpson, *British dragons*, 2nd edn (London, 2001), pp. 73–88.   21 For example, the vagina dentata (toothed vagina) is a widespread symbol of the paradigmatic male fear that the penis will be severed during sexual intercourse. Apostolos-Cappadona, *Dictionary of women in religious art*, p. 372.

being depicted, for the grotesque contortionist creature which displays its anus is a staple of the range of drolleries who appear in medieval carvings – and, to a lesser extent, other formats – much to the discomfort of some people in later, more prudish times. These carvings invariably depict humans or humanised creatures, which make direct comparison with the defiantly bestial dragon rather difficult, but a closer analogy can be drawn with some of the more fantastical animals who appear in contemporary bestiaries and other works of 'natural history'. One good example is the 'Bonnacon', a monster which had a particularly unpleasant weapon to employ against any hunter foolish enough to pursue it.[22] The creature, it is claimed, would void the contents of its bowels in the general direction of its enemies: its excrement could cover an area of several acres and it was noxious enough to cause trees to burst into flames spontaneously. Interestingly, the Bonnacon may have had some links to the dragon, for it is claimed that the Tarasque, the dragon killed by St Martha at Aix-en-Provence,[23] was the product of a coupling between Leviathan (whose progeny were legion) and a Bonnacon.

When considering the remaining possibility – that the orifice is intended to be read as female genitalia – it is important to remember that no one today knows what a dragon's pudendum is actually *supposed* to look like. As a reptile, the dragon's genitalia should, in theory, be hidden inside a cloaca, the cavity in the pelvic region into which the alimentary canal and the genital and urinary ducts open in all vertebrates other than the higher mammals. It is difficult to interpret the extent to which this type of information would have been available to natural historians and the compilers of bestiaries, far less the designers, artists and patrons of images which apparently depict gendered dragons. However, there is clear evidence that at least some people thought that dragons had humanised genitalia.[24] For example, the *Grimani Breviary* (1480–1520) depicts a male dragon which evidently has a scrotum hanging down underneath its tail:[25] this is a very important finding which goes some way towards supporting the identification of a dragon with a definite orifice as female, for it is obvious that the artist of this work was not seeking to represent a 'realistic' reptile with its genitalia hidden inside a cloaca.[26]

22 Anne Clark, *Beasts and bawdy* (London, 1975), p. 92.   **23** The story of St Martha and the Tarasque, a creature described as 'half animal and half fish, larger than an ox, longer than a horse' is related by Jacobus de Voragine in *The Golden Legend*, trans. William Granger Ryan (Princeton, 1993), vol. 2, pp. 23–4.   **24** One factor which may underlie this trope of is a belief in the power of genital display. Sigmund Freud, writing on the Medusa, commented on a tradition that display of the female genitalia was sufficient to frighten off the Devil himself: 'Das Medusenhaupt', cited in Jørgen Andersen, *The witch on the wall: medieval erotic sculpture in the British Isles* (London, 1977), p. 135. The intrinsic power of genital display fits well with an understanding of dragons as both sexual and malevolent.   **25** Bibliotheca Marciana, Venice, fol. 538v. I am indebted to Dr Wendy Larson for drawing my attention to this image.   **26** The example of a 'gendered dragon' which is perhaps

This identification of the orifice as female genitalia is substantiated by certain compositional traits of these treatments of the combat between the saint and the dragon. In virtually every case the dragon lies supine beneath the saint, whether he is on foot or mounted on a horse, with her legs spread apart.[27] This stance is very reminiscent of the position that women are often expected to adopt during internal medical examinations, a position which gives a sense of extreme vulnerability. It could also be argued that the dragon is depicted in a position for face-to-face sexual congress, a form of intercourse that is human rather than animal (indeed, some animals, including the rhinoceros, the elephant and the hermaphrodite hyena, were believed by medieval people to mate back-to-back, a position known as 'retrocopulation').[28] It may be that St George has forced the dragon into this position, but it seems more likely that the message of the imagery is that the depraved creature is offering herself to him sexually as a way of trying to save her own life. We should not overlook the phallic nature of the weaponry St George uses, particularly the way that it often functions as a pointer to the orifice itself: figure 7 has a typical format, with the broken lance passing underneath the dragon's tail directly beneath the orifice. Other versions have a broken lance, or other pointer, such as a discarded femur, pointing directly towards the orifice,[29] or aligned alongside the dragon's tail.[30] In each case the viewer's eye is inevitably drawn towards the creature's pudendum, and approaches it in company with an aggressively masculine object.

Figure 7, a treatment of St George and the dragon c.1515 by the German artist Leonard Beck, depicts the motif of the gendering orifice alongside the *topos* of the monstrous mother. In the foreground St George, mounted, is about to cut off the dragon's head with his sword. The creature is already wounded through the throat with a broken lance, and the remainder of the weapon lies

---

most persuasive has two orifices: the identification of this as a female monster seems irresistible. It occurs in a French book of hours dated 1430–40, Bodleian MS Auct D. inf. 2 11.   **27** By contrast, this posture is by no means typical of images of St George and the dragon *per se*. Studies of the iconography of the combat, such as J. Roosval, *Nya Sankt Görans Studier* (Stockholm, 1924) and Georges Didi-Huberman et al., *St Georges et le dragon* (Paris, 1994) indicate that the dragon can adopt a wide range of postures. The postioning of the beast on its back is not confined to images where there is a visible orifice, but is considerably more common in 'gendered' images than in the iconography of the combat more generally.   **28** Clark, *Beasts and bawdy*, p. 77.   **29** The device of the broken lance as a pointer occurs in a treatment of the combat by the Master of the Calvary (fifteenth-century). Albrecht Dürer's 'St George on Foot' c.1500, has the hero's scabbard pointing directly towards the dragon's orifice, and a horse's hoof and a femur both act as pointers in one of Israhel van Meckenem's versions of the fight (late fifteenth-century). All these images are reproduced in my book *St George: hero, martyr and myth* (Stroud, 2000), figures 5.16; 5.13; 5.15.   **30** Another image by the Master of the Calvary uses the motif of the broken lance aligned alongside the dragon's tail. It is reproduced in Riches, *St George*, figure 5.12.

7   Leonard Beck, *St George Fighting with the Dragon* (*c.*1515) by permission of Kunsthistorisches Museum, Vienna.

behind the dragon's tail, closely aligned with a clearly-drawn, oval orifice which lies horizontally across the base of the tail. A dragonlet, with a wound in its chest, lies alongside the adult, surrounded by skulls and bones. The princess and her lamb watch from rocky outcrop, and in the background we see the city amongst verdant fields and woodland. In the middle distance St George and the princess make their way back towards the city; the horse looks round towards the lamb which the princess still leads, in a variant of the more usual subject of the subdued dragon being led on her girdle. Whilst this latter aspect of the image is of some interest, the most important elements are undoubtedly the presence of the dragonlet and the obvious orifice on the pudendum of the adult dragon. The first of these motifs offers positive proof that the dragon is a parent, whilst the second strongly suggests that the monster is female. The juxtaposition of offspring and orifice carries the clear implication that the dragon is a mother, that she has spawned a terrible brood who must also be killed, if the heroic knight is to win ultimate victory. The fact that the adult dragon is placed in the classic position for a 'female-gendered' dragon – on her back, beneath the hooves of the saint's horse, with her pudendum clearly visible – demonstrates that it is very likely that other dragons who are depicted in this pose were intended to be understood as sexualised, female monsters.

If we are correct in our reading of these images of dragons with orifices as monsters who are feminised and sexualised through the portrayal of external female genitalia, it is clear that this imagery defines the dragon in a quite specific way, both as an obscene creature and also, crucially, in her relationship to St George. A complex paradigm is set up of an act of penetration by the aggressive male that overthrows the sexuality of the female (he refuses to have actual coition with her) and at the same time sublimates his own sexual desires through the use of phallic weaponry. St George is presented as the antithesis of the dragon: human to beast, good to bad, male to female. But given the quite specific overtones of sexuality, we can argue that St George is presented as chaste in opposition to the dragon's obvious sexuality.[31] Within figure 7 the dragon (female, sexual, evil, bestial) is placed, both literally and figuratively, in opposition not only to St George (male, chaste, good, human), but also to the rescued virgin princess (female, chaste, good, human). The relative positions of the dragon and the princess – who watches the slaughter from a promontory directly above the dragon – seem to be intended to embody the polar opposites inherent in late medieval attitudes to women. They represent the nadir and the epitome: the evil, sexual, bestial creature and the good, virginal, saintly creature.

---

31 The identification of St George as a figure of chastity is a significant theme in the medieval cult, and seems particularly important in relation to his construction as a martyr. On this topic see my paper 'St George as a virgin martyr' in Samantha J.E. Riches and Sarah Salih (eds.), *Gender and holiness: men, women and saints in late medieval*

The image of the feminised, sexualised monster was in evidence throughout the fifteenth century, and into the sixteenth century, in a wide variety of media.[32] One of the most interesting aspects of the trope is that it does not appear to be constrained geographically: there are extant examples of feminised dragons from England, France, Germany, Italy, the Netherlands and Romania, and very probably elsewhere too. Whilst it is obvious that simple misogyny informs the construction of the gendered monster, we must be careful not to see these creatures simply as female. Rather, they stand for a specific type of femininity that is sexual and bestial, everything that is worst about women to the late medieval mind. In figure 7 a chaste woman (the virginal princess) is rescued by an embodiment of chastity (St George), who saves her from an embodiment of sexual evil (the dragon). The images accompanying this paper demonstrate the extent to which it is possible to manipulate both iconography and hagiography to make a specific argument in the arena of sexual politics. Perhaps this is the ultimate purpose of monsters: they exist to serve the needs of the societies which conjure them up.

Europe (London, 2002), pp. 65–85.   [32] Whilst Reformation engravings and woodcuts provide a rich source of examples of these monsters, my research into 'gendered dragons' has uncovered specimens in stained and painted glass, sculpture in wood and stone, panel and wall paintings, and manuscript illumination. A selection of these images is reproduced and discussed in Riches, *St George*, figures 3.23; 4.8; 5.9; 5.11–5.16; 5.21; 5.24; 5.25; 5.28–5.30, pp. 158–64; 169–72.

Bibliography

Note: Individual items contained in large well-known collections, such as the *Monumenta Germaniae Historica* or *Patrologia Latina* have not been listed separately in the Bibliography.

PRINTED PRIMARY MATERIAL

Acta Sanctorum. Antwerp, Brussels, 1643–1940.
Acte des religieuses de Port-Royal. Du 28. Aoust 1665, contenant leur disposition à la vie & à la mort touchant la signature du Formulaire, & leurs sentimens en cas de refus des sacramens à la mort. No place indicated, 1722.
Ancient charters, royal and private, prior to A.D. 1200, ed. J.H. Round. Pipe Roll Society 10, 1888.
Angélique de Saint-Jean Arnaud d'Andilly, *Memoires pour servir à l'histoire de Port-Royal, et à la vie de la Reverende Mere Marie Angelique de Sainte Magdeleine Arnaud Reformatrice de ce Monastere*. 2 vols., Utrecht, Aux depens de la Compagnie, 1742.
—— *Relation de la captivité de la M. Angélique de St-Jean*. No place indicated, 1711.
Annála Connacht, the Annals of Connacht (A.D. 1224–1544), ed. A. Martin Freeman. Dublin, 1944.
Annála Ríoghachta Eireann, being annals of the kingdom of Ireland by the Four Masters, ed. J. O'Donovan. 7 vols., Dublin, 1851.
Annála Uladh, Annals of Ulster, ed. W.M. Hennessy and B. MacCarthy. 4 vols., Dublin, 1887–1901.
Annals of Innisfallen, ed. S. MacAirt. Dublin, 1951.
Augustine of Hippo, Saint, *Confessions*. Tr. Maria Boulding, London, 1997.
Avitus of Vienne, Alcimus, *Alcimi Aviti opera*, ed. Rudolph Peiper. Monumenta Germaniae Historica, AA 6, 2. Berlin, 1883.
—— *Avitus: the Fall of Man – De spiritalis historiae gestis libri I–III*, ed. Daniel J. Nodes. Toronto, 1985.
—— *The poems of Alcimus Ecdicius Avitus: translation and introduction*, ed. and tr. George W. Shea. Medieval and Renaissance Texts and Studies, vol. 172, New York, 1997.
—— *Histoire spirituelle, Tome I (Chants I–III)*, ed. and tr. Nicole Hecquet-Noti. Sources Chrétiennes, 444, Paris, 1999.
Biblia Sacra: iuxta latinam vulgatam versionem, ed. Henry Quentin. Rome, 1926.
Boutemy, A., 'Deux pièces inédites du manuscrit 749 de Douai', *Latomus* 2 (1938), pp. 123–30.
—— 'Notice sur le manuscrit 749 ... de Douai', *Latomus* 3 (1939), pp. 183–206, 264–98.
—— 'Trois œuvres inédites de Godefroid de Reims', *Revue du Moyen Âge Latin* 3 (1947), pp. 335–66.
Bracton, *De legibus Anglie*, ed. Sir T. Twiss. 6 vols., London, 1878–83.
Branca, V. (ed.), *Mercanti scrittori: ricordi nella Firenze tra Medioevo e Rinascimento – Paolo da Certaldo, Giovanni Morelli, Bonaccorso Pitti, Domenico Lenzi, Francesco Datini, Lapo Niccolini, Bernardo Machiavelli*. Milan, 1986.

Bulle ou Constitution de Nostre S. Pere le Pape Innocent X. Par laquelle sont declarées et definies cinq propositions en matiere de foy. Avec le Bref de sa Sainteté aux Archevesques & Evesques de ce Royaume. Et le Mandement de Monseigneur l'Archevesque de Paris, pour la publication & observance de la dite Constitution. Paris, Pierre Targa, 1653.

Brucker, G.A. (ed.), *The society of Renaissance Florence: a documentary study.* New York, 1971.

Byrne, M.J. (ed.), *Ireland under Elizabeth ... being a portion of the History of Catholic Ireland by Don Philip O'Sullivan Beare.* Dublin, 1903.

Calendar of charter rolls. 6 vols., London, 1903–27.

Calendar of documents relating to Ireland, 1171–1307, ed. H.S. Sweetman and G.F. Handcock. 5 vols., London, 1875–86.

Calendar of entries in the papal registers relating to Great Britain and Ireland. 19 vols., London and Dublin, 1893–1998.

Calendar of inquisitions post mortem. 16 vols., London, 1909–74.

Calendar of Ormond deeds, 1172–1603, ed. E. Curtis. 6 vols., Dublin, 1932–43.

Calendar of state papers Ireland. 1860–.

Calendar of the close rolls, 1272–1509. 47 vols., London, 1892–1963.

Calendar of the Gormanston register, 1175–1397, ed. J. Mills and M.J. McEnery. Dublin, 1916.

Calendar of the justiciary rolls of Ireland, Edward I (1295–1307), ed. J. Mills. 2 vols., Dublin, 1905–14.

Calendar of the liberate rolls of Henry III. 6 vols., London, 1916–64.

Calendar of the patent rolls, 1232–1509. 55 vols., London, 1891–1971.

Cartulaire de l'abbaye de Conques en Rouergue, ed. G. Desjardins. Paris, 1897.

Cartulaire de l'abbaye de Marmoutier pour le Dunois, ed. E. Mabille. Châteaudun, 1874.

Cartulaire de l'abbaye de Molesme, ancien diocèse de Langres, 916–1215, ed. J. Laurent. Paris, 1907–11.

Cartulaire de l'abbaye de la Sainte Trinité de Tiron, ed. L. Merlet. Chartres, 1883.

Cartulaire de l'abbaye de Saint-Père de Chartres, ed. B.E.C. Guérard. 2 vols., Paris, 1840.

Cartulary of Cirencester abbey, Gloucestershire, ed. C.D. Ross, 2 vols., London, 1964, Vol. 3 ed. M. Devine, Oxford, 1977

Cartulary of Darley abbey, ed. R.R. Darlington. 2 vols., Kendal, 1945.

Cartulary of Haughmond abbey, ed. U. Rees. Cardiff, 1985.

Cartulary of Oseney abbey, ed. H.E. Salter. 6 vols., Oxford Historical Society 89–91, 97–8, 101, 1929–36.

Cartulary of the priory of St Denys, ed. F.O. Blake. 2 vols., Southampton Record Series 24–5, 1981.

Cartulary of Shrewsbury abbey, ed. U. Rees. 2 vols., Aberystwyth, 1975.

Cartulary of the Wakebridge chantries at Crich, ed. A. Saltman. Derbyshire Archaeological Record Series 6, 1976.

Chamillard, G., *Response aux raisons que les religieuses de Port-Royal proposent contre la signature du Formulaire avec leurs maximes et leur esprit.* Paris. F. Muguet, 1665.

Charters of the Anglo-Norman earls of Chester c.1071–1237, ed. G. Barraclough. Lancashire and Yorkshire Record Society 126, 1988.

Chartularies of St Mary's abbey, Dublin, ed. J.T. Gilbert. 2 vols., Rolls Series, London, 1884, 1886.

Chartulary of Cockersand abbey, ed. W. Farrer. 7 vols., Chetham Society, new series 38–40, 43, 56–7, 64, 1897–1909.

Chester, A. (ed.), *Selected sermons of Hugh Latimer*. Charlottesville, Virginia, 1968.
Chrysostom, John (Saint), *Saint John Chrysostom: homilies on Genesis 1–17*, tr. Robert C. Hill. The Fathers of the Church vol. 74, Washington, D.C., 1986.
Chronicle of the Third Crusade. A translation of the 'Itinerarium Peregrinorum et gesta regis Ricardi', ed. H.J. Nicholson. Aldershot, 1997.
Clarke, E.A. and Hatch, D.F. (eds. and tr.), *The golden bough, the oaken cross: the Virgilian Cento of Faltonia Betitia Proba*. Chico, CA, 1981.
Clement VI, *Lettres se rapportant à la France*, ed. E. Déprez and G. Mollat. 3 vols., Paris, 1901–1961.
Copeland, Robert, *The seven sorrowes women have when theyr husbandes be deade* (London, 1568), in M. Prior (ed.), *Women in English society, 1500–1800*. London, 1985.
Curia regis rolls. 17 vols., London, 1922–99.
Declaration des Religieuses de Port-Royal, touchant leurs actes qui ont été imprimez. No place indicated, 1664.
Divers actes des religieuses de Port-Royal du saint Sacrement. Touchant l'Ordonnance de Monseigneur l'Archevesque de Paris, par laquelle il exige la foy humaine du fait de Jansenius. Et les étranges violences qui leur on estés faites en consequence de ce commandement. No place or date indicated [1664].
Divers actes, lettres et relations des religieuses de Port-Royal du Saint Sacrement touchant la persecution & les violences qui leur ont été faites au sujet de la signature du Formulaire. No place or date indicated [1724]
Documents on the affairs of Ireland before the king's council, ed. G.O. Sayles. Dublin, 1980.
Dracontius, Blossius Aemilius, *Œuvres*, vol. 1 ed. Claude Moussy and Colette Camus. Paris, 1985.
Du Bartas, Guillaume, *The works of Guillaume de Salluste, Sieur du Bartas*, ed. Urban T. Holmes Jr. 3 vols., Chapel Hill, 1935.
Early Yorkshire charters, ed. W. Farrer, 3 vols. Edinburgh, 1914–16 and C.T. Clay, vols., 4–12, Yorkshire Archaeological Society extra series, 1935–65.
Emerton, E. (ed.), *The letters of Saint Boniface*. New York, 1940.
English historical documents, vol. 2, 1042–1189, ed. D.C. Douglas and G.W. Greenaway. London, 1953.
English historical documents, vol. 3, 1189–1327, ed. H. Rothwell. London, 1975.
Feet of fines for the county of York 16–30 Henry III, ed. Col. J. Parker. Yorkshire Archaeological Society Record Series 67, 1925.
Feet of fines for the tenth year of Richard I, A.D. 1198 to A.D. 1199. Pipe Roll Society 24, 1900.
Fineschi, V., *Memorie istoriche degli uomini illustri del Convento di S.Maria Novella*. Florence, 1787, reprint Rome, 1977.
Gairdner, J. (ed.), *The Paston letters*. 6 vols., London, 1904; reprinted in one volume, Gloucester, 1983.
Gerald of Wales [Giraldus Cambrensis], *The history and topography of Ireland*, ed. J.J. O'Meara. Mountrath and London, 1982.
—— *The journey through Wales and the description of Wales*, ed. L. Thorpe. London, 1978.
—— *Expugnatio hibernica. The conquest of Ireland*, ed. A.B. Scott and F.X. Martin. Dublin, 1978.
Gilbert, J.T. (ed.), *The register of the abbey of St Thomas the Martyr, Dublin*. London, 1889.

Glanvill, Tractatus de legibus et consuetudines regni Anglie qui Glanvilla vocatur, ed. and tr. G.D.G. Hall. Selden Society, London, 1965.
Goez, E., *Beatrix von Canossa und Tuszien: eine Untersuchung zur Geschichte des 11 Jahrhunderts*. Sigmaringen, 1995.
Goring charters, ed. T.R. Gambier-Perry. Oxfordshire Record Society 13, 1931.
Great chartulary of Glastonbury, ed. A. Watkin. 3 vols., Somerset Record Society 59 and 63–4, 1947–56.
Guicciardini, F., *Storie fiorentine dal 1378 al 1509*, ed. A. Montevecchi. Milan, 1988.
Hilary of Arles, *Metrum in Genesin ad Leonem Papam*, ed. Rudolph Peiper. Corpus scriptorum ecclesiasticorum latinorum, vol. 23. Vienna, 1891.
Hilbert, K. (ed.), *Baldricus Burgulianus, Carmina*. Heidelberg, 1979.
Holinshed's Irish chronicle, ed. L. Miller and E. Power. Dublin, 1979.
Hugh the Chanter, *The history of the Church of York, 1066–1127*, ed. C. Johnson, rev. by M. Brett, C.N.L. Brooke and M. Winterbottom. Oxford, 1990.
Hungerford cartulary. A calendar of the earl of Radnor's cartulary of the Hungerford family, ed. J.L. Kirby. Wiltshire Record Society 49, 1994.
Irish monastic and episcopal deeds, 1200–1600, ed. N.B. White. Dublin, 1932.
Isidore, *Etymologiarum sive originum, libri xx*, ed. W.M. Lindsay. 2 vols., Oxford, 1911.
Jacobus de Voragine, *The golden legend*. Tr. W.G. Ryan, Princeton, 1993.
James, M.R., Brooke, C.N.L. and Mynors, R.A.B. (eds), *De nugiis curialium*. Oxford, 1983.
Jennings, B., 'Brussels Ms 3947: Donatus Moneyus Provincia Hiberniae S. Francisci', *Analecta Hibernica* 6 (1934), pp. 12–131.
—— (ed.), *Wadding papers*. Dublin, 1953.
Joinville and Villehardouin, *Chronicles of the crusades*, ed. M.R.B. Shaw. London, 1963.
Jordan Fantosme's chronicle, ed. R.C. Johnson. Oxford, 1981.
Kavanagh, S. (ed.), *Commentarius Rinuccianus, de sedis apostolicae legatione ad foederatos Hibernaie catholicos per annos 1645–9*. 6 vols., Dublin, 1932–49.
Kew, G. (ed.), *The Irish sections of Fynes Moryson's Unpublished Itinerary*. Dublin, 1998.
Kingsford, C.L. (ed.), *The Stonor letters and papers*. 2 vols., Camden Third Series 30, London, 1919.
Kirkconnell, W. (ed. and tr.), *The celestial cycle: the theme of Paradise Lost in world literature with translations of the major analogues*. New York, 1967.
Landucci, Luca, *Diario fiorentino dal 1450 al 1516*, ed. I del Badia. Florence, 1883.
Lanyer, Aemilia, *Salve Deus rex Judæorum*, ed. Suzanne Woods. Oxford, 1993.
Leclerc, P. (ed.), *Histoire des persecutions des religieuses de Port-Royal, écrite par elles-mêmes*. Villefranche, 1753.
Leclercq, J., *Yves de Chartres: Correspondance*. Paris, 1949.
Letters and papers of the reign of Henry VIII, foreign and domestic. 21 vols., London, 1895–
Littlejohn, Col. R. Pudsay (ed.), *The Pudsay deeds*. Yorkshire Archaeological Society Record Series 56, 1916.
Mabillon, J. (ed.), *Acta sanctorum ordinis Sancti Benedicti in saeculorum classes distributa*. Paris, 1680.
Magdelaine de Ste Melthide Thomas du Fossé, *Lettre de la Sœur Magdelaine de Ste Melthide, R. de P.R. A Monseigneur l'Archevesque de Paris. Au sujet de la retraction de sa signature du Formulaire*. No place indicated, 1664.

—— *Lettres de la Sœur Magdeleine de Sainte Melthide, religieuse de Port-Royal, a Monseigneur l'Archevesque de Paris et aux religieuses de Port-Royal ses sœurs. Par lesquelles, elle témoigne la douleur qu'elle a d'avoir retracté sa premiere signature, & la disposition où elle est de signer tout du nouveau, sans jamais estre capable de retomber en sa premiere faute*. Paris, F. Muguet, 1665.

Magnusson, M. and Pálsson, H. (eds), *The Vinland sagas: the Norse discovery of America*. London, 1965.

Mansi, J.D., *Sacrorum conciliorum nova et amplissima collectio*. 31 vols., Florence, 1759–98.

Marchionne di Coppo Stefani, *Cronica fiorentina* ed. N. Rodolico. Rerum Italicarum Scriptores 30, Città di Castello, 1903.

Marmoutier cartulaire blésois, ed. C. Métais. Blois, 1889–91.

Martène, E. and Durand, U. (eds), *Veterum scriptorum et monumentorum amplissima collectio*. 9 vols., Paris, 1724–33.

Martin, J. (ed.), *Commodianus, Claudius Marius Victorius*. Corpus Christianorum series latina vol. 128. Turnhout, 1960.

Mère Agnès de Saint-Paul, *Les constitutions du monastère de Port-Royal du Saint-Sacrement*. Mons, 1665.

Meyer, P. (ed.), *L'histoire de Guillaume le Maréchal*. 3 vols., Paris, 1891–1901.

Migne, J.-P. (ed.), *Patrologia Latina*. 221 vols., Paris, 1844–64.

Monumenta Germaniae Historica

More, Thomas, *Complete Works*, ed. T. Lawler, G. Marc'hadour and R. Marius. New Haven, 1981.

Morelli, 'Ricordi', in V. Branca (ed.), *Mercanti scrittori; ricordi nella Firenze tra Medioevo e Rinascimento – Paolo da Certaldo, Giovanni Morelli, Bonaccorso Pitti, Domenico Lenzi, Donato Velluti, Goro Dati, Francesco Datini, Lapo Niccolini, Bernardo Machiavelli*. Milan, 1986.

Mullally, E. (ed.), *The deeds of the Normans in Ireland. La geste des Engleis en Yrlande*. Dublin, 2002.

Nelson, W. (ed.), *The life of St George by Alexander Barclay*. Early English Text Society, Original Series 230, London, 1955.

Niccolini di Camugliano, G., *Chronicles of a Florentine family, 1200–1700*. London, 1933.

Nicholls, K.W. (ed.), 'The Lynch Blosse papers', *Analecta Hibernica* 29 (1980), pp. 115–30.

Niermeyer, J.–F., *Mediae latinititis lexicon minus*. Leiden, 1976.

Orderic Vitalis, *The ecclesiastical history of Orderic Vitalis*, ed. M. Chibnall. 6 vols., Oxford, 1969–1980.

Original charters relating to the city of Worcester, ed. J.H. Bloom. Worcester Historical Society 27, 1909.

Orpen, G.H. (ed.), *The song of Dermot and the earl*. Oxford, 1892.

Pedes finium eboracensis regnante Johanne, ed. W. Brown. Surtees Society 94, 1897.

Peiper, R. (ed.), *Cypriani Galli poetae heptateuchos accedunt incertorum de Sodoma et Iona et ad senatorem carmina et Hilarii quae feruntur in Genesin, de Maccabaeis atque de Euangelio*. Corpus scriptorum ecclesiasticorum latinorum, vol. 23. Vienna, 1891.

Prosper of Aquitaine, *The Carmen de providentia Dei attributed to Prosper of Aquitaine: a revised text with an introduction, translation and notes*, ed. and tr. by Michael P. McHugh. The Catholic University of America Patristic Studies, vol. 98, Washington, D.C., 1964.

Prior, M., *Women in English society, 1500–1800*. London, 1985.
Prudentius, *The poems of Prudentius*, tr. By Mary Clement Eagan. 2 vols., Fathers of the Church, vols. 43, 52, Washington, D.C., 1962, 1965.
Receuil des chartes de l'abbaye de Cluny, ed. A. Bernard and A. Bruel. 6 vols., Paris, 1876–1903.
Receuil des historiens des croisades, historiens occidentaux. 5 vols., Paris, 1841–1906.
Receuil des pièces concernant les religieuses de Port-Royal des Champs qui se sont soumises à l'Eglise. Paris, de l'Imprimerie Royale, 1710.
Reflexions de la R. Mere Angelique de S. Jean Arnaud, Abbesse de P.R. des Champs, pour préparer ses Sœurs à la persecution, conformément aux Avis che la R. Mere Agnès avoit laissés sur cette matière aux Religieuses de ce Monastère. No place indicated, 1737.
Relation de la vie et de la mort de la Réverende Mère de Ste Anastasie, dernière prieure de P.R. des Champs. No place or date indicated.
Requeste presentée au Roy par les Religieuses du Port-Royal des Champs en mars 1707. No place indicated, 1707.
Requeste presentée à son Eminence Monseigneur le Cardinal de Noailles Archevêque de Paris par les Religieuses du Port-Royal des Champs au mois d'octobre 1707. No place indicated, 1707.
Rich, Barnaby, *A new description of Ireland*. London, 1610.
Richa, G., *Notizie istoriche delle chiese fiorentine divise ne' suoi quartieri*. 10 vols., Florence, 1754–62.
Riley, H.T. (ed.), *Annales monasterii S. Albani a Johanne Amundesham monaco, ut videtur, conscripto A.D. 1421–1440*. 2 vols., Rolls Series 28, London, 1870–1.
Roger of Howden, *Chronica*, ed. W. Stubbs. 4 vols., Rolls Series, London, 1868–71.
Rucellai, Giovanni, *Giovanni Rucellai ed il suo Zibaldone. Il Zibaldone Quaresimale*, ed. A. Perosa (Studies of the Warburg Institute, 24). London, 1960.
Rymer, T., *Foedera*. 10 vols., The Hague, 1739–45.
Robinson, Rev. J.L. (eds), 'Of the ancient deeds of the parish of St. John's, Dublin, preserved in the library of Trinity College Dublin', *Proceedings of the Royal Irish Academy*, C, 33 (1916–1917), pp. 175–224.
Schenkl, C. (ed.), *Poetae Christianae minores*. Corpus scriptorum ecclesiasticorum latinorum, 16. Vienna, 1888.
Schimmelpennick, M.A., *Select memoirs of Port Royal*. 5th ed., 3 vols., London, 1858.
Sibton abbey cartularies and charters, ed. P. Brown. 4 vols., Suffolk Record Society, Suffolk Charters 7–10, 1985–8.
Sidney, Sir Philip, *Sir Philip Sidney, the Oxford authors*, ed. Katherine Duncan-Jones. Oxford, 1989.
St Thomas the martyr, Dublin: register of the abbey, ed. J.T. Gilbert. Rolls Series, London, 1889.
Statutes and ordinances and acts of Parliament of Ireland, King John to Henry V, ed. H.F. Berry. Dublin, 1907.
Steele, R. (ed.), *Medieval lore: an epitome of the science, geography, animal and plant folk-lore and myth of the Middle Age: being classified gleanings from the encyclopaedia of Bartholomew Anglicus on the properties of things*. London, 1983.
Stenton, D.M. (ed.), *The earliest Lincoln assize rolls A.D. 1202–1209*. Lincolnshire Record Society 22, 1926.
—— *Rolls of the justices in eyre, being the pleas and assizes for Yorkshire in 3 Henry III (1218–19)*. Selden Society 56, London, 1937.

Strozzi, Alessandra Macinghi negli, *Lettere di una gentildonna fiorentina del secolo XV*, ed. C. Guasti. Florence, 1877.
Suplément au Nécrologie de l'Abbaïe de Notre-Dame de Port-Roïal des Champs, Ordre de Cîteaux, Institut du St-Sacrement. No place indicated, 1735.
Tertullian, *The writings of Tertullian*, vol. III, ed. Alexander Roberts and James Donaldson. Ante-Nicene Christian library, Vol. 18, Edinburgh, 1870.
La toilette des femmes, tr. Marie Turcan. Sources Chrétiennes, 173, Paris, 1971.
The register of John Swayne, archbishop of Armagh and primate of Ireland, 1418–1439, ed. D.A. Chart. Belfast, 1935.
The rule of St Benedict: in Latin and English with notes, ed. T. Fry et al. Collegeville, Minnesota, 1981.
Thomson, I. and Perraud, L. (eds. and tr.), *Ten Latin schooltexts of the Later Middle Ages: translations and selections*. Lewiston, 1990.
Vasari, Giorgio, *Vite de'più eccellenti pittori, scultori ed architettori*, ed. G. Milanesi. 9 vols., Florence, 1878–85.
Velluti, Donato, *Cronica domestica di messer Donato Velluti*, ed. I. del Lungo and G. Volpi. Florence, 1914.
Visitations of the diocese of Norwich, 1492–1532, ed. A. Jessopp. London, 1888.
Walsh, R. (ed.), 'Miscellaneous documents', *Archivium Hibernicum* 6 (1917), pp. 60–8.
Ward, B. (tr.), *The sayings of the Desert Fathers*. London and Oxford, 1975.
Westpfahl, H. (ed.), *Vita Dorotheae Montoviensis Magistri Johannis Marienwerder*. Cologne-Graz, 1964.
White, C. (ed. and tr.), *Early Christian Latin poets*. London and New York, 2000.
William of Malmesbury, *Gesta regum Anglorum*, ed. R.A.B. Mynors, R.M. Thomson and M. Winterbottom. Oxford, 1998.
Williamson, E.W. (ed.), *The letters of Osbert of Clare*. Oxford, 1929.
Windeatt, B. (ed.), *The book of Margery Kempe*. London, 2000.

SECONDARY SOURCES

Adair, P., 'Countess Clemence: her power and its foundation' in T.M. Vann (ed.), *Queens, regents and potentates* (Dallas, Texas, 1993), pp. 63–72.
Adam, A., *Du mysticisme à la révolte: les jansénistes du XVIIe siècle*. Paris, 1968.
Adams, R.G. and Allen, G. (eds), *Placing friendship in context*. Cambridge, 1998.
Allen, G.A., *A sociology of friendship and kinship*. London, 1979.
Alster, B., 'Tiāmat' in K. van der Torn and others (eds), *Dictionaries of deities and demons in the Bible* (Leiden, New York and Cologne, 1995), cols. 1634–9.
Ames-Lewis, F. and Rogers, M. (eds), *Concepts of beauty in the Renaissance*. Aldershot, 1998.
Amusson, S., 'Punishment, discipline and power: the social meanings of violence in early modern England', *Journal of British Studies* 34 (1995), pp. 1–34.
Andersen, J., *The witch on the wall: medieval erotic scupture in the British Isles*. London, 1977.
Anderson, B.S. and Zinsser, J.P., *A history of their own: women in Europe from Prehistory to the present*. vol. I, London, 1988.
Apostolos-Cappadona, D., *Dictionary of women in religious art*. Oxford, 1998.

Atkinson, C.W., '"Your servant, my mother": the figure of St Monica in the ideology of Christian motherhood', in C.W. Atkinson, C.H. Buchanan and M.R. Miles (eds), *Immaculate and powerful: the female in sacred image and social reality* (Boston, 1985), pp. 139–72.
Baldwin, J.W., *The language of sex: five voices from Northern France around 1200*. Chicago, 1994.
Bartlett, T. and Jeffery, K. (eds), *A military history of Ireland*. Cambridge, 1996.
Barnard, T.C., Ó Crónín, D. and Simms, K. (eds), *'A miracle of learning': studies in manuscripts and Irish learning in honour of William O'Sullivan*. Aldershot, 1998.
Baxendale, S. F., 'Exile in practice. The Alberti family in and out of Florence, 1401–1428', *Renaissance Quarterly* 44 (1991), pp. 720–56.
Benton, J.F., 'Clio and Venus: an historical view of medieval love' in F.X. Newman (ed.), *The meaning of courtly love* (Albany, New York, 1968), pp. 19–42.
Besoigne, J., *Histore de l'abbaye de Port-Royal*. 6 vols., Cologne [Amsterdam], 1752–3.
Binns, J.W., 'Biblical latin poetry in Renaissance England', in F. Cairns (ed.), *Papers of the Liverpool Latin Seminar*, vol. 3 (Liverpool, 1981), pp. 385–416.
Bisson, T. (ed.), *Cultures of power: lordship, status and process in twelfth-century Europe*. Philadelphia, 1995.
Blamires, A., *The case for women in medieval culture*. Oxford, 1997.
Bloch, M., *Feudal society*. Tr. L. Manyon. 2 vols., Chicago, 1961.
Bond, G.A., *The loving subject: desire, eloquence and power in romanesque France*. Philadelphia, 1995.
Borsje, J., 'Omens, ordeals and oracles: on demons and weapons in Early Irish texts', *Peritia* 13 (1999), pp. 224–48.
Bossy, J., *The English Catholic community, 1570–1850*. London, 1975.
Bradley, J. (ed.), *Settlement and society in medieval Ireland. Studies presented to Francis Xavier Martin O.S.A.* Kilkenny, 1988.
Bradshaw, B., *The dissolution of the monastic orders in Ireland by Henry VIII*. Cambridge, 1974.
Brady, J., 'Funeral customs of the past', *Irish Ecclesiastical Record* 78 (1952), pp. 330–9.
Branca, V., *Boccaccio: the man and his works*. New York, 1976.
Brand, J., *Observations on popular antiquities*. Newcastle, 1777.
Bright, D.F., *The miniature epic in Vandal Africa*. Norman, Oklahoma and London, 1987.
Brooks, E. St. J., *Knights' fees in counties Wexford, Carlow and Kilkenny (13th–15th century)*. Dublin, 1950.
—— 'The de Riddelsfords', *Journal of the Royal Society of Antiquaries of Ireland* 81 (1951), pp. 115–38; 82 (1952), pp. 45–51.
Broude, N. and Garrard, M. (eds), *The expanding discourse: feminism and art history*. New York, 1992.
Brown, D.A., *Virtue and beauty. Leonardo's Ginevra de' Benci and Renaissance portraits of women*. Princeton and Oxford, 2001.
Brown, J.C. and Davis, R.C. (eds), *Gender and society in Renaissance Italy*. London, 1996.
Brown, P., *The body and society: men, women and sexual renunciation in early Christianity*. New York, 1988.
Brucker, G.A., *Giovanni and Lusanna: love and marriage in Renaissance Florence*. Berkeley, 1986.
—— *Florence: the Golden Age, 1138–1737*. Berkeley, Los Angeles and London, 1996.

Bryce, J., 'Performing for strangers: women, dance and music in Quattrocento Florence', *Renaissance Quarterly* 54 (2001), pp. 1074–1107.
Bugnion-Secretan, P., *La Mère Angélique Arnauld 1591–1661 d'après ses écrits abbesse et réformatrice de Port-Royal*. Paris, 1991.
Bullough, V.L., 'Prostitution in the later Middle Ages' in V.L. Bullough and J. Brundage (eds), *Sexual practices and the medieval church* (Buffalo, 1982), pp. 176–86.
—— and J. Brundage (eds), *Sexual practices and the medieval church*. Buffalo, 1982.
Butler, G., 'Red Piers Butler of Ormond', *Journal of the Butler Society* 1 (1968), pp. 37–44, 113–19.
Cadden, J., *Meanings of sex difference in the Middle Ages*. Cambridge, 1993.
Canny, N., *From Reformation to Restoration in Ireland, 1534–1660*. Cambridge, 1993.
Cassidy, M., Hickey, H. and Street, M. (eds), *Deviance and textual control: new perspectives in medieval studies*. Melbourne, 1997.
Cheyette, F.L., 'Women, poets and politics in Occitania', in T. Evergates (ed.), *Aristocratic women in medieval France* (Philadelphia, 1999), pp. 138–77, 225–33.
Chibnall, M., *Empress Matilda: queen consort, queen mother and lady of the English*. Oxford, 1991.
—— 'Women in Orderic Vitalis', *Haskins Society Journal* 2 (1990), pp. 105–21.
Clark, A., *Beasts and bawdy*. London, 1975.
Coerver, C., '*Donna/dono*: chivalry and adulterous exchange in the Quattrocento', in G.A. Johnson and S. F. Matthews (eds), *Picturing women in Renaissance and Baroque Italy* (Cambridge, 1997), pp. 196–221.
Cohn, S.K. Jr., *Women in the streets: essays on sex and power in Renaissance Italy*. Baltimore and London, 1996.
Corblet, J., *Notice sur quatre religieuses de Port-Royal des Champs exilées dans divers monastères d'Amiens*. Amiens, 1861.
Corish, P., 'Women and religious practice', in M. McCurtain and M. O'Dowd (eds), *Women in early modern Ireland* (Dublin, 1991), pp. 212–20.
Cosgrove, A. (ed.), *A new history of Ireland II. Medieval Ireland, 1169–1534*. Oxford, 1989.
—— and D. MacCartney (eds), *Studies in Irish history presented to R. Dudley Edwards*. Dublin, 1979.
Cousin, V., *Jacqueline Pascal: premières études sur les femmes illustres et la société du XVIIe siècle*. 3rd ed., Paris, 1856.
Cottret, M., *Jansénisme et lumières: pour un autre XVIIIe siècle*. Paris, 1998.
Cregan, D., 'The social and cultural background of a Counter Reformation episcopate, 1618–60', in A. Cosgrove and D. MacCartney (eds), *Studies in Irish history presented to R. Dudley Edwards* (Dublin, 1979), pp. 85–117.
Crouch, D., 'Oddities in the early history of the marcher lordship of Gower', *Bulletin of the Board of Celtic Studies* 31 (1984), pp. 133–41.
—— 'The hidden history of the twelfth century', *Haskins Society Journal* 5 (1993), pp. 111–30.
—— *William Marshal: court, career and chivalry in the Angevin Empire*. London, 1990.
Damian-Grint, P., *The new historians of the twelfth-century Renaissance. Inventing vernacular authority*. Woodbridge, 1999.
Dauphiné, J., 'Le "Chevallier" Du Bartas: lettre inedite de Jacques VI d'Écosse', *Bibliothèque d'Humanisme et Renaissance* 59 (1997), pp. 63–6.
Davidsohn, R., *Storia di Firenze*. 8 vols., Florence, 1957–73.

Davis, N.Z., *Society and culture in early modern France*. Stanford, 1975.
Davis, R.C., 'The geography of gender in the Renaissance', in J.C. Brown and R.C. Davis (eds), *Gender and society in Renaissance Italy* (London, 1996), pp. 19–38.
Delumeau, J. and Cottret, M., *Le Catholicisme entre Luther et Voltaire*. 6th ed., Paris, 1996. First published 1971.
De Beauvoir, S., *The second sex*. London, 1980.
Del Lungo, I., *Women of Florence*. Tr. Mary G. Steegman, New York, 1908.
Dempsey, C., *The portrayal of love: Botticelli's 'Primavera'*. Princeton, 1992.
Den Boeft, J. and Hilhorst, A. (eds), *Early Christian poetry: a collection of essays*. Leiden, 1993.
Dennehy, W., 'Irish Catholics in the seventeenth century', *Irish Ecclesiatical Record* 4th series, 18 (1905), pp. 410–420.
D'Evelyn, C. and Foster, F.A. (eds), *A manual of writings in Middle English*. Hamden, Ct., 1970.
Dhondt, J., 'Sept femmes et un trio de rois', *Contributions à l'histoire économique et sociale* 3 (1964–5), pp. 35–70.
DiBernardino, A. and Cipriani, N, 'Christian poetry', in Angelo DiBernardino (ed.), *Patrology*, vol. 4, tr. Placid Solari. Westminster, Md., 1986.
Didi-Huberman, G. and others, *St Georges et le dragon*. Paris, 1994.
Dizionario Biografico degli Italiani vols. 1–, 1960–
Duby, G., 'Women and power', in T. Bisson (ed.), *Cultures of power: lordship, status and process in twelfth-century Europe* (Philadelphia, 1995), pp. 69–85.
—— *Women of the twelfth century, vol. 2: remembering the dead*. Tr. J. Birrell. Chicago, 1997.
Duncan-Jones, K., *Sir Philip Sidney: courtier poet*. New Haven and London, 1991.
Elm, S., *'Virgins of God': the making of asceticism in Late Antiquity*. Oxford, 1994.
English, B., *The lords of Holderness, 1066–1260*. Oxford, 1979.
Erler, M. and Kowaleski, M. (eds), *Women and power in the Middle Ages*. Athens, Georgia, rev. ed. 1988 (first published 1973).
Ettlinger, H.S., *'Visibilis et invisibilis*: the mistress in Italian Renaissance court society', *Renaissance Quarterly* 47 (1994), pp. 770–92.
Evenpoel, W., 'The place of poetry in Latin Christianity', in J. Den Boeft and A. Hilhorst (eds), *Early Christian poetry: a collection of essays*. Leiden, 1993.
Evergates, T. (ed.), *Aristocratic women in medieval France*. Philadelphia, 1999.
Fabbri, L., *Alleanza matrimoniale e patriziato nella Firenze del '400: studio sulla famiglia Strozzi*. Florence, 1991.
Facinger, M., 'A study of medieval queenship: Capetian France, 987–1237', *Studies in Medieval and Renaissance History* 5 (1968), pp. 3–48.
Ferrante, J.M., *To the glory of her sex: women's roles in the composition of medieval texts*. Bloomington, Indiana, 1997.
—— and Economou, G.D. (eds), *In pursuit of perfection, courtly love in medieval literature*. Port Washington, New York, 1975.
Filoramo, G., *A history of gnosticism*, tr. Anthony Alcock. Oxford, 1990.
Fineschi, V., *Memorie storiche degli uomini illustri del convento di S. Maria Novella*. Florence, 1787, reprinted Rome, 1977.
Fitzgerald, W., 'Notes on Lady Margaret Fitzgerald who married Pierce, 8th Earl of Ormond in 1485', *Kildare Archaeological Society Journal* 8 (1915–17), pp. 503–11.

Flanagan, M.T., 'Irish and Anglo-Norman warfare in twelfth-century Ireland' in T. Bartlett and K. Jeffery (eds), *A military history of Ireland* (Cambridge, 1996), pp. 52–75.
—— *Irish society, Anglo-Norman settlers, Angevin kingship: interactions in Ireland in the late twelfth century.* Oxford, 1989.
Fontaine, J., *Naissance de la poésie dans l'occident chrétien: esquisse d'une histoire de la poésie latine chrétienne du IIIe au VIe siécle.* Paris, Études Augustiniennes, 1981.
Ford, A., 'Reforming the Holy Isle: Parr Lane and the conversion of the Irish' in T.C. Barnard, D. Ó Crónín and K. Simms (eds), *'A miracle of learning': studies in manuscripts and Irish learning in honour of William O'Sullivan* (Aldershot, 1998), 137–63.
Freeman, E., 'The medieval nuns at Watton: reading female agency from male-authored didactic texts', *Magistra* 6 (2000), pp. 3–36.
Gamber, S., *Le livre de la 'Genèse' dans la poésie latine au Ve siècle.* Paris, 1899.
Garrard, M., 'Leonardo da Vinci: female portraits, female nature', in N. Broude and M. Garrard (eds), *The expanding discourse: feminism and art history* (New York, 1992), pp. 58–85.
Gastellier, F., *Angélique Arnauld.* Paris, 1998.
Gibson, W., *Women in seventeenth-century France.* Basingstoke, 1989.
Gilbert, J.T., *History of the confederation and war in Ireland.* 7 vols., Dublin, 1882–91.
Gillespie, R., *Devoted people: belief and religion in early modern Ireland.* Manchester, 1997.
Gillingham, J., 'Conquering the barbarians: war and chivalry in twelfth-century Britain', *Haskins Society Journal* 4 (1993), pp. 67–84.
Goldin, F., 'The array of perspectives in the early courtly love lyric', in J.M. Ferrante and G.D. Economou (eds), *In pursuit of perfection, courtly love in medieval literature* (Port Washington, New York, 1975), pp. 51–100.
Gregory, H., 'Daughters, dowries and the family in fifteenth-century Florence', *Rinascimento* ser. 2, 27 (1987), pp. 215–37.
Gres-Gayer, J., *Le jansénisme en Sorbonne, 1643–1656.* Paris, 1996.
Gwynn, A. and Hadcock, R.N., *Medieval religious houses: Ireland.* Dublin, 1970.
Hagger, M.S., *The fortunes of a Norman family: the de Verduns in England, Ireland and Wales, 1066–1316.* Dublin, 2001.
Halbwachs, M., *On collective memory*, ed. and tr. with an introduction by Lewis A. Coser, *The heritage of sociology.* Chicago and London, 1992.
—— *Les cadres sociaux de la mémoire.* Paris, 1952.
Hall, D., 'Immoral and contemptuous: the trial of Elicia Butler, abbess of Kilculliheen, in sixteenth-century Kilkenny', in M. Cassidy, H. Hickey and M. Street (eds), *Deviance and textual control: new perspectives in medieval studies* (Melbourne, 1997), pp. 17–33.
—— *Women and the church in medieval Ireland.* Dublin, 2003.
Hall, V. Jr. and others, 'Renaissance poetics', in A. Preminger and T.V.F. Brogan (eds), *The Princeton encyclopedia of poetry and poetics.* 3rd ed., Princeton, 1993.
Hanawalt, B., *Growing up in medieval London: the experience of childhood in history.* Oxford, 1993.
Hannam, J., 'Women, history and protest', in V. Robinson and R. Richardson (eds), *Introducing women's studies: feminist theory and practice* (2nd ed. Basingstoke and London, 1997. 1st ed. 1993), pp. 77–97.

Harrison, K., 'Rich friendships, affluent friends: middle class practices of friendship' in R.G. Adams and G. Allen (eds), *Placing friendship in context* (Cambridge, 1998), pp. 92–116.
Harrison, S.J., 'cento', in S. Hornblower and A. Spawforth (eds), *The Oxford classical dictionary*. 3rd ed., Oxford, 1996.
Harvey, M., *The English in Rome, 1362–1420: portrait of an expatriate community*. Cambridge, 1999.
Hibbert, C., *The rise and fall of the house of Medici*. London, 1974.
Hogarth, P. with V. Clery, *Dragons*. London, 1979.
Holloway, J.B., Bechtold, J. and Wright, C.S. (eds), *Equally in God's image*. New York, 1990.
Holmes, M., *Fra Filippo Lippi the Carmelite painter*. New Haven and London, 1999.
Holt, J.C., 'Feudal society and the family in early medieval England: II. Notions of patrimony', *Transactions of the Royal Historical Society* 5th series 33 (1983), pp. 193–220.
Honeycutt, L., 'The idea of the perfect princess: the *life* of St. Margaret in the reign of Matilda II (1100–1118)', *Anglo-Norman Studies* 12 (1989), pp. 81–97.
Hore, H.J. and Graves, J. (eds), *The social state of the southern and eastern counties of Ireland in the sixteenth century*. Dublin, 1870.
Hornblower, S. and Spawforth, A. (eds), *The Oxford classical dictionary*. 3rd ed., Oxford, 1996.
Hufton, O., *The prospect before her: a history of women in Western Europe. Volume one, 1500–1800*. London, 1995.
Hughes, D.O., 'From brideprice to dowry in medieval Europe', *Women and History* 10 (1985), pp. 13–58.
Johnson, G.A. and Matthews Grieco, S.F. (eds), *Picturing women in Renaissance and Baroque Italy*. Cambridge, 1997.
Kaeuper, R., *Chivalry and violence in medieval England*. Oxford, 1999.
Kelly, J., 'Did women have a Renaissance?', in her *Women, history and theory: the essays of Joan Kelly* (Chicago and London, 1977) pp. 19–50.
P. Kilroy, 'Women and the Reformation', in M. McCurtain and M. O'Dowd (eds), *Women in early modern Ireland* (Dublin, 1991), 179–96.
Klapisch-Zuber, C., *Women, family and ritual in Renaissance Italy*. Tr. L. Cochrane, London and Chicago, 1985.
Kleinhenz, C., 'Texts, naked and thinly veiled: erotic elements in medieval Italian literature', in Joyce E. Salisbury (ed.), *Sex in the Middle Ages: a book of essays* (New York, 1991), pp. 83–109.
Krautheimer, R., *Lorenzo Ghiberti*. Princeton, 1956.
Kuehn, T., *Illegitimacy in Renaissance Florence*. Ann Arbor, 2002.
—— *Law, family and women: toward a legal anthropology of Renaissance Italy*. Chicago and London, 1991.
Latzke, T., 'Die Fürstinnenpreis', *Mittellateinisches Jahrbuch* 14 (1979), pp. 22–65.
—— 'Robert von Arbrissel, Ermengard und Eva', *Mittellateinisches Jahrbuch* 19 (1984), pp. 116–54.
Laqueur, T., *Making sex: body and gender from the Greeks to Freud*. Cambridge, Mass., 1990.
Laven, M., *The virgins of Venice*. London, 2002.
Lawless, G., *Augustine of Hippo and his monastic rule*. Oxford, 1987.
Lennon, C., *The lords of Dublin in the age of reformation*. Dublin, 1989.

Levi d'Ancona, M., *Due quadri del Botticelli eseguite per nascite in casa Medici*. Florence, 1999.
Lewis, R.E. and others (eds), *Middle English dictionary*. Ann Arbor, 2000.
Lifshitz, F., 'Is mother superior ?: toward a history of feminist Amtscharisma', in J.C. Parsons and B. Wheeler (eds), *Medieval mothering* (New York and London, 1996), pp. 117–138.
Livingstone, A., 'Aristocratic women in the Chartrain', in T. Evergates (ed.), *Aristocratic women in medieval France* (Philadelphia, 1999), pp. 44–73, 200–7.
LoPrete, K.A., 'Adela of Blois and Ivo of Chartres: piety, politics and the peace in the diocese of Chartres', *Anglo-Norman Studies* 14 (1991), pp. 131–52.
—— *Adela of Blois, countess and lord, c.1067–1137*. Dublin, forthcoming.
—— 'Adela of Blois: familial alliances and female lordship' in T. Evergates (ed.), *Aristocratic women in medieval France* (Philadelphia, 1999) pp. 7–43, 180–200.
—— and Evergates, T., 'Introduction', in *Aristocratic women in medieval France* (Philadelphia, 1999), pp. 1–5, 179–80.
Luttrell, A., 'Englishwomen as pilgrims to Jerusalem: Isolda Parewastell, 1365', in J.B. Holloway, J. Bechtold and C.S. Wright (eds), *Equally in God's image* (New York, 1990), pp. 184–97.
Lydon, J. (ed.), *Law and disorder in thirteenth-century Ireland*. Dublin, 1997.
McCurtain, M., 'Women, education and learning in early modern Ireland', in M. McCurtain and M. O'Dowd (eds), *Women in early modern Ireland* (Dublin, 1991), pp. 160–78.
—— and D. Ó Corráin (eds), *Women in Irish society*. Dublin, 1978.
—— and O'Dowd, M. (eds), *Women in early modern Ireland*. Dublin, 1991.
McLaughlin, M., 'The woman warrior: gender, warfare and society in medieval Europe', *Women's Studies* 17 (1990), pp. 193–209.
McClure, J., 'The biblical epic and its audience in Late Antiquity', in Francis Cairns (ed.), *Papers of the Liverpool Latin Seminar*, vol. 3 (Liverpool, 1981), pp. 305–21.
McNamara, J.A. and Wemple, S., 'The power of women through the family in medieval Europe, 500–1100' in M. Erler and M. Kowaleski (eds), *Women and power in the Middle Ages* (rev. ed., Athens, Georgia, 1988, first published 1973), pp. 83–101.
Maddern, P., *Violence and the social order: East Anglia, 1422–1442*. Oxford, 1992.
Maire, C., *De la cause de Dieu à la cause de la nation: le jansénisme au XVIIIe siècle*. Paris, 1998.
Maisières, Maury Thibaud de, *Les poèmes inspirés du début de la Genèse à l'époque de la Renaissance*. Louvain, 1931.
Makowski, E., *Canon law and cloistered women: Periculoso and its commentators, 1298–1545*. Washington, D.C., 1997.
Mannini, M.P. and Fagioli, M. (eds), *Filippo Lippi: catalogo completo*. Florence, 1997.
Mazzi, M.S., *Prostitute e lenoni nella Firenze del Quattrocento*. Milan, 1991.
Meek, C.E. (ed.), *Women in Renaissance and early modern Europe*. Dublin, 2000.
—— and Simms, M.K. (eds), *'The fragility of her sex'? Medieval Irish women in their European context*. Dublin, 1996.
Michel, M.-J., *Jansénisme et Paris, 1640–1730*. Paris, 2000.
Miles, M., 'The Virgin's one bare breast: nudity, gender and religious meaning in Tuscan early Renaissance culture', in N. Broude and M. Garrard (eds), *The expanding discourse: feminism and art history* (New York, 1992), pp. 27–37.
Molho, A., *Marriage alliance in late medieval Florence*. Cambridge, Mass. and London, 1994.

Muir, E., *Civic ritual in Renaissance Venice*. Princeton, 1981.
Mulder-Bakker, A. (ed.), *Sanctity and motherhood: essays on holy mothers in the Middle Ages*. New York, 1995.
Mulholland, J., 'The trial of Alice Butler, abbess of Kilculliheen', *Decies* 25 (1984), pp. 45–6.
Mullaly, E., 'Hiberno-Norman literature and its public' in J. Bradley (ed.), *Settlement and society in medieval Ireland. Studies presented to Francis Xavier Martin O.S.A.*, (Kilkenny, 1988), pp. 327–44.
—— 'The portrayal of women in the *Histoire de Guillaume le Maréchal*', *Peritia* 10 (1996), pp. 351–62.
Newman, B., *From virile woman to WomanChrist: studies in medieval religion and literature*. Philadelphia, 1995.
Newman, F.X. (ed.), *The meaning of courtly love*. Albany, New York, 1968.
Newton, W.R., *Sociologie de la communauté de Port-Royal: histoire, économie*. Paris, 1999.
Nicholas, K.S., 'Countesses as rulers of Flanders', in T. Evergates (ed.), *Aristocratic women in medieval France* (Philadelphia, 1999), pp. 111–37, 220–5.
Nip, R., 'Godelieve of Gistel and Ida of Boulogne', in A. Mulder-Bakker (ed.), *Sanctity and motherhood: essays on holy mothers in the Middle Ages* (New York, 1995), pp. 191–223.
Noble, T. and Head, T., *Soldiers of Christ: saints and saints' lives from Late Antiquity to the early Middle Ages*. London, 1995.
Nodes, D.J., 'Benevolent winds and the spirit of God in *De laudibus Dei* of Dracontius', *Vigiliae Christianae* 43 (1989), pp. 282–92.
—— *Doctrine and exegesis in biblical Latin poetry*. ARCA vol. 31, Leeds, 1993.
Ó Cléirigh, C., 'The absentee landlady and the sturdy robbers: Agnes de Valence', in C.E. Meek and M.K. Simms (eds), *'The fragility of her sex'? Medieval Irish women in their European context* (Dublin, 1996), pp. 101–118.
—— 'The problems of defence: a regional case study' in J. Lydon (ed.), *Law and disorder in thirteenth-century Ireland* (Dublin, 1997), pp. 46–55.
O'Connor, P., *Friendship between women*. Hemel Hampstead, 1992.
—— 'Women's friendships in a post-modern world', in R.G. Adams and G. Allen (eds), *Placing friendship in context* (Cambridge, 1998), pp. 117–35.
O'Dowd, M., 'Women and war in Ireland in the 1640s', in M. McCurtain and M. O'Dowd (eds), *Women in early modern Ireland* (Dublin, 1991), pp. 91–111.
O'Loughlin, T., 'Giraldus Cambrensis and the sexual agenda of the twelfth-century reformers', *Journal of Welsh Religious History* 8 (2000), pp. 1–16.
Orcibal, J., *Port-Royal entre le miracle et l'obéissance: Flavie Passart et Angélique d'Andilly*. Paris, 1957.
Origo, I., 'The domestic enemy: eastern slaves in Tuscany in the fourteenth and fifteenth centuries', *Speculum* 30 (1955), pp. 321–66.
Orpen, G.H., *Ireland under the Normans, 1169–1333*. 4 vols., Oxford, 1911–20. Reprinted Dublin, 2003.
—— 'The Fitz Geralds, barons of Offaly', *Journal of the Royal Society of Antiquaries of Ireland* 44 (1914), pp. 99–113.
Otway-Ruthven, A.J., 'The dower charter of John de Courcy's wife', *Ulster Journal of Archaeology* 3rd ser. 12 (1949), pp. 77–81.
Palmer, R.C., 'Contexts of marriage in medieval England from the king's court circa 1300', *Speculum* 59 (1984), pp. 42–67.

Palmer, W., 'Gender, violence and rebellion in Tudor and early Stuart Ireland', *Sixteenth Century Journal* 22 (1992), pp 699–712.
Parker, R. and Pollock, G., *Old mistresses: women, art and ideology*. London, 1987.
Parsons, J.C. and Wheeler, B. (eds), *Medieval mothering*. New York and London, 1996.
Partner, N., *Serious entertainments: the writing of history in twelfth-century England*. Chicago, 1977.
Passerini, L., *Genealogia e storia della famiglia Altoviti*. Florence, 1971.
Perosa, A. (ed.), *Giovanni Rucellai ed il suo Zibaldone. Il Zibaldone Quaresimale*. Studies of the Warburg Institute, 24, London, 1960.
Pieraccini, G., *La stirpe de' Medici di Caffagiolo*. 3 vols., Florence, 1924–5.
Phelan, M., 'An unidentified tomb in St Canice's cathedral, Kilkenny', *Old Kilkenny Review* 48 (1996), pp. 40–4.
Platelle, H., 'Le problème du scandale: les nouvelles modes masculines aux XIe et XIIe siècles', *Revue Belge de Philologie et d'Histoire* 53 (1975), pp. 1071–96.
Pollock, F. and Maitland, F.W., *The history of English law before the time of Edward I*. 2 vols., Cambridge, 1911.
Power, E., *Medieval English nunneries, c.1275–1535*. Cambridge, 1922.
Preminger, A and Brogan, T.V.F. (eds), *The Princeton encyclopedia of poetry and poetics*. 3rd ed., Princeton, 1993.
Prescott, A.L., *French poets and the English Renaissance: studies in fame and transformation*. New York and London, 1968.
Prestwich, M., Britnell, R. and Frame, R. (eds), *Thirteenth-century England VIII*. Woodbridge, 2001.
Rae, E.C., 'Architecture and sculpture, 1169–1603', in A. Cosgrove (ed.), *New history of Ireland* Vol.II (Oxford, 1987), pp. 737–80.
Raby, F.J.E., *A history of Christian latin poetry from the beginnings to the close of the Middle Ages*. 2nd ed., Oxford, 1953.
Rauer, C., *Beowulf and the dragon: parallels and analogues*. Cambridge, 2000.
Riches, S.J.E., 'St George as a virgin martyr', in S.J.E. Riches and S. Salih (eds), *Gender and holiness: men, women and saints in late medieval Europe* (London, 2002), pp. 65–85.
—— *St George: hero, martyr and myth*. Stroud, 2000.
—— and S. Salih (eds), *Gender and holiness: men, women and saints in late medieval Europe*. London, 2002.
Roberts, M., *Biblical epic and rhetorical paraphrase in Late Antiquity*. ARCA vol.16, Liverpool, 1985.
—— 'The prologue to Avitus' *De spiritalis historiae gestis*: Christian poetry and poetic licence', *Traditio* 36 (1980), pp. 399–407.
Robinson, V. and Richardson, R. (eds), *Introducing women's studies: feminist theory and practice*. 2nd ed., Basingstoke and London, 1997 (1st ed., 1993).
Rochon, A., *La jeunesse de Laurent de Médicis (1449–1478)*. Paris, 1963.
Rocke, M., *Forbidden friendships: homosexuality and male culture in Renaissance Florence*. Chicago, 1997.
Roosval, J., *Nya Sankt Görans Studier*. Stockholm, 1924.
Rowland, B., *Animals with human faces: a guide to animal symbolism*. Knoxville, 1973.
Ruda, G., *Fra Filippo Lippi*. London, 1993.
Rudolph, K., *Gnosis: the nature and history of gnosticism*, tr. Robert McLachlan Wilson. Edinburgh, 1983.

Ruggiero, G., *The boundaries of Eros: sex crime and sexuality in Renaissance Venice*. Oxford, 1985.
Saint-Beuve, C.A., *Port-Royal*, ed. M. Leroy. 3 vols., Paris, 1955.
Salisbury, J.E. (ed.), *Sex in the Middle Ages: a book of essays*. New York, 1991.
Scott, J.W., 'Gender: a useful category of historical analysis', *American Historical Review* 91 (1986), pp. 1053–75.
Scribner, R.W., *For the sake of simple folk: popular propaganda for the German Reformation*. Cambridge, 1981.
Searle, E., 'Women and the legitimisation of succession at the Norman Conquest' in R. Allen Brown (ed.), *Proceedings of the Battle conference on Anglo-Norman Studies* 3 (1980), pp. 159–70, 226–9.
Sedgewick, A., *The travails of conscience: the Arnauld family and the ancien régime*. Cambridge, Mass. and London, 1998.
Seidel Menchi, S., Jacobson Schutte, A. and Kuehn, T. (eds), *Tempi e spazi di vita femminile tra Medioevo ed Età Moderna* (Annali dell'Istituto Storico Italo-Germanico in Trento, 51). Bologna, 1997. English translation as *Time, space, and women's lives in early modern Europe*. Kirksville, Missouri, 2001.
Short, I., 'Patrons and polyglots: French literature in twelfth-century England', *Anglo-Norman Studies* 14 (1991), pp. 229–49.
Simms, K., 'Women in Norman Ireland', in M. MacCurtain and D. Ó Corráin (eds), *Women in Irish society* (Dublin, 1978), pp. 14–25.
Simons, P., 'Women in frames: the gaze, the eye, the profile in Renaissance portraiture', *History Workshop Journal* 25 (1988), pp. 2–29.
Simpson, G.G., 'The *familia* of Roger de Quincy, earl of Winchester and Constable of Scotland', in K.J. Stringer (ed.), *Essays on the nobility of medieval Scotland* (Edinburgh, 1985), pp. 102–29.
Simpson, J., *British dragons*. 2nd ed., London, 2001.
Smith, B., 'Irish politics, 1220–1245', in M. Prestwich, R. Britnell and R. Frame (eds), *Thirteenth-century England VIII* (Woodbridge, 2001), pp. 13–22.
—— 'The concept of the March in medieval Ireland: the case of Uriel', *Proceedings of the Royal Irish Academy* 88C (1988), pp. 257–69.
Stafford, P., *Queens, concubines and dowagers: the king's wife in the early Middle Ages*. Athens, Georgia, 1983.
Stone, L., *The past and present revisited*. London, 1987.
Strickland, M., *War and chivalry: the conduct and perception of war in England and Normandy, 1066–1217*. Cambridge, 1996.
Stringer, K.J. (ed.), *Essays on the nobility of medieval Scotland*. Edinburgh, 1985.
Strocchia, S., 'Gender and rites of honour in Italian Renaissance cities', in J.C. Brown and R.C. Davis (eds), *Gender and society in Renaissance Italy* (London, 1996), pp. 39–60.
Stuard, S.M., 'Fashion's captives: medieval women in French historiography', in S.M. Stuard (ed.), *Women in medieval history and historiography* (Philadelphia, 1987), pp. 68–76.
—— (ed.), *Women in medieval history and historiography*. Philadelphia, 1987
Tait, C., *Death, burial and commemoration in Ireland, 1550–1650*. Dublin, forthcoming.
Talbot, C.H., *The Anglo-Saxon missionaries in Germany*. London, 1954.
Thompson, K.H., 'Dowry and inheritance patterns: some examples from the descendants of Henry I', *Medieval Prosopography* 17 (1996), pp. 45–61.

Tinagli, P., *Women in Italian Renaissance art: gender, representation, identity*. Manchester, 1997.
Trexler, R.C., *Public life in Renaissance Florence*. New York, 1980.
—— *The children of Renaissance Florence. Power and dependence in Renaissance Florence*, vol. 1. Asheville, 1998.
—— *The women of Renaissance Florence. Power and dependence in Renaissance Florence*, vol. 2. Asheville, 1998.
Turner, R.V., *King John*. London, 1994.
Van der Torn, K., Becking, B. and van der Horst, P.W. (eds), *Dictionary of deities and demons in the Bible*. Leiden, New York and Cologne, 1995.
van Houts, E.M.C., 'Latin poetry and the Anglo-Norman court, 1066–1135: the *Carmen de Hastingae Proelio*', *Journal of Medieval History* 15 (1989), pp. 39–62.
Van Kley, D.K., *The religious origins of the French Revolution, from Calvin to the Civil Constitution, 1560–1791*. New Haven and London, 1996.
Vann, T.M. (ed.), *Queens, regents and potentates*. Dallas, Texas, 1993.
von Moos, P., *Hildebert von Lavardin, 1056–1133: Humanitas an der Schwelle des höfischen Zeitalters*. Pariser Historische Studien, no. 3, Stuttgart, 1965.
Walker, S.S., 'Proof of age of feudal heirs in medieval England', *Medieval Studies* 35 (1973), pp. 306–23.
Warner, M., *Monuments and maidens: the allegory of the female form*. London, 1996.
Weaver, F.E., *The evolution of the reform of Port-Royal, from the rule of Cîteaux to Jansenism*. Paris, 1978.
Webb, D., 'St James in Tuscany: the Opera di San Jacopo of Pistoia and pilgrimage to Compostela', *Journal of Ecclesiastical History* 50 (1999), pp. 207–34.
—— *Pilgrims and pilgrimage in the medieval West*. London, 1999.
Wind, E., *Pagan mysteries in the Renaissance*. Oxford, 1980.
Wittke, C., *Numen litterarum: the old and the new in Latin poetry from Constantine to Gregory the Great*. Mittellateinische Studien und Texte, V. Leiden, 1971.
Young, G.F., *The Medici*. New York, 1910.
Zaccaria, R.M., 'Documenti e ipotesi sulla madre di Giulio de' Medici', *Interpres: Rivista di Studi Quattrocenteschi* 18 (1999), pp. 234–43.
Zanelli, A., *Le schiave orientali a Firenze nei secoli XIV e XV*. Florence, 1885.

THESES

Cottrell, J., 'Leinster, South Wales, Bristol and Angevin politics, 1135–1172. Some influences on the earliest English in Ireland'. Unpublished Ph.D. thesis, University of Bristol, 2000.
de Trafford, C., 'The contract of marriage: the *maritagium* from the eleventh to the thirteenth century'. Unpublished Ph.D. thesis, University of Leeds, 1999.
Duignan, A., 'For the preservation of religion and the safety of the nation: the Connacht Group, 1625–42'. Unpublished M.A. thesis, National University of Ireland, 2000.

Contributors

CAROL BAXTER   A graduate in History and French she is completing a Ph.D. at Trinity on the nuns of Port-Royal. She is a civil servant in the Department of Foreign Affairs.

CLAIRE DE TRAFFORD   A graduate of University College London and Durham, she obtained her Ph.D. from the University of Leeds for a thesis on the *maritagium*. She now teaches History and IT at a school in England.

JOHN FLOOD obtained his Ph.D. from Trinity for a thesis on the figure of Eve in early modern literature. He is a Senior Lecturer in the Department of English at Bishop's Grosseteste's College, Lincoln.

DIANNE HALL   A graduate of the University of Queensland, she obtained her Ph.D. from the University of Melbourne for a thesis on women and the church in medieval Ireland, which was recently published by Four Courts Press. She is now a Research Fellow in the Department of History at Melbourne.

GILLIAM KENNY   A graduate of UCD, she is completing a Ph.D. at Trinity on medieval Irish women.

CATHERINE LAWLESS   A graduate in History and History of Art, she obtained her Ph.D. at Trinity for a thesis on the figure of St Anne in Florentine painting. She now teaches at the University of Limerick, where she is the Director of the M.A. course in the History of Art and Architecture.

KIMBERLY LOPRETE graduated from the University of Chicago and obtained her Ph.D. for a thesis on Adela of Blois. She is a Lecturer in History at NUI Galway, specialising in medieval French history and the history of women.

CHRISTINE MEEK   Associate Professor in the Department of Medieval History at Trinity, she is a specialist on Italian history. She has written several books on the history of Lucca and edited collections of essays on medieval and early modern women.

SAMANTHA RICHES   With a Ph.D. from the University of Leicester, she is the author of a book on St George. She has taught at Leicester and

Huddersfield, and is at present in the Department of History of Art at St Andrews.

BRENDAN SMITH   A graduate in History, he obtained his Ph.D. from Trinity for a thesis on medieval Louth. The author of several books on medieval Irish history, he has also edited a collection of essays. He is a Senior Lecturer in History at the University of Bristol.

DIANA WEBB is a Senior Lecturer at King's College London. A specialist on late medieval social and religious history, especially of Italy, she has recently worked on the significane of pilgrimage, on which she has produced several studies and collections of translated texts.

Index

Aachen, 75, 81, 83, 84
abbesses, 14, 120, 131, 133, 135, 157, 158, 169
abbots, 134
Abraham, 21
Acciaiuoli, Antonio di Neri, Neri di Jacopo, 119
Acevedo, Alonso de, 19; see also *Creación del mundo*
Adam, 8, 23, 25–32, 34, 106, 143, 180, 181
Adams, Rebecca, 156
Adela of Blois, 12, 90ff
Adelphius, Clodius Celsinus, 23
adultery, 10, 62, 119, 122, 151
Aelred of Rievaulx, 135
Aeneid 24, commentary on, 105; *see also* Virgil
Agli (degli), Jacopo, 125
Agnes of Ponthieu, 97
Aífe, daughter of Diarmait Mac Murchada, 52, 54–5, 57
Alberti, Carlo, Leon Battista, Lorenzo, 118
Albizzi (degli), Giovanna, 114, Uberto di Giovanni, 123
Alethia, 27, 29–30
Alfani, Niccolò, Nigio, 119
Alice of Abervenny, 9, 49–50, 52, 58
Aline, daughter of Strongbow, 56
Allen, Graham, 156
Altdorfer, Albrecht, 185, 188; see also *St George and the Dragon*
Alton (de), Alex, Roesia, 74
Altoviti, Giovanna di messer Ugo, 121
Aluet, Emma, William, 41
Ambrose of Milan, St, 18, 26
Amiens, 175
anchoresses, 78, 112
Anges (des), Isabelle, Pelagie, 168
Annals, Irish, 139–40
Annals of Connacht, 51
Anne of Bohemia, 76
Anselm of Canterbury, 94, 107
Antichrist, 190
Antoninus, archbishop of Florence, St, 120

Apeldrefeld (de), Avice, William, 64
Apsu, 179
Ardinghelli, Niccolò, 115–16
Ardnurcher, 69
arianism, 31
Armagh, 69, 137
Arnauld, Anne-Eugénie, 170
Arnauld, Antoine, 159, 161
Arnauld d'Andilly, Mère Angélique de Saint-Jean, 157–8, 163, 165, 167, 168–70
Arnauld d'Andilly, Sr Angélique-Thérèse, 169
Arnauld d'Andilly, Sr Marie-Angélique de Sainte-Thérèse, 172–3
Arnauld, Marie-Claire, 163
Arnauld, Mère Agnès, 157–8, 163–4, 174
Arnauld, Mère Angélique, 157–8, 162–3
Arsenius, Abba, 78–9
Ashton, Elizabeth, Sir Robert, 85
ass head, 184
Assisi, 83–4, 87
Aston (de), Emmeline, Hugh, 64
Athlone, 139
Aud the Deep-Minded, 77–8
Audley (de), Adam, Henry, Leyra, 65
Audoein, Roger, 63
Augustine, St, 20, 30–2, 105, 133, 160; see also *Confessions*
Augustinian rule, 133–4, 137; theology, 158–9
Augustinus, 15, 155, 158–60; *see also* Jansen, Cornelius
Auters, Galfrid des, 70
Auxerre, St Germain, 103
Avitus, Alcimus of Vienne, St, 8, 18, 22, 31–5; see also *De spiritalis historiae gestis*
Aylward, Lucy, Nicholas, 73

Baginbun, battle of, 9, 49–50, 52
Bagnesi, Bartolomea, Filippo di Rosso, 118

Bagod, Roger, 62
Balaam, Michael, 42
Baldi, Pongano, 124
Baldovinetti, Niccolò, 124
Ball, Margaret, 142
Bar le Duc, Joan of, countess of Warenne, 83
Bardi, Alessandra, 117
Bardolf, Agnes, 86
Barducci, Lorenzo, 127
Baron, Milo de, 131, 133, 136, 140
Bartas, Guillaume du, 19; see also *La seconde semaine*
Bataille, John de la, 68
Beauchamp, Elias de, 40
Beaufort, Joan, countess of Westmoreland, 89
Beck, Leonard, 193–4; see also *St George Fighting with the Dragon*
Bede, 79
Bembo, Bernardo, 116
Benci, Bartolomeo, 117–18; Damiano di Giovanni, 127; Ginevra, 116, 130; Giovanni d'Amerigo, 127
Benciatti, Giuliano di Agnolo, 127
Benedictine Rule, 133–5, 162
Beowulf, 190
Bermingham, Margaret, 142; Piers, 138
Bermondsey, St Saviour, 88
Bernard of Tiron, St, 98, 102–3
Berotti de Cimegne, Serena, 119
Bertrand, Sr Marie-Magdelaine de Sainte, 175
Besoigne, Jérôme, 164
Betson, Thomas, 88
Bigod (le), Hugh, 64; Joan, 64–5
Bigot, Margery le, 73
Biliotti, Giovanozzo, Tommaso, 127, 129
Birgitta of Sweden, St, 83
Bischeri, Filippa di Nofri, Francesco di Bartolo, 119
Bischofsheim, 80
Blanchevil (de), Agnes, William, 42
Blathac, 69

217

Blound (le), Joan, Roger, 67
Boccaccio, 21, 122; see also *Genealogiae deorum gentilium*
Bohemond of Antioch, 98
Boiscervoise, Anne de Sainte-Cécile, Sr, 155, 175
Bona of Pisa, St, 82
Boniface of Wessex, S., 79–81
Boniface VIII, pope, 80
Bonnacon, 192
Bonneval, St Florentin, 103
Borehard, Simon de, 44
Bossy, John, 142
Botticelli, 115–16; see also *Primavera*
Bourne, Henry, 180
Brant, Sebastian, 185–6; see also *Narrenschiff*
Brégy, Eustoquie de Flécelles de, Sr, 157, 165–6, 168, 174
Breifne, 57
Bret, Ennison le, 40
Breton, Emma, Walter, 42
Bretonn, Elena, 70
Brideprice, 43
Bridgwater, 87
Bridlington Priory, 37
Brionie, Matilda de, 87
Briquet, Sr Christine, 160–1, 165–6, 167–8, 174
Briver, Mrs, 145
Brucker, Gene, 113
Brun, Arnold, John, Robert, 41
Brundeye (de), John, Marsilia, 65
Bryce, Judith, 117
Buckingham, Andrew de, 67
Bulkley, Launcelot, 145
Bullough, Vern L., 124
Burges, Mariota, Ralph, 66
Burhont (de), Emma, Walter, 47
Buti, Antonio di Francesco, 120; Lucrezia di Francesco, Spinetta di Francesco, 120–1
Butler, Elicia, 14–15, 131–3, 135–7, 139–40
Butler, James, 132
Butler, James, abbot of Inishlonaght, 134
Butler, Katherine, 139–40
Butler, Margaret, 73
Butler, Philip, 38
Butler, Piers, 14, 132, 139
Butler, Theobald, 73

Cadden, Joan, 105
Caen, Holy Trinity convent, 93
Calcagnini, Theophilo, 118
Camera (della), Ser Jacopo di ser Paolo, 123
Camera, Geoffrey de, 73
Camões, Luiz de, 19; see also *Da creacao e composicao do homen*
Canny, Nicholas, 141
Canons, 37, 100, 104, 122
Canterbury, 81, 83, 89
Canterbury, Anselm, archbishop of, 94, 107
Canterbury, Cuthbert, archbishop of, 79–80
Carew, Raymond de, 71
Carlow, 62, 71
Carnesecchi, Amerigo di Simone, 125
Carthage, 30–1
Casa, Giovanni della, 113
Casciatelli, Giovanni, 129
Cashel, archbishop of, 142
Castleroche, 57
Catesby, priory, 136
Catholic, Reformation, 15, 141–2, 151; see also Counter-Reformation
Cavan, 148
Cenini, Mona Papera di Cienni, 128
Cento, 21–3; see also Proba, Faltonia Betitia
Chalcore, Gilbert de, 44
Chamillard, Gaston, 160, 166
Chanbini (Cambini), Bernardo, 127
Chartres, 12, 93, 97, 103
Chen, John le, 65
Chepstow castle, 52
Chetwynd, Adam de, 42
Chrysostom, John, St, 33; see also *Homilies on Genesis*
Cicely, duchess of York, 88
Cicero, 20, 22
Cingatti, Piera di Nuto di Grazia, 119
Cistercian, 57, 134
Cittadino (del), Andrea Maddalena di Antonio di Michele, Antonia, 123–4; Antonio di Michele, Fioretta, 124
Ciucci, Fruosino d'Ugolino, 122
Clare, Basilia de, sister of Strongbow, 10, 54–7, 71
Clement VI, pope, 81
Clement VII, pope, 123–4
Cleri, Anne, 131
Cockersand Abbey, 42

Cod, Richard, 70
Cogan (de), Eustace, Margaret, Miles, 57
Cohn, Samuel K. Jr., 113
Collier, Agnes, Alice, John, Walter, 39
Cologne, 82, 86
Columbanus, St, 79
Communion, 146, 171, 173
Como, Cathedral, 184
Concubinage, 113, 129, 150, 151
Confederates, 149, 151
Confessions, 20; see also Augustine, St
Connacht, 51
Constitutions de Port-Royal, 163–4
convents, 10–16, 48, 80, 112, 116, 120–1, 131–3, 136, 162–3
Corbinelli, Vieri di Tommaso, 127
Cordwainer (Cordwaner), Affreca, John, 63
Cork, 70, 72, 143
Corsini, Filippo, 117
Coulommiers, 102–3
Council of Trent, 162–3
Counter-Reformation 141, 143, 151, 153; see also Catholic Reformation
Courcy (de), Affreca, John, 60
Cousturier, Sr Marie de Sainte Anne, 175
Coventry, 86
Cranach, Lucas, the Elder, 181–2, 184
crannog, 148
Creación del mundo, 19; see also Acevedo, Alonso de
Creation, 18, 20, 24–5, 28–9, 32, 178–9
Cressy, Roger de, 45
Crucci, Francesco di Ruggieri, Lisa di Ruggieri, Ruggieri, 128
Crusade, 10, 12, 50, 93–4, 98, 103; see also Holy Land; Jerusalem; Holy Sepulchre
Culchet, Richard de, 42
Cusack, John, 137
Cyprian, 8, 18, 24–7, 31, 35

Da che'l lauro, 115; see also Medici, Lorenzo de'
Da creacao e composicao do homen, 19; see also Camões, Luiz de
Dai, Basilia de, 38

Daiuill, John de, 42
Dante, 21, 114–15
Danzig, 83–4
Darcy, Patrick, 152
Darley Abbey, 38
Dati, Giorgio, 122; Goro, 128
Daundon, John, 62
Davanzati, Vieri di Antonio, 127
David, baron of Naas, 61
Davis, Natalie Zemon, 146
Davis, Robert, 112
Day, Ascelinus de, 38
De donis, 37, 47, 61; see also Statute of Westminster
De Laudibus Dei, 29; see also Dracontius, Blossius Aemelius
De rerum natura, 20; see also Lucretius
De spiritalis historiae gestis, 32; see also Avitus, Alcimus of Vienne, St
Dearbhfhorgaill, daughter of Maghnus O Conor, 138
Delvin, baron of, 57
Dempsey, Charles, 115
Derbforgaill, daughter of the king of Meath, 57
Derby, 38
Derneford (de), Emery, Margery, 62
Deti, Marietta, Tommaso, 121
Deveneys, William le, 64
Devil, 32, 34, 111, 135, 180, 190; see also Serpent
Diacceto (da), Pagolo, 127
Dittochaeon, 23; see also Prudentius, Aurelius Clemens
Divinae institutiones, 20; see also Lactantius
Dodington (de), Adam, Aveline, 42
Dol, Richard de, 44
Donati, Costanza, 115; Lucrezia, 115–17, 130; Marchione di ser Marchione, 129; Piccarda, 115–16
Donatists, 31
Dorothea of Montau, St, 83
Dorset, 80, 87, 89
Dowdall, Lady, 145
dower, 8–11, 36ff
dowry, 8, 16, 35, 64, 71, 93, 121, 127, 162
Dracontius, Blossius Aemelius, 8, 18, 29–31, 35; see also *De Laudibus Dei*

Dragons, 17, 147, 177 ff
Drogheda, 69–70, 145–6
Drumcliffe, 138
Dublin, 10, 54–6, 57, 64, 69, 71, 74, 76, 145–6, 148
Dunston, William, 7
Dyloun, Ismannia, Nicholas, Thomas, 67

Eadburga of Minster in Thanet, 80
Ecclesiastical History, 97; see also Orderic Vitalis
Eclogues, 20; see also Virgil
Eden, 17, 32–3, 180, 189; see also Paradise
Edward I, king of England, 66
Edward IV, king of England, 88
Einsiedeln, 83
Eirik the Red, 77
Elisabeth-Agnès, Sr, 166
Elslack, 39
enclosure, of male religious, 81
enclosure of nuns, 16, 80, 120, 135, 156
Erasmus, 19
Eriksson, Leif, 77
Eriksson, Thorstein, 77
Essex, 41, 86
Ettlinger, Helen, 113
Eustace, Janet, 138
Evangeliorum libri IV, 21; see also Juvencus, Caius Vettius Aquilinus
Evans, J.M., 28
Eve, 7–8, 18–19, 22–35, 106, 180, 181, 184
Everwin of Tintagel, 39
Expugnatio hibernica, 51–2; see also Gerald of Wales
Eztergom, 75

Fall (from Eden), 8, 22–6, 29, 32, 34–5, 106, 143, 180–1
Fall of Man, 182; see also Cranach, Lucas, the Elder
Fantosme, Jordan, 53
Fechin, St, 51
Felp, John de, 45
Ferns, 55, 142
Ficino, Marsilio, 116
Fieschi, Bianca di Carlo, 118
Fitz Gerald, Margaret, 133, 139; Maurice, 54–6, 68
Fitz Griffin, Matthew, 62
Fitz Henry, Meiler, 56, 58
Fitz Maurice, Margaret, Thomas, 72
Fitz Pons, Bertha, Richard, 43

Fitz Stephen, Robert, 54, 55, 71
Flécelles, Sr Marie-Madeleine de Sainte Sophie de, 175
Fleshhewer, Henry, Ralph, 86, Sara, 86
Florence, 13, 111 ff
Florentyne, Dame Margaret, 84
Foleville, Walter de, 46
Fontaine, Jacques, 27
Formulary, 16, 159–60, 165, 169–75
Forth, barony of, 71
French, Mary, 154
Frescobaldi, Stoldo, 129
Freydis, 77–8
Freynes (de), Matilda, William, 74
friars, 13, 84, 111, 122, 142, 145, 150
Friuli, synod of, 79
Frung, Sir George, Margaret, 84
Fulda, 80
Furneys, William de, 47
Fusc, Magnus, 131–2

Gall, Elicia, 131
Galway, 151, 153
Gant, Emma de, 37
Garrard, Mary, 116
Gaul, 22, 102, 107
gender, 7, 12, 24, 81, 90–2, 97, 101, 104, 109–10, 112, 143, 179, 189
Genealogiae deorum gentilium, 21; see also Boccaccio
Genesis, 8, 18–19, 21–8, 30–1
genitalia, 26, 30, 185, 191–3, 195
Genoa, 86, 116, 118
George, St, 17, 177–80, 185, 190–1, 193–6
Gerald of Wales, 51, 52–4, 56, 57; see also *Expugnatio hibernica; History and topography of Ireland; Journey through Wales*
Geraldines, 55–6, 58
Ghiberti, Cione, Lorenzo, 129
Ghibertine monastery, 135
Ghirlandaio, 116
Giffard, Elias, 43
Gilbert, son of Strongbow, 57
Glenscarraig, 71
Godarville, Walter de, 69
Goes, Isabella, John, 62
Goring, 44–5

Gorini, Fioretta, 124
Gosefeud, Ralph de, 41
Gottland, Peter, 177, 180, 185, 190
Grace, 28, 32, 108–9, 153, 158, 160, 167, 170, 172
Graenlendinga Saga, 77
Grandmesnil, Peronelle de, 54
Greenland, 11, 76, 77–8
Grimaldi, 118
Grimani, breviary, 192
Grimston, William de, 38
Gros (le), John, 43, Raymond, 55–7
Guasconi, Cosa, 125
Gunthamund, Vandal king, 29
Gwenllian, 53

Halbwachs, Maurice, 163
Hamartigenia, 34; see also Prudentius, Aurelius Clements
Hamburg, 81
Hardenacke, Gerhard, 82
Harvey, Margaret, 76
Hautvillers, 102
Haydock, John, 42–3
Haye, Walter de la, 62
Haytesbury, 41
Healy, Francis, 145
Heidenham, 80
Helena, St, 102
Henry I, king of England, 12, 53, 94–5, 98, 107
Henry II, king of England, 43, 50, 53, 55
Henry V, emperor, 94
Heptateuch, 24, 27
Hercules at the Crossroads, 186
Hereford, 50
Heresy, 158–9, 179
Hibbert, Howard, 124
Hilary of Poitiers, 20
History and topography of Ireland, 51, 55; see also Gerald of Wales
Holderness, 46–7
Holinshed, 139
Holy Land, 85–7, 93, 98
Holy Sepulchre, 87
Homilies on Genesis, 33; see also Chrysostom, John, St
Hugh the Chanter of York, 107
Hughes, Diana Owen, 43
Hufton, Olwen, 146
Hungary, 75

Iceland, 11, 77–8
Idrone, barony of, 71

Ipswich, 84, 88
Isaiah, 33
Isidore of Seville, St, 105
Isobel, daughter of Strongbow, 9, 57, 58
Israel, 174
Italy, 83, 149, 184, 196
Itinerarium peregrinorum et gesta regis Ricardi, 50
Ivo of Chartres, bishop, 99–101, 104, 109

Jambe, Alice Bela, Walter Bela, 67
James, St, 82
James VI (king), 19
Jansen, Cornelius, 15, 155, 158–60, 169, 173; see also *Augustinus*, Jansenism
Jerusalem, 12, 81, 83–4; see also Crusade, Holy Land; Holy Sepulchre
Jesuits, 124, 142–3
Joanna, illegitimate daughter of King John, 44
John, king of England, 44–5, 68
Jointures, 11, 59, 65
Joinville, Jean de, 50; see also *Life of St Louis*
Journée du Guichet, 163
Journey through Wales, 53; see also Gerald of Wales
Juvencus, Caius Vetetius Aquilinus, 21, 25; see also *Evangeliorum libri IV*

Kaerdif (de), Joan, Matilda, 68
Kantitun, Nicholas de, 57
Karlsefni, 78
Katherine, wife of Henry V, 76
Kavanagh, Sadhbh, 132
Kelly, Joan, 114
Kellystown, church of St Patrick, 62
Kempe, Margery, 12, 83–5
Kenmare Bay, 147
Ker, David, 64
Kerry, 72, 148
Keynes, Elizabeth de, 87, 89
Kidwelly Castle, 53
Kilculliheen, convent of, 14, 131, 133, 135–6
Kildare, 51, 58, 60, 138–9
Kilfenny Castle, 145
Kilkenny, St Canices's Cathedral, 132
Killaloe, 62, 150–1
Killeen, lord, 146

Kings (book of), 107
Kirkby Wharfe, 38
Knights of Rhodes, 84
Kuehn, Thomas, 113, 119

La Giostra, 115; see also Pulci
La seconde semaine, 19; see also Bartas, Guillaume du
Lacey, Roesia de, 57
Lactantius, 20–1; see also *Divinae institutiones*
Lacy (de), Hugh, 51, 56–7, Margery, 68–9, Walter, 68–9
Landino, Cristoforo, 116
Lane, Parr, 142
Laqueur, Thomas, 105
Latimer, Hugh, 84–5
Le Féron, Sr Elisabeth Agnès, 170
Le Féron, Sr Marguerite Elizabeth, 174
Le Juge, Sr Françoise de Sainte Agathe, 175
Le Mans, Hildebert, bishop of, 101
Le sette giornate del mundo creato, 19; see also Tasso, Torquato
Leicester, earl and countess of, 53–4
Leinster, 55, 57–8, 71, 149
Leonardo da Vinci, 116
lesbian, 164, 181
Leviathan, 192
licences to travel, 85–6
Liège, 75–76
Life of St Louis, 50; see also Joinville, Jean de
Lilith, 17, 180
Limerick, 62, 139, 144
Lippi, Alessandra, 121, Filippino, Fra Filippo, 120–1
Lisle (de), Bartholomew, Elizabeth, 86
Llywelyn, 44
Loch Key, 51
Lodge, Thomas, 19
London, 41, 84–9
Louis VI, king of France, 94, 97, 107
Louis XIV, king of France, 159, 160
Louth, 11, 57, 69
Lübeck, 81–2
Lucca, 82
Lucretius, 20; see also *De rerum natura*

Index

Ludyngton, William de, 43–4
Luther's Game of Heresy, 185, 187
Luttrell, Beatrice, 86
Lynch Blosse correspondence, 151, 153
Lynch, Ellis, Harry, Henry, Mary, Robert, Roebuck, Stivine, 151–4
Lysaght, Catherine, 144

Mac Murchada, Diarmait, 52, 54–5, 57, 133
McOdo, John, 14, 132, 140
Machiavelli, Bernardo, 129; Giovanni Angelini, 120; Niccolò, 129
Magna Carta, 62
Manetti, Giovannozzo, 118
Mangioni, Michele di Piero, 120
Mannelli, Francesco di messer Arnaldo, 129
Map, Walter, 50
March, Christina de la, 42
Marcigny, 94, 106–7
Marduk, 179
maritagium, 8, 9, 36–9, 40 ff; *see also* dowry
Marmoutier, 103–4, 106
Marshal, Richard, 58, William, 9–10, 57–8
Martelli, Braccio, 115
Martha, St, 192
Martin, Richard, 152
Mary (Virgin), 8, 24, 82, 87, 102, 116
Massari, Dionysio, 148
Matilda, wife of William the Conqueror, mother of Adela of Blois, 93
Mazzi, Serena, 113
McKesky, Catherine, 137
Meath, 51, 57, 67–9; *see also* Colp; Drogheda; Fore
Meaux, 12, 93
Medici (de'), Carlo, 125; Cosimo, 121; Giovanni, 124; Giovenco di Giuliano, 125; Giuliano, 114, 116–17, 123–4; Giulio (*see:* Clement VII, pope); Lorenzo, 114–17, 123–4
Melancthon, Philip, 184
Mellifont, 57
Mesnil, Mère Louise de Sainte Anastasie du, 175
Metamorphoses, 20

Michael, St, 181
Migliorati, Ruberto, 124
Milan, 115
Minerbetti, Ippolita, 121
Miracles, 51, 80, 95, 102
monastery, 14, 37, 43, 93, 97, 99, 102–6, 133–4, 137, 155, 161, 163, 166–8, 175, 184
Monsters, 16, 177 ff
Montaigne, Nicholas de, 70
Montmorency, Hervey de, 56
More, Thomas, 85
Morelle, Guillaume, 18
Morelli, Bernardo, Simona, 128
Moronti, Gimignano, 120
Mortimer, Thomas, 86
Moryson, Fynes, 142–3
Mothing, Katherine, 131, 133
Mountgarrett, viscount, 149
Moycreddin, 64
Moyl, Agnes, John, 139
Muir, Edwin, 112
Munster, 149

Naas, 56, 61
Naples, 117–18
Narrenschiff [Ship of Fools], 185–6; *see also* Brant, Sebastian
Naunton, Sir Thomas, 84
Neroni, Alessandro, 148
Nest, daughter of Maurice Fitz Gerald, 56
Netherlands, 196
Neubourg, Henry of, 41
Neville, Ida lady, of Essex, 86
Newcastle, 69, 180
Niccolini, Caterina di Paolo, 121; Ginevra, 125; Giovanni 119; Giuliano di Otto, 125; Jacopo, 128; Lapo di Giovanni, 118, 119; Luigi di Bernardo di Lapo, 116; Otto, 125, 127; Paolo, 125, 129
Nicholas V, pope, 120
Noiseux, Sr Denise de Sainte Basilisse, 175
Norfolk, 39, 88; *see also* Norwich; Stiffkey
Normandy, 52, 94, 102
Norway, 11, 78
Norwich, 64, 88, 136
Nugent (de), Gilbert, 57, widow, 145
nuns, 11, 13–16, 79–80, 94, 98–9, 106–7, 112, 120–2, 129, 131–6, 140, 149, 155ff

O'Cléirigh, Cormac, 7
O Conchobair, Aed, 51, 56; Toirdelbach, 51
O Conchobháir Failghe, 138
O Conor, Maghnus, 138
O'Connor, Pat, 157
O'Neill, Owen Roe, 148–9
O'Queely, Malachy, 150–1
O Ruairc, Tigernán, king of Breifne, 57
O'Sullivan Beare, 146
Oconoyl, Nevok Inyn, 139
Olaf the White, king of Dublin, 77
On the apparel of women, 35; *see also* Tertullian
Orderic Vitalis, 54, 97–9, 103, 109; *see also Ecclesiastical History*
Origo, Iris, 113, 125
Orkney, 77
Osbert, prior of Westminster abbey, 107
Oseney Abbey, 45
Ossory, bishop of, 131, 151; *see also* Baron, Milo de
Ottavanti, Pagolo, 128
Ovid, 20
Oxfordshire, 44, 87–8; *see also* Goring; Stonor

Page, Nicholas, 70
Palagio (del), Niccolò di Jacopo, 119
Panna (del), Giovanna di messer Jacopo, 129
Papal Ass, 183; *see also* Wenzel of Olmutz
Paradise Lost, 34
Paradise, 20, 29–30, 32–3, 106, 115; *see also* Eden
Parenti, Ginevra di Piero, 121
Parewastel, Isolda, 87
Paris, 159, 164–6; *see also* Péréfixe, Hardouin de 168–72
Parker, Roszika, 112
Pascal, Sr Jacqueline de Sainte-Euphémie, 161
Paschal II, pope, 94, 98
Passart, Sr Flavie, 168–70
Paston, John, Margaret, Margery, 88
Paulinus of Nola, 20, 22
Pazzi conspiracy, 117, 122; Costanza de', 115
Pecher (le), Christina, Emma, Galliana, Gilbert, John, Margaret, Margery, 44

Percy family, 37; Agnes, 42; Joanna, 47; Walter, 37–8; William, 47
Péréfixe, Hardouin de, archbishop of Paris, 159, 174
Periculoso, 80
Peruzzi, Brigida, 121
Pesenhall, William de, 42
Petriboni, Fascello, 119
Philip VI, king of France, 81, 98
Pico della Mirandola, 114
pilgrimage/pilgrims, 11–12, 75, 78–81, 83–6, 89, 98, 145
Pineau, Sr Geneviève, 168–70
Pisa, 82
Pistoia, Opera of San Jacopo, 81, 86
Pius II, pope, 121
Pliny the Younger, 22
Plunkett, Suzanna, 146
Poer, Richard le, 139
Pole, Joan de la, duchess of Suffolk, 88–9
Polet, Simon le, 46
Poliziano, Angelo, 116; see also *Stanze per la giostra*
Pollock, Griselda, 112
Pontchartrain, M. de, 175
Pontefract, 46
Porcellini, Giovanni di Noldo, 111
Port-Royal, convent of, 15–16, 155 ff
Port-Royal Des Champs, 159–60, 167, 173
Portiuncula, 84
Portugal, 19
Prato, 120, 125
Prendergast (de), Maurice, Philip, 55
Primavera, 115–16; see also Botticelli
Proba, Faltonia Betitia, 8, 21, 23–4; see also *Cento*
prostitutes, 50, 112, 113, 120, 127
Prudentius, Aurelius Clemens, 23, 34; see also *Dittochaeon; Hamartigenia; Tituli historiarum*
Prussia, 84
Pseudo-Hilary of Arles, 18
Psychomachia, 33
Pulci, 22
Pulle, John de la, 70
Pupplynton, John, 45

Quency (de), family, Maud, Robert, 55
Quincy, Roger de, earl of Winchester, 55
Quintilian, 22

Racine, Jean, 169
Racine, Sr Marguerite de Sainte Thècle, 169
Ralph of Norwich, 64,
Rapenteyn (de), Bertram, Ismaya, 66
Rebais, 102
rebellion of 1641, 141, 151
Recha (del), Lionardo di Zanobi, 127
Redlingfield convent, 136
Reformation, 14, 16–17, 177, 184, 185
Rendi, Maria, 119
Rhys ap Gruffydd, 53–4
Ricci, Antonio, Filippo d'Ardingo, 128
Rich, Barnaby, 142
Richa, Giuseppe, 124
Richard II, king of England, 76, 86
Rimington, 37, 44
Rinuccini, GianBattista (papal nuncio), 15, 147–9
Rinuccini, Piero di Jacopo, 125
Rocamadour, 82, 86
Roche, Henry de la, 73
Roche, Joan, 142
Rocheford (de), Beatrice, 46–7, William, 46
Rocke, Michael, 113
Rokele, Joan de la, 73
Rome, 12, 23, 76, 78–81, 83–4, 86, 148, 150, 184
Rossi, Rosso del Boneca, 129
Rucellai, Andrea, 129; Bernardo, 115; Giovanni, 118, 128; Santi di Andrea, 129
Rudolf of Fulda, 80
Ruggiero, Guido, 113
Russel, Reginald, 72
Ruston (de), Richard, William, 38
Rya, Margery de, 45
Ryley (de), Edelina, Pagan, 43

sacraments, 16, 155, 159–60, 171–3
St Albans, 89
St Brigid's, 51

St George and the Dragon see also Altdorfer, Albrecht, 188
St George Fighting with the Dragon, 194; see also Beck, Leonard
St Marie du Faubourg, convent of, 167
St Quentin (de), family, 46; Herbert I, 47; Herbert II, 46–7
St Satur-sous-Sancerre, 103
Sainte-Melthide Thomas du Fossé, Sr Magdeleine de, 169–73
salvation, 27, 29, 81, 96, 100, 158, 160, 167, 172, 174
Salviati, Bernardo, 125
San Gallo (da), Antonio, 123
San Piero a Grado, 82
Sancto Amando (de), Guy, Lucia, 64
Sancto Laudo (de), John, Rohese, 46
Sancto Mauro, Miles de, 46
Sandiacre, Peter de, 38
Santiago de Compostela, 12, 81–7
Sasse, Heinrich, 81–8
Sassetti, Federigo di Pierozzo, Letta di Federigo, 111
Schof, Geseke, Johann, 81
Scotland, 11, 55
Scott, Joan, 90
Scryneyn (le), Ermellina, Richard, 45
Serpent, 8, 16–17, 23, 26, 28–30, 32–3, 179–81, 184, 189; see also Devil
Servius, 105
Sexton, Alison, Edmund, the elder, Edmund the younger, Joan, Mary, 144
Sézanne, 102
Shank, Gilbert, Isabella, 70
Sheppey, Agnes, John, 86
Ship of Fools, see *Narrenschiff*
Shrewsbury, 42
Sidney, Sir Philip, 19, 21
Simons, Patricia, 112
Skraelings, 77
slavery/slaves 13, 112–13, 118, 123–8
Sligo, 51
Soderini, Giovanni di Francesco, 124; Lorenzotto di Tome, 119; Tome, 119
sodomy, 113, 122

Index

Somerset, 40, 87
Sommaia (da), Caterina di Chimenti, 118, 129; Chimenti, 118
Song of Dermot and the Earl, 49–50, 52, 54–5, 57
Southampton, 42
Spain, 76
Spini, Salvestro, 126
Stanze per la giostra, 116; see also Poliziano, Angelo
Statute of Merton, 64
Statute of Westminster, 8–9, 37, 48, 64; see also De donis
Statutes of Gloucester, 65
Stephen, king of England, 12, 93, 95, 107
Stephen-Henry, count of Blois, 12, 93, 94–5, 102–3, 106–7
Stiffkey, 39
Stone, Laurence, 122
Stonor, Elizabeth, 87–9, Sir William, 87–8
Strinato (dello), Belfredello, 127
Strocchia, Sharon, 112
Strong, Anastasia, 142
Strongbow, 9–10, 51–2, 54–5, 56–8
Strozzi, Alessandra Macinghi, 115; Filippo di Matteo, 117; Francesco, 127; Lorenzo di Matteo, 117–18; Lorenzo di Palla, 117; Marietta, 13, 117–18
Stufa (della), Andrea, 125, 127
Sweden, 83
Sweyn, Walter, 139
Sylvester, Joshua, 19

Talenti, Piero, 119
Talmud, 180
Tani, Filippo di Jacopo, 128; Jacopo, 125, 128
Tarasque, 192
Tasso, Torquato, 19; see also *Le sette giornate del mundo creato*
Tauber, 80
Tertullian, 67; see also *On the apparel of women*
Thanet, 80
Thebes, 119
Theodosius, emperor, 78
Thibaud III, count of Blois, 93
Thibaud the Great, count of Blois-Champagne, 12, 93, 95

Thorstein the Red, 77–8
Thurstan, archbishop of York, 107
Tiāmat, 178–9
Tiber, 184
Timahoe, 56
Tipperary, 134
Tiron, 102–3
Tituli historiarum, 23; see also Prudentius, Aurelius Clemens
Tolachtyper, 61
Tornabuoni chapel, S. Maria Novella, 116; Lisabetta, 118 Lorenzo, 114
Tours, 103
Trapani, 119
Trexler, Richard, 112–13
Trier, 81–2
Trim, 67, 71
Trite, John, 42
Trubleville, Ralph de, 63
Tuyt, Nichola de, 71

Ubertini, Giovanni di Luca, 125, 128
Ufford, Joan, 73, Robert, 72–3
Ulster, 60, 147–9
Ursulines, 157

Valence, Agnes de, 7, 74
Vasari, Giorgio, 116
Vavasour, Mauger le, 39
Velescines, Michael de, 41
Velluti, Agnola, Donato, 119
Venice, 83, 113, 122
Verdun (de), Nicholas, 11; Roesia, 11, 57; Theobald, 67–8
Vernun (de), Cecilia, 70–1; Rodolf, 71
Verrocchio, 115
Vescy (de), Isabella, William, 60
Vespasiano da Bisticci, 117
Vespucci, Marco, 116, Piero, 117, Simonetta, 115–17, 130
Victorius, Claudius Marius, 8, 18, 27–9, 31, 33
Vienne, 22
Vifilsson, Thorborn, 77
Viking, 11, 76
Vinland, 11, 77–8
Virago, 99, 104–7
Virgil, 8, 20–1, 24, 32; see also *Aeneid*; *Eclogues*
Visdomini, Andrea, 126

Visitandine order, 159
Visitation, by Ghirlandaio, 116,
Visitation order, 155, 166, 168, 172
Voluptas, 185–6

Wakebridge chartulary, 43
Wales, 49, 52–3, 55
Waleys, Isabella de, 45
Walloon, 75
Walpurgisnacht, 80
Walsh, Walter, 44
Walsingham, 89
Walter, Theobald, 11
Waterford, 55–6, 68, 72, 140, 143, 145
Watton monastery, 135
Welend (de), Thomas, William, 65,
Wenzel of Olmutz, 183–4
West Rasen, 40
Wexford, 54–6, 71; see also Glenscarraig, Ferns
Whitechurch, Moldina, 69
Wickenham, Wakelin of, 41
Wife of Bath, 87
Willesden, Our Lady of, shrine, 85
William the Conqueror, 12, 93, 95–6, 102–7
Wilsnack, 84
Wimborne, 80
Winchester, 12, 55, 93, 107
Wind, Edgar, 114
Windsor, 88,
Wogan, John, 73
Wolbot, Stephen, 67
Wold Newton, 37
women:
 and authority, 93, 101, 104, 132, 151;
 and beauty 8, 30, 32, 35, 72, 76, 96, 108, 113–14, 116–17, 148;
 and chastity, 97, 108, 114–16, 130;
 and crime, 113, 138, 140;
 and crusades, 10, 50;
 and daughters, 37, 39, 41–2, 45–7, 68, 76, 81, 88, 110, 137, 141–2;
 and education, 101, 154, 157;
 and family, 9, 36–7, 47–8, 67–8, 87, 92, 94, 108, 111–12, 139, 144, 163;
 and friendship, 156–7, 163–4, 173;

women: *(cont.)*
    and inheritance, 7–10, 36–7, 44, 48;
    and law, 9, 11, 33, 46, 62–3, 66–70, 80, 86, 96, 100, 102, 104, 135;
    and marriage, 7, 9, 11, 13;
    and patronage, 12–13, 57, 67, 70–1, 87, 93, 95, 97–8, 102–104;
    and perceived weakness, 8, 32, 75, 80, 82, 91, 105, 143, 184;
    and pilgrimage, 11–12, 75, 78–9, 81–9;
    and priests, 143, 150;
    and property, 8–11, 16, 35ff., 83, 88, 135, 152, 162;
    and religion, 14, 78–80, 133, 141–5, 147–8;
    and resistance to authority, 16, 153, 155ff., 163, 166–9, 173–6;
    and social roles, 92, 96, 101, 106, 108;
    and sons, 37–41, 42, 45–8, 53, 76–8, 93–4, 97–8, 107, 119, 142;
    and the church, 14, 70–1, 74;
    and travel, 11–12, 75ff;
    and violence, 14–15, 49–50, 77, 100, 131ff;
    and warfare, 9, 11, 14, 49–53, 131, 151

Worcester, 45
Wulfric, 40

York, 47, 84, 88
Yorkshire, 37–9, 46–7

Zaccaria, Raffaella Maria, 124
Zanelli, A., 113
Zita, St, 82